WITNESS TO THE FIRE

WITNESS TO THE FIRE

CREATIVITY AND THE VEIL OF ADDICTION

Linda Schierse Leonard

Shambhala
Boston & London
2001

Shambhala Publications, Inc.
Horticultural Hall
300 Massachusetts Avenue
Boston, Massachusetts 02115
www.shambhala.com

9 8 7 6

Printed in the United States of America
♾ This edition is printed on acid-free paper that meets the American National Standards Institute Z39.48 Standard.

Distributed in the United States by Random House, Inc., and in Canada by Random House of Canada Ltd

The Library of Congress catalogues the hardcover edition of this work as follows:

Leonard, Linda Schierse.
Witness to the fire: creativity and the veil of addiction / Linda Shierse Leonard.—1st ed. p. cm.
Bibliography: p. 1. Compulsive behavior. 2. Creative ability. 3. Archetype (Psychology). 4. Jung, C. G. (Carl Gustav), 1875–1961. 5. Dostoyevsky, Fyodor, 1821–1881.
1. Title. RC533.L47 1989 153.3'5—dc20
ISBN 0-87773-393-7 ISBN 0-87773-588-3 (pbk.) 89-42634 CIP

For my mother, Virginia May Herrmann-Schierse,
whose love and inner strength have been a source of inspiration

Without suffering, happiness cannot be understood. The ideal passes through suffering like gold through fire.

—Fyodor Dostoevsky

And did you get what
you wanted from this life, even so?
I did.
And what did you want?
To call myself beloved, to feel myself
beloved on the earth.

—Raymond Carver,
"Late Fragment"

CONTENTS

ACKNOWLEDGMENTS

Thanks and gratitude to all the people who helped me along the journey of recovery and creativity and the writing of this book and especially to:

Keith Chapman, who was always present as a creative companion, offering his wisdom and experience as a shamanistic and existential and Jungian-oriented psychiatrist, both in workshops and throughout the long, challenging process of writing this book.

Phyllis Kenevan, whose love of Dostoevsky and the existential philosophers first inspired me and who read each chapter with care as it was written.

Emily Hilburn Sell, my editor, who performed the enormous task of cutting and pruning the manuscript without losing its depth.

Lindy Steele, who typed the manuscript with loving attention, offering many insights about the recovery process, and Steven Capan and Gerri Ganter, who also contributed to the typing process and creative input.

Arthur E. Colton, whose wisdom, experience, and hope were a great source of strength, guiding me throughout the recovery process, and whose insights infuse this book.

Misty Thornton, whose faith and guidance in recovery were a great gift.

Nancy Frank and the Women's Network Group for their emotional support and earthy wisdom about applying the steps to everyday life.

Bill Steele and Rennick Stevenson, from whom I learned so much about the twelve steps in relation to creativity.

Don Sandner and Jane and Joe Wheelwright, whose presence helped along the Jungian journey.

Pat Bixby, Janine Hunter, and Mary Sullivan, whose feminine spirit and élan vital lightened the hard work phase.

Harold Booth, Karen Chamberlin, Robert Chamberlin, Lynn Foote, Marjorie Foster, Chuck K., Doug van Koss, Rae Ellen Holland, Christina Loeffel, Betty Meador, Lara Newton, Ron Ruggles, Peggy Walsh, Ph.D., and Don Williams, who shared their ideas and suggestions and/or read the manuscript at various stages.

And especially to all the "witnesses to the fire" who so generously shared their stories.

PREFACE

I WAS DESTINED to deal with the issue of addiction. Born into a family of alcoholics and co-addicts, I lived in this environment until I was twenty. My first book, *The Wounded Woman*, came out of this experience. In my twenties, fearing that I might be like my alcoholic father, I drank only occasionally. If anything, I had many of the attitudes that I now recognize as codependency.[1] But, as a river inevitably cycles to its source, so my life unpredictably took me back to the overt world of addiction, and thus began my "nightsea journey." My thirties were years of opening up creatively through Jungian analysis, years of exploration, adventure—and of drinking. These were the years of Romance—a romance with wine, my Ghostly Lover, which became the Demon Lover described in *On the Way to the Wedding.*[2] These years lived on high mountain peaks led to the dark descent into the valley of death and depression.

My forties were full of horror and reckoning—and confrontation of my drinking. Acknowledging my denial of the deadly disease I had inherited, I finally broke through it. With the exception of my traumatic childhood, these were the most painful years of my life. Yet, they were also the most creative years. I wrote three books and underwent a profound spiritual transformation. I was truly forced to face my mortality, the possible loss of my profession, my relationship, and my life. In the end, I was led to make the vow to lead a creative and spiritual life.

The turning point of my addiction was at the bottom of an unfathomable abyss—in a detox ward. There I faced my death, and I also clearly heard the call to life. After years of trying by myself to stop drinking, I felt helpless and humiliated. At that moment, on my knees in prayer, I admitted I was powerless. So I turned and asked for help from others whom I knew had sunk to similar depths, yet who were recovering. Up until then I was so angry at God for having "let me down" that I was in rebellion. I could not open myself to any higher power at all. But with other recovering addicts I felt the miracle that happens when people come together to share the stories of their suffering, their descent toward death, and their return to life. In those meetings, I felt the higher power of love. These stories inspired me and opened my heart with hope. Hearing them, I felt the courage of daily struggle in the face of a lethal disease and the wisdom and serenity that emerged. I learned that this required daily commitment, a vow to life each day, and that the ultimate issue was not merely to stop the physical act of drinking but to face the very meaning of my life—not conditionally as I had done before, but with my very blood. The entire experience of addiction forced me to face directly the human condition, to acknowledge my mortality, and in the face of this to make a vow to life—a vow to create a new way of being.

Looking back, I was shocked by the history of drinking in my family, which was shrouded in the dark romance of alcohol. Both my grandfathers were immigrants and both were alcoholics. Each was an exciting figure. Yet, one was dark, while the other was happy-go-lucky. The dark figure, my father's father, is said to have been wild and Dionysian, but with a brutal edge. He died by fire during a drunken debauch when the stove in his room overturned. Repeating death by fire, my father accidentally burned down the house when a cigarette fell from his hand while he was drunk, and my grandmother was killed. My mother's father ran booze during the Prohibition, hiding it under my mother's mattress and selling the forbidden booty at a German drinking and dancing club. This is where my father and mother met, dancing and drinking in the romance of the forbidden. And so, while my child's consciousness saw and felt the shame and horrors of addiction, from the shadows of our family history loomed the overwhelming figure of the Romantic in addiction.

As I began to write this book, various archetypal figures of addiction arose in my dreams and in my waking life: The Moneylender, The Gambler, The Romantic, The Underground Man, The Outlaw, The Trickster, The Madwoman, The Judge, The Killer, The Hostage. While some of these figures could be related to specific addictions, the more I talked to other addicts and understood my own addictions, the more I saw that they are archetypal aspects functioning generally in all addiction—whether to substances, control, activities, debt, or romance. Encountering these figures allows the reader to enter into the drama of addiction and see some of the characters and dialogues that occur. Of course, there are many figures in addiction that are not portrayed here, for I had to narrow down the cast of characters to the ones that seemed most central. As if to stress the confusing process of addiction, a disease in which the sufferer ceases to think clearly and to feel the genuine impulses of the heart, these characters intermeshed and interrupted one another as I wrote. I often felt overwhelmed. I had to face the force of each archetype and learn how to turn its energy toward creativity.

Just as the gambler stands before the roulette table, excited by the risk of living on the edge, so was I drawn into writing a book on the very experience that had already nearly cost my life. All my fears and terrors were rekindled, my past securities devoured in the blazing fire. I dreamt of an arsonist, an angry red-haired rebellious man, who threatened to burn down my retreat, a log cabin nestled in the dark quiet of the woods. I was angry too. I reacted by resentfully telling this man to "burn the house down." Flippantly he tossed a match into the house, setting the place ablaze. I realized that I would be held responsible for the fire, for I held in my hands an implicating book. Then out of the house came a kindly man, who showed me a book cover—with the word *Witness* printed boldly on it. It was he who saved the house from burning down. From this dream came the title of this book.

As I wrote I realized the "witness" image referred to the survivors—the recovering people who shared their stories. Each of these stories was an inspiration to me, as I hope it will be to others. Each bears witness to the flight and fall into the hellfire of addiction and also to the fire of the creative process, the struggle to endure the purging fire of spiritual recovery, and to the work to re-create a new being. This process—sharing the personal story of what happened in the addiction, what brought the person to change, and what life is like in recovery—is a ritual that enables the holy presence to come forth. This ritual acknowledges the death every addict faces. It affirms life and the possibility of rebirth.

Every addict who recovers chooses life and makes this existential choice daily. The addict's recovery depends upon an acknowledgment of his powerlessness over the unmanageable depths to which he has fallen through his disease, upon his surrender to allow a higher creative power to guide his life, and on a daily commitment to work to lead a creative life and to give to others. This process of recognition, surrender, work, and choice is the basis of the twelve-step program of recovery and parallels the experience of a creative artist such as Dostoevsky, who was also addicted to gambling.

Many addicts fear they will lose their creativity if they give up the drinks or drugs, romance or power, that they feel takes them to the creative source. Of these, many who hold onto their addictions die an early death or find their creative spring has gone dry or soured. In contrast, many recovering addicts, after enough healing time has passed, find new energy and open spaces in themselves for a creative life. Both need to know there is a way down and back from the creative depths without recourse to addiction.

The relationship between addiction and creativity, as I see it, is not causal.[3] Rather, there is a parallel process occurring in the psyche of the addict and the creative person. Both descend into chaos, into the unknown underworld of the unconscious. Both are fascinated by what they find there. Both encounter death, pain, suffering. But the addict is pulled down, often without choice, and is held hostage by addiction; the creative person *chooses* to go down into that unknown realm, even though the choice may feel destined. Artists who are addicted have a "double descent"—the one of their addiction and the other of their creativity; their situation is compounded and complex, and they respond in different ways. Some creative artists descend with the help of drugs or alcohol and continue to create. Some find they must give up their addictions in order to create. And others continue their addictions to the early loss of their creativity and/or their lives. But once in the realm of the underworld mysteries, they must eventually choose to find form and meaning from the chaos and to return to life and society.

For example, Tennessee Williams and Carson McCullers claimed that alcohol helped them write; Jean Rhys often finished her novels with the help of a bottle or two of wine. In contrast, Eugene O'Neill and John Cheever gave up drinking to continue to create, and Raymond Carver said that writing "under the influence" made his work inferior, adding that he considered giving up drinking to be one of his greatest achievements. Still other artists such as Jack London, Rainer Werner Fassbinder, and Jackson Pollack died young due to their addictions.

Who are the characters in the psyches of these creative people who were also addicts? Who are these figures in ourselves? In literature, one can find vivid and insightful descriptions of these figures—the same inner characters that I found in myself as an addict. In every chapter I have presented a portrait of the archetypal figure through a literary work that describes such a character in detail. This portrait may help the reader recognize him or herself and better understand the inner psychodynamics of the drama of addiction. Often the author was an addict who was struggling with that interior figure. For example, Jack London, who was an alcoholic, describes the way he was tricked by alcohol in *John Barleycorn*, a classic study of denial. Jean Rhys, who was addicted to love and in her later years to alcohol, describes the paranoid feelings of rejection of the Madwoman in *Good Morning, Midnight*. And Dostoevsky, who was addicted to gambling and love, as well as getting into debt, describes these syndromes in *The Gambler* and many of his other works. Although most of these figures came up independently in my psyche and corresponded as well to the experiences of other recovering addicts, later I found them all described in Dostoevsky's works, particularly in *The Brothers Karamazov*. I have presented an analysis of that novel as reflecting the inner patterns of addiction and its transformation as well as a brief story of Dostoevsky's life showing his own transformation from the bondage of addiction to creative faith.

This book has three parts. "The Flight" is the initial stage of the addictive process, which is seductive. In this phase we fly high, just as we do in the early soaring of creative inspiration. "The Fall" is the descent into darkness. This is the ominous stage of possession in which the inner patterns solidify, turn cold, hard, and threatening. In the creative process, this is when we most often feel blocked, criticized, and are tempted to abandon our work. But this darkness must be faced in order to transform the destructive course and to create. "The Creation" is the turning point, where the wounds are accepted, understood, and transformed; this is where healing can occur and life can be created anew.

Since the archetypal figures of addiction are dark and frightening, I want to emphasize the importance of hope for recovery and creativity. Thus, this book includes many personal stories of recovering addicts who identified with the archetypal figure described in the chapter in which their story appears and knew intimately the other inner characters and images as well. It is important to understand these patterns in the psyche of the addict. When we can see the symbolic spiritual meaning which the soul is seeking and which the literal addiction obscures, then creative life can be realized as a gift.

In addition to the literary and personal portraits presented, I have woven into this book the threads of meaning and insight, of faith and hope, that have helped me to survive and have illumined my own way through this dark and fiery journey of the soul. In particular the writings of the existential philosophers—Heidegger and Camus, Kierkegaard and Nietzsche, Tillich and Buber—have been most helpful because they boldly confront the death that stares every addict in the eyes. The insights of Jung, too, have helped, for he took the creative journey into the depths of the unconscious and showed others how to travel in these fearsome regions. Jung also envisioned the hope of spiritual recovery for addicts that eventually was embodied by the original founders of Alcoholics Anonymous. Yet, he was humble enough to admit that psychotherapy and medicine alone were insufficient to help addicts recover. I also found myself returning to the poets and the religious writings of the mystics and the spiritual traditions of the East. And, always, I returned to Dostoevsky, who dared to explore his experience of addiction and creativity as well as doubt and faith, and who directly confronted the question of good and evil, neither shirking from the demons nor forgetting there were angels.

This book is not meant to be a "how to" or "self-help" book about either addiction or creativity. Transforming an addiction is not a "do it yourself" project. There is no "quick fix" for addiction. The twelve-step program, which is frequently mentioned, requires spiritual labor and sacrifice—both are essential to the creative process.

The first three steps entail surrender—a leap into the unknown. Trust, faith, and hope in a creative process that is higher than ego control enable transformation from addictive patterns to creative ones. Then comes the work—steps 4–9—reviewing one's life, digging into the shadow, sorting and sifting, making reparations and changes in one's life. Creativity, too, demands such work and discipline. All this must be done on a daily basis to enable embodiment and integration, just as artists set aside a sacred time and place daily to enact the ritual of creative work. This involves steps 10 and 11, the steps of daily renewal, the daily choice to journey through the cycle. And finally, via the twelfth step, one gives back, contributes to the world by showing that the darkness of addiction can be transformed into creative life.[4] Spiritual recovery, like the creative process, is a daily commitment, a unique blend of receptivity and hard work.

Writing this book has helped me in my own transformation from an alcoholic life in bondage to the Demon Lover to recovering—a life in search of the creative spirit of the cosmos. And it has helped me to understand the underlying meaning of my addiction—the waters of the spiritual life for which I was always thirsting. I hope that it will help others who want to understand the meaning of addiction either in themselves or those they love.

PART ONE: THE FLIGHT

You've just told me some high spots in your memories. Want to hear mine? They're all connected with the sea. . . . I became drunk with the beauty and singing rhythm of it, and for a moment I lost myself—actually lost my life. I was set free! I dissolved in the sea, became white sails and flying spray, became beauty and rhythm, became moonlight and the ship and the high dim-starred sky! I belonged, without past or future, within peace and unity and a wild joy, within something greater than my own life, or the life of Man, to Life itself! To God, if you want to put it that way. . . . Dreaming, not keeping lookout, feeling alone, and above, and apart, watching the dawn creep like a painted dream over the sky and sea which slept together. Then the moment of ecstatic freedom came. The peace, the end of the quest, the last harbor, the joy of belonging to a fulfillment beyond men's lousy, pitiful, greedy fears and hopes and dreams! And several other times in my life, when I was swimming far out, or lying alone on a beach, I have had the same experience. Became the sun, the hot sand, green seaweed anchored to a rock, swaying in the tide. Like a saint's vision of beatitude. Like the veil of things as they seem drawn back by an unseen hand. For a second you see—and seeing the secret, are the secret. For a second there is meaning! Then the hand lets the veil fall and you are alone, lost in the fog again, and you stumble on toward nowhere, for no good reason!

He grins wryly.

It was a great mistake, my being born a man, I would have been much more successful as a sea gull or a fish. As it is, I will always be a stranger who never feels at home, who does not really want and is not really wanted, who can never belong, who must always be a little in love with death!

—Eugene O'Neill, *Long Day's Journey into Night*

1: THE HOSTAGE

> Keep awake, keep awake, artist,
> Do not give in to sleep . . .
> You are eternity's hostage
> And prisoner of time.
> —Boris Pasternak

ONE NIGHT I AWOKE in darkness to find myself hostage in a hospital ward. I had only scattered moments of memory. For the last ten days I had been on a drinking binge. In horror of what I had done, and in terror of what I might do in the future, I struggled for hope. Was there any meaning to be found in this dark event? In that moment, the inspiration for this book was born.

As hostage in the detox ward, I was forced to come to terms with the brute reality of a deadly disease—alcoholism. I was also forced to confront the meaning of my life. No longer could I deny that I was powerless over alcohol. I had taken the first drink and could not stop. Finally, I had ended up in this humiliating state, aware of the threat to my life. And so I was forced to "name" my addiction. Naming it, acknowledging the demon within me by using the word, enabled me to ask the following questions with the fevor of necessity.

Is there meaning in addiction? Does the addiction want something from me? Is it a cry from the soul, a call that is challenging my being? Suddenly the word *creativity* entered my mind. I remembered a similar experience of being hostage to the creative process. While writing, I had also experienced terror, anxiety, and desperation. I had been thrown into darkness, abducted into the underworld, engulfed in a nightmare while writing *The Wounded Woman*, when I had been forced to re-experience my life as the child of an alcoholic. It dawned on me that my addiction might give me insight into the creative process, and that understanding creativity might help me deal with my addiction. Perhaps the journey of the creative person and the addict were similar. Perhaps both the addict and the creator were drawn into the dark regions of the soul. Perhaps this was the way of the mystic, too. I remembered the words of St. John of the Cross: "The Night darkens the spirit, but only to illumine it." Here was my hope! I had fallen through the black, dark tunnel toward death as an addict, but I had also traveled part of that way at other times, through creativity and moments of mystical fervor.

Later, when I looked up the word *addiction* in the dictionary, I found a connection between addiction and creativity buried in the original etymological roots. The Latin for addict, *addictus,* means to devote, surrender, deliver over, or give oneself up habitually. Although the word was often used generally in a pejorative sense, originally it had a spiritual meaning—dedication to the gods—stemming etymologically from *addicere:* to say. Thus, inherent in the meaning of addiction is the sense of dedication or bearing witness to creative energies. Among the Romans, addiction also signified a making over of goods to another by sale or legal sentence and an assignment of debtors in service to their creditors.[1]

Is addiction, then, the act of giving oneself over to something as one's master—be it a substance, object, person, or activity—so totally that one's entire being and meaning become possessed by it? This sense of being possessed corresponded to my experience as an addict. Some of the things we give ourselves over to in this way are alcohol, drugs, food, cigarettes, gambling, shopping, romance, sex, work, money, power, and control. None of these things are bad in and of themselves. But if one is *possessed* by them, if one gives up one's whole being to something else, allowing oneself to be ruled by something external, one's freedom and personal integrity are lost. In this kind of giving up or delivering oneself over, one loses one's soul. And unless one wrests it back there is no transformation.

In the story of Dracula the victim offers himself, exposing his neck before Dracula sucks the blood. Once bitten, he is Dracula's slave.[2] Here there are two aspects to the phenomenon of addiction—giving oneself over and being taken and possessed. They are inseparable. For example, alcoholism is a physical, mental, and spiritual disease. A process takes place in the body and psyche of the alcoholic so that he is no longer predictably in control if he takes a drink. But he does have a choice to take the first drink. And to take the first drink is like offering his neck to Dracula—it is insanity! (This also applies to codependency, romance addiction, etc.) The problem, of course, is that he has already taken too many "first drinks," that he has become habitually predisposed to do so. He is in a vicious circle. The addict is caught in a state of possession not unlike the vampire's bondage to Dracula. The addict is bound by a Demon Lover who has taken possession of his soul. And he lives in the realm of the "living dead."

When I found myself in the detox center there was nothing I could do or appeal to in terms of my usual defenses or ways of operating. My education, my professional success, my possessions—all these meant nothing. I was just a drunk like the others around me, and I was facing death! I felt utterly trapped when doctor after doctor told me I had three possibilities: to die, to go mad, or to stop drinking. My defenses were gone. There was no way to work, or to please, or to extricate myself from this situation and diagnosis. At that moment I knew I was a hostage to my disease and to the terrorizing inner figures that held my soul captive. I also knew I had to face these inner demons and that I could not do it alone. In helplessness and humiliation I got down on my knees and prayed for help. I surrendered my ego desire to be all powerful and in control. Finally I was able to accept help from others similarly afflicted yet who had recovered. Gradually I regained my faith in the greater power of love.

The addict is held hostage through denial. One woman told the following story. She had been alone on a cocaine and alcohol binge in her house for several days. Once during this period she woke up momentarily and absent-mindedly gazed in the mirror. What she saw horrified her—the bloated red face, the dirty disheveled hair, the glazed eyes staring back with the devilish look. Unable to bear seeing herself this way, she reached for a drink to escape, plunging back into blackness until she ended up in a drug treatment center a few days later. Looking in the mirror and taking a drug or a drink (or a romance or power fantasy) to escape the devil who looks back is typical of the addict. In this way the act of reaching for an addictive escape becomes so habitual that it takes possession of the addict until he forgets who he is and begins to be unable to recognize himself any longer. Finally, he begins to lose his soul. One of the characteristics of Dracula is that he casts no reflection in the mirror. Symbolically, this happens finally to the addict who, in the later stages of his disease, deep in denial, can see himself no longer. The man who obsessively borrows money to buy what he doesn't need and cannot afford, the woman who falls in love with man after man who rejects her or whom she rejects after she has won his love, the couple caught in a power relationship ruled by jealousy and possessiveness instead of love—all are hostage to addictive patterns archetypally ruled by the Demon Lover within.

A woman who suffered from love addiction felt hostage to her uncontrollable desire for an unattainable love—the love her father was never able to give her. She repeated this pattern in every love relationship. She *had* to have the absolute love of a man. But then, if the man did happen to fall in love with her, she would lose interest and reject him. And soon she would find another man whom she could not have. She reached bottom in humiliation as she saw this pattern repeat itself over and over again and knew she was powerless over it. Suicidal feelings of hopelessness began to overwhelm her. But she also knew she was being confronted with the meaning of her own existence and her freedom to choose between life and creativity or her capacity for self-destruction.

Addiction, when confronted, brings a person face-to-face with his or her own dark side—the capacity for the horrible and destructive. It brings the addict down to confront the inner demons, forcing one to one's knees in humiliation. It invokes the agony of Job crying out in anger against God for the injustice of a horrible affliction. Addiction brings one face-to-face with evil. And finally, if acknowledged, it brings one before one's mortality and the death of ego desires.

Recently, in a workshop on addiction and creativity, I asked the participants, many of whom were artists and/or recovering addicts, what characterized addiction for them. One person said, "Addiction brings me to face the void." Another said it brought him before death. Fear, anger, and anxiety were the dominant feelings of most. And one woman emphasized pain as the focal point of her experience, which, when denied, disintegrated into indulgence and self-pity. Another woman, who characterized herself as "addicted to the addict," felt that addiction came from "wanting order, perfection, and control but being unable to get it." Still another saw addiction as a power struggle with reality—denying "what is" and the flow of time and being. And another person added that his addiction finally absolutized everything and reduced his experience to the quantitative level—"I wanted one more, and still one more after that." Though all agreed that addiction brought them to the utter depths of darkness, they also emphasized that it brought them to awakening. As one man, a writer, expressed it: "It's a paradox. You learn you can't serve two masters. Yet, the creative force comes out of the experience of duality and the vivid presence of good and evil. For me, the suffering of addiction was a spur to the creative process, expressed by Milton and Dante. I found that too much unity and bliss does not produce the fire for creation." And a woman who was a sculptor added, "Facing my addiction both awakens me and grounds me. It sets the limits of [illegible]ality before me every time I might reach for a cigarette or a [illegible] And it helps me accept the material limits of actualizing [illegible]sion."

[illegible]rtist who began to find herself hostage to the refrigerator had felt basically in control of her tendency to overeat until she entered her most creative period. Then, just as she began to feel the flood of her creative energy, she also found herself compulsively overeating and losing control of her willpower. When she looked within, she realized she was experiencing terror before the awesome power of the creative process happening through her, and that she was overeating to escape experiencing her fear of being overwhelmed by the creative force. Once she became conscious of this, her addictive tendency to overeat acted as a reminder that she needed to ground herself, in order to face the creative fire and live in its tension. So she began a practice of meditation and breathing to center and ground herself. Thus she was able to dialogue imaginatively with the work to come, and her creative activity both deepened and increased.

As I was gradually recovering and was able to face with more serenity the questions I had asked myself in the detox ward, I had the following dream, which provided an image of the hostage in relation to addiction and creativity.

> It was time to begin my book on addiction and creativity, so I sat down in a café at a round table and ordered a few beers so I could start to write. But just then my lover approached, and I remembered I wasn't supposed to be drinking. We were on a trip and we drove through a deserted canyon to see a Tibetan Buddhist village that was now an abandoned town. As we drove through the empty street toward the mouth of the dead-end canyon, suddenly we were taken hostage. From out of nowhere a huge iron hook and hoist dropped from the blue sky and lifted the car in the air, finally funneling us into a huge bus where a Vietnamese couple held us captive. The woman was very cold and unfeeling. There were many others in the bus too. Eventually the woman ordered us all out in a line to be registered. As I stood in line, I saw several people I knew, to my surprise. They were all writers with whom I had participated in a conference on creativity, focusing on the Orpheus myth. When I lamented that we were all prisoners here, one of the woman poets said that she had voluntarily chosen to go on this retreat. I woke up in amazement, wondering why anyone would choose such a fate.

For a long time this dream intrigued me. I knew it involved the challenge of this book. Formerly it had been my practice to write in cafés, drinking wine while I wrote. The wine, I had always felt, loosened up the creative flow of my writing. There were many models for my practice, I had told myself. Had not Tennessee Williams said that he never wrote without first drinking wine? And so many of m favorite authors—Carson McCullers, Dylan Thomas, Thomas Wolfe, Eugene O'Neill, William Faulkner, F. Scott Fitzgerald, Ernest Hemingway, Theodore Roethke—all were drinking writers. In the dream I was only doing what I always did when I began a book. But now, in reality, I could no longer drink and write.

The dream showed I was heading for a dead end, like the dead end "spirits" of my drinking. I was also taken hostage without warning "from out of the blue," just as I had been taken "hostage" in the detox center. Yet there seemed to be a spiritual significance to being lifted up from and to the sky, which seemed confirmed by the ending of the dream. A creative woman writer from the conference on Orpheus and the creative process had voluntarily chosen this retreat. This dream reminded me that one could *choose* the creative process with all its unexpected shocks, as had this woman writer, or one could be taken hostage, as when one drinks. Of course, I knew the path was not quite so clear. For we are taken "hostage" as creative beings too. And it is possible to drink and create, as my drinking and writing models had shown, although many of these creative people had died from their addictions. But to choose to be taken by the creative call—was this not the challenge of creativity? Was not my urge to drink the "spirits" of the alcohol ultimately a desire for the higher spirit of the creative? Immediately, this brought to mind the paradox of creativity and the ancient concept of the Creative Daimon.

Down through the ages the creative person has acknowledged the power of the Creative Daimon. Socrates said it was an inner voice that guided him. The poet, Rilke, once said that he did not want to undergo psychoanalysis, for though it might remove his "devils," he might also lose his "angels," i.e., his creativity. Eugene O'Neill—who started drinking at fifteen—had to choose between the Creative Daimon and the Demon Lover when, by midlife, his drinking left him incapacitated for longer and longer periods, interfering with his writing. The Creative Daimon won; he stopped drinking and his writing deepened. In his later plays, *Long Day's Journey into Night* and *The Iceman Cometh*, he was able to give expression to the ravages of addiction and the effect on family and human relationships in a way that uniquely touched and opened the heart and soul of his audience.

The daimon is an inner force, a spirit within that energizes us and calls upon us to be and become creatively. The dictionary describes it as an indwelling power or spirit that possesses human beings with extraordinary drive and enthusiasm. It can also be an evil spirit. The original

Greek sense of the word connoted both the divine and the diabolical energies—hence the notion of the danger of creativity and Plato's notion of creativity as the "divine madness." According to Jung, the libido itself, the energy of the psyche, is by nature daimonic: it transcends consciousness and carries the tension of good and evil. Jung said, "If evil were to be utterly destroyed, everything daimonic, including God himself, would suffer a grievous loss. . . ."[3] Many creative artists see this struggle—the call to live in the tension between good and evil and to bear witness to the good—as the challenge of human existence, and the meaning art bears is to reveal this universal struggle. As Andrey Tarkovsky, the Russian film director, has said about his struggle to create:

> . . . the artist cannot be deaf to the call of truth; it alone defines his creative will, organizes it, thus enabling him to pass on his faith to others. An artist who has no faith is like a painter who was born blind . . . the subject grows within him like a fruit, and begins to demand expression. It is like childbirth. . . . The poet has nothing to be proud of: he is not master of the situation, but a servant. Creative work is his only possible form of existence, and his every work is like a deed he has no power to annul. . . . The aim of art is to prepare a person for death, to plough and harrow his soul, rendering it capable of turning to good.[4]

The daimon brings us the unusual intensity of creative fire. But it can also destroy us. To distinguish between these two possibilities—the creative and the destructive—Rollo May refers to the way a person relates to the daimon. The person who integrates the daimon, thereby becoming more whole, has a state of being that Rollo May calls the eudaimonic. This is the way of the creative person: an ever-deepening and broadening process whereby one becomes more whole and centered in one's being. In contrast, in the dysdaimonic state of being, the person becomes possessed, monomaniacal, and fanatical to the point where all life is reduced to that person's ever narrowing ego power drives. An example of someone in this state is Hitler, whose daimonic energy came to serve the forces of evil. There is also a third way to relate to the daimonic, according to May. This is the way of the antidaimonic person, who represses the daimonic and whose life energy becomes apathetic, mediocre, and dull. This is the image of the "mass man," the collectivized person who has become one of the crowd. Such a person, having repressed the daimonic, fears its energy and to maintain control tends to ward off its attending dangers as well as its possibilities.[5] It is then that the destructive energy of the dysdaimonic can surge up and seize us by surprise, as in the case of Nazism.

Using the above distinction, addiction leads to dysdaimonic possession because it reduces the person's wholeness to a monomaniacal obsession. But the same energy that serves addiction can be transformed into creative fire. The addict, in his very experience of the daimonic and the way it can destroy, can learn the supreme necessity of transforming that energy in the service of something higher.

If we look within the psyche, we find two archetypal figures corresponding to addiction and creativity—the Demon Lover and the Creative Daimon. In my experience, it is the archetypal figure of the Demon Lover to whom one gives oneself in addiction. For the Demon Lover seduces and can possess the soul as a slave. In contrast to the addictive possession by the Demon Lover, the process of recovery and creativity requires devoting oneself to the higher power within, the Creative Daimon. Often these two figures are confused. Distinguishing between these two images in myself has helped me to understand and sort through my confusions between addiction and creativity.

There are two stories that show the contrast between the way of addiction and the way of creativity. In the stories, both characters were taken hostage. But one died uselessly, while the other gave a gift to humankind. One is the story of Icarus, who, intoxicated with the power of flight, flew too high and lost his life. Thus he was never able to bring his newfound powers of flight to creative fruition. The other, which I relate in the last chapter, is the ancient Russian legend of the firebird, who broke the possession of the Demon Lover by sacrificing her life so her creative gifts could be free for all.

The myth of Icarus symbolizes the course of addiction—from its desire to flee an imprisoning situation, to the heights of euphoric escape and freedom, to the consequent fall—and the burning and the drowning that ensue. Icarus had been imprisoned with his father, the inventor Daedalus, in the very labyrinth Daedalus had designed for the king. Since escape by land or sea seemed impossible, Daedalus made two pairs of wings—one for himself and one for Icarus—of feathers threaded together and held in place by wax. Before they flew off he cautioned Icarus not to fly too high or too low. Having wrested many new creations from matter, he knew their limits. But shortly after, intoxicated by the great heights and the uplifting power of his new and wonderful wings, Icarus soared toward the sun. Lost in ecstasy, he forgot his father's advice and flew higher and higher until the sun melted the wax, whereupon the wing feathers came off and Icarus fell into the sea and drowned.[6]

In the creative process there is also a sort of "possession," a giving oneself over to the call of creativity. This kind of possession can be negative and narrowing, but it can also be deepening and transformative. In the process of creating, both sides are often felt. Their tension must be borne if one is to actualize the vision. The addict tries to escape the tension of existence. The creative person honors the tension by living in it and creating out of it.

The novelist Thomas Wolfe describes the state of possession he felt when writing his novels.

> I cannot really say the book was written. It was not constructed word by word or line by line or chapter by chapter. It came from me like lava pouring from the crater of a volcano. It was constructed on a scale in which the words were reckoned not by thousands, but by millions. It was something that took hold of me and possessed me, and before I was done with it—that is, before I finally emerged with the first completed part—it seemed to me that it had done for me. The tenement of one man's heart and brain and flesh and bone and sinew, the little vessel of his one life, could not possibly endure, could not possibly be strong enough or big enough to hold this raging tempest of his creative need.[7]

But he also emphasizes over and over how hard he struggled and worked to contain the raging creative energies and put them in form via the word. Creativity requires living in the tension of the opposites, while the Demon Lover seduces us by promising to take the tension away. That is why, when uncomfortable feelings come up, the addict reaches for drinks or drugs or food or romance or power or buys possessions—whatever erases the tension—instead of living through the tension, looking at the uncomfortable feelings, naming them, recording them, and sharing the insights with others, as does the creative person.

While possession by the Demon Lover in addiction leads to monomania—a narrowing of life and vision, reducing the addict to the status of an object defined by its craving—possession by the Creative Daimon ultimately can lead to a broadening of life, opening one up and furthering transformation. Erich Neumann distinguishes between the creative transformation of the total personality and the initial eruption of creativity. Creative transformation is guided by the wholeness of the psyche and centers the individual, leading to a new relationship with the self, the thou, and the cosmos. This is what happens in the recovering process of the addict.

What Neumann has said of the closeness of the creative man to suffering and sickness can also be said of the recovering addict.

> Consequently, the individual history of every creative man is always close to the abyss of sickness; he does not, like other men, tend to heal the personal wounds involved in all development by an increased adaptation to the collectivity. His wounds remain open, but his suffering from them is situated in depths from which another curative power arises, and this curative power is the creative process. As the myth puts it, only a wounded man can be a healer, a physician. Because in his own suffering the creative man experiences the profound wounds of his collectivity and his time, he carries deep within him a regenerative force capable of bringing forth a cure not only for himself but also for the community.[8]

Out of the wounds of addiction, consciously and courageously faced, can come creativity and healing. This is the call that challenges the recovering addict—the call to creativity. It is a call that requires courage—transforming one's addictive afflictions to creativity. Whether one creates a new spiritual self, an act of love that opens up the possibility of recovery and transformation to an other, or a work of art per se, it generously gives back the life it has received.

One of the chief differences between the Demon Lover and the Creative Daimon is generosity. The Demon Lover drains, sucks the life blood out of the addict, who finally becomes one of the "living dead," unable to contribute or give back anything to others or to the world. Addiction is linear, a progressive, degenerative disease. But creativity is regenerative and cyclical, a process of death and rebirth. Even though its energy may first be experienced as a kind of possession, ultimately, if integrated, the Creative Daimon brings new being. The creative person gives regenerative energy to the world, for his own transformation moves toward wholeness. A miracle happens in creativity—receiving becomes giving and giving becomes receiving. This is the key to the creative process.

Alexander Pushkin, Russia's most beloved poet, knew the power of both the Demon Lover and the Creative Daimon. A gambler and love addict, he was shot to death in a duel over love. In this poem he gives expression to the call of the Creative Daimon and the sacrifice required for this poetic gift.

> Like a corpse I lay in the waste land,
> And I heard God's voice cry out:

"Arise prophet, and see and hear,
Be charged with my will
And go out over seas and lands
To fire men's hearts with the word."[9]

2: THE MONEYLENDER

MEPHISTOPHELES: In this world I will bind myself to cater.
For all your whims, to serve and wait on you;
When we meet in the next world, some time later,
Wages in the same kind will then fall due.

FAUST: The next world? Well, that's no great matter;
Here is a world for you to shatter—

. . .

If ever to the moment I shall say:
Beautiful moment, do not pass away!
Then you may forge your chains to bind me,
Then I will put my life behind me . . .

—Goethe, *Faust*

WHEN I WAS THIRTY I fell in love with an artist. As our eyes met over candlelight he offered me a glass of red wine. Wondering if I would share the fate of the woman drinker in the film *Days of Wine and Roses*, I nevertheless accepted. Until then I had been very cautious whenever I drank, and that was seldom. Suddenly, with this drink, I experienced a euphoria that I had never imagined possible, a romantic high that was irresistible. If wine could open up the world this way, give me ecstasy whenever I wanted, who could refuse such a gift? It was as though, after all my years of hard work and study, a Moneylender suddenly had given me a million dollars free of interest for a while and urged me to spend it and enjoy it as I wished. But I did not read the terms of the loan contract. The interest would be exorbitant when the money was due. And I would be so indebted and dependent on the lender that my life would be my own no longer.

While I was flying high on wine I did not question my good luck to have found such a panacea—a beautiful, soothing liquid that inspired me to creativity, that infused me with courage in social situations and even allowed me to enjoy them, that first gave a warm romantic glow to my life and later a dramatic melancholic flair (*Liebestod*).

Like Icarus I soared toward the sun with my wings of wine, not realizing that by flying so high I would fall as deeply into the sea as had Icarus and my alcoholic father before me. My unimpeded flight lasted only a few years. By thirty-five I was already falling—at parties I suffered humiliating episodes of drunkenness made worse by blackouts, not even able to remember what I did or said, whom I had insulted or seduced. But the euphoric moments were so powerful that the guilt and humiliation through which I paid for them seemed minimal.

As is the way of an addiction, I came to need more wine to give me that ecstatic high. Now I needed two or three glasses of wine for that incomparable moment; one glass of wine was no longer enough. The three glasses of wine soon increased to four, then to a bottle, then to a liter daily. And the time of ecstasy decreased. The interest payments became higher—the nights of drunkenness increased; the hangovers were more painful. There were some warnings and an arrest, even a night in jail. The debt of guilt mounted so high I could no longer comprehend its infinite progression!

By now I was addicted. If truth be told, I would have sold my soul to the devil for a glass of wine. On one level I knew of my predicament, but my body and psyche were so dependent on alcohol that I tried to deny it. After all, I could function. I could work. I didn't drink in the morning. I might have a drinking problem, but I was *not* an alcoholic, *not* an addict. And so I made desperate attempts to control my drinking to prove to myself that I was still in control. The Jungian approach did not seem to help me in my efforts at control. So I tried behavioral methods and numerous plans for controlled drinking. I even consulted a hypnotist. But nothing worked. Sometimes I could limit my drinking for a period, and in relief thought I was getting better. But sooner or later the night of drunken humiliation occurred. The energy I devoted to my drinking and to trying to control it was enormous. The thought of the next drink was always on my mind—the wine with lunch or dinner, the aperitif at intermission at a concert, the drink with a friend after work, the beer après skiing or hiking or while traveling, soon became more important than the meal or the concert or the activity or the trip or the friend.

As a moth circles around a light, now flying into the flickering fire, then away as if to escape, only to fly back in again and finally to die in flames, so I hovered above the edge of an unfathomably dark abyss, flying high for a short time, then down, then up again only to fall into the waters of fire below. For about five years I lived in this way, always seeking the ecstatic high, drawn to wine as the moth to light, finally to burn and drown in its fiery waters. During these years there were still times of excitement, pleasure, and romance with wine. But compared to the periods of depression and anxiety, the moments of horror, and the increasing hopelessness about my life, they were dim flashes in the dark night of my soul. Still, I continued to drink.

Secretly, I was hoping that by transforming my father complex, I would also transform my drinking problem so that I could be a controlled normal drinker and live my life like others. But finally I knew my hopes were false. Though the father complex did transform, my drinking did not. I took a last fling, traveling and drinking all over Europe. Most of that time was lost in blackouts and an alcoholic haze. When I returned I tried to stop drinking.

During this period I was in debt to the Moneylender in my psyche. After one particularly humiliating incident I woke up and spontaneously wrote a fairy tale that showed the bondage of myself and my parents to this dark demonic figure. In the beginning of this story, the connection between the Moneylender and the Demon Lover gradually emerged, and I recognized this figure as the one who had haunted and chased after me throughout repeated dreams in my childhood.

> In the heart of a great forest lived a young girl who was very much alone. Although she had carved out a hole in a tall tear tree for her home, the tree was often cold—damp from the torrential rains that showered upon this great wood. She had gone into this forest to live when her parents were mysteriously bewitched by a tall, thin man who was dressed in black clothing. His cloak and high hat added to the mysterious power he seemed to have, and her father, in fear for his life, agreed to do whatever this man demanded.
>
> How this man came to have so much power was unknown to the townspeople, but all agreed that he was very clever. Instead of demanding that her father work for him or give him money, he gave her father delicious potions to drink, potions that made her father initially feel strong and powerful, but later weakened him and made him feel sick. Because the potions were so delicious and because initially he felt so strong after drinking them, he wanted more and more, and the tall, thin man in the black cloak and hat soon became his master. The potions also made her father lose his memory, and eventually he forgot that he had a daughter.
>
> While the tall, thin man was giving her father the irresistible potions, he offered her mother delicious desserts, which made the mother feel better after she came home from a hard day's work to support the family. The sweetness of these desserts so pleased her mother that she craved sweetness wherever she could find it, and, when she discovered the daughter's sweet and gentle personality, she fed upon it until one day the daughter was afraid she would be eaten up. That night the daughter dreamt that a tall, thin, threatening man dressed in black was chasing her and she ran for her life up some steps, over a bridge that spanned the railroad tracks, and down again to the other side. When she awoke she rushed to her father for help, but he had just drunk his potion for the night and could not see or hear her. She turned to her mother, who was tired after her hard day's work and in the midst of eating a rich chocolate cake, and the mother said, "Don't be silly, dear, there are no tall, thin men as you describe. That was just a dream."

> Desperate for help, she ran to her grandmother, who lived in the same house. When she told her grandmother about the tall, thin man, the old lady said, "Yes, I know the dangers of such men because I have been chased by them, too. You can stay with me and I will protect you." From then on, the little girl lived in her grandmother's room, and from this wise old lady she learned much. Her grandmother read her poems and told her stories of nature and of a magical world in which animals could speak, women could fly, and men could sing and dance. The old lady shed a tear and said, "Although I know there is such a kingdom, I myself have never been able to go there because it is a long journey and in my day women had to stay at home. But, also, I am very afraid of the tall, thin man, and before one can enter the magical kingdom, one must pass through a dark forest where this man lives. I have avoided this man and have never eaten the fruits from his trees nor drunk from his magical streams. But to get to the wonderful kingdom on the other side of this dangerous wood one must first face this man."

Despite this message from the psyche showing the bondage of my soul to the devil, I continued to drink. But I knew someday I would write about this tall, thin man whom I then called the Moneylender.

The Moneylender lures us to addiction through a high, through a fast rush to ecstasy. Most of us have experienced this allure in the fast energy charge of sugar and caffeine, or the delicious euphoria of wine, or the rush of cigarettes, or the dreamy other worldliness of marijuana, or the stimulating excitement of cocaine. Sometimes these experiences are so extraordinary that we want to repeat them—we want more and more, again and again. The substance that gives us so much pleasure and excitement becomes our Demon Lover and ever more the one we turn to in time of need. For soon we are indebted to it for the extraordinary energy and ecstasy it gives us. Sometimes it even seems that all meaning rests in it. For these substances can inspire us to new heights of creativity, take us into unknown depths of experience, intensify erotic pleasure, give us courage and energy, and even calm us when we are anxious and afraid. With them we seem to become more than human. Money, power, success, ambition, romance, work, gambling, and shopping are among the other things that can also give us this high. When we begin to love these substances or things as the only or major source of our meaning, when they become so powerful in our lives that we are willing to give up all else, even our lives, for and to them, then they have become the master and we are indebted to them. We are in bondage to the addiction.

The Moneylender stands behind the experience of addiction—the irresistible high, the shortcut to ecstasy, and the insurmountable debt we owe in the end. Eager to entice us he offers a good deal, gives us what we want at no initial cost; we pay only later. He gives us wonderful things, offering shortcuts to pleasures and experiences that might take years of work to achieve. He is imbedded in the American economy, in the lure of the credit card, behind advertisements, in entertainment. We see his image constantly in literature and films—the devil in Goethe's *Faust*, or in the Russian legend that Stravinsky put to music in "The Soldier's Tale."[1] But first of all he is in our psyche—that figure in us who convinces us we can have something for nothing, a free ride to paradise, a shortcut to creativity. For an addict, he is behind every glass of wine, every line of cocaine, every cigarette, every mounting debt, every romance that keeps us spellbound and remains untransformed into love, every power play. In the beginning the Moneylender may seem friendly, even kindly. But once we are in debt his cruelty and demonic power often astound us. In the end we pay far more than we receive. And sometimes we pay with our lives.

The Moneylender is a frequent figure in dreams. Here is the dream of a young woman who was addicted to cocaine, addicted in her love relationships, and, underneath it all, addicted to an intense idealism that finally threatened her life. The dream shows the initial allure of the Moneylender, the terrible price the dreamer had to pay, and the sadistic deception involved in the transaction.

> I am a princess and have a penis. I have been away to college and have just returned to my father's kingdom. I have a meeting with a man who is the Moneylender of the kingdom, and he agrees to a loan that will enable me to complete my study at the School of Music. My father walks up to me as the Moneylender walks away and smiles, saying he is glad I have accomplished this transaction on my own.
>
> I have a boyfriend and am developing toward sexual awareness. But I realize that I have an abnormality. I am afraid for my boyfriend or my father to know. I go to the Moneylender to rid myself of the penis. Immediately, I am guilt-ridden because I know that both my boyfriend and my father know about the penis and would be angry that I have consulted the Moneylender.
>
> I am standing, doubled over, and the Moneylender is beside me. I have just about decided to leave when I realize that he has piano wire wrapped around the penis, and he cuts it off at this instant. I feel a terrible loss, and I believe the Moneylender has deceived me and I have deceived both father and boyfriend. Also, I know that with the penis cut off I cannot hide my deception from them. I'm afraid and am mentally considering a sex change (to give myself a real vagina).

> I walk away from the Moneylender and around a building, which he goes into. My boyfriend is also in the building. I start to look at a picture album of close-ups of my boyfriend, who is also a famous rock star. He looks very contemplative and intelligent in the pictures. A voice is saying to me, "We had hoped he would have shown more maturity in dealing with the present situation." I am aware that my boyfriend is in the building with the Moneylender, who has now transformed into a motorcycle gang leader, and my boyfriend has started a fight with him. The Moneylender has badly injured my boyfriend, whose legs are now paralyzed.
>
> In the final scene, my boyfriend is sitting on a country roadside with a few little children around him. They are little black kids who have been his friends for a long time. These children are now his only remaining friends, and they are curiously asking what he'll do now. He is obviously helpless but is filled with resentment. He says, "Someone had better do something about my legs." I am poignantly aware of the pathos and know that no one is listening to him except the children.

In the dream the Moneylender first appears as helpful. He can loan the dreamer the money she needs to embark upon the most creative venture in her life—to complete her professional training in music. Her father, in whose kingdom the Moneylender rules, is glad she has accomplished this transaction on her own. Carol, the dreamer, said her father was an eternal boy, a "puer" who lived in a make-believe world. A romantic who lived in fantasy, he was never happy once he actualized a dream and always skipped on to another dream. It is in this world—the world of the romantic dreamer who never actualizes fantastic ideals or accepts their worth—that the first transaction with the Moneylender is made.

The dreamer was a romantic too, a very creative woman who idealized relationship above all else. Since adolescence, relationship had been a "religion" for her. Like her father, Carol was an eternal youth who lived in the realm of possibilities. In the dream she was a princess, an eternal girl with potential not yet developed. For her the penis symbolized the creative phallus, a masculine aspect of creativity. In the dream she is ashamed of it, sees it as an abnormality, and does not want her boyfriend and her father to know. She is in a panic! Her budding sexuality and the creative potential do not seem compatible. In her life she had always suffered a terrible conflict between her creativity and relationship. She wanted relationship so intensely and so ideally that she always sacrificed her creativity for her lover, so the relationship would last. But of course it never did.

At the time of the dream Carol had been consulting the Moneylender in herself. She had been trying to overcome her addiction to cocaine, but as yet she had been unsuccessful. She saw the Moneylender as the figure in herself who urged her to take cocaine in order to create. When she took the drug she felt she could compose brilliant music with a speed and energy that seemed to be spectacular. She also used drugs of various sorts to travel deeply into her unconscious mind. She knew that going too far could kill her and her creativity, but in fascination she was always drawn to the destructive edge. She was under the illusion, she said, that the destructive way actually helped her to create. But it was not long before the shortcut to creativity became a pact with the devil. Soon she was dependent on the drug to create, and the interest she was paying was exorbitant in terms of her time, energy, money and self-respect. Later she saw that what she first—on drugs—had thought was so creative was a letdown to her sober mind. The Moneylender, she realized, had deceived her, had given her the illusion of an easy way, a shortcut, but one that made her pay too dearly by cutting off the creative phallus. She was paying with a guilt that almost paralyzed her. In the dream she considered a sex change to hide the deception, but on waking she realized that this was just a way to avoid the issue, to sidetrack herself. It was seeking an external solution to the inner conflict she felt about her creativity—her ambivalence between commitment to creativity versus commitment to relationship, and her ambivalence between the discipline required for creativity and the shortcut that she had hoped drugs could give her. The sex change also symbolized an external solution that would allow her to avoid dealing with feelings of anger.

After her transaction with the Moneylender, she discovers that her boyfriend and the Moneylender are in the same building. Now the identity of her boyfriend emerges. She saw him as an immature side of herself who by fighting with the Moneylender holds onto a no-win, deadly relationship. The dream shows the Moneylender to be a vicious, sadistic character—a motorcycle gang leader who injures and paralyzes the boyfriend. To Carol the connection between the boyfriend and the Moneylender was clear. The boyfriend was her own angry and resentful martyr-victim side holding onto the relationship with the Moneylender by fighting instead of realizing there is no deal to be made with the devil. Instead of putting her energy into the work of transforming herself, she continued to fight a losing battle. Years later, after much work on herself, she said, "If you make a deal with the Moneylender, (the Devil), you give away your soul, your creativity. If you fight with the Moneylender, you still stay in connection. The connection with the Moneylender—be it alcohol, cocaine, or an illusory ideal—must be severed. If in the dream I could have turned away from the Moneylender and said, 'No! You can't have my creativity!' then I could have transformed." But the path she took was to give up her creativity and to struggle for the next ten years with drugs and romanticized relationships, trying to hold on to an impossible ideal. Just as in the dream the boyfriend fought and was paralyzed, so she stayed crippled in bondage to the Moneylender.

The final scene of the dream gives a picture of this condition—the boyfriend paralyzed, helpless, filled with resentment. He says, "Someone had better do something about my legs." He is a victim, not taking responsibility for his paralysis, denying his part in it. Here is an image of what keeps the addictive cycle going—the denial that one is in the grips of an addiction and the resentment that someone else did it and someone else had better help. This resentment makes the addict continue to drink or use drugs or gamble. But the dream shows a hopeful ending, for the dreamer feels the pathos of this condition. The black children who listen and befriend the paralyzed boyfriend symbolize the spontaneous creative instincts in touch with the natural world and the unconscious.

Eventually Carol was able to overcome her addiction to cocaine. But her addiction to the ideal—especially to the ideal relationship—continued for ten more years. She fell in love with a sensitive, creative man, who—when he drank—told beautiful stories. They had numinous philosophical and spiritual conversations, drunk with the beauty of meaning. Before, she had taken cocaine to achieve this kind of illumination, for it had helped her express the ideal ad infinitum. Now this wonderful beauty was happening in the relationship. Carol lived for these intense conversations, but they became less and less frequent as her boyfriend started drinking more and more. She married him anyway, because she saw his beautiful potential and she knew she could save him. In the beginning the relationship had a creative energy that was like a drug, intense and exciting. But then the energy became crazy—a draining and destructive force, just like the drugs she had taken earlier. Even though the relationship wasn't working, she wanted to save it and her husband. She even started drinking with her husband, hoping he'd see how much *she* was suffering from it and stop it for both of them. But of course her "savior ideal" did not work, and her husband's drinking got worse.

When he threatened to kill her if she left him, she finally hit bottom. The verbal threats and abuse turned into physical realities. He locked her in a room and threatened her with a weapon. Facing death in this way, she realized that saving him was an illusion and that she had to leave the relationship to save herself. Her belief that she alone could win the battle against her husband's alcoholism, that her love, her commitment to the ideal of the marriage could make the relationship work, was crushed. The threat of physical death from her husband brought her to face the death of her own ego ideals.

Remembering the Moneylender dream, she realized that the Moneylender was involved in her relationship. She had been living off the high of her idealism about the relationship's potential. But the price she had to pay to keep this relationship was exorbitant: she had been sacrificing her creativity. Just as in the dream her boyfriend had fought with the Moneylender, she had been fighting with her husband and his alcoholism for "taking her creativity away," when she had given it away herself.

The threat of death brought all this before her. In taking responsibility for her addiction to this illusory ideal, she faced the death of the ideal itself. Realizing that she and her idealism were not more powerful than her husband's alcoholism, she went to Al-Anon. There she learned detachment. She learned that she could not control or save the relationship, no matter how fine her ideals might have been. She learned to accept her own mortality and the limits of human existence. And she realized that despite her love for him, she had to separate from her husband. She began to work with her creativity and to live in the tension between the infinite possibility and its finite realization. Finally she began to compose again, this time without drugs, without the high (and the high price) of the Moneylender. About her new relation to creativity, she said:

> I've gradually come to accept my own creativity—that the ideal is not out there, but in me to express. I no longer look *only* for potential, but I want to be with people who are actualizing their potential every moment in their lives. Now it's easier to accept the finitude, but the finitude also looks better to me. Before, my composing was never good enough. Now I can look at what I do and love it.

The Moneylender operates through the cycle of inflation and deflation. The inflation of the woman in the story above was the inflation of the ideal that she, by herself, could save her husband and the relationship. While she was taking drugs she suffered from the inflation of the drug regarding her creativity. Her deflation came from the guilt and humiliation of being dependent on the drugs and later from the crash of her ideals. The inflation a few drinks brings makes one feel charming, funny, interesting, brilliant, courageous, creative. A few wins at the gambling table bring a feeling of elation, cleverness, triumph, power. Drugs often provide the feeling of great insight, facile contact with the unconscious, the feeling of shamanic vision. And when we are in love, romance brings the soaring flight of merger with the universe. We are so high that no one can touch us. But once the flight is over there is usually a fall. Then comes the terrible humiliation, the hopeless depression, the irreparable guilt and emptiness.

The way inflation and deflation alternate and turn into each other has been dramatized by Eugene O'Neill. O'Neill grew up in a family engulfed in addict/co-addict patterns—his mother was addicted to drugs, his brother died of alcoholism at forty-five, and his father was a heavy drinker and a slave to money. O'Neill portrays their guilt and the way they blamed and depended on one another for their own addictions in his semi-autobiographical drama, *Long Day's Journey into Night*. In *The Iceman Cometh* he shows the unendurable tension of the inflation of the "pipe dream" and the deflating guilt that follows. As Larry, one of the drunken characters, says, "The lie of a pipe dream is what gives life to the whole misbegotten mad lot of us, drunk or sober."[2] In the same play, O'Neill exposes the lie of the pipe dream for both the addict and the codependent partner. The main character, the salesman Hickey, has returned to Harry Hope's bar, a haven where he goes for his periodic drunks. All the lost souls who hang out at this bar are addicted not only to alcohol but to the dream that they will pay up "tomorrow," that tomorrow they will change and start their lives anew. But "tomorrow" is always a day away and never comes. It is Harry Hope's birthday, and all the barflies are drinking cheap whiskey or sleeping in a drunken stupor when Hickey arrives. He is popular at the bar for his humor and affability. As he says about himself, he is a master moneylender of the pipe dream. "It was like a game, sizing people up quick, spotting what their pet pipe dreams were, and then kidding 'em along that line, pretending you believed what they wanted to believe about themselves. Then they liked you, they trusted you, they wanted to buy something to show their gratitude."[3]

When Hickey comes this time he is not drinking and he tries to sell them on his cure—a cure for their pipe dreams so they "simply won't give a damn! Any more than I do!"[4] Hickey persuades some of the bums in the bar to try to stop drinking and go back out in the world again to get the job they say they'll get tomorrow. At first they scoff at Hickey, but then a few get their hopes up and try. The others watch and wonder if there is hope for them, too. Hickey knows they will fail and be "cured," knocked cold of their pipe dreams. For Hickey is the Iceman who brings death. As he says to the disillusioned drinkers:

> By rights you should be contented now, without a single damned hope or lying dream left to torment you! But here you are, acting like a lot of stiffs cheating the undertaker! . . . Don't you know you're free now to be yourselves, without having to feel remorse or guilt, or lie to yourselves about reforming tomorrow? Can't you see there is no tomorrow now? You're rid of it forever! You've killed it! You don't have to care a damn about anything any more! You've finally got the game of life licked, don't you see that? Then why the hell don't you get pie-eyed and celebrate?[5]

At the bar where everyone now is disillusioned and back to cynical drinking, Hickey tells the story of what a pipe dream did to him and his late wife, Evelyn. They had loved each other. But Hickey was always drinking and running around. Nothing daunted Evelyn's love; no matter what he did she always forgave him, making excuses for him and defending him against himself. Then he would promise not to do it again. Nothing could shake her faith in him because "she was a sucker for a pipe dream."[6] She knew she could make him happy, so happy he wouldn't want to do any of the bad things anymore. He believed her dream, but he continued to drink and run around with other women. Evelyn continued to forgive him. Hickey's guilt kept mounting. In anguish, Hickey bursts out revealing the anger and hatred inside him, the guilt that finally drove him so crazy that all he knew to do was to kill her.

> Christ, can you imagine what a guilty skunk she made me feel! If she'd only admitted once she didn't believe any more in her pipe dream that someday I'd behave! But she never would. Evelyn was stubborn as hell. Once she'd set her heart on anything, you couldn't shake her faith that it had to come true—tomorrow! It was the same old story, over and over, for years and years. It kept piling up, inside her and inside me. God, can you picture all I made her suffer, and all the guilt she made me feel, and how I hated myself! If she only hadn't been so damned good—if she'd been the same kind of wife I was a husband.[7]

Hickey tells his defensively callous listeners that finally he felt relieved of all his guilt, for he knew that killing her was the way to give Evelyn peace from the misery of loving him. He even knew she would forgive him. Suddenly he heard himself saying what he had always wanted to tell her. "Well, you know what you can do with your pipe dream now, you damned bitch!"[8] Shocked, he stops the nightmarish story he has been telling and bursts into frantic denial of the horror his life has become. His drunken listeners try to deny what they have heard too, for Hickey represents the icy death-dealer of their own addictions. When Hickey is taken away by the police who, disguised, have been in the bar, all the drunks but Larry try to excuse him, saying he was insane. They try to pretend they were only humoring him, that they had no real hopes of changing all along. They sink into drink and partying as they had before Hickey arrived. Only Larry understands fully the icy death that Hickey was selling; only he understands that Hickey finally sold his soul to the Devil, to the ultimate Moneylender, for a pipe dream of absolute freedom to drink that brings only death instead. And Larry, unable to choose life, stares blankly at the wall in bitter self-derision as the play ends.

Just as the inflation of the pipe dream feeds the addiction of the characters in *The Iceman Cometh*, so does the way they relate to guilt. Either they identify with guilt as do the drunks who drink to forget their guilt, or they identify with guiltlessness as did the codependent wife, Evelyn, whose love was so martyred and sacrificial that she seems almost inhuman, shadowless and unreal. She, too, is in denial of addiction. Hickey, the pivotal character, shows these two sides in the conflict that drives him crazy. First he feels so totally guilty for abusing his wife that he murders her to end the pain. But the result is the cold, pathological guiltlessness of the iceman who feels remorse no more. This play of opposites around guilt is a feature typical in relationships patterned in the addict/codependent mold. The addict typically plays the "guilty one" the morning after succumbing to the addiction. But while the addict is drinking or using or gambling or romancing, he or she is in a state of denial that does not acknowledge the guilt. The partner who is the co-addict (addicted to controlling and blaming the addict) also alternates between the guiltless self-justification of the martyr who is sacrificing for this "no good," and a terrible guilt for having failed in the relationship to "save" the partner. In this pattern the codependent gets a feeling of power and virtuousness from the addict's guilt and dependency while the addict depends on the co-addict for survival and often projects his own strength and goodness on the partner. A vicious cycle of guilt and the Moneylender's promise of relief from the pain of this guilt ensues, and neither party faces directly the paradoxical nature of the union of opposites in their human condition.

The following story of a rock musician shows how the "high" of severe drug and love addiction can be transformed into a serene and centered life. It emphasizes how the Moneylender's seductive offer of euphoria colludes with the Romantic's wish for ecstasy and merger in a paradisal Garden of Eden. But it also shows the enormous debt of guilt incurred from the Moneylender who, for this man, had a feminine image, The White Lady.[9] Although the man who told this story nearly died of his addiction, through his intensive commitment to the work of recovery via the twelve steps and *zazen* (Zen meditation), he is now free of his bondage to The White Lady, the former mistress of his addiction to cocaine and romance.

Michael's early family history is typical for many addicts. There was some addiction on the paternal side; his grandfather was an alcoholic and his father reacted by being a compulsive worker (workaholic). The immediate family patterns were also dysfunctional. Everything at home revolved around taking care of his mother, who was subject to devastating hysterical fits. As a small boy he found this very frightening: he felt not only abandoned and helpless but also responsible for rescuing her. To this also was added the confusion of being spoiled and overprotected by his mother. The father was away from home much of the time, and his emotional energy went into protecting and trying to please the mother. If he fought with his mother, he was always held in the wrong by his father too. Michael was caught in the conflict of wanting to protect his mother, but also felt angry. The resulting guilt and confusion was enormous.

He had his first "drink" at ten at a party given by his parents. He liked neither the taste nor the effect—it made him feel sick. But he wanted to drink because he wanted to be "cool" and join in with older boys. At thirteen a friend gave him some Dexedrine and Benzedrine, bought on the streets. These drugs made him feel powerful and in control. They gave him a grand feeling about himself. With drugs, he didn't need other people. At fourteen he first tried cocaine and immediately loved it. "It was euphoric, and I was getting away with something I wasn't supposed to do. It was a way of rebelling against my possessive mother." He remembers the thrill of driving around in a stolen car; it was a romantic feeling that he later associated with the seduction of the Demon Lover.

Even more powerful than the allure of drugs was the allure of women. "The woman in my life was always a 'drug' to me." In his teen years Michael had two long-term relationships. During this time he described his drinking and drug usage as minimal. But when the second relationship broke up, he went full fire for drugs, smoking much marijuana and taking LSD every day. Both drugs and women were addictive for him. "They got me out of myself, erased reality, and I didn't have to deal with who I was. My fears were gone." The drugs had another advantage for him, too. They relieved him of his parents' possessiveness, a heavy burden for many only children. "When I took the drugs I was out of my parents' power. I felt free." Although he was extremely bright and gifted, due to his drug usage his grades were poor, so he quit school and angrily retaliated against his parents for not paying for his education. He wanted to be a musician, but he was not serious about practicing music.

At twenty-two he met "the great love of his life," a woman he married the following year. Soon they were in a typically addictive relationship: he was the wild acting-out romantic drug user while she became the practical martyred judge who kept control and maintained order.

During the sixties he made a conscious decision to be "high." A hippie, he played drums in rock and roll bands and was part of the conscientious objector movement protesting injustices—the war in Vietnam and the conditions in the Watts and fillmore ghettos. But being high was his major goal.

> I smoked marijuana like cigarettes. It changed my reality, mellowed me out. Everything was cool. My philosophy was 'Don't bug me, I'm OK.' Being high was a career.

Since he was constantly high, he noticed very little about what was going on in his marriage and neglected his wife. But underneath this apparent lack of concern was an enormous sense of guilt, which the marijuana, like a good soft earth mother, covered over and mellowed out.

When he broke his leg in a motorcycle accident, Michael's addiction took over his life. Lying around in a body cast, he was totally dependent. He was on welfare, and his wife was taking care of him. All day long he smoked dope, joint after joint. Now it was really a "habit."

After recovering from the accident he joined a band that was backed by a drug dealer who was all too eager to have the musicians playing on a high. With a new unlimited access to cocaine, it became his drug of choice, and it helped him to escape. By now Michael had given himself up to The White Lady and could no longer hear the music in his heart.

> Cocaine was The White Lady, the one woman who never says no. I could always depend on it, or so I thought at the time. It's a romantic drug. It's an aphrodisiac and induces sexual prowess. When I had my cocaine everything was OK. So it became my drug of choice and a habit. It made me feel "up." First things first—getting it became the most important thing. The physical process of snorting, the head mucus, all that was important. Snorting made me feel erotic and eventually compulsively erotic. So having sex with many women became part of my addiction. Sensual feeling was my priority. At first climaxes were easy and great. But later they were hard to get and hold onto. Later, too, I couldn't hold onto a thought. I was so toxic I couldn't pay attention to anything except cocaine and sex. In the end I even lost sex because it became difficult to reach orgasm with a partner. Physically it was difficult to climax because of the toxicity. I was snorting a quarter ounce of cocaine a day. When I masturbated the first orgasm came fast, but then, as happened eventually with a line of cocaine, the effect was short-lived and I would have to repeat the process over and over again for hours and hours. I was snorting every couple of minutes always chasing the high. I was sick! I had to take so much cocaine I couldn't take enough. Finally, I wasn't eating. I couldn't sleep. I'd be up five days and nights in a row. I was grouchy and then I'd be in tears, nervously breaking down, crying in front of my wife and daughter because I felt so powerless and trapped in a vicious cycle of addiction. I knew I was dying. But I kept trying to cover it all up with more drugs and beer. I gained a lot of weight from drinking beer, but my whole physical system was suffering from malnutrition.
>
> Emotionally, the shame was overwhelming. On the recording scene, hookers were always available, paid for by the drug-dealing manager. I was betraying my wife and myself. I knew I didn't want to be doing this, but I couldn't stop doing it. I felt trapped because I didn't see a way out. I didn't think I could go through the withdrawal. If I had to take all these drugs to be even remotely "sane" and function, to get off them would be fatal. I was afraid that I'd explode and go crazy and die, that my body would burst and I'd jump out of my skin.

The turning point came for him one night when his wife calmly confronted him. She said it simply: "I can't live with a drug addict anymore." This time Michael knew she meant it. Before she had begged, cajoled, nagged, threatened, withheld love and sex. To her desperate pleas, he would lie about what he had done, promising to change and be different the next day. As a codependent, she was hooked into her side of the dysfunctional relationship, accepting the deception. But this time he knew she was fed up and meant what she was saying. So, he went to a doctor who recommended he go to Narcotics Anonymous (NA). A few days later he went to a meeting and immediately knew he was in the right place. He knew the people there were all drug addicts like himself, but they weren't using. Although he didn't get off all the drugs immediately, he continued to go to meetings. When he got a sponsor and started to work the twelve steps, eventually he was able to stop using. This is his view of the effectiveness of the twelve-step program.

> With a client suffering from substance abuse any therapist who doesn't explore the possibility of finding recovery in a twelve-step program is wasting the time of therapy: the addiction must be treated first, directly and on a daily basis, and no therapist has the same power as God. The twelve-step program is a springboard for spiritual practice. But the challenge it gives to many is to go further. Keeping the foundation of twelve-step meetings on a *regular basis* is the essential groundwork for any addict. And they are an excellent basis for creativity. But, for me, combining the twelve steps with Zen meditation and Jungian individuation work has been a powerfully deep transformer.

After Michael had some "clean time" and his mind and body cleared up, he was able to see that he had to face his addiction as a disease—a combination of physical, emotional, and spiritual factors. Looking back he could see that as the addiction progressed, he had stopped feeling the music he had inside him. With all his energy directed toward getting the drugs, he had none left for either love or creativity. At the same time he now felt that without drugs he couldn't play at all. Toward the end he had even lost the capacity to have the "high" for which he had given up his soul, and he was in deep bondage to the Moneylender. The intense feeling of shame and guilt from which he suffered are symptomatic of the exorbitant interest demanded by this inner figure in the psyche.

At a later point in his recovery, he began analysis and his initial dream showed that guilt was an overriding issue. In the dream he was in a department store to return a sweater he had purchased. He had lost the receipt and was worried that he would be accused of stealing the sweater. Some of his possessions were also in the store. At the desk was an older woman who was authoritative, judgmental, and suspicious. Even though he had not stolen he felt guilty, not knowing how to explain why his things were in the store. But he fought the guilty feelings in order to retrieve his things. In the dream there was also a helpful figure, a younger woman who was sympathetic and more trusting. At first he thought the dream was insignificant. But the accusing, judgmental woman kept appearing in his dreams, just as angry and scolding as he had experienced his wife in the days of his using and his mother when he was a child. Reflecting on his childhood, he realized he had received a mixed message from his parents: "You're our good little boy, but you do things the wrong way." From this he had concluded he couldn't ever please them, and in reaction he tried to fill this hole of hurt with drugs and love. Now, as the guilt-provoking woman kept reappearing in his dreams, he had to look within to find and confront that judgmental figure in himself. In a later dream this actually happened. In this dream his wife was making cross-stitches on a masklike face. As he watched his wife's hands at work, light danced over the mask-face so he could see it clearly. Just then the same authoritative lady from the initial dream appeared, and he realized she was part of himself and also the mask. When he realized she was part of himself, he understood he could direct her actions. In the process of talking with this inner figure, he began to feel more confident and free. Finally she agreed to leave the place of power behind the desk and to be easier on him, to let go and not be so demanding.

This judging guilt-provoking woman was an inner figure that had formed developmentally from his upbringing. But she was also one of the faces of a mask for the Moneylender to whom he had sold his soul in the forms of both his drug and love addictions, which made him feel guilty all the time.

> Guilt was my constant companion—for years and years. One might say that the addiction fed off incessant guilt, a vicious cycle of guilt and the Moneylender's promise of relief from the pain of this guilt. For me it was very important to understand this vicious circle inherent in my days of using: Feel guilty about wanting to use. Feel guilty about spending money to use. Feel guilty about using. Feel guilty about the aftereffects of using. Feel guilty about lying about using. The only cure—use more! Stop using tomorrow.

As Michael worked on the steps in his NA program, he cleared away the debris of excessive guilt. He began to become more honest with himself, and his obsession to use drugs was lifted. Taking responsibility for his own negative feelings, he made amends for the emotional debts he owed. He also participated actively in the twelfth step, work of service—volunteering at recovery houses, speaking at meetings, and helping others as he himself had been helped. He gave of his new understanding about the disease of addiction by going to San Quentin prison and helping chair some NA meetings there. All of this service, in turn, helped him. For it reminded him of what it had been like to use drugs and constantly alerted him to his own denial.

Although he had loosened the grip of the Moneylender over his drug addiction, he was still in bondage through his obsession with being loved. About three years into his recovery, his wife, who had been working on her own addiction of codependency through Al-Anon, decided she wanted to leave. The threat of separation threw him down the abyss to a new bottom. For underneath his drug addiction lay a far deeper addiction to love. Had he not, after all, given up the drugs for his wife and to try to save the relationship? Now he had to look deeply within himself. Suicidal thoughts overwhelmed him. The cravings for drugs and alcohol, which had been lifted earlier through his work on the twelve steps, reappeared.

Because he had been so fully committed in his twelve-step work and knew it had worked to transform his drug addiction, Michael had faith that it could work on this much deeper and more difficult addiction. So he got a new sponsor and reworked the steps, with the focus on his dependency on women, and doubled his efforts at NA meetings. Before the decision to separate was made, the couple had decided to go into therapy with a Jungian orientation so they could see what their dreams were saying about their relationship and about the inner growth process of each one separately. For a short time they came together; then each decided to work individually. In therapy he looked within to see the developmental reasons for his excessive dependency, and he realized he had been projecting his capacity for love on his wife and on women in general rather than seeing the love in himself and taking responsibility for it.

After giving up drugs, he had decided to leave the world of rock music, for it is a dangerous place for a recovering addict. But he knew that as his recovery progressed he would be playing from the heart and would enjoy it—something the drugs had made impossible for him before. Now, in recovery, he had begun to experience life itself as creative. This creative process became aligned with his own unique individuation process. The practice of meditation helped him see things better, particularly how guilt had kept him in a vicious circle of addiction—to both drugs and to love relationships. In order to ease the guilt, Michael had made half-hearted apologies but had not truly amended to change his life. When his partner, through the guilt of her own codependency, accepted the apology also half-heartedly, then the two were hooked in the vicious circle of half-truths. He came to see that if either partner accepts a romantic projection that is related to addiction, it hooks the other in the addictive cycle. (Wanting to be *the* "anima woman" or *the* "inspiring animus guide" are examples of such addictive inflation.) Only a whole-hearted commitment, without hidden resentment and power drives, could break the cycle of addictive love. As he said, "Addiction is a family disease and recovery can begin anywhere in the circle—recovery starts when one person refuses to go along with the denial game."

When his wife left, three years into his recovery, Michael was forced to get to the deeper layers of his addictions, because then his addiction to her was revealed. In the beginning he tried to avoid this revelation through the quick fix of developing crushes on other women. At the same time he was enormously jealous of her relationships with other men. But eventually he came to see that one of his major issues was separation.

> I never learned to be truly independent as a man. There is a lack of male initiation in our culture. I was addicted to a woman who would provide a home and who would be there for me as mother and the mother of my child. When my wife left, at first I felt I had nothing left. I wasn't prepared to be alone because I hadn't looked within. But I did have the resources of the program. I lived and breathed the program. I relied on the twelve steps as a source of spiritual strength. I had a way to receive help from a group of people who understood and had a way to give back. I also started to meditate—*zazen*. After a short time I became committed to this process of meditation. The practice I do helps me to let go of the guilt of the past and of the expectations of the future. I also had to let go of my wife and my projections on her as the meaning of my life. Now I try to acknowledge my own inner eros, and I'm learning to live in the moment.

Finally, in the process of looking within, he was graced with the following dream.

> I fell asleep—lying on my bed—while reading the introduction to the *I Ching* by Carl Jung. A picture of Jung sitting at his desk in a three-piece suit appeared and he said to me, sitting across from him, "I don't know if I've ever told you this but I'm your father." Jung and I then somehow changed into full-length, white robes. These robes seemed holy—no buttons, not flashy but absolutely clean, linen-type robes. We were walking together down a path made from redwood humus. Jung seemed slightly larger than life and I was the size of a five- or six-year-old child, although I looked as I do today. Jung was saying things to me like "You are God-like. You are blessed. You are a healer." He was communicating in a

> nonverbal way all the types of things a father might communicate to his son over a lifetime.
>
> The path was lined with the houseplants from our home. There was a white light beginning at the edge of the path that encircled the entire scene. This light was infinite yet sort of foggy.
>
> Suddenly I heard a voice calling my name. I wasn't sure if this voice came from the dream. As it turned out, the voice was not from the dream. My friend was calling me from outside my apartment, and the dream was interrupted. This was early afternoon. When I went to sleep that night, the dream continued precisely where it had left off, and Jung and I continued walking down the path, communicating in this nonverbal manner.
>
> We came to a clearing that was lined with the same houseplants plus larger versions of the very crystals in my therapist's living room. Jung took a seat on a low bench and I sat at his feet. As I looked up at him, I realized Jung was actually me—there were two of me. My wife appeared for an audience with Dr. Jung. She looked tense, apprehensive, mistrusting, afraid, agitated, and more. Jung said to her, "See the love in your husband." She looked at me and a wave of serenity came over her. She became truly happy, joyous and free. Then I heard a voice calling my name again, the same as in the afternoon. I awoke. It was three-thirty in the morning and no one was there. I was astounded!

This dream overwhelmed him with awe for the gift of the growth process that was happening within him, and it helped him see the love in himself. This love, he realized, was the gift of divine love, an unconditional love that he felt in the giving of his twelfth step work. Now he was able to affirm that healing love within himself. The initial image of his wife as unhappy, tense, and untrusting showed to him the state of his own feminine side when he projected it externally on his wife. But as soon as he saw the love that was within him, this inner feminine figure became joyous and serene. Jung, he felt, was the healing masculine side of himself, the inner father who could guide a son to wholeness the way his own father never could. The dream focused clearly for him the necessity to become his own authority and to transform the inner critical judge that made him feel so guilty, by consciously accepting the higher powers of wisdom, love, faith, and compassion. The dream also suggested an important way toward this goal—the path of meditation (symbolized by the white robes), which is emphasized by the eleventh step. Accepting the dream suggestion, he began to meditate. Soon he was sitting daily for long periods of time. Through his practice of meditation he has learned to let his worries, fears, guilts, and expectations come up and let them go. He has learned to breathe deeply and allow the breath of the cosmos to flow through him. The combination of the twelve-step work, meditation, and his work in therapy has given him many insights about the nature of addiction in his life and about the course of recovery and creativity. These are some of his reflections.

> In addiction there is always a descent, *a fall*! The stories one hears in meetings all acknowledge that descent, and they say, in effect, "Remember! Feel it again!" The people present share the dark journey once more, but this time with love and hope to transform the suffering together. And thus comes the part about recovery, the ascent into creativity. Recovery is not just to stop taking a drug. The problem is that we give up our identity and power not only to substances, but also to people, places, and things. Before, I gave it up to rock stars, all the people I wanted to be, including my wife. When I was using I felt *enslaved* by the creative process. I felt there was no other way to live, and that one had to be totally spontaneous to follow an idea or impulse whenever it came. Now I realize there is another essential part of the creative process—the daily routine of work, which I had previously been denying. Before I lived on the high and didn't do the work. Now I know that in order to be creative I need to be there in the moment with openness and with discipline. I also learned that I don't have to "act out" everything. Before I felt a compulsion to act out all my fantasies, particularly those that were sexual. Whereas now I feel the fantasies are valuable *as fantasies* and more creative as such. Acting them out takes away from the mystical values and makes the mystical mundane.
>
> Recovery is learning to be true to oneself and realizing that one can't do it all alone by one's own ego powers. In recovery a spiritual practice is imperative, for at the deepest level the disease of addiction is based in the spirit. It is a "dis-ease." It requires faith in a divine plan and that there is a connection between all human beings. One learns the power of giving and forgiveness. I had to learn to forgive myself and not obsess on the guilt of the past. Of course, I had to take responsibility for what I had done, and step four, which takes stock of one's own wrongdoings and negative attitudes, helped me to do that. But I also had to let go of the guilt of the past and move on to accept the unknown future and to live in the present moment. Part of learning to let go required a grieving process, parallel to that described by Kübler-Ross in her book *On Death and Dying*. I had to grieve for the old me, like grieving for the death of an old friend. I had to let that old addictive one go. This required going into the void, into a complete emptiness. Recovery comes from that abyss. There one encounters the Zen paradox of having and experiencing the feelings, turning them over, and letting things go. One learns to live with the tension of opposites. In the end, if you can acknowledge it, addiction paradoxically is a "blessing" because to recover you have to live a spiritual and creative life. The "highs" that I got from my addictions cannot

compare with the serenity of calm, peace, and repose that now center me daily.

As Michael's story shows, the Moneylender in our psyche tries to be the master controller, manipulating us through particular debts and accusations of guilt. This figure tries to persecute us morally by tempting us to think we could be fully free of debt. As long as we listen to the Moneylender, to the sadistic, controlling voice of the Demon Lover instead of the call of the Creative Daimon, which comes in silence from the open center of our being, we will be subject to guilt we believe we can remove and control.

Guilt is a lack, a debt, but not one that can be made up or paid off, although traditionally guilt has been understood in this way. Heidegger points out that the German expression for guilt, *Schuld*, refers to "owing, or having something due on account," as well as "being responsible."[10] This sense of Being-guilty as having debts, as failing to pay up the claims that others have made on us, brings up the image of the Moneylender. We think we can pay off our debt to the Moneylender, thereby becoming free of guilt as though we were objects that could be completed. But, as Heidegger says, our existential guilt does not stem primarily from committed or omitted acts. We are not the source of our own being, nor do we have total control. We are not able to be perfect.

There is a debt that we all share—the debt we owe our human existence, the responsibility to actualize our human potential. This debt cannot be "paid off": we are never free of it. Moreover, because we will die we cannot actualize everything. Every decision and every act limits the way in which the potential of our being can be actualized at any given moment. This debt is the paradoxical guilt that must be accepted as part of the human condition. Conscience calls us to accept this existential guilt—to acknowledge it daily. To do so requires constant watchfulness—the wisdom to discriminate, the serenity to accept what cannot be changed, and the courage to change what we can. To be aware of this tension calls upon all that is within us. No wonder we seek easy solutions, ones we can control. To settle into an objectified identity with respect to a particular guilt or into a self-justified guiltlessness is an attempt to avoid the tension of being human.

The addict, who has given him or herself over to another master, who is in debt to the demonic Moneylender, is substituting a debt to the devil for the existential debt of the human soul. Instead of acknowledging the daily debt to the mystery of life, the addict tries to master and control his debt by making "bargains" with the devil. This is an inauthentic relation to guilt, and the Moneylender—that figure in ourselves who tempts us to cover up the nothingness, the gap in our being—plays on it. Just as the first drink leads the alcoholic to think he is absolutely free, that his limitations can be surpassed, just as the gambler thinks if he keeps on gambling he will eventually be able to "pay up" and cover all his debts, and just as the co-addict seeks self-justification, so are we as humans tempted by the Moneylender in our psyche to think we can be perfect. The Moneylender takes the paradoxical mystery we are and attempts to reduce it to a debt that can be paid off. But the payment he exacts is "a pound of flesh" or our very soul, as Mephistopheles did to Faust.

In our addictions we experience the temptation to make ourselves into objects, into a medium of exchange. We are tempted to play either "the guilty one" (taking all the blame, absolute guilt) or its opposite, "the self-justified guiltless one." In both cases we objectify ourselves and avoid the mysterious opposition of finitude and potentiality, as did Hickey, who tried to avoid guilt through murdering his wife (the Moneylender of forgiveness), as did Evelyn, who tried to avoid guilt by perfect love, as did the drunks, who tried to escape guilt by drinking to forget. In addiction we avoid facing the nothingness—the open place that is also the dark face of wholeness. Conscience calls us to this open space, where we face death. Only in this space can we choose to live authentically as the paradoxical creative beings that we are.

Recovering addicts who are in the twelve-step programs acknowledge their powerlessness and turn their lives over to a power greater than ego wishes. In doing so they acknowledge their existential debt. Driven to the bottom by their addiction, they face a humiliation that can be transformed only through humility, through accepting that they are no longer in control or the masters of their own being. In the course of the twelve steps, they make a searching and fearless inventory of themselves—admitting the nature of the specific wrongs done and praying to have the negative feelings behind them removed—which directly acknowledges the specific guilts for the wrongs done in their addiction. At the same time, the acknowledgment of the existential guilt is made in humility, and this process is continued every day in personal inventory, daily prayer, and meditation. In this way recovering addicts experience a spiritual awakening and, accepting the wound of addiction and its redemptive force in their lives, they turn outward to help other addicts.

Thus, their addiction becomes a source of healing for themselves and others. They begin to experience the existential guilt as a gift, for by changing their attitude from ego control to acceptance, the debt becomes the healing force and the creative challenge of giving. Their energy turns from the egoistic search for the pleasurable high, from the tight bondage of the Moneylender, toward the open space of creative being.

3: THE GAMBLER

> I believe I had something like
> four thousand gulden in my hands
> within five minutes. That's when
> I should have quit. But a funny feeling
> came over me, some sort of desire to
> challenge Fate, an uncontrollable urge to
> stick my tongue out at it, to give it a
> flip on the nose.
>
> —Fyodor Dostoevsky, *The Gambler*

THE NOVELIST FYODOR DOSTOEVSKY was in bondage to the Moneylender. He was addicted to gambling. One of his publishers, Stellovsky, used his addiction to try to gain ownership of Dostoevsky's novels. Dostoevsky was given an advance, which he often gambled away, and then he had to quickly write his novel by a deadline, for under the terms of the contract if he didn't finish he would lose the rights to the rest of the royalties. Dostoevsky wrote his novel *The Gambler* under such a contract to this unscrupulous Moneylender-publisher.[1]

Like the first drink for the alcoholic, Dostoevsky's first gambling venture was to lead to eight years of despair, his soul at the mercy of the roulette table. As early as the fall of 1863, he had conceived the idea of a novel about gambling. In a letter to a friend, he describes the central character, the gambler, as follows:

> The main point is that all his vital sap, all his energies, his impetuosity and boldness will be absorbed by roulette. He is a gambler, but not just an ordinary gambler, just as Pushkin's Stingy Knight is not just an ordinary skinflint. . . . My hero is, in his way, a poet, but he is ashamed of the way his poetic feelings are expressed and he feels its ugliness deeply. Nevertheless, his need to risk something ennobles him in his own eyes. The story will cover three years, during which he plays roulette. . . . It is a description of a sort of hell.[2]

Dostoevsky wrote *The Gambler* three years later in despair, barely making the deadline in which he would have lost everything to the Moneylender-publisher. And, all the while, he continued to gamble. While his original idea for the novel was that the gambler, though lost in the habit of gambling and wasting his talents for three years, would eventually be redeemed, in the actual novel the gambler says he will quit as soon as he gets even. The reader is left with the damnation of his denial. Letters written after he finished this novel show Dostoevsky still trying to justify his gambling. If only he could "think and keep control," if only he could "play cooly, using his head," if only he didn't have "weak nerves," then he could win. Pawning his wife's jewelry, borrowing money from publishers, friends, and even enemies, Dostoevsky continued to gamble. Regularly, he promised to stop, to be through with gambling once and for all, and, just as regularly, he broke his promises. It was not until five years after he had written *The Gambler* that he finally was able to keep his vow to stop gambling. He had just lost the rescue money his wife had sent him, as he had so often before. He was down at the bottom. Somehow, a miracle happened. He was finally released from his addiction. He admitted in a letter to his wife: "Anna, Anna, you must understand that I am not just an unscrupulous creature—I am a man devoured by the passion for gambling. But I want you to know that now that mirage has been dispersed once and for all and I feel I have been released from this delusion."[3]

Like so many characters in Dostoevsky's novels, Alexei, the Gambler, tries to go beyond all limits—not only the limits of the established social order but of the human condition. He is a Russian expatriate, living abroad, educated and sophisticated, yet incomplete, immature. He has lost his faith and his contact with the native soil of Russia. In Roulettenberg, when we meet him, Alexei is in the employ of the General and is working as a tutor. He is also in love with the General's neice, Paulina, a love that he believes is impossible. An addict in love as in gambling, he pledges he will risk his life for her—he will dive head first from the cliff of the Schlangenberg if she says the word. On her dare, he insults the Baroness, thus risking his job. He also defies the social hierarchy when he is rude to a guest of the General at the dinner table. Alexei is an extremist; he plays the game of all or nothing.

Before he even puts down a coin on the roulette table, Alexei feels the pull of gambling. Paulina has ordered him to gamble for her and to win at all costs. When he first walks into the gaming room, he doesn't dare to play. He describes his initial reactions.

> I confess that my heart was pounding in my breast and that I didn't feel at all cool and detached; probably I had felt for a long time already that I would leave Roulettenberg a different man and that something was about to happen which would radically and irrevocably change my life. I felt that it was bound to happen. Although it may seem ridiculous to say that I expected so much from roulette, I find the generally accepted opinion that it is stupid to expect anything from gambling even more ridiculous.[4]

Alexei begins to stake all his hopes on roulette. It seems to him to be his only hope and salvation, starting even to supersede his love for

Paulina. Intuitively he knows that "in starting to gamble for Paulina, I was going to wreck my own life."[5] On his first throw, he loses and feels sick. But he tries again and wins, and for the rest of that evening he continues to win until he leaves the roulette table with the money for Paulina and with a strange, unbearable sensation as well. By now, Alexei's energy is with the game of roulette. The money itself is not the goal. What draws him is the gambling, playing the game that defies Fate. On his second day of gambling, he cannot quit while he is ahead but feels compelled to challenge Fate. He loses everything.

The next encounter that Alexei has with the roulette table occurs after the arrival of Paulina's seventy-five-year-old grandmother, a rich, feisty lady confined to a wheelchair. Her arrival surprises the General, who had been anticipating her death and his inheritance. But the Grandmother is very much alive and decides, to everyone's chagrin, to experience gambling. Alexei goes with her. Once at the roulette table, she gambles with passion, deciding to play the zero, the longest shot. She plays the zero and loses again and again. But she is determined to play the long shot. As she says:

> If you're afraid of wolves, you'll never go into the forest. What? We've lost it? Put another one on it! . . . What is it waiting for, that miserable little zero! But even if it costs me my life, I'll sit it out here, waiting for it to come up.[6]

Suddenly, the zero comes up and the Grandmother is elated. Again, she plays the zero and loses. But when Alexei tries to explain that the zero is most unlikely to come up again, she persists, wins, and turns to him with a shriek of incredible triumph. At that moment Alexei knows he too is a gambler.

> I too was a gambler, and I became aware of it that very moment: my hands shook, my legs trembled. I felt as if something had struck me on the head.[7]

After many more wins, the Grandmother leaves. But, the next day, she is irritable and impatient to return, unable to wait until later. At the table, she plays in a frenzy until finally she loses everything she has brought with her and must return to Russia penniless. Able to accept her losses, she returns to the land she loves in Russia. In contrast, from this point on, Alexei finds he cannot leave gambling, not even for his love for Paulina.

After the Grandmother leaves, Paulina confides to Alexei that she had asked him to gamble for her to pay off a debt to a man who had taken advantage of her. Instead of taking her in his arms, Alexei rushes out to try to win by gambling the money to pay off this old lover. He bets all his remaining money and wins, bets it again, and keeps winning. So given over to the gambling, he is hardly aware of what he is doing. As he writes in his notebook:

> In a daze, I pushed all that pile onto the red, but then I suddenly came to my senses. And that was the only time that night that cold fear ran down my spine and made my hands and legs tremble. With horror I realized what it would mean to lose at that moment—my whole life was at stake.[8]

By this time, Alexei, possessed by the gambling, has forgotten about Paulina. Betting on impossible odds, possessed by a mad desire to take risks, he gets higher and higher on the intensity of the drama he has created at the table of chance.

The "high" of risk, of staking oneself and all one has, and the continual need to increase the risks for greater excitement because less will not suffice—this becomes Alexei's life. As he rushes home, his mind in a vacuum, he feels the power of his gambling triumph. Forgetting the reason he had gone gambling in the first place, he now knows only that something is starting anew. When he reaches the room, he throws the money on the table and, suddenly obsessed with all the coins and bills, starts sorting the money, forgetting all about Paulina, who sits there staring at him. Mortified by Alexei's lack of understanding of her love for him and why she had confided in him, Paulina rushes off hysterically, throwing the fifty thousand he has given her back in his face. Although he tries unsuccessfully to bring her back, later he realizes that "from the very moment I had reached the roulette table the night before and had started raking in money, my love for her had receded into the background."[9]

From this point on, Alexei's life loses its order—he spins with the whirl of the roulette wheel. He goes to the gambling spas of Europe, sometimes winning, then losing all he has, living the life of a beggar, even locked up in jail for unpaid debts. Working at odd jobs, he manages to survive and save some money for one more turn at the wheel of fortune. One moment of risk and winning is worth the constant anxiety that pervades his life. As a friend he meets by chance on the streets of Hamburg tells him: "You've turned into a log of wood. You've not only lost contact with reality and lost all interest in world events, in your civic duties, in yourself, in your friends (and you did have friends), you've not only lost all goals in life, except for winning at roulette—you've even renounced your memories."[10] While Alexei wishes for recovery, wishes to come back to life, when he talks of giving up gambling it is always "tomorrow," always "if only," and tomorrow never comes. Alexei's life has become reduced to the spin of the roulette wheel itself; an apt metaphor for the ring of power twirled by the Demon Lover. As the novel ends, Alexei still gambles, hoping that the next turn of the wheel of fortune will change his life for him.

Outwardly, the Moneylender has become the roulette wheel while inwardly the Moneylender is the figure in Alexei driving him to risk more and more, and more is never enough. The Gambler and the Moneylender spin together in the psyche. For without the gamble to get something for nothing, the Moneylender would have no power. And what would motivate the Gambler without the Moneylender's enticement that there are shortcuts to ecstasy, that one single turn of the wheel could change everything so that one wouldn't have to make the long effort of work and build patience and character? Dostoevsky has described how his gambling urges were like the seductive temptation of the devil, how the devil played games with his exaggerated tendency to go to the uttermost extreme, and how he agonized in the hell brought on by betting on the shortcut.

> Since Baden was not too far out of my way, I took it into my head to stop over there. A tempting idea plagued me: to risk 10 louis d'or in the hope that I might wind up with an extra 2,000 francs, which, after all, would take care of us for 4 months, everything included, and would also cover my expenses in Petersburg. The most disgusting thing about it is that I had won on some previous occasions. And the worst part of it is that I have a vile and overly passionate nature. Everywhere, and in everything I drive myself to the ultimate limit, all my life I have been overstepping the line. And right away the devil played a trick on me: In three days or so, I won 4,000 francs with incredible ease. Now let me tell you how I visualized the whole situation: On the one hand there was that easy win—in three days I had turned a *hundred* francs into four thousand. On the other hand debts, lawsuits, anxiety, the impossibility of going back to Russia. And finally the third and most important point—the gambling itself. You know how it ensnares you. No, I swear it was not just avarice, although I did need money for money's sake above all . . . I took the risk, went on playing and lost. I went on to lose every *last* thing I had; in my fevering exasperation, I lost. I started pawning clothes. Anna Grigorevna pawned *everything* she had . . . we had the most awful seven weeks in that hell.[11]

Essential to the Gambler are the elements of risk taking, fear, danger. The Gambler has a remarkable ability to cope with dangers while lacking the ability to control the impulses that precipitate these dangers. So he creates dangers to keep himself stuck and to give the illusion of his own power (when he, once again, faces this danger). For the Gambler, excitement is an exalted end in itself. Euphoria and anguish alternate in the Gambler's soul.

> The excitement makes the stress and distress of life disappear and nullifies the basic needs of affection, sex, safety, hunger, and sleep. Then, in turn, it generates agonizing, unbearable pain.[12]

The transition of changing from a recreational gambler into a pathological gambler is subtle. It is analogous to being in a canoe that is floating gently in the water. Ahead is a whirlpool, but the canoe is at its outer periphery and the water seems calm and safe. For the addictive gambler, a change in the waters occurs. The addictive gambler ceases to control the canoe's direction. As the canoe begins to gather speed, first slowly but then with frightening rapidity, the passenger can be carried toward his doom.[13] This illustrates the way addictions usually begin; they seem to be pleasurable and harmless, but they can progress into something destructive and deadly.

While the urge to gamble is central to the addictive process, it is also central to recovery and creativity. This can be seen in the following story of a man, an artist, who was addicted to drugs, alcohol, and gambling for most of his adult life, and who used the image of the Gambler in his art and in his recovery. As he said:

> Whether in jobs, relationships, art, or life in general, I always gambled. I tried to take things to the limit, to the edge of the precipice and at the last dangerous moment I would try to reel it back in. I always liked to "sweat the cards," to play a blind hand, and I played this way in "the game of life." Can you cheat Death? Can you beat the Devil? This is the thrill. Now that I'm not drinking or drugging anymore, now that I'm in the recovery process, I find that every day is a gamble. The gambling has to do with life and death. Are you going to take the risk of life and be a maximum service to the life force, to God and to your fellows? The risk of the light, the risk of the creative, is feeling good, feeling success, feeling love, believing that there really is someone or something that loves us. It's easy to feel terrible and be a failure as I did when I was drinking and drugging. Now I take the risk that I feel good today and that it will get better. I take the risk of gambling on our unlimited resources.

This man's drinking career started at thirteen. His first drink felt "great!" At fifteen he started drinking a lot and going on long speed and whiskey runs, and he started painting. Always high, on a rush, "it was like I discovered the mother lode." His creativity burst forth. Paul was glad to leave home, a small town in Texas where his father drank and worked and was seldom present and his mother was cool, controlling, and never pleased with anything he did. He and a friend traveled around, drank a lot, and got into violent gun fights when they got drunk—"It was a miracle nobody got killed." When he was eighteen he joined the Air Force. He continued to drink, was popular, manipulated to get out of duty, and eventually met and married an older woman who was hooked on drugs, had a lot of junkie friends, and turned him on to everything but heroin. In England his wife gave birth to a child and he went to the hospital so drunk and crazy that he had to be handcuffed in the hospital, taken to jail, and finally put in a psychiatric ward, the first of many jailings and hospitalizations. Finally he was discharged from the military as unfit. Looking back, he said that his emotional growth had stopped when he started getting loaded in his teens.

For the next few years he lived like Jack Kerouac, "on the road." Heavy into drink and drugs he went to Greenwich Village for a while, then back to Texas, and up to see his wife who had moved to Spokane and was pregnant again. The responsibility of a child was too much, and he insisted the child be put up for adoption. He painted there for a while, living on welfare, but the urge to move hit him again and so he went to San Francisco, where he lived and painted in a wino hotel in the Mission district. For a short time he tried to go clean, but eventually he headed for North Beach where he hung out with the Beat poets, painters, and musicians. On an impulse he left for Los Angeles where he went to college on the GI Bill and studied acting. All the time Paul was partying and playing around with other women. He and his wife, he said, were in a typical pattern of addict/co-addict. She would follow him when he left, then throw him out, and take him back in again. But finally she threw him out for good, so he quit school and left for Texas. There he painted murals in coffee houses, played the guitar, worked as an artist and display director for stores and advertising agencies, and married for a second time. But his wild life continued, and after more drunken craziness and subsequent arrests and hospitalizations, this marriage broke up, too.

Risk became his "god." He continued his drinking, drugging, and gambling and started on the rodeo circuit, riding raging bulls and bucking horses. "My life kept getting crazier and crazier," he said. Somehow he managed to get two women pregnant on the same night, and nine months later they gave birth to children on the same day. By this time he had been hospitalized several times for breakdowns due to alcohol and drug abuse. Suicidal and in despair, he deliberately got loaded and rode a wild bucking horse one night, ending up in a coma with a fractured skull. But he recovered and returned to California, where he married a third time.

This was California in the sixties; he added hallucinogenics to his repertoire of drugs. The drinking and drugging continued to get worse, but his art was getting better. He started having shows throughout the state and his paintings started to sell. Now he could support himself through his art. He was invited to be artist-in-residence at a university in the Bay Area, taught drawing and composition at an experimental college there, and continued to take what he called "unreasonable risks."

> All the creative folks I hung out with worshipped "The Lady," and the lady was Death. Going to that space and seeing how you could come out with any marbles left, whether life marbles or sanity marbles, was the big gamble. The more the odds, the bigger the rush. Going to the dark side, hanging out with underworld characters, trying to cheat death and beat the devil—this was the thrill. Betting on the "wild card" that knows no limits and can't be controlled, the wild card that can suddenly change your whole hand in a game as in life, gambling that all things are possible with that card—this was our gamble with Death. If you're going to live on the Dark Side, you have to not care about life, yours or other people's. The darkness is so seductive, slick, sensual, that you think you can play with it and control it. But Darkness is secret and covert. And, you can't control the wild card.

The wild card in his life started to wear the devil's costume. By this time he was dealing drugs and taking mescaline every day. In the late sixties he almost got busted for dealing, so he moved again, ripping off his partner "so I'd have a good reason to leave and not return." His third marriage had broken up by this time, and he found a new woman, his final drinking and drugging mate. "For the next six years I lived a dual life, like Doctor Jekyll and Mr. Hyde, until I finally turned into Mr. Hyde." As Doctor Jekyll he opened a studio in Denver. He taught and worked in community projects with children on neighborhood murals. As Mr. Hyde he was running around with women, drinking and drugging at a feverish pitch, abusing the woman with whom he lived. Finally, she stabbed him. In critical condition he was taken to an intensive care unit where he nearly died because he went into withdrawal. They didn't know he was an alcoholic. But he survived and continued on his crazy path. His paintings were selling faster than he could paint them. He couldn't deal with the success, he said, and all of a sudden his art took a turn. Before, he had painted spiritual paintings in warm earth tones. Suddenly he started painting in violent reds, oranges, pinks, and silvers. The images were icy, ripping apart, hard-edged images, like his painting of a woman's bright red lips parted by a double-edged razor blade. One day he walked drunk into a restaurant gallery in which his paintings were hanging, tore them off the walls, returned to his studio, trashed the paintings and the studio, and left. From that day on he gave up painting and got down to serious drinking, drugging, and debauching. He became a street drunk. His friends took him to dry out at a ranch where there was no alcohol. However, there were drugs. Because he didn't get completely clean, several months later he was back to drinking again. By this time, Paul knew his number was up. By now he'd had about fifteen breakdowns and hospitalizations. "The Lady (of Death) was smiling and beckoning me. Those bright red lips with the double-edged razor were hers!"

Finally, some twenty-eight years after he had started drinking and drugging, he voluntarily went into a hospital to recover. At first he was very resistant to the process. Even though he knew he had to stop, he was still in denial. "Finally they put me on the 'Synanon hot seat.' About forty people told me what an asshole I was. I cried for three days after that, and then I started praying." He went through the three-month-long treatment program and joined AA. Then he began to work in alcohol rehabilitation. Part of his recovery process was to work with other drunks and drug addicts like himself. He also started to work for Outward Bound, taking troubled adolescents on wilderness trips. The challenge of rock climbs and long-distance trail runs over snowfields and through rivers provided the risk and the gamble he needed—the risk of life and death in Nature. For the first two years he had to stop painting because the temptation to drink and use drugs in that situation was too great. But eventually, as his life improved in sobriety and his confidence centered in his new spiritual path, he began to paint again and had a successful show.

Reflecting on the Gambler inside of him as it related now to his recovery and creativity, he said:

> Before I always thought I could beat the game. But now I knew I couldn't. A professional gambler can set limits about what he's willing to lose and

stop. An addict can't predict what will happen after the first drink, or line, or hand. The addict's risk is foolhardy and uneducated. He risks at random and is messing with someone's life. Before I was gambling for the wrong stakes—the stakes of darkness. Now I'm gambling to transform my life and contribute to a better world. In my art I take the risk to be responsible for the good and the bad of my work. This is how one becomes well. It's a one-day-at-a-time existence. In the recovery process every day is a gamble. As in a painting, you can always cover the paint and start again.

After his recovery he had a series of gambling dreams. He was at the roulette table and bored. His association to his boredom was that now he was bored with the dark side. It no longer seduced him. His descent into darkness, he said, had been important because it had given him an understanding of the depths of human hell. He compared his journey to Plato's parable of the cave in *The Republic*.

I don't ever want to forget the dark because if I do I'll get cocky, complacent. I'll lose my compassion. My descent into the dark gave me knowledge, but it also almost killed me. Now that I have some understanding of the dark, it holds nothing for me anymore. The dark has lost its seductive power. Not that I think I can avoid the dark. You can't separate the black and white of the Yin-Yang wheel of life. But I choose to live in the light as much as possible. The dark changes costumes as I go on living. It gets more subtle. Dark used to be selling drugs, cheating life, gambling with the devil. Then it was manipulating, hustling, cheating. The dark can be a holier-than-thou hypocrite. Now the dark involves self-deception, bad faith, and the challenge is a daily inventory to be true and straight with myself, to be responsible for what I do each day. I used to have dreams that people were chasing me and going to kill me. I was always hiding in my dreams as I was in reality. Now I try to live my life without hiding. I'm gambling on faith and openness and the quiet excitement of serenity.

4: THE ROMANTIC

> His love was the only thing left to her and she wanted to love him. "You must understand that from the day I loved you everything has changed for me. There is only one thing in the world for me: your love. If that's mine, I feel so uplifted and so determined that nothing can be degrading to me. I am proud of my position because, well, I am proud of being proud . . ." She could not say what she was proud of. Tears of shame and despair choked her. She stopped and burst into sobs.
>
> —Leo Tolstoy, *Anna Karenina*

THE ROMANTIC IS one of the most entrancing, yet dangerous figures in the psyche of the addict. If untransformed, the Romantic can draw us into death. Yet the Romantic can draw us also into creativity and toward spiritual transformation, for its energy takes us from the grip of the practical world into the "forbidden" unknown realms. The Romantic is the archetypal figure who wants absolute merger with the loved one, who longs to fly "somewhere, over the rainbow" or to dissolve into the night sea to experience union with the infinite. When this desire to merge with the infinite possesses one's life and reduces it to the futility of insatiable longing alone, then romanticism has become an addiction. Bound by a longing that is insatiable and ultimately does not satisfy, the Romantic is behind all addiction. But behind the restless longing of the Romantic is the soul's thirst for the divine fire of creativity. Therein lies the possibility for transformation.

Not only is the Romantic a powerful figure in the psyche of addicts; addiction itself is often romanticized in our culture. Consider the romantic image of the drinking writer or the rock star who is a drug addict. Quite often the early deaths of creative persons suffering from addiction are romanticized, drawing those who admire creativity along a similarly addictive path. For example, the artist Jackson Pollock's alcoholism was often romanticized. Yet Pollock ended up "dead drunk" from this disease, in a car accident that killed him and a passenger. Nevertheless, Pollock, through his nightsea voyage into the unconscious, bequeathed humankind a vision via his art. The tragedy is that he did not live longer in the service of creativity.

The Romantic often begins as a dreamer who feels the soul as a bird
s wings and flies off into the unimaginable spaces of
is, an early German Romantic, describes this dreamy
novel *Heinrich von Ofterdingen*, the dream image of the
vs the romantic, Heinrich, toward its fragrant center, its

mysterious blossom revealing a delicate face as he gazes on in sweet astonishment. Then he awakens from the dream to hear his mother's voice. Nearby, his father says: "Dreams are bubbles . . . you would do well to turn away from such useless and harmful things."[1] Heinrich replies:

> Is not every dream, even the most confused, a unique phenomenon that, without thinking of divine providence, is a significant rent in the mysterious curtain that falls into our inner being with a thousand folds? . . . Dreams seem to me to be a bulwark against the regularity and ordinariness of life, the free refreshment of a fettered imagination that tosses about all the images of life, and interrupts the constant earnestness of adults with a cheerful child's game. Without dreams we would surely age sooner. . . . The dream I dreamed last night is surely no ineffectual coincidence in my life, for I feel it meshing into my soul like a broad wheel and driving it on with a mighty turn.[2]

Heinrich's love for the dream image shows the great creative potential of the Romantic—the longing to travel to the mysterious realms where creative imagination can take us. But this same longing, when unfulfilled, can result in withdrawal from reality in cynical disillusion. Thus, in German Romantic literature the yearning for paradise often leads to a bitter feeling of homelessness, alienation from the day world, and an addiction to night that promises the bittersweet experience of unattainable love or forgetting. In love with the night, the Romantic can still have the "dream," if not the embodied reality. But often, the addiction to the night turns into the "last night," into *Liebestod*, where love is possible only in death.

Nietzsche, who distinguished romanticism from creative openness—which he called the "Dionysian"—had this to say:

> *What is romanticism?*—Every art, every philosophy may be viewed as a remedy and an aid in the service of growing and struggling life; they always presuppose suffering and sufferers. But there are two kinds of sufferers: first, those who suffer from the *over-fullness of life*—they want a Dionysian art and likewise a tragic view of life, a tragic insight—and then those who suffer from the *impoverishment of life* and seek rest, stillness, calm seas, redemption from themselves through art and knowledge, or intoxication, convulsions, anaesthesia, and madness. All romanticism in art and insight corresponds to the dual needs of the latter type.[3]

Romanticism is, Nietzsche adds, "Revenge against life itself—the most voluptuous kind of frenzy for those so impoverished!"[4] It is this revenge against life, coming from a sense of poverty, which constitutes resentment. When the Romantic becomes disappointed with life because the longing for absolute merger is frustrated, then romanticism can degenerate into the cynical, life-denying resentment of the Underground Man, which Dostoevsky describes and to which Nietzsche refers. The addictive Romantic refuses to live in the tension, absolutizes love and mystery, and withdraws from the ordinary world by seeking escape in *Liebestod.* When addicted, the Romantic often fails to bring back the sense of mystery to the world and thus leaves no creative gift. But if the Romantic can endure the tensions of the soul's thirst for the divine abundance and learn to dwell on earth, then, like the firebird, his or her creative visions can glow transcendentally upon the earth.

The man in the following story felt the Romantic to be at the very core of his being. As a young boy, like Novalis, he lived in his fantasies, gave wild flowers to the mother he adored, played in the swings atop the tall trees surrounding his home, wrote poems, and painted his magical world in many colors. As he grew up he glowed in the love of the feminine and devoted himself to a series of women who embodied various aspects of the soul for him. Later in life he discovered that his romanticism veiled his search for divine creativity. This romanticism became a wild Dionysian orgy of dancing and drink, which ended in the fatal feelings of the *Liebestod.* As a Romantic he frequently set himself up for this tragedy. For example, whenever a relationship was going well, inexplicably he would threaten it by becoming jealous and angry. Then he would drink. One night after such an orgy, he found himself in the emergency critical care unit of a hospital because his heart had stopped beating. This incident broke through his denial: he realized that his romanticism had become enmeshed with a pattern of episodic alcoholism that now endangered his life. About the Romantic and its relation to addiction, he said:

> Romance has to do with the flight of fantasy. I always used the image of two birds flying as a signature to all of my letters. The two birds are flying into the unknown, somewhere other than here. The Romantic in a man's psyche is to want the woman to be a muse, to inspire him and share in his creative flight and the celestial union between heaven and earth. Underneath all of his endless yearning and longing for ecstasy with the loved one, the Romantic really wants the mystical union with the divine presence. Transformed, the Romantic leads to the flight toward creative imagination and the divine wedding. I think Romantics tend to have a different sensitivity of feeling. They feel the profound passionate poignancy and ecstasy of all life. But the overwhelming feelings lay them

> open to the Demon Lover—both to plunge into and to escape these intense feelings. The Romantic seeks the celestial cosmic union with the lover in a moment of ecstasy that will last forever. It's an addiction to ecstasy. If this goes too far, you can feel so inflated, flying so high, that you feel separate and greater than God. But humans can't hold the supreme peak that the romantic wants to possess *at any cost*! That's the addiction! The soaring for me was often ignited by alcohol, which released the obsessive-compulsive, overly responsible side of my personality, and freed me, or so I thought, for the Dionysian union. Drinking enables the Romantic. When wine and roses and feelings flow in the rosy glow of candlelight, you can forget about all of the burdens, tensions, and responsibilities of the real world. In love with love, you never want to return. You want to soar and stay up there forever and never return to earth and its limitations. The practical world becomes a big intrusion.

Born in the deep south, Eric was the youngest son of a highly artistic, brilliant, and creative family. Books, music, flowers—beauty of all kinds and the exciting flow of ideas formed the atmosphere in which he grew up. As a child he was immersed in the King Arthur legend and in the Grimms' fairy tales. To him, Merlin was a living presence and his home was an alchemical vessel of transformation.

His mother was a lay analyst and writer. She loved music and literature, and read Shakespeare, Poe, and stories of the great heroes to her son. She was a woman who could intuit the heart of a person's life, expressing to them their innermost feelings and thoughts in a few pungent words. Since she was a wonderful listener with a charismatic personality, people from all walks of life were drawn to her, and their home was a creative meeting place. This was a source of great inspiration to her son, as well as a source of conflict: frequently he felt abandoned by her as she listened to her many admirers. In addition, she had serious bouts of depression that caused her to withdraw her emotions unpredictably, which fostered feelings of insecurity and jealousy in her introverted son. So the early romance he had with his mother was a volatile combination of flights of fancy with the fear of abandonment and loss—a preparation for his later dark fascination with the *Liebestod*, feelings that love draws one inevitably into night and death.

A shy and loving child, he had a vivid imagination and an entire world of imaginary playmates with whom he conversed. His special perch was a little tree house high in the branches of a tall beech tree, and he loved to float there in fantasy, drifting in the world of possibilities, high in the luscious leafy arms of the tree goddesses. For him, the tree became an important symbol of life and shamanic knowledge in his dreams.

Eric's father was also a creative, sensitive man who had always dreamed of travel but had grown up poor and later suffered in the Depression. "Ah, Sweet Mystery of Life," was his favorite song. He created this sweet mystery by gardening flower fields and designing the house and a cascade of natural pools with water lilies, tropical fish, and moon roses. He even set up a stand by the road and gave free floral sprays to anyone who wanted them. Eric's sister, seven years older, always valued his creativity. In many ways, in his early boyhood, she too was like a mother to him.

As Eric grew older his bond with his mother remained unbroken. When he was as old as eight, his mother often slept with him. This angered his father, who became jealous and resentful. About this time the Depression hit America, and his father lost all his money and property, including the beautiful stone house that he had personally designed and landscaped. His father chose a creative solution by building a small log cabin on the remaining acres of land. Even though the family had lost all their money, they still were surrounded by the trees, running water, birds, and wild animals that they loved.

However, as a teenager growing up in an area where everyone else was wealthy, secretly Eric was ashamed of being poor, even though he was attractive, athletic, and popular. Even while dancing with debutantes to big-name bands in country clubs, he felt like an outsider. This was in the late thirties. There was a drifty, dreamy quality to life, and the war added the sense of *Liebestod* to the feeling of romance. The boys were all ready to join the army, and leaving for war seemed heroic. Romance included a plaintive quality of leaving the beloved, who would wait at home while the man went off on heroic adventures. At sixteen he had read Richard Halliburton's *The Royal Road to Romance*, a book that strongly influenced his life. The author had followed the heroes of the world and dared to take many exotic, dramatic, and "forbidden" journeys, the last on a Chinese junk sailing from San Francisco to Shanghai. On this journey he disappeared at the age of thirty-five. "I found this highly romantic and wanted to go on similar night sea journeys." So Eric left home and signed up as a seaman on a tanker and sailed to South America. As an outsider to the rich social milieu, he compensated by being different and unpredictable. He valued the eccentric, the rebellious, the heroic, and the mysterious.

The Romantic, for him, was the conquering of death and danger. In college he excelled at one of the most dangerous sports, pole vaulting.

Each time he flung himself off the pole into the air, he seemed to be testing death, returning to the ground a hero. When war was declared, continuing to seek adventure, he left college and joined the naval air corps as a cadet officer. During this period he sought love in a poetic way—he longed for bliss and rapture with his loved one—but the possibility of death was always included in the ecstasy.

When he fell in love, he would become like "one possessed." He was intensely loyal. But at the same time, he was always afraid he'd lose the loved one, around whom his entire life evolved. Then he would become depressed and unable to eat. This became a pattern: falling in love, he would feel the ecstasy of drifting in eternity; but then he would fear the loss of the beloved and would become jealous and possessive, sometimes destroying the relationship by his clinging and anger at the possibility of abandonment. This pattern of jealousy and possessiveness was one he had to work on transforming for most of his life.

At twenty-three he married for the first time, a woman whom he saw in a nightclub and with whom he fell in love at first sight. He began studying to become a doctor, a healer like his mother. After medical school, he moved to California—a romantic place at the edge of the sea—where he interned and set up practice. Although he loved his work, Eric did not feel at home with material success, being the head of a family, or the secure and comfortable suburban life that his wife so liked. In compensation he became a compulsive workaholic, which went against the soul of his romantic nature. As a result he became depressed and anxious. In order to deal with the symptoms, he went into Freudian analysis, then in its halcyon days of popularity. He was now in his late thirties—in the abyss of a midlife crisis.

Through analysis he began to uncover old childhood hopes and dreams as well as the "incestuous aspect of the mother-son lover relationship." As many repressions from early childhood were lifted, he unexpectedly began to act them out. At this time he began a pattern of episodic "Dionysian" drinking that romanticized everything. After having been faithful to his wife for sixteen years, he now had an affair with one of his students. This was the start of the break-up of his marriage, which seemed to have lost its romance in the shackles of materialistic suburban life. The desire for poetry and mystery in his life and for a creative, spiritual connection like the one he had had with his mother took him through a series of romantic relationships, usually with "beautiful, charismatic, dramatic but rather wild Madwomen, hungry for love."

Drinking, dancing, dating young girls, driving wildly in his white Jaguar convertible, became his passion. One night he drove to Mexico. On the beach in Acapulco he fell in love with a twenty-year-old traveling musician who was engaged to a Mexican aristocrat, a very jealous man. He imagined himself to be a great matador and lover—a Hemingway man capable of a duel. Love-drunk and death-drunk, made paranoid by the combination of tequila and mescal, he began to imagine her lover would kill him. Visions began to overwhelm him: he saw the great Aztec sun calendar in the sky. Fearing he was going mad, he returned to California to consult his analyst.

A typical addict, he wanted it all—the security of a wife and family, home and a stable job, but also the wild romance, the Dionysian life, and the continual drama. At first his wife, who had helped support him through his professional education, hoped he would come out of this crisis. As a result, she went to therapy herself. But when he continued in his wild ways, she sought a divorce. In the meantime his drinking increased, and he became totally addicted to making love, to being in love and to being loved. His romantic addiction also had a creative side—he went to art school, painted, wrote poetry, and danced. Finally he fell in love with a Danish ice skater and artist who had a dreamy, faraway quality. For a year the couple drank, danced, and partied up and down the coast, playing out wildly the F. Scott and Zelda Fitzgerald life-style. But eventually ennui set in because there was nothing new left to do; they had burnt themselves up. Since the relationship was based on romantic projection and Dionysian drinking—even though both persons were very creative and had a deep thirst for the spirit—it finally ended. The work necessary to make love spiritual and creative had been left undone. By this time Eric was addicted episodically to alcohol and to the Ghostly Lover (the unknown, unattainable stranger who would give his life and soul infinite meaning). Like Cassanova, he continued to add to his "list" of erotic adventures. This was a time of great poetic output, during which he also had mystical visions. But because these poems were written from the night world of wine, roses, song, and ecstatic merger, in the daylight they were never fully finished and refined.

As each relationship fell into pieces, he knew he could not continue in this manner. He was immersed not only in the *Liebestod*—the death in romantic love—he was also suffering from the loss of his children, whom he loved very much. But he was still frantically running away from his conflicts through his frenetic drinking and Dionysian orgies. He had broken all the rules; he felt guilty and punished himself by drinking more and more. This orgiastic period lasted about three years. His analyst commented that at bottom he was running away from the depression that was due to an early traumatic abandonment by his mother.

Then he met a brilliant, beautiful young woman who became his new great love. Gradually he abandoned his Dionysian life-style, but he was still addicted to love. His romantic projections had passed from the artistic Madwoman to this bright and competent southern belle. With her, he settled into a marriage that lasted twelve years. The first part of the marriage was romanticized: he was the older man, like her father, on his way up the ladder of financial and professional success, and she was the young beauty, the brilliant muse who inspired him. They were living out the archetype of Prince Charming and the Special Princess. Once more his life was full of material success and social recognition. Eric was very proud of showing off the young beauty he had married; he was possessive and in some ways treated her like "a beautiful object." But the relationship lacked spirituality. Instead of embarking on the Romantic's inner spiritual journey to the divine wedding, he allowed the pressure of work and the boredom of their social life to drive him to episodic overuse of amphetamines and alcohol. During these periods he would stay up all night writing poetry, making pottery, painting, listening to music, and doing chemical experiments that fascinated his children. From a deeper viewpoint, he was engaged in an alchemical process, trying to embody his creativity, which was lacking in the relationship with his wife. He felt alone and in despair. Meanwhile, his wife drew away from him, eventually falling in love with another man and leaving the marriage. He entered a "nightsea journey," during which he became very depressed.

For the next three years he was plunged deep into the abyss. Life was icy, like the vodka he was drinking. Finally he met a cowgirl, an earthy wild woman, who brought him back to his own wildness, via drinking and dancing. This wildness diverted his depression for a while. He tried to reconnect with his children, but his children were angry at him, for they thought he had abandoned them. Alienated, depressed, questioning whether God existed, periodically he drank heavily. The Romantic in him had now turned into the alienated Underground Man. Off and on, the wild Dionysian life-style continued, via drinking and a series of affairs. But inside he was miserable. He felt life was passing him by.

Amidst all this confusion and inner turmoil, Eric could not work. He was homeless, living on welfare. Then he heard about a priest in the country to whom he turned for help. This man told him to accept his helplessness and ask for God's guidance. Helping the priest in his work by gardening at the church, restoring the earthen pathways for the stations of the cross, and accompanying the priest on his parish rounds was essential to his recovery. At this time he had a mystical experience of conversion and even considered entering the monastery. But tragedy struck: he learned he had a high-risk malignant melanoma. Through prayer, meditation, and soul searching he was able to get through this crisis. Eventually he recovered from the cancer. Participating in a three-day retreat of initiation into the ancient Christian mysteries, he went on a *cursillo* honoring agape love. This gave him the spiritual strength to take a university post in Persia as associate professor of psychiatry, working also as a flight surgeon and medical director. During this time in Persia, he did not drink, honoring the Moslem religious customs. Also, he felt he was on a hero's journey.

Returning to America, he began Jungian analysis to continue work on his soul's journey. He started running in marathons, and he met a woman who was an athletic, nature-oriented woman, both a feminist and mother, a woman interested in many facets of the world. He fell in love, and it seemed like the Garden of Eden. He began to reach rapprochement with his children and became more stable. Although he still drank episodically, it was not in the cold, icy way of before. However, the relationship broke up because his drinking bothered the woman, who also needed to lead a freer feminist life than was possible in their relationship. Devastated once more, his jealous demons resurfaced. But this time, because he was working on his relationship to the feminine in analysis, the incapacitating depressions did not occur.

After some time in analysis, his own dream images inspired him to go on a journey to Asia to study shamanic rituals and practices. There he encountered a woman who was on a similar soul-searching journey. She, too, was deeply involved in the individuation process and in the creative life. Mystics both, they found they shared the same romantic longings and thirst for the divine. They traveled, climbed mountains together, explored opera, ballet, film, literature, mythology, and art. But both partners discovered eventually that their romantic natures had become possessed by alcohol. The woman hit bottom first, and went to AA, where she found the help she needed to stop drinking. This helped her transform her romanticism into a deeper spiritual commitment. At first, seeing his partner as "the addict," he denied his own episodic alcoholism. But as she became stronger in the process of her recovery, his episodic drinking increased. Feeling abandoned once more, he returned to his former patterns. But now he justified his "Dionysian life-style" as a "creative, ecstatic, shamanic flight." He fell in love with a woman thirty years younger, and together they danced, drank, and smoked marijuana. About this last period of possession by the Demon Lover through alcohol and romance, he said:

> I feel there are times in a person's life when he feels the drudgery, lifelessness without meaning. A Romantic ascends into the clouds with the one he loves and feels the celestial. When he has to return to the bourgeois, bureaucratic mentality, he feels the loss of youthfulness and romantic ecstasy. To escape the loss of romance, I took alcohol and marijuana and got involved with an attractive young woman who represented the possibility of continuing the romantic life forever. But I was killing my current relationship and then the young woman decided to leave me too. I fell into a big black pit. I was depressed and suicidal, yet caught into the Romantic fantasies of youthful "in loveness forever," and also the Sturm and Drang of the *Liebestod.* I even made a dramatic suicide attempt. This was when the Romantic turned into the Killer.

About this time Eric had a number of warning dreams. In one dream he and his soul mate were trapped on the edge of a cliff. To the left was a drunken, reckless teenager, who crashed his car and was killed. Eric was accused of the murder. To the judge he said, "I am not responsible." In the dream the verdict was that he was not guilty of the teenager's death. But the police officer told him he should go to AA. In another dream he was a prisoner even though he was outside the prison walls. Sitting atop the prison wall was a judge dressed in black. The judge asked him about his drinking. He answered honestly. Immediately the prison became a castle, with a grand celebration of wonderful food and gifts for everyone. Both dreams, he knew, were warning him about his drinking and trying to help him cut through his denial.

Other dreams warned him of the dangers of his addiction to romance. These images included a man in black who was taking him and his soul mate to the graveyard. The man held a faded, dying rose (symbolizing the dying love relationship) and said to the dreamer ominously: "I am the collector of lost souls." In recurring dreams, this Mephistophelean figure dressed in black was frequently linked with a seductive young woman. His romantic passion for being "in love" drew him to romances with young women, but his dreams were warning him of the danger to his soul. About this fascination he said:

> My love had to change from this immature romantic love to mature caring. Also I had to honor the many shamanic visions—both waking dreams and night visions that had been given me. For example, one day at the beach I felt the wind blowing, heard the roaring of the sea and the sounds of the seals, and I looked up and saw a flight of pelicans, which I felt was a divine visitation. At that moment I asked God for a dream vision to continue this divine presence. That night and the nights following I had a series of mysterious dream images: by the sea a carven ram in the cliff came alive and spoke to me; an old man with long flowing hair was walking along a beach with the bag of mysteries on his back. I knew I was related to him. Then I saw a "soul tree" with birds; in a forest I encountered an elephant who looked into my eyes; I also battled on a nightbridge to the underworld with the big black dogs of Hades. All these images—both the divine and the demonic—came calling me to accept my creative healing powers as a doctor with shamanic vision. But my romanticism and my episodic drinking were preventing me from responding to this creative call.

Having been warned by many dreams and bad experiences while drinking, nevertheless he continued his disastrous love-drunk plunge in the abyss of addiction. Only a week earlier, the angel of death had appeared to him in a dream, as though to warn him. One day he went to church to receive communion. Afterwards he had lunch and remembered drinking only one glass of wine. He awoke in the intensive cardiac care unit. The doctors told him his heart had stopped for fourteen seconds. At this moment, behind his left shoulder, he felt a dark ghostly presence—a large black cat. As he turned, he saw the cat's eyes fix upon his own. The cat bounded away; he knew that he would live. This was his turning point. Face to face with death, his heart literally stopped. He could deny his self-destructive path no longer. He felt relieved and liberated. Finally, he was free to devote his energies to the spiritual union for which he had been thirsting his whole life. About his spiritual experience he said:

> The spiritual transformation can happen only when you've lost everything. In the hospital I realized I had upped the ante too many times. In drinking, I'd played my last card. I was aware I was gambling with life and love, but I really didn't want to hurt anyone else. I truly loved all the women, felt the divine mystical presence in each. In the course of my Jungian analysis I came to learn that each outer woman symbolized an aspect of myself that needed integrating. For example, the wild, beautiful

Madwoman who was hungry for love was a rejected feminine part of myself needing love. The artistic woman symbolized my own need to create. The young woman symbolized my need to play creatively. The motherly woman showed I needed to nurture myself. All I really wanted was to love and to be loved. But I failed to realize I had to do this for myself instead of projecting that task on others. After the many warnings from my dreams and now, facing death, I had reached the point of total loss, of not being and not having, of nothingness. Suddenly I had another chance to live. Then I began to feel the presence of loving and caring friends. I realized the love of friendship with women was one way of transforming my romantic longing. Now I appreciate every day of my life as a gift. I've come to terms with my age and I'm not trying to deny it. I've accepted that my episodic drinking binges were one manifestation of the many varied patterns of the disease of alcoholism. And I've also accepted that my romanticism was covering up my deeper yearning for spiritual transformation and creativity. The creative search has replaced the romantic longing now, and I have found other kinds of loves—the love of friendships and an inner spiritual love and ecstasy found only in inner silence and the sacred space where the divine presence dwells.

Archetypally, the legend of Tristan and Isolde shows the dark doomed love of romanticism. Wagner's operatic expression, which most of us have heard and loved, is one in which German Romanticism reaches its greatest culmination. I tell Wagner's version here to illumine the meaning of the Romantic in addiction and how, if untransformed, romanticism leads to death.

The musical prelude of *Tristan and Isolde* expresses one single emotion—endless insatiable longing. This longing is the longing of addiction. The longing almost has a drugged quality, being based in the love potion that seals their passion, which Tristan and Isolde at first try to control. From the beginning their love is impossible; that impossibility—once they have delivered themselves to it—constitutes their addiction. The love philtre is the symbol of the fire of passion and the inextinguishable longing through which addictive lovers are possessed.

As a composer trying to express this in music, Wagner felt the same endless difficulty of this longing—"how to impose restraint on himself, since exhaustion of the subject is impossible."[5] Of the "Prelude," Wagner said that he

> let that insatiable longing swell forth from the first timidest avowal to sweetest protraction, through anxious sighs, through hopes and fears, laments and desires, bliss and torment, to the mightiest forward-pressing, the most powerful effort to find the breach that will open out to the

> infinitely craving heart the path into the sea of love's endless delight. In vain! The exhausted heart sinks back, to pine away in a longing that can never attain its end, since each attainment brings in its wake only renewed desire, till in final exhaustion the breaking eye catches a glimpse of the attainment of the highest bliss—the bliss of dying, of ceasing to be, of final redemption into that wondrous realm from which we only stray the farther the more we struggle to enter it by force. Shall we call it Death? Or is it not the wonder world of Night, whence as the story tells, an ivy and vine sprang of old in inseparable embrace over the graves of Tristan and Isolde?[6]

The bittersweet quality of the Prelude announces the predestined doom of the lover's romance. When Tristan and Isolde first met, they had looked into each other's eyes and fallen in love. Tristan was a wounded hero from the enemy country and had been brought for help to Isolde, who was skilled above all others in the magic art of healing. Even though Isolde had recognized Tristan as the one who had killed her betrothed, with that look her heart melted, and she saved his life, and he in turn had pledged undying loyalty to her.

Tristan and Isolde are from warring lands, so political expediency dictates their separation. To help bring peace between the two nations a practical marriage is arranged between Isolde and King Mark, Tristan's uncle. Isolde is torn between love and hate for Tristan: he had killed her betrothed and conquered her country, and now, by taking her as a captive bride for his king, he ignores the love through which she saved his life. Tristan, too, is caught in a hopeless conflict: the honour and loyalty that he has vowed to his uncle now battles in his soul with his love for Isolde, his uncle's bride-to-be. Thus each of the lovers bears within a conflict of opposites—loyalty to the homeland and its practical needs versus loyalty to the love of the infinitely craving heart. The former is symbolized by the light-world, day, while the latter is the "Wonder-world of night."

Though Isolde's sorceress mother brews a love philtre to ensure the union of her daughter with the old king, Mark, to overcome the breach between the two day-world nations, Isolde chooses the night-world of death rather than betray her heart. This choice comes out of her rage at Tristan's betrayal: she aims to kill them both with a death potion. But when the servant Brangäna substitutes the love philtre for the death potion, Tristan and Isolde are liberated from their rational worldly restraints and plunged into the night-world of love. While the death potion would have liberated them from their inner conflict, the love potion frees them to confess the love that they have felt for each other and almost concealed from themselves. In this way, the conflict between "day" (the practical world) and "night" (the wondrous world) is brought to consciousness.

After Tristan and Isolde drink the love philtre, longing for the night-world takes over. Daytime enforces their separation. Night seals their oneness and blots out their torment. Even though she is now King Mark's wife, Isolde secretly meets Tristan in the night when she extinguishes the torch, symbolically extinguishing the light of day and consciousness and the servitude of their love to the day's demands.

For the lovers the practical world of the day is filled with deceit, false value, superficiality, and transitoriness, while the night-world holds the mystical, eternal truth of oneness. From the moment when they first looked into each other's eyes, even before the love philtre sealed the meaning of this look, the light of day, which rules the world outside, ruled their separation and their suffering. The lovers sing out their defiance of the day, crying out to be enfolded in love's night, which can give them oblivion of the world. They sing an ecstatic hymn to eternal night through which their individual separate identities will be lost. Even death, they now believe, is not powerful enough to part them. As lovers they become the world.

When Brangäna who is watching from the tower, warns them to take care, that the night is passing and day is coming, the lovers defy her words and resolve to enter the darkness forever. In doing so they reduce the meaning of existence to one thing only—the desire that their love be infinite. But that love is finite, limited by the approaching demands of the day-world. This reduction of the total mystery of their lives to their love alone *is* the Romantic's addiction, in which the love object finally becomes the whole world, with all else sacrificed to this one end.

Brangäna represents the servant of consciousness, ever present at the border of dark and light, night and day. In the first scene of the opera, while Isolde broods on the voyage to the marriage she does not desire, Brangäna reminds her again and again of the light-world of reality, although she is at first unaware of the storm of Isolde's inner feelings. It is also Brangäna who substitutes the love philtre for the death potion, through which the inner conflicts of the lovers are raised to consciousness. Thus Brangäna symbolizes the figure of the watchman in us, who must always be alert and heed the opposing principles in ourselves. This constant attention to the "border," the realm of tension between consciousness and unconsciousness, must be alertly tended. Without this caring attentiveness to all that is, human life becomes split into warring dualities. Romanticism can end in murderous fanaticism or total withdrawal from the practical world; then the genuine mystery of the divine romance is lost.

This same image of the watchman or "shepherd" has been evoked by Heidegger. The human challenge, as he sees it, is to participate with care in the mysterious creative process of Being. This requires standing in the tension of two intermeshing modes of existence. There is the practical "everyday" world, which requires us to act and get things done, and there is the mysterious movement of Being, which asks for our surrender in the awesome appreciation that we humans are the place of openness and revelation where Being unfolds. Creative life affirms both modes of being. Most of humankind, Heidegger maintains, opts for the practical mode because it is safer and seems secure; it is controllable. Through such control we attempt to avoid the ultimate unknown: death. In this way the person who tries to relate to the practical alone finally denies all mystery and all meaning in an attempt to control life.

In contrast to the practical person, the Romantic seeks mystery. Longing for the infinite, the dark moment, the dangerous look, the Romantic wants to merge, to dissolve in the unknown, to drink of love forever, even unto death. In such intensity, the Romantic disdains the everyday world and its practical affairs. To survive, he or she may rely on others to do this practical work. We see this in marriages in which one partner seeks adventure and excitement while the other partner tends to the business of survival—this pattern is typical for the addict/co-addict relationship. In such relationships the two realms—the practical day-world and the romantic night-world—are opposed and embodied by the partners, who are often at war with each other. If these opposites are not integrated in a relationship and within an individual, eventually the soul of love and creativity will become cold and hardened, and the love between the couple will be killed.

As the Watchman in the tower, Brangäna cares and notes the border between night and day. She warns Isolde to leave some light during the night in order to be alert to the danger of being discovered. For she suspects Tristan's friend Melot of jealousy and betrayal. From the watch-tower, the caring Brangäna calls to Isolde to summon the lovers to the light of consciousness. But the lovers would rather be united in death than be parted by the light of day. Thus Tristan says to Isolde, "Let the day to death be given."[7]

At this crucial point in the drama, the lovers choose death instead of life. Although they hear Brangäna's caring call, they refuse to waken to the light, for they want no separation. Instead they opt to die because the all-encompassing absolute love that they desire can be had only in the realm of death and night. Thus Tristan sings the romantic *Liebestod* ode:

> So let us die
> And never part,
> Die united,
> Heart to Heart,
> Never waking,
> Never fearing,
> Nameless,
> Endless rapture sharing,
> Each to each devoted,
> In love alone abiding![8]

In chemical addiction, the preferred substance always becomes the end to which all else is sacrificed. In the addiction to romance, the corresponding "substance" is the passion to merge. Addicts, in giving themselves over to alcohol, drugs, power, idealism, or romantic love, try to escape the conflicts and tensions of life. For they want to forget whatever keeps them from the absolutized object of their desire. Thus, they leave the paradox of opposites that is part of the human condition on earth and try to live at one pole, for the tendency in addiction is to live at the extremes: either total idealism and perfection or total despair and cynicism. In romance, that pole usually first appears as bright and "dreamy"—hence all the angelic projections in the beginning of a romantic relationship. But both the light of consciousness, i.e., the practical day-world, as well as shadowy jealousy and possessiveness, eventually intrude upon romantic lovers. Unless the lovers choose to deal consciously with these factors that interfere with their idealistic projections, they are thrown over to the dark romantic night pole. That is, they try to keep their pure love in the unconscious realm, away from the confronting light of day. If that is impossible, sometimes they opt for suicide rather than sacrifice their ideals. Archetypally, the *Liebestod* is what Tristan and Isolde choose.

In either case, the lovers try to avoid participating consciously in the entire cycle of conflict that exists in human life and love. The Romantic is "hooked" on a fantasy of love that usually is projected on an outer finite person, although the fantasy can also be attached to an inner Ghostly Lover. Romantics often protest that they experience the tension of opposites more strongly than others. Since the suffering from the loss of the beloved is so intense, the Romantic is ready to give up life and die. But death here is merely an attempt to escape conflict, whereas to live would be precisely to come to terms with the opposites of the ideal and its negation.

In romantic passion the jealous fantasy or feeling betrays the romance and is the killer of love. So, on the archetypal level in this drama, the treacherous figure of Melot, who betrays Tristan, now appears. Tristan projects that Melot, blinded by Isolde's glance, betrayed him out of jealousy, thus excusing Melot's treachery. Melot symbolizes the treacherous, jealous, possessive side of the Romantic, the dark side that seeks to kill genuine love.

In a romantic relationship, if one lover is jealous and projects infidelity upon the loved one, trust is killed. The jealous lover tries to control love by possessing the beloved. Often the Romantic projects *all* meaning onto the loved one, believing that the beloved could make him or her totally happy. With this fantasy of absolute bliss projected on one person, the Romantic then tries to possess the beloved and thereby secure happiness and meaning forever. With the impossible expectation that the lover will fulfill all desires, the Romantic becomes more and more possessive, which in turn leads to increased jealousy, feelings of betrayal and abandonment, anger and resentment against the partner, and sometimes to murderous feelings either toward the partner or oneself. Thus, by holding the lover responsible for life's very meaning, the Romantic can turn into the Killer, a frequent scenario in addiction. At bottom jealousy is really a denial of life's finitude and is a self-betrayal, which kills fidelity to oneself and to the life force. Ultimately, by wanting the absolute merger, by wanting to possess all happiness and meaning in the loved one, the Romantic pits himself against "God," against the greater divine mysterious life force of the universe that cannot be controlled. In wanting to secure love, to hold onto it and control it, in wanting to possess love and to dominate, the Romantic, like Lucifer, becomes possessed by the Demon Lover, the force in the psyche that kills love and life. All of this is inherent in the *Liebestod*.

Tristan would have let Melot kill him, but King Mark, who symbolizes the principle of honor and forgiveness that can redeem, interferes and holds Melot back. Even though he has himself been betrayed by Tristan, King Mark does not carry the betrayal further. Cast into his own wound by Tristan's breach of loyalty, King Mark is left to face his vulnerability without defense. He reflects that Tristan's gift of Isolde brought him love and opened up his heart. When he learned of the betrayal his trusting heart was tortured by doubt. His spying on Tristan and Isolde has brought him only breach of honor. Cast into his own dark night of the soul, King Mark asks Tristan:

> Why this hell must I suffer?
> With no hope of cure,
> Why must I bear the shame?
> The deep
> Mysterious source,
> The causes of my woe,
> Who'll tell me where they flow?[9]

But Tristan's only reply is "what, you ask, that can never be answered."[10] Mark is left to face his own darkness in the tension of the dark mystery. He does not objectify it by killing Tristan in punishment or revenge. King Mark symbolizes the person who dwells in the tension of the day and night worlds, the tension of the practical and romantic, the tension of the mystery.

In the final act Tristan is separated once more from Isolde. Seeking union in death, he allows himself to be attacked by Melot. But Tristan is wounded, not killed. Taken by his faithful servant across the sea to his native Brittany, Tristan floats in and out of unconsciousness. He wants to remain in the night-world of the unconscious, to escape the pain of separation from Isolde. Tristan longs to live in the eternity of "forgetting." He wants to withdraw from life because it mars the perfect union with Isolde. Thus he wants to dissolve into

> The boundless realm
> of endless night,
> And there we know
> One thing only:
> Endless godlike
> All forgetting![11]

But even there he is separated from Isolde, for she still lives. Even the night-world of forgetting gives him no peace. Finally, love drives him back in agony to find her.

The Romantic is addicted to ecstasy—and his yearning for rapture becomes agony as he realizes the insatiability of his desire. Seeking absolute union he comes upon the pain of separation. And feeling unable to bear this pain, he longs to forget. Thus ultimately, the longing for merger becomes the *longing to forget*, which is typical for the addict. Sometimes the pain of separation from wine, from the lover, from whatever possesses, is so unendurable that the addict longs to forget forever. The addiction actually helps the addict forget for a while by drawing him into unconsciousness. But eventually the addict needs more and more to forget, so much that the addictive substance or activity ceases to help him. Instead it turns him back upon himself in agony. If finally the addict faces the agony, plunges down into the darkness with open eyes, surrenders the ego desire totally in order to receive what is really there, his consciousness can reach a turning point. But if he continues to deny the pain and the conflicting tension between the practical day-world and the mysterious night-world, the path leads instead to death and stagnation. Forgetting the question of Being, as Heidegger has emphasized, is the ultimate denial of our age and of western thought, a denial that has led us into inauthenticity and self-betrayal. Denial, forgetting, self-betrayal—these are at the root of addiction, which keeps us from our genuine questioning and questing for life's meaning.

Tristan is driven back by love to the light. There he faces even more intensely the agony of his life of yearning. In a partially delirious memory he recalls his parents—his father already dead, his mother dying at his birth. In the ache of loneliness, he perceives his own dark fate and the fate of all humankind. He now realizes the pain into which he had been born and which he had hoped would be soothed by the love of Isolde, even cured by the philtre. This pain is the fate of yearning and dying. To such a fate all humans, as creatures of will and desire, are born. In self-torturing agony, Tristan realizes that through his desire for limitless rapture—his desire to escape the human condition—he himself had brewed the "poison" of the fatal drink from which he can find no rest or escape. In anguish he curses the drink and its brewer.

In Wagner's operatic version of the ancient legend the lovers are united for a brief moment. Isolde makes her way back by ship, crossing the sea to be with Tristan. But by now, from all his unfulfilled longing, pain, and despair, Tristan is driven to madness. Wildly tearing the bandages from his wounds, he dies in Isolde's arms. At this point

Brangäna and Mark arrive with messages of forgiveness for the lovers. But it is too late. Seeing Tristan in a vision, Isolde sinks into his arms to die with him.

Tristan's agony—that life is an oscillation between yearning and dying—is the agony of the human condition. The substance addict, in his craving, experiences this agony because he comes to know that his craving is insatiable and that at a certain point *more* means physical death. The love or control addict, faced with the same insatiability, encounters the limits of existence. Both face "existential" death.

This oscillation between yearning and dying is the despair that Kierkegaard describes in *Sickness Unto Death*. To be a human being, he says, is to be a movement between two opposite poles—the finite and the infinite, limitation and possibility, matter and spirit. If we try to stay at either of these poles, we cut ourselves off from the movement we are and split ourselves in two. This is what despair means—to be split in two away from our center of movement. The Romantic in us, who longs to merge into the infinite, wants to live in possibility, yearning for the spirit and infinity. But by denying limitation and finitude, the Romantic cuts himself off from the matter that could *embody* possibility. In contrast, the more practical person (who is frequently afflicted with co-addiction), opts for the other side of the opposition—control and limitation—thereby suffering the despair of alienation from the transcendent side. Insofar as we live at either one of these poles at the expense of the other, Kierkegaard says, we live a life of despair. Most of humankind lives this way unconsciously. We live in denial of the paradox of being human, not even acknowledging our pain. It takes a crisis to break through the denial and bring this to consciousness. Both consciousness and the free choice and acceptance of ourselves as this movement of being between these opposites are requisite to living our lives meaningfully.

Thus, Romanticism can be a potent form of addiction. The archetypal figure of the Romantic, the one who wants absolute merger with the loved one, is present when the addict seeks to escape the stresses of the everyday practical world through a drink, a love fantasy, or whatever helps to give the absolute feeling of being at one with the universe. Though the Romantic's search is an essential part of creative life, when it is absolutized or held tightly in an attempt to control and possess, the mystery of transcendent life is objectified and destroyed. The Romantic is caught in a paradox. In trying to possess and eternalize the feeling of oneness, he loses it altogether. For example, when love becomes objectified in the form of jealousy, its creative mystery is lost, sacrificed to the Demon Lover. What once was the uplifting, open expansive relation to the universe becomes constricted in self-pitying feelings of abandonment and rejection. In the face of his desire for absolute merger, love seems impossible, and he sinks into the opposite—the despair of eternal separation from the loved one. The only solution the Romantic can imagine is love eternalized in death, *Liebestod.* The Romantic swings perpetually from the longing for unity to the fear of separation. For transformation he needs to learn to live in the tension of these opposites, the mystery of unity in difference—a possibility that a genuine relationship with an "other" always presents.

In romantic addiction, the loved person is just like a drink or a drug for a substance addict. If the romance has been lost, the longing for the "lost lover" is similar to the longing for a drink. After the break up of an addictive relationship, there is often a tendency to want to get back into it, even though it would be self-destructive. To do so, for the love addict, would be analogous to the alcoholic taking the first drink. The addict would be possessed and trapped in the old feeling. (One form of this love addiction for women is to want to be the "anima" or the inspiring muse for the man.) In addiction there is always the desire that the substance or love will deliver something that is impossible. This is the Romantic's link with the Moneylender. The bottom, too, is similar. The addicted lover feels powerless, humiliated about the endless repetition and impossibility of having the loved one and faces an existential death—either to give up the addictive love object or to lose the soul. Sometimes this is acted out in suicide. At this point, like any addict, the love addict has the existential choice to choose authentic life or to be one of the "living dead."

When the Romantic experiences his own agony, as Tristan did, he begins the voyage of self-discovery. This is true also for the addict when he or she breaks through denial. Then the addict has started consciously on the "nightsea journey," or the "long day's journey into night," as Eugene O'Neill expressed it. Through suffering, the addict discovers that ego desire for power and control or for limitless love is doomed to frustration. Only surrender to the greater forces of life and death are transformative. In *Tristan and Isolde*, the "journey" is symbolized by the sea and the night, the cosmic dimensions of Wagner's opera. The lovers are on a sea voyage when the love philtre is taken; the sea separates their countries and the lovers in Act III; the mournful piping tune that reminds

Tristan of his life of sorrow is played at the sea's edge. It is also by the sea that Isolde finally comes to join Tristan as he is dying. Night, the realm into which the lovers long to merge, together with the sea, symbolizes the deeper realms of the divine mystery of the soul.

But when literalized in an outer relationship, the desire for ecstasy and infinite reality, symbolized by the romantic love of Tristan and Isolde, is doomed to frustration and failure. The addiction to this impossible romantic love really expresses our restlessness for the divine. Only when this desire is understood symbolically to be a desire for the wedding with the divine, can it take us beyond our familiar everyday experiences and open us to mystery and its creative expression in the world.

The romance of addiction can take us deep into our primal longing, deep into the unconscious desires that conventional society would have us repress. But there in that deep night we experience—along with the depths of our unconscious feelings—the primal energies of creation, the urge for ecstasy that takes us beyond the ordinary and familiar world we often take for granted as the only reality. Thus, the restlessness and longing of the Romantic, if genuinely understood, is like the mystic's quest to be aflame with the fire of divine love. If the Romantic can endure this fire and bring the mystical vision back to earth by embodying it in creative life, then the addictive quality of romance can be transformed into a creative gift.

5: THE UNDERGROUND MAN

> Resentment is the "number one" offender. It destroys more alcoholics than anything else. From it stem all forms of spiritual disease, for we have been not only mentally and physically ill, we have been spiritually sick. When the spiritual malady is overcome, we straighten out mentally and physically.
>
> *Alcoholics Anonymous*

> The Child is innocence and forgetting, a new beginning, a game, a self-propelled wheel, a first movement, a sacred "Yes." For the game of creation . . . a sacred "Yes" is needed.
>
> —Friedrich Nietzsche, *Thus Spake Zarathustra*

WHEN ADDICTS BOTTLE UP their angry feelings, their rage congeals into resentment, a destructive force that can be aimed toward others, themselves, and the universe itself. In Dostoevsky's *Notes from Underground* there is an analysis of resentment as the chief attitude that smolders in the Underground Man, killing his love and creativity. Nietzsche, in *The Genealogy of Morals*, calls resentment the sickness of the *Untermensch*, the person who fears creativity and who tries to kill it in themselves and others. Resentment is also underlined in the Big Book of Alcoholics Anonymous as the "number-one offender" that destroys more alcoholics than anything else. There resentment is seen as the major force behind recovering addicts' return to their addictions. From resentment stems all forms of spiritual disease. The founders of AA state plainly:

> It is plain that a life which includes deep resentments leads only to futility and unhappiness. To the precise extent that we permit these, do we squander the hours that might have been worthwhile.[1]

Dostoevsky, Nietzsche, and the founders of AA are all saying the same thing: resentment is the killer of creativity, life, and recovery.

Nietzsche saw resentment to be the antithesis of creativity. Resentment, he said, is the attitude of a human being when he lives a life of impotence and slavery, when he does not live out of the creative challenge of his existence but instead from the "impoverishment of life." And while resentment often expresses itself in a respectable facade of morality, from resentment stems hatred and envy that seek revenge—the revenge of the needy victim who is jealous of the strong creative person. Thus Nietzsche contrasted noble morality, which grows out of a natural and creative self-affirmation, with slave ethics, which is based on reaction rather than action and begins by saying "no" to an "other" while requiring a sphere hostile to its own. Those subject to slave morality live with bottled-up aggressions in a state of drugged tranquility that hides their impotence. It is this passive state that breeds the "poisonous eye of resentment," according to Nietzsche, whether it be the resentment of the condemning moralist and executioner or the sufferer who seeks the escape of intoxication.

In *The Genealogy of Morals* Nietzsche describes the difference between the person who can live creatively and openly and the one who must live underground with secret, hidden resentment.

> Whereas the noble lives before his own conscience with confidence and frankness, the rancorous person is neither truthful nor ingenuous nor honest and forthright with himself. His soul squints; his mind loves hide-outs, secret paths, and back doors; everything that is hidden seems to him his own world, his security, his comfort; he is expert in silence, in long memory, in waiting, in provisional self-depreciation, and in self-humiliation.[2]

When a nobleman feels resentment, Nietzsche says, he acts and does not brood upon it, hence it does not poison him. But the man who is in bondage lets resentment fester inside until he has "the smell of failure, of a soul that has gone stale."[3] The person devoured by resentment seeks revenge, seeks to punish his enemies. The moralistic judge, the martyred victim, the frenzied addict—all three are at bottom consumed by revenge, born of the same devouring resentment.

To the judge Nietzsche says:

> I do not like your cold justice; and out of the eyes of your judges there always looks the executioner and his cold steel. Tell me, where is that justice which is love with open eyes? Would that you might invent for me the love that bears not only all punishment but all guilt! Would that you might invent for me the justice that acquits everyone, except him that judges![4]

Resentment and power are behind the severity of the moralistic judge; the shadow of the judge is the killer as executioner.[5]

The martyr, too, is motivated by resentment and power, and Nietzsche sees this figure as no different in kind than the barbarian. For while the barbarian seeks power by torturing his neighbor, the martyr tortures himself, thereby torturing others.

The person who is slave to a demonic master, who is possessed by craving something outside himself for fulfillment, who lives out of this impoverished hunger, is the person ruled by resentment. Both the addict ruled by his substance and the co-addict ruled by the need to project the shadow on others in order to control and judge them are, by Nietzsche's standards, excellent examples of slave morality bound in resentment. They are qualitatively different from the creative person who lives from the inner generosity of his being, who responds to the inner call of the Creative Daimon. It is the creative mode of being which is truly Dionysian, according to Nietzsche, in contrast to the slavelike, addictive, hedonistic way of being that so often is mistaken for it.

The following story portrays the resentment of one Underground Man and shows how it figured in his drinking and affected his relationships and creativity. This man had always felt like an outsider, a misfit who didn't belong. There had been no known history of alcoholism in his family, but the atmosphere of his Irish Catholic home was gray and heavy. James's father was emotionally withdrawn; his mother, overworked. As a child he had been ill much of the time, and so he was never able to join in and play regularly with other children. He was handsome, intelligent, and always first in his class, and this too set him apart. He felt inadequate in social situations. It was during his particularly painful teenage years that he took his first drink. Even though he passed out from that drinking episode and woke up with a hangover, he knew he loved to drink. Because initially it made him feel lighter and better.

"From the start," James said, "I was an obvious drunk." He drank to escape from his highly active and often dark imagination, his extreme sensitivity, his brooding temperament, his resentments, and his pervasive sense of guilt. At sixteen he left home on a scholarship. Although he didn't get the opportunity often enough, he drank whenever he could and usually got drunk. Then he went into the army and was able to drink a lot, and when he drank he usually had blackouts. After the army, he went to college and studied literature. It was then that he started drinking every night and then, too, that he discovered Dostoevsky. For him, Dostoevsky was a brother, and *Notes from Underground* a mirror of his soul.

> I had lots of sour feeling about the world. I felt I was a misfit. I remember the absolute joy of these first words of the Underground Man when I read them in my twenties—"I'm a sick man. I'm a spiteful man. I have a disease of the liver." The miracle of Dostoevsky is that everyone finds himself in his novels. He was a brother!

Like the Underground Man, he always had a double consciousness—there was him and that "other" who was always watching, always observing, most often a sharp and excruciatingly perceptive critic—usually of others, above all of himself. Drinking helped wipe that double consciousness out—for a while. But as he saw in one of his dreams, that other was always to be found "alone, drinking in a corner."

At twenty-seven he made the first of three marriages to which he brought a touch of the poet, but also his drinking, resentments, guilt, fear, and increasing emotional withdrawal. He learned to isolate himself until he disappeared. "Because I didn't have a belief that things would really work out, I destroyed these relationships," he said. He also quit college several times, and although he was finally within reach of his doctorate, he didn't finish his thesis, thus fulfilling his sense of incompletion and failure. After this, he taught in college, and though he drank every night, he was able to teach and function effectively. But he didn't do the extra research or creative writing that is the unseen part of that job. Instead he drank, fantasized, and brooded. James could function off of his brilliance. But the drinking absorbed his creative process. He imagined that some "magic event" would solve all his problems. All this time he had dream after dream that announced his alcoholism to him. He even had a vision, a waking dream, in which he saw that he had been an alcoholic in all of his past lives. But despite his brilliance and his perceptive double consciousness, despite his theorizing and rational understanding, despite his telling dreams, he was caught in denial. As he said: "I don't know why I drank alcoholically. And no theory helps the alcoholism."

In the last years of his drinking, in his thirties, in his third marriage, he literally moved underground. In the basement of his house, drinking and brooding, he lived with the withdrawn one in himself. He could not share with his family. James knew he was in despair, and that when he picked up the first drink it would send him into oblivion. Previously, after a blacked-out drinking binge, he would wake up to find himself in a strange city. Now he would wake up to find that there was no one there in himself. Finally one day, when he looked in the mirror, he truly *saw* himself. He contacted someone he knew in AA, went to a meeting, and stopped drinking for the next eight months. But he couldn't stand success. One night, at the time of his customary AA meeting, just at the time his fellow recovering alcoholics were saying the Serenity Prayer, he sat down and raised a cup of whiskey to them in silent sardonic salute. Once again his drinking became so terrible and isolating that, months later, he went back to AA.

In AA he discovered that he was not alone. Instead he found himself sitting in a room feeling human equality. There he found a possibility of transformation for the Underground Man. As he said:

> We're all misfits sharing the human condition. We shared the addiction and now we share the possibility to go beyond that. We hear each other. In AA people acknowledge their resentments and the sharing helps. AA respects the freedom of others. If I feel like a malcontent corner of being, I can go there and still be loved and heard. I still feel the double presence and I think I always will, but now the two of me can go there and even the critical one can laugh. So when things disturb me, I go to AA. But now I can also reach out and witness to other drunks that I'm an alcoholic just like them, and today I'm not drinking. I find my creativity now in being present to help other people. Instead of being tormented by my creative imagination, now I enjoy it. I still have my battles with the demons, even though it has been eighteen years since I've had a drink. Five years after I stopped drinking, I quit smoking, and at the time smoking seemed an even greater demon than booze.

In *Notes from Underground*, Dostoevsky reveals the torment of a man suffering in the abyss of resentment. Like so many addicts, he is suffering from a "disease of the liver," a sick relation to life. As the *Notes* begin, he confesses:

> I am a sick man. . . . I am a spiteful man. I am an unattractive man. I believe my liver is diseased. However, I know nothing at all about my disease, and do not know for certain what ails me. I don't consult a doctor for it, and never have, though I have a respect for medicine and doctors. . . . No, I refuse to consult a doctor from spite. That you probably will not understand. Well, I understand it, though. Of course, I can't explain who it is precisely that I am mortifying in this case by my spite: I am perfectly well aware that I cannot "pay out" the doctors by not consulting them; I know better than any one that by all this I am only injuring myself and no one else. But still, if I don't consult a doctor it is from spite. My liver is bad, well—let it get worse![6]

Through his spite the Underground Man has chosen to live in a corner, believing that an intelligent man like himself has no place in society; only the stupid succeed. Yet he has served in society in the government service and was an official who took delight in intimidating petitioners. Now at forty, in midlife, the Underground Man is full of paradoxes, conscious of the opposing elements in himself but unwilling to reconcile them or live in their tension.

> I felt them positively swarming in me, these opposite elements. I knew that they had been swarming in me all my life and craving some outlet

> from me, but I would not let them, would not let them, purposely would not let them come out. They tormented me till I was ashamed: they drove me to convulsions and—sickened me, at last, how they sickened me![7]

Suffering from the conflict of opposites in himself, in bittersweet cynicism he calls consciousness a disease. For is it not true, he asks, that often at the very moment when one feels all that is "good and beautiful," one sinks immediately into perverse thoughts and commits a loathsome, ugly act. And just when one feels conscious of utter degradation, intense enjoyment occurs, for example, in those moments of despair when one actually enjoys the hopelessness of one's position. Such is the curse of consciousness. The Underground Man is a dreamer-romantic gone cynic. He compares himself to an insulted, crushed, ridiculed mouse, but with consciousness—a creature that contemptuously becomes consumed in cold, malignant, everlasting spite. Remembering every injury to the smallest ignominious detail, tormenting itself with its own imaginings that invent even more insults, such a creature forgives nothing and wants revenge. But he seeks revenge in trivial ways, incognito and piecemeal, knowing that it is he himself who will suffer more than the one upon whom he wreaks the revenge. This is the absurd hell of resentment in which the Underground Man indulges.

> But it is just in that cold, abominable half despair, half belief, in that conscious burying oneself alive for grief in the underworld for forty years, in that acutely recognized and yet partly doubtful hopelessness of one's position, in that hell of unsatisfied desires turned inward, in that fever of oscillations, of resolutions determined forever and repented of again a minute later—that the savour of that strange enjoyment of which I have spoken lies.[8]

There is enjoyment in pain, voluptuous pleasure in a suffering moan. Just listen to the sounds of a refined person suffering from a toothache, challenges the Underground Man. Even though he knows his moans bother others, who begin to loathe him, the pleasure in this martyrdom is intoxicating. It is the same with the intoxicating suffering of jealousy.

The human being is a strange, absurd creature of paradox, Dostoevsky points out. Humans are "sometimes extraordinarily, passionately, in love with suffering."[9] Even for a "palace of crystal," or for the secure mathematical certainty that "twice two makes four," the Underground Man will not renounce his paradoxical freedom to choose what is destructive, chaotic, injurious to himself, for that is the same freedom that grounds his individuality and his creativity. The rational man will shout: "It is no use protesting: it is a case of twice two makes four! Nature does not ask your permission, she has nothing to do with your wishes, and whether you like her laws or dislike them, you are bound to accept her as she is, and consequently all her conclusions. A wall you see is a wall."[10] But the Underground Man will reply:

> Merciful heavens! but what do I care for the laws of nature and arithmetic, when, for some reason, I dislike those laws and the fact that twice two makes four? Of course I cannot break through the wall by battering my head against it if I really have not the strength to knock it down, but I am not going to be reconciled to it simply because it is a stone wall and I have not the strength.[11]

To the rational man, who believes in control, who thinks there is proof that an enlightened and developed man cannot consciously desire what is disadvantageous to himself, who hopes for a controlled and ordered society where all is predictable, the Underground Man contends that reason is only part of life whereas will is a manifestation of the whole of human life, including reason and all the impulses. Life is not mathematical; life is more than simply extracting square roots. The history of the world is not rational. And even those who make it their object to live all their lives as morally and rationally as possible sooner or later play a queer trick on themselves and err. In rebuttal to the man of reason and control, the Underground Man points to the dark side of human nature.

> Now I ask you: what can be expected of man since he is a being endowed with such strange qualities? Shower upon him every earthly blessing, drown him in a sea of happiness, so that nothing but bubbles of bliss can be seen on the surface; give him economic prosperity, such that he should have nothing else to do but sleep, eat cakes and busy himself with the continuation of his species, and even then out of sheer ingratitude, sheer spite, man would play you some nasty trick. He would even risk his cakes and would deliberately desire the most fatal rubbish, the most uneconomical absurdity, simply to introduce into all this positive good sense his fatal fantastic element. . . . And if he does not find means he will contrive destruction and chaos, will contrive sufferings of all sorts, only to gain his point! He will launch a curse upon the world, and as only man can curse (it is his privilege, the primary distinction between him and other animals) it may be by his curse alone he will attain his object—that is, convince himself that he is a man and not a piano-key! If you say that all this, too, can be calculated and tabulated—chaos and darkness and curses, so that the mere possibility of calculating it all beforehand would stop it all, and reason would reassert itself—then man would purposely go mad in order to be rid of reason and gain his point.[12]

As the Underground Man points out, the strange paradox of being human is that resentment and the potentiality for destruction are part of the price we pay for freedom; we are free to choose destructive modes of being.

While the Underground Man criticizes the normal man mercilessly, rejects the idea of mathematical certainty and rational control, and desires the unobtainable palace of crystal, while he prefers to retreat into his underground hole rather than compromise, and to live in conscious inertia rather than adapt, in his heart he hopes there is another possibility, something different that he cannot find. He will not stay in bourgeois normality, but he does not want to be in the underground either. Finally, the Underground Man admits: "I know myself that it is not underground that is better, but something different, quite different, for which I am thirsting, but which I cannot find! Damn underground!"[13]

After confessing the torment of his soul, the Underground Man recounts a haunting memory of his intoxication with resentment. This story externalizes his inner struggle with the "normal man." He was twenty-four—a solitary, gloomy, savage soul. A Romantic who believed in the "good and the beautiful," furtively at night he indulged in "filthy vice." One night, he felt like picking a fight, but when an officer rudely jostled him without apology, instead of protesting he retreated. For several years he brooded upon this indignity until spite and hatred choked him with resentment. Obsessed, he followed the officer around for two years, imagining challenging him to a duel. Finally, he devised a plan to pass him in the street in such a way that the officer would move over and give way. But every time they passed it was he himself who moved over. The humiliation he felt each time this happened was so enjoyable, he felt such a rush of pleasurable pain, that he was drawn there at every possible opportunity. Every time he was humiliated, he gloated in his resentment at making way for the officer. He fantasized he would not move aside the next time and obsessively made elaborate plans as to what he would wear, and so on. Finally, the officer was transferred. But his resentment continued. As he was with the officer, he would be obsessed with revenge and resentment whenever anyone humiliated him. And, of course, *he* was the one who sought out the humiliation. He would alternate between his dreams of the good and the beautiful and his dissipation. Either he was a hero or he groveled in the mud. There was nothing in between. And it was often just when he was at the very bottom in his dissipation when the true and beautiful visited, not banishing the dissipation but highlighting it by contrast. The contradictions and suffering, the agonizing inward analysis, even gave a piquancy and a significance to the dissipation.

One of these "romantic humiliations" occurred when he encountered an old school friend, Zherkov, a "normal man" of whom he was jealous for his self-confidence and popularity. He maneuvered an invitation to a dinner in honor of Zherkov, planning to get the upper hand and humiliate him when all along he knew that it was he who would be humiliated. But he could not stop or control himself in this matter. Without enough money, in stained trousers and having taken a drink that was too much for him, he joined the party and insulted Zherkov. Ignored by the others, he strode about the room alone, rejected and angry, looking foolish. When the others set out for a house of pleasure, he followed them, drunk and in despair. Once there, he spent the night with a prostitute, Liza. The next day he tried to help her by painting a picture of the horror of her life, showing her that she was in debt to the madam (a Moneylender). "It's like selling your soul to the Devil."[14] He described how it could be otherwise, talked of fathers who love their daughters, talked of the idyllic family life, of married love and love of children. But though he talked with great emotion, to the point where Liza, at first sarcastic and distrustful, was overwhelmed with tears and became open and childlike, though he knew he was "turning her soul upside down and rending her heart,"[15] inside he knew he had killed his feelings, killed his love and his capacity to live life. He even began to blame Liza for his own sorry state. " 'She is the cause of it all,' I thought."[16] As Liza surrendered her heart openly to him, something hideous in him stifled all compassion and provoked him to greater venom. Ruthlessly he told her how from his own humiliation he wanted to humiliate her and show his power. The killing cynicism of his words overwhelmed her, but she returned his cruelty with love and compassion. But for him it was too late. The only love he had been able to imagine was a love that tyrannized and showed his moral superiority. Even in his dreams of beauty love started with hatred and was always a struggle with the loved one, who became a subjugated object. Realizing that he was by now incapable of love, he finally killed his love by shoving money into her hands, a cruelty from an evil brain, as he put it. Hysterically remorseful, he ran after her and found she had thrown away the money. She was lost to him. Perhaps she was better off to keep the resentment of the insult forever, he projected.

> Resentment—why, it is purification; it is a most stinging and painful consciousness! Tomorrow I should have defiled her soul and have exhausted her heart, while now the feeling of insult will never die in her heart, and however loathsome the filth awaiting her—the feeling of insult will elevate and purify her . . . by hatred . . . h'm! . . . perhaps too, by forgiveness.[17]

So ends the Underground Man's musings with this evil memory and the pain of remorse. He reminds his readers that he has only carried to the extreme in his life what they have not dared to admit in themselves and have carried only half way. Yet he also hints at a hope for transformation. Resentment may congeal into hatred and destruction. But it can also be transformed by forgiveness into creative love. Had he been able to acknowledge the necessity of steps six through nine, i.e., ask that his inner resentment be removed and make amends to the person harmed, he would have been open to receive and give love.

A betrayer of "living life," the Underground Man accuses us all of this crime. As he says to the reader, "the normal man" to whom he writes:

> Why, we don't even know what living means now, what it is, and what it is called! Leave us alone without books and we shall be lost and in confusion at once. We shall not know what to join on to, what to cling to, what to love and what to hate, what to respect and what to despise. We are oppressed at being men—men with a real individual body and blood, we are ashamed of it, we think it a disgrace and try to contrive to be some sort of impossible generalized man.[18]

The Underground Man has objectified two extremes in himself and retreated into one of them rather than bearing the tension of many opposing forces. In his rebellion against rationality and control, he has prescribed his own existence in an almost mathematical manner. He is unable to reconcile the raging paradoxes of human existence. Opting out of society, he envies the normal man's ability to deny suffering and despair, but his rebellion is in itself a way of denial. His extreme sensitivity to insult and humiliation congeal into resentment that is as cold and unrelenting and as hard as the stone wall of reason he decries.

Every addict knows these raging paradoxes—the scorn for the "normal" man yet the envy to be like others, the rebellion against control that is replaced by the controlling power of the addiction, the martyrdom in depression and anxiety that denies the suffering inherent in the human condition, the fact of the addiction and the denial and/or refusal to accept this limitation. Like the Underground Man, the addict is all too conscious of the human power to self-destruct and of the perversity that lies within.

The "normal man," who is not aware of these dark, raging forces within, or denies them in himself, or thinks he can control them through reason and sheer willpower, lives in a delusion. His is a disease of self-deception, of "bad faith" as Sartre calls it, or inauthenticity as described by Heidegger. Neither the "normal" man nor the addict, the one who lives "underground," lives in the tension of existence. The "different" way for which the Underground Man thirsts is to accept and *live* in this paradoxical tension of opposites. This includes the paradox of control and freedom. The addict who is not in denial and who is trying to recover is faced with this paradox from moment to moment. He knows he cannot control his addiction, yet he must choose not to succumb even while being continually assailed by temptation. His dignity rests in the consciousness of his choice to bear the tension of his being. The addiction actually brings him before the possibility of his being whole by thrusting him into the choice to bear life's paradoxes. Thus the addict is also thrust into a confrontation with his own death (mortality) and existential guilt.

The Underground Man inside us can keep us from creating. And he can also keep us from putting our creative ideas, feelings, and deeds out into the world. Dictums such as: "Why try, the world's not worth it" or "Your work will never be accepted by the stupid fools in control" are typical Underground Man statements. Giving up due to fear of criticism and/or rejection is also within the province of the Underground Man's grip over our psyche. Many of the voices that prevent us from having the faith and the daring to create can be traced back to this inner figure.

If one remains caught in the Underground Man's despair, resentment against existence can block all creativity. For it is the Underground Man in us who, from resentment and cynicism, refuses to create and/or to love. After I finished my first book, I found myself in such a state. During the course of writing *The Wounded Woman* I learned I could not drink. I was angry and resentful at the creative powers for having assigned to me this fate. So, I put down my pen as though in strike. I tried to stop drinking by myself, but I was not successful. For I was still caught in resentment and lived as a "dry drunk." So I denied myself not only creative expression but also the love and support I could have received from other human beings. Then I found myself falling into relapses. As Nietzsche says of the person caught in resentment, I was revengeful of the passing of time because my resentment kept me from living in the moment. Personally, I was not able to write again until I had surrendered and taken the first three steps. I acknowledged that I was powerless over alcohol and that my life had become unmanageable; I affirmed faith in the higher power that could restore me to sanity; and I tried to turn my life and my will over to this greater creative force. That is, I broke out of my resentment and despair of defiance and opened myself up once more to listen to the call of the Creative Daimon. Then I heard six words, "On the Way to the Wedding," and from these words I began to write again. In less than a year's time, I had given birth to a second book.

The Underground Man is not only simply detrimental to creation. This energy within the psyche also has a positive function in the process of creative transformation. For, having broken from the status quo of "normalcy," the Underground Man has started the descent into the dark chaotic realms from which the new creation springs. His black, bitter burning rage reminds one of the "Dark Night of the Soul" phase of spiritual creation. St. John of the Cross compares the soul to a burning log that gets blacker, looking abominable and ugly as it burns. Yet this burning process is essential to clear away the impurities so the soul (the log) can become one with the divine fire of creation. The Underground Man is caught via resentful rage in this black, bitter, burning process. But this is an essential part of the soul's journey and cannot be bypassed. Thus the Underground Man pulls us away from our entrancement with the collective images of material success, down toward something deeper.

Redemption, for Nietzsche, comes from willing every moment, while revenge comes from resentment over "what was." Resentment is the will's "ill will" against time. If you can will each moment, i.e., if you can say a creative "Yes" to it, then you can take responsibility for your life instead of festering in addictive resentment at the past which says: "if only." The child is an image of creativity, for it can say the "sacred Yes." In Nietzsche's view, Dionysus is symbolic of the life-affirmative forces that can bear the human condition, that can affirm life despite its inherent tragedy. Dionysus was connected with addiction, as the god of wine and revelry, and with creativity, as the god of drama. The addict, like Dionysus, is dismembered, torn into pieces, through the addictive process. But as Dionysus is reborn in a new cycle of creation, so is the addict in recovery. For Nietzsche, who struggled with the dark forces of resentment and succumbed to madness, the burning questions were:

Can the human being be reborn from his own darkness and disease? Can the creative be born from the destructive forces in human existence? How is the sick man to become whole and healthy? For an addict the same questions sear the soul when he hits bottom and faces his own powerlessness and capacity for destruction. But we are given images that point to the possibility of rebirth: the sun sets each evening to rise the following morning in all its burning glory; the phoenix emerges from its own ashes; Dionysus is reborn. So too can a human being transcend the burning fires of humiliation and resentment to find a life of creativity and transcendence.

6: THE OUTLAW

> . . . to learn to live and die, and, in order to be a man, to refuse to be a god.
>
> —Albert Camus, *The Rebel*

THE OUTLAW IS A glamorous, dangerous, and romantic figure, symbolizing the human being at odds with society, one who dares to be different. Like the creative artist who is often romanticized and feared for his difference, so is the Outlaw. Frequently addicts, as they tell their stories, express how, even in childhood and adolescence, they felt different from others. Many felt like "strangers in a strange land," thrown into a materialistic society they did not create and with values that they did not approve. Some came from alcoholic families and were set apart from normal society through shame about their parents. Others felt this way even in the midst of normal families. A common fantasy that such people have in childhood is that they are really orphans, born of mysterious, perhaps divine parents. According to Jung, this fantasy expressing a feeling of difference is at its source a first call from the greater Self. It is an expression of "the divine child archetype," of the deep thirst for creative spirit.

Many novelists and philosophers have given expression to this feeling of difference, these first stirrings of the call to creativity. For example, Herman Hesse in *Demian* and *Steppenwolf* expressed the call to an individual existence higher than the one to which most people aspire. But he also portrays the protagonists of these novels as suffering the conflicts of opposing desires in themselves—to be like others and belong, yet to be different and true to themselves. Hesse believed that suffering this opposition was requisite for the creative person. In his last novel, *Magister Ludi*, Hesse affirmed the necessity for the unique and creative individual to rejoin society to transform it.

Kierkegaard and Nietzsche, forerunners of existential philosophy, protested the course of Western philosophy, which leveled the individual through abstract rational systems of thought. Such systems ignored the mystery of individual uniqueness and human emotions because emotions were irrational and did not fit the system. Kierkegaard and Nietzsche brought personal feelings into the open by writing about their own experiences, daring to descend into the dark chaotic abyss in human existence. All of these thinkers—Kierkegaard, Nietzsche, Hesse, and Jung—were "misfits" in their time, at odds with conventional society, creative individuals who had to break free from the prevailing rational dualism of contemporary Western thought.

Sometimes it seems that to be a creative person it is imperative to be a rebel or misfit or outsider. But this holds a dangerous possibility. For this can be manifested in feeling "above the law" or "beyond all morality." When absolutized and taken to the extreme, this striving, which originates from the innate call to be creative, can be turned upon itself into an alienated position of contempt for one's fellowman. In this way the misfit can become an Outlaw and a Killer. Dostoevsky, in his novels, showed the way that the Underground Man's resentment ultimately turned into an attitude that could justify murder, as Raskolnikov did in *Crime and Punishment.* Thus the feeling of being special and unique that originates in the call to the creative can be diverted from its course by losing the tension of relating to society and taking that specialness to the extreme.

Many individuals who originally felt the urge to creativity have dared to be different through the path of addiction. The drink or the drug gives them "liquid courage" to do the forbidden as well as an inflated sense of their own importance. The romance of the Outlaw captures the imagination in this desire for danger and glamour and its opposition to an increasingly urban and technological society. The Outlaw links with many of the other archetypal figures in addiction—the Romantic, the Gambler, the Trickster, the Killer, and the Underground Man.

References to the Outlaw mentality abound in the literature of addiction. In the AA Big Book, the phrase "self-will run riot" attests to the centrality of the Outlaw archetype. Those who are addicted to illegal drugs automatically become Outlaws. Other addicts often find themselves at odds with the law in various ways. Drunk drivers are an example. But whether or not the archetype of the Outlaw is enacted on the outer level, the psyche of the addict usually contains an Outlaw in the inner cast of characters.

The Outlaw archetype is prominent in the psyche of the following man, a recovering addict and former thief who now expresses the Outlaw creatively by working with psychotic people. His addiction also "tricked" him into individuation and creativity. For the process of acknowledging his addiction forced him into spiritual growth beyond his wildest imagination.

The family in which Gary grew up was extremely dysfunctional. When he was five, his father, a heavy drinker who later quit, abandoned the family. Although as a little boy he was close to his father, after his father left he did not see him at all. His mother, also a heavy drinker who later quit, functioned in the family primarily as a co-addict vis-à-vis himself: after his father left home, she transferred her anger toward her husband to her son, often telling him he was bad like his father.

The first time he stole something was when he was four years old. During a time of much friction and fighting in the family, just before his father left home, he took some tip money from a restaurant table. From then on he committed minor thefts and shoplifting. Life at home with his mother, who moved a lot and had a number of boyfriends, was difficult. His ambivalent feelings toward her corresponded to the mixed message she gave him: "Now come here; then go away"—typical behavior for the co-addict. Eventually he came to hate her for abandoning him, but he also longed for the missing mother. When he was twelve, she remarried, and resenting his stepfather, he went to live with his sister.

His sister was heavily into drugs and drink, and Gary started using marijuana and amphetamines with her. He loved his sister and idolized her boyfriend, who had an Outlaw persona and belonged to a motorcycle gang that valued self-assurance and decisiveness. It also demanded a commitment not to use heroin or be an intravenous drug user. At this time, since he was free to do what he wanted, he became "streetwise." Yet he got good grades in school. "There were two people in conflict inside me," he said, "the good student and the rebel. I had two different ideals of manhood and both were macho—The Outlaw motorcycleman versus the western cowboy 'good guy' like John Wayne or Roy Rogers." This fostered a split masculine image. Partly, he wanted to be normal, like the other kids. But he always also was drawn to the unsavory exciting characters of the underworld. To be a "good thief," and later a "good convict," became a status symbol and had its own code—always to share the spoils with his friends and not to betray them.

By ten Gary had already started to steal on a bigger level, burglarizing bars for beer and wine. Often, after the heist, he and his friends would drink all night. Eventually he was caught, and from the age of twelve and a half on he was on continuous probation for various offenses. In his early teens, between arrests he shuttled between living with his mother and sister. His mother would take him in for a while and then, in disgust and anger, send him back to his sister.

Eventually he was stealing cars, using stolen credit cards, and making forgeries. At the same time, he started using heroin and selling drugs.

When, at seventeen, he was put in a youth camp and told he was a heroin addict, he asked to be put in a drug recovery program. But instead he was sent to a prison camp where he learned to jump right "into the fire" from helicopters. Although in many ways he learned from this training, he resented that he had been refused professional help for recovery from his addiction. He did get his high school equivalency diploma, which he valued.

The pattern of drugs and thefts continued. At eighteen he spent a year in the county jail's honor farm. He was out of jail for seven days when he was arrested again for assaulting two cops. This time he spent another thirty days in a county jail that was more frightening because of racial tension among the prisoners. Now he was beginning to experience the "real thing."

After his release, his mother refused to take him in, and his brother, who lived in another state, stepped to the rescue. He offered him a place to live and taught him to dance so he could get a job as an instructor in ballroom dancing. Thus began a new identity as a handsome, smooth-talking young man, now well-dressed in Italian shirts, who could charm lonely women into buying thousands of dollars' worth of dance lessons. In many ways, Gary said, selling dance lessons felt like stealing, for he was taught to play on people's emotions, find out their secret dreams, and put together a dance program that offered them fulfillment. Often he had to bring the customer to tears to make the sale. Soon he was so successful he was driving around in Cadillacs. Since drinking was part of the job, alcohol became his drug of choice. But soon his drinking got out of hand and he lost his job. So he went home and got back into burglarizing drugstores. When he sold some barbiturates to a narcotics agent, he was arrested. Instead of jail, he went into a halfway house that offered young offenders vocational rehabilitation and counseling. Here, through his photojournalism course, he was able to steal camera equipment and sell it to buy more drugs.

Then he committed his one and only armed robbery, an experience that gave him such a high and overwhelming sense of power that now, these many years later, he understands how criminals get hooked. The man he robbed was the boyfriend of a girl he had been dating, and he was filled with jealousy and resentment toward him. So he kicked in his door and robbed him at gunpoint. Although he was suspected of the robbery, charges were eventually dropped. Realizing he could have gotten fourteen years to life in prison for this crime deflated the "high" of the experience, however, and he never tried it again. But there were still charges against him for drug sales, so he jumped bail and moved to another state.

After confronting the possibility of a long jail term, he wanted to change. But by this time, his disease had progressed very far. A short marriage didn't agree with him, so he moved again to take another dance studio job, this time as manager. Back into the Cadillac and three-piece suit routine, he had lots of money and prestige. But since he also had no external or internal controls, he started drinking to the point of severe blackouts. He also began shuttling back and forth between his wife and a girlfriend, repeating the scenario he had experienced with his mother and sister. Finally, due to his drinking, Gary couldn't get a job as a dance instructor, so he started driving a cab and living with his wife, a co-addict like his mother. Again his role was the "bad boy" who was always rescued and taken back. During this period he got back into drug dealing. He was drunk most of the time and played dangerous practical jokes. He also got into fights, committed many infidelities, and terrorized his wife so badly that finally she filed for divorce.

By this time none of his friends could tolerate him. So on stolen money he went to visit the father he had not seen for twelve years. Now twenty-two, he arrived in LA blacked out and he left blacked out. For a few months he worked with his father, but most of his time was spent in a lonely Hollywood hotel room drinking and doing bizarre things like stealing bikes for a joke. The loneliness and isolation were intense.

Finally, he went back home. When he got there, his old roommates didn't want him back, nor did his mother or brother, whom he had beaten up in a drunken rage. Desperately lonely, he tried to drown himself, but was pulled from the water at the last minute by a passing boat. Finding himself still alive, back he went to what he knew best, drinking and selling drugs.

Now he became paranoid—with good reason, for there was a warrant out for his arrest. He moved, started to shoot heroin again, and was taking amphetamines every day. He felt crazy and paranoid, and nothing could relieve the emotional pain. At this point Gary had in his wallet five different IDs. When necessary, he could act the persona of these "normal" other people. But he didn't know who *he* was. Even his charm with women worked no longer. When one last woman asked him to leave, he felt like he'd suffered rejection from every human being on earth. Nothing was working; he seemed no longer to be a part of the human race. He hit bottom.

In this condition Gary called up an old counterfeiter friend who he knew had gotten clean through NA and now worked at a recovery center as a counselor. At first he could only brag about his recent crimes, but finally, for the first time, he told another human being just how desperate he was. The friend helped him get into a residential treatment center, where he stayed for three months. There he was introduced to the twelve-step program of AA and NA, which he took on blind faith. Only twenty-four, with most of his life ahead of him, Gary genuinely wanted to get better. But he was still not willing to do the work the steps required, i.e., "to do whatever it takes."

After Gary left the facility, he felt anxious about going to work. Since his job skills were poor, he had trouble with the eight-to-five work routine. And he was still looking for a "quick fix" in his relationships with women. Feeling anxious and sorry for himself, he got drunk, but luckily this slip scared him. The only way to save himself at this point, he thought, was to work in the recovery field himself. So he started training for a job at a drug abuse center. He also got a sponsor who helped him go to meetings and start working the steps. Now he had to look within himself, work on his "shadow side," and clear out the negativity that led to his drinking and drugging. One of his primary issues was feeling victimized by women, a pattern that had started early in his childhood with the mixed messages from his mother. He worked on this issue with his sponsor, and for the sake of clarity, he stayed out of relationships with women for six months.

> I knew I was an addict and an alcoholic. I also knew the twelve-step program would work. But at first I wasn't willing to do the necessary work on myself. I was doing the classic "I'm a victim" number, and I wasn't taking responsibility for my actions. Instead I wallowed in my memories of women's betrayal, starting with my mother. To get better, I had to do a fourth step inventory on my relationship with women and look at my own part in these encounters. When I looked at my abandonment issues, which had a real basis early in my childhood, I discovered that now, as an adult, I actually set things up to be abandoned. I found people who would abandon me, and I set it up for them to leave.

As he worked inwardly on the patterns that led him to drink and use drugs, he started to learn carpentry, which helped him become more independent. However, six months after he had started on the inner work of the steps, he got into another relationship, which brought up all the old cravings and fears of abandonment. But this time he had more resources to deal with those fears: the genuine friendship of his sponsor, the fellowship of the meetings, and the increasing integrity and true self-expression that result from inner work. All this time he was doing twelfth step work, helping other addicts who were newcomers. The help he gave to others helped himself.

Progress in his spiritual recovery continued for two and a half years. He was working hard, paying bills, living with a woman in the program. Both partners were doing their inner work and consciously practicing good communication. But then he was laid off from his job. They started arguing about money. When he tried to start his own business, it failed. Angry at this turn of events, he felt abandoned by God, and also by his sponsor, who had moved away. In resentment, he rebelled. He quit praying, and he quit doing twelfth step work with new people. The resentment built up and he became bitter. One by one the old negative patterns re-emerged, including his sexual promiscuity, leading to the end of the relationship. Although he still felt a responsibility toward his recovery program, gradually he started using drugs, which brought back full force all his misery and paranoia. Gary had to steal the money to support his drug habit, and to steal he had to be loaded. He was caught in a very vicious circle, exacerbated by paranoia about getting caught. Now he forged about $10,000 worth of checks on the account of a man he knew and resented and used the money to buy drink and amphetamines and cocaine. He was on a wild roll. But again nothing worked—neither drugs, drink, women, nor aggression could relieve his emotional pain. For, down deep, he knew the person he was betraying was himself. In the midst of all this a program friend telephoned and told him he loved him and to call when he was ready to sober up again. This touched him deeply. One night he woke up from a blackout and had a moment of clarity. He got down on his knees and prayed to God for help to get clean. The downward path he was taking was not what he wanted. He flushed his remaining drugs down the toilet and called a program friend, who took him in. Then he phoned his NA sponsor, who invited him to visit and got him a job in the Deep South. Even though Gary was still a misfit, riding his motorcycle and wearing a golden ring in his ear, he found that at meetings even the yuppies accepted him just as he was. Eventually, he was able to drop some of the more reactively offensive hard-core biker traits. Soon, he fell in love with a woman and they lived together, working hard on the relationship. Gary focused on inventory work on his relationship issues. His confidence was renewed, as was his self-esteem. Then he had another test of faith. Suddenly his girlfriend starting using again and left him. This time he did not give in to self-pity or resentment. Instead he increased his program work and went to meetings three times daily, working with newcomers and reaching out. He did not deny his feelings of grief, but despite the abandonment he kept his faith. Another test of faith occurred when his sponsor had a relapse after ten years of sobriety. Instead of giving in to his own abandonment feelings, he redoubled his twelve-step work to solidify his own sobriety.

Finally Gary decided to fulfill his desire to do meaningful healing work, completing a program to be a psychiatric technician. Since then he has been working at a large state hospital with a wide variety of psychotic patients. He loves his work. As a former addict and thief, he understands that the people he works with don't have control over what they do. Because of his past, he can tell when someone is "conning" him, and he can recognize the ones who are acting crazy to avoid prison or the outside world. When necessary, he can consciously return to his former underworld persona and use it as a bridge for communication with patients who are still caught there.

The stories told at NA meetings continually remind him that "this is what it was like, this is what happened, and this is what it is like now in recovery." Just as these stories give him hope, so he can give hope to others, particularly the substance abusers with whom he especially likes to work. One of the greatest joys of his life now is to see people get better. Having learned how to be patient and understanding with himself, he can give that understanding to others. The Outlaw-Trickster that before used, conned, stole, and dealt, now helps in healing.

Because of the extremes of his drug usage and stealing, Gary had a heavy list of amends to deal with. In the course of his recovery, as he worked the steps, he was prepared to make all appropriate and possible financial and emotional amends. In doing so he tried to be open and honest about his problems with drugs and alcohol and own up to the resentment behind his behavior. Most people, he said, were glad that he was clean and sober and responded very supportively. During blackouts he did things that he doesn't remember; to amend for these actions he gives to charity programs for users. He also cleared all his court charges.

About the amends he said: "When I make the amend, it reaffirms for myself that I'm an OK, honest person. I still have to deal with the old feelings that I'm not a good person because a good person wouldn't have done such things. But if I am willing to make the amend I feel better about myself. I discovered I couldn't force the amends; often I had to wait for the appropriate time. And, also I have to make amends to myself, too, for the terrible way I treated myself. Just as I have to learn to forgive others, so I have to forgive myself. Forgiveness is essential!"

Now he likes himself, so he doesn't have to have people like him at any cost. In being honest with himself, he can be honest with others. Instead of feeling the Outlaw's alienation from the human race, he has become a contributing member. As he said of his addiction and its transformation:

> My addiction actually "tricked" me into becoming a growing person. Because I had to face all the dark side of life and of myself, I had to look inside in order to recover, and that's what helps me help others. Now I put all the energy that formerly went into drugs, rebellion, and thieving into recovery and helping others heal. The Outlaw energy has been transformed into the solidarity of helping other recovering addicts in the twelve-step program. The trickery that goes into denial and destruction can also go into creativity and healing.

In his analysis of the rebel, the existentialist Albert Camus shows the transformational possibilities of the Outlaw. According to Camus, the rebellion brought on by feeling alienated comes from the confusion of values in a seemingly absurd and sterile society. Yet, if it is consciously understood, rebellion requires human solidarity to transform what has gone awry. According to Camus, rebellion is the very foundation of human solidarity. But without solidarity with others, rebellion degenerates into the very thing it abhors—tyranny or servitude. If the Rebel remains alienated, he turns into the Outlaw-Killer and acquiesces to murder. Camus expresses this as follows:

> Man's solidarity is founded upon rebellion, and rebellion, in its turn, can only find its justification in this solidarity. We have, then, the right to say that any rebellion which claims the right to deny or destroy this solidarity loses simultaneously its right to be called rebellion and becomes in reality an acquiescence in murder. In the same way, this solidarity, except in so far as religion is concerned, comes to life only on the level of rebellion. And so the real drama of revolutionary thought is announced. In order to exist, man must rebel, but rebellion must respect the limit it discovers in itself—a limit where minds meet and, in meeting, begin to exist. Rebellious thought, therefore, cannot dispense with memory: it is a perpetual

> state of tension. In studying its actions and its results, we shall have to say, each time, whether it remains faithful to its first noble promises or if, through indolence or folly, it forgets its original purpose and plunges into a mire of tyranny or servitude.[1]

In rebelling through addiction, many addicts plunge into the very tyranny and servitude they sought to escape. They become self-justified in their rebellion, alienated from their fellow humans, and lost in their own indulgences. Thus they embody the very thing they are protesting—the carelessness of a society that fails to honor the unique creative being of individuals and aggrandizes nature for its own uses.

Camus contrasts rebellion with resentment (a chief attribute of the addict) in order to distinguish between the passive-negative mode of resentment, which closes upon itself in "autointoxication," and the liberating active energy of rebellion. He points out that resentment is like an evil secretion of prolonged impotence in a sealed vessel. In contrast, rebellion "breaks the seal and allows the whole being to come into play. It liberates stagnant waters and turns them into a raging torrent."[2] The resentful person takes delight when someone he envies suffers humiliation and pain. But at bottom the resentment is really resentment at himself. The resentful person wants to be other than he is. This resentment often turns into unscrupulous ambition if he is strong or bitterness if he is weak. In contrast, the Rebel defends who he is and does not allow others to violate him. Rebellion is always a passionate affirmation of the integrity of the human being.

Camus reminds us of the original meaning of the spirit in rebellion—that sharing of strangeness and solitude from which human solidarity is born. This paradoxical acknowledgment of the strangeness that unites people can be seen in the communal sharing of recovering addicts—in meeting and sharing their suffering with humility, a kind of miracle happens. The humiliated estranged "I" of the suffering addict becomes the "We" of recovering addicts transforming themselves and others. As Camus says: "I rebel—therefore we exist."[3]

According to Camus, rebellion is a principle of human existence. Taken to its utmost limits, it implies a positive value to society and a hope for the creation of new ways to realize this value, as opposed to conformity to rigid, destructive social structures. Rebellion implies the acceptance of suffering within our human limits and, ultimately, the decision to endure. This decision does not come from obedience to outer religious or political dictates but from a stark intelligent confrontation with human limits. Viewed in this way, rebellion ultimately brings us not to excess, as in the Outlaw syndrome, but rather to the restraint and moderation that affirm our continual struggle as humans. Camus puts it this way:

> Whatever we may do, excess will always keep its place in the heart of man, in the place where solitude is found. We all carry within us our places of exile, our crimes and our ravages. But our task is not to unleash them on the world; it is to fight them in ourselves and in others.[4]

Overcoming the Outlaw's contamination by resentment, which "denies life," "dashes toward destruction," and ends in "rancor, malice and tyranny," finally becoming the "murderer," the Rebel lives life on this earth, enduring the tensions of time in order to give meaning to the moment.

> But he who dedicates himself to the duration of his life, to the house he builds, to the dignity of mankind, dedicates himself to the earth and reaps from it the harvest that sows its seed and sustains the world again and again. Finally, it is those who know how to rebel, at the appropriate moment, against history who really advance its interests. To rebel against it supposes an interminable tension and the agonized serenity of which René Char also speaks. But the true life is present in the heart of this dichotomy. Life is this dichotomy itself, the mind soaring over volcanoes of light, the madness of justice, the extenuating intransigence of moderation. The words that reverberate for us at the confines of this long adventure of rebellion are not formulas for optimism, for which we have no possible use in the extremities of our unhappiness, but words of courage and intelligence which, on the shores of the eternal seas, even have the qualities of virtue.[5]

The transformation of the Outlaw into the Rebel is an act of courage and dignity that takes us beyond nihilism. The Rebel overcomes the obsessions of the outlaw and "indefatigably confronts evil."[6] The Rebel does not abandon society and live in resentment, inflation, and rancor against or above the law, as does the Outlaw. Instead, the Rebel returns to life and generously gives with a "strange form of love" to the present, refusing injustice and hoping to bring dignity to the humiliated.[7] Thus, through rebellion, the alienated Outlaw can reaffirm the love within himself that was striving for uniqueness and creativity but was lost through excess and through escaping the creative conflict by living at only one pole of his being. The Outlaw can transform his hatred of society into love and generosity which makes:

> no calculations, distributing everything it possesses to life and to living men. It is thus that it is prodigal in its gifts to men to come. Real generosity toward the future lies in giving all to the present. Rebellion proves in this way that it is the very movement of life and that it cannot be denied without renouncing life. Its purest outburst, on each occasion, gives birth to existence. Thus it is love and fecundity or it is nothing at all."[8]

The challenge for humans, according to Camus is "the only original rule of life today: to learn to live and to die, and, in order to be a man, to refuse to be a god."[9] This means sacrificing one's ego and instead applying one's unique creativity to the struggles and destiny of all. For Camus the transformative and healing power is not in a higher divine order but in humans themselves sharing in the struggle to affirm and create. With the passionate affirmation and fervor of the rebel, Camus concludes with an expression of hope for the transformation of the adolescent Outlaw into the creative spirit that returns to the earth, accepts the supreme tension of life and death, affirms the present, and participates in remaking the soul anew.

> In the light, the earth remains our first and our last love. Our brothers are breathing under the same sky as we; justice is a living thing. Now is born that strange joy which helps one live and die, and which we shall never again postpone to a later time. On the sorrowing earth it is the unresting thorn, the bitter brew, the harsh wind of the sea, the old and the new dawn. With this joy through long struggle, we shall remake the soul of our time. . . . At this moment, when each of us must fit an arrow to his bow and enter the lists anew, to reconquer, within history and in spite of it, that which he owns already, the thin yield of his fields, the brief love of this earth, at this moment when at last a man is born, it is time to forsake our age and its adolescent furies. The bow bends; the wood complains. At the moment of supreme tension, there will leap into flight an unswerving arrow, a shaft that is inflexible and free.[10]

7: THE TRICKSTER

> It is a trick of John Barleycorn to turn the smile to a sneer without an instant's warning.
>
> —Jack London, *John Barleycorn*

> The so-called civilized man has forgotten the trickster. He remembers him only figuratively and metaphorically, when, irritated by his own ineptitude, he speaks of fate playing tricks on him or of things being bewitched. He never suspects that his own hidden and apparently harmless shadow has qualities whose dangerousness exceeds his wildest dreams. As soon as people get together in masses and submerge the individual, the shadow is mobilized, and, as history shows, may even be personified and incarnated.
>
> —C. G. Jung, "On the Psychology of the Trickster-Figure"

BEFORE I REACHED the turning point in my life, I had a series of relapses. In every single relapse there was a cunning and powerful archetypal figure working against me instead of with the creative forces of my psyche: the Trickster. Every addict knows this figure well. The Trickster is the highly seductive energy at play in the beginning of addiction. As the disease progresses he pops up whenever denial, hiding, and self-deception take place. In addiction the seductive Trickster frequently allies himself with the other underworld characters—the Moneylender with his high, the Gambler with his urge for risk and excitement, the Romantic with his longing, the cynical Underground Man, the rebellious Outlaw, the chaotic Madwoman, the critical Judge, and ultimately the Killer. But, as with the energy of all of these figures in the psyche, the Trickster's energy can be turned toward creativity. The Trickster can be allied with the "god" as well as with the "devil." Jung points out that the shaman, or the medicine man, has many characteristics of the Trickster.

The creative side of the Trickster is at work when, through our addictions, we are "tricked" out of our unconscious, materially oriented lives into awareness and individuation. When the addictions overwhelm us and bring us face-to-face with mortality, we can take responsibility for our inner potential for destruction. Acknowledging this demonic force in ourselves and the ego's powerlessness to fight it alone may lead us to reach out for help, thereby breaking through the imprisoning ring of power into the ring of love. Then we are able to stop projecting evil onto others and realize the universal fellowship of humankind. But just as the Trickster aspect of addiction can lead to individuation, so can it keep the addict in denial as well as lead to relapse.

The dual aspect of the Trickster archetype has been described by Jung, who points to the unpredictability inherent in this mythical figure. Just like addictive substances, the Trickster is a "shape shifter" who can both wound and heal. Jung sees the trickster as a primitive daimonic figure in the psyche that originally functioned autonomously and could even cause possession. So called "primitive" peoples have always acknowledged the Trickster, carefully giving him his due as both demon and savior in their myths and rituals. It is only "civilized" society that rationally rejects the Trickster when he is seen personified. For his unpredictability is disturbing to the person who thinks he is in control. It is natural to want to disassociate from such a disagreeable figure and to deny him in oneself. But as Jung points out:

> The trickster is a collective shadow figure, a summation of all the inferior traits of character in individuals. And since the individual shadow is never absent as a component of personality, the collective figure can construct itself out of it continually. Not always, of course, as a mythological figure, but, in consequence of the increasing repression and neglect of the original mythologems, as a corresponding projection on other social groups and nations.[1]

Some of the characteristics of the trickster are a hermaphroditic sexual appearance, a mixture of divine, human, and bestial qualities, a lack of body unity, and a phallus that he can remove and from which he can create. In mythology he turns up as a thief with special powers—Hermes and Krishna are examples. One finds him at the carnival, in parapsychological experiences, and in magical rituals of healing all over the world. In our time he may show up as a clown at the circus or in a drunken revelry. One frequently encounters him on a shopping spree and while buying a house. And in the disrupting and disturbing orgies of any addiction, the trickster is always present.

Jack London described the trickster's relationship to addiction in his "alcoholic memoirs," *John Barleycorn*. In this confessional novel the Trickster aspect is linked with its darkest demonic side—denial—and with what London calls "white logic," the inner pessimistic argument that he equates with the "absolute zero of the spirit."[2] In contrast to the inner dialogue between the opposites that Jung sees as part of the individuation process or that Nietzsche sees as creatively constituting the act of being, the white logic spoken by John Barleycorn (alcohol) as Trickster is a devilish discourse that brings sickness to the soul. With the white logic the Trickster takes the Romantic's longing, the Gambler's excitement, the Underground Man's cynicism, and the Killer's destructiveness and twists them into a cosmic "joke." " 'Drink' says the White Logic. 'The Greeks believed that the gods gave them wine so that they might forget the miserableness of existence.' "[3]

John Barleycorn portrays the inner working of the mind of the drinker. From the start, London describes John Barleycorn as a Trickster. As the book begins, his mind already "lit up" by a few drinks, the book's protagonist describes John Barleycorn's influence on the writing process itself.

> My brain was illuminated by the clear, white light of alcohol. John Barleycorn was on a truth-telling rampage, giving away the choicest secrets on himself. And I was his spokesman. There moved the multitudes of memories of my past life, all orderly arranged like soldiers in some vast review. It was mine to pick and choose. I was a lord of thought, the master of my vocabulary and of the totality of my experience, unerringly capable of selecting my data and building my exposition. For so John Barleycorn tricks and lures, setting the maggots of intelligence gnawing, whispering his fatal intuitions of truth, flinging purple passages into the monotony of one's days.[4]

As London describes him, John Barleycorn is both the enemy of life and the way to naked truth, a "red handed killer" and a slayer of youth. London describes the influence of this Trickster and the various ploys he uses. For "it is a trick of John Barleycorn to turn the smile to a sneer without an instant's warning."[5]

The protagonist recounts how John Barleycorn beckoned him, even in his early childhood when he first drank the forbidden beer, and how it made him sick. Each time he drank he entered the excitement of the grown-up world, but physically he loathed the alcohol. Still, in the saloon was good cheer and good spirits, which lured him, and the men who were there fascinated him and implicitly put society's seal of social approval on the saloon and on drinking. How could he, an impressionable lad, know "what these men sought was forgetfulness of jaded toil and stale grief."[6] Moreover, as he entered the teenage years, men laughed at those who took soda instead of beer. So he learned how to gulp down the distasteful beer and to enjoy the wild man's world and the tales of romance and adventure.

Yearning for adventure and dreaming of romance, he set out to sea at fourteen. Sailors proved they were men by the way they drank. "Drink was the badge of manhood. So I drank with them, drink by drink, raw and straight, though the damned stuff couldn't compare with a stick of chewing taffy."[7] Still, his brain blew open and now he could live the adventures of his dreams, brag about his exploits with his loosened tongue, and pledge eternal friendship with these young and tipsy comrades.

> Oh, it was brave. I was beginning to grasp the meaning of life. Here was no commonplace, no Oakland Estuary, no weary round of throwing newspapers at front doors, delivering ice and setting up ninepins. All the world was mine, all its paths were under my feet, and John Barleycorn, tricking my fancy, enabled me to anticipate the life of adventure for which I yearned. We were not ordinary. We were three tipsy young gods, incredibly wise, gloriously genial, and without limit to our powers. Ah!—and I say it now, after the years—could John Barleycorn keep one at such a height, I should never draw a sober breath again. But this is not a world of free freights. One pays according to an iron schedule—for every strength the balanced weakness; for every high a corresponding low; for every fictitious god-like moment an equivalent time in reptilian slime. For every feat of telescoping long days and weeks of life into mad, magnificent instants, one must pay with shortened life, and, oft-times, with savage usury added.
>
> Intenseness and duration are as ancient enemies as fire and water. They are mutually destructive. They cannot co-exist. And John Barleycorn, mighty necromancer though he be, is as much a slave to organic chemistry as we mortals are. We pay for every nerve Marathon we run, nor can John Barleycorn intercede and fend off the just payment. He can lead us to the heights, but he cannot keep us there, else would we all be devotees. And there is no devotee but pays for the mad dances John Barleycorn pipes.[8]

But the above is only aftersight. On this first great drinking voyage he discovered he could hold his liquor and outdrink grown-up men; he was proud. Only later did he learn that the man who can outdrink his fellow man and hold his liquor without a sign *must* take increasing numbers of drinks to get a "high." As he says, John Barleycorn is a "strange friend" whom one comes to hail and to hate at the same time.

> And yet—and here enters the necromancy of John Barleycorn—that afternoon's drink on the "Idler" had been a purple passage flung into the monotony of my days. It was memorable. My mind dwelt on it continually. I went over the details, over and over again. . . . I had got behind men's souls. I had got behind my own soul and found unguessed potencies and greatness.[9]

When at fifteen the protagonist of *John Barleycorn* returns to land, working ten-hour days at a cannery, he feels his life has been reduced to that of a work beast. Again he turns to the sea and John Barleycorn. "Wherever life ran free and great, there men drank. Romance and adventure seemed always to go down the street locked arm in arm with John Barleycorn."[10] For the price of this warm glowing comradeship where men shared spirit and revolt, he would drink with them. But he still didn't really like the stuff.

Even so, heavy drinking overtook him—not out of desire but out of an intellectual conviction. One could make good friends out of a gloomy grouch just by buying him a drink. This way, John Barleycorn could win him his manhood spurs, convert enemies into friends, and eventually inhibit his moral guilt about spending all the money he owed his mother on booze. With John Barleycorn's help he could leave his boyhood behind and win his way to manhood. Finally, buying and accepting drinks became "a social duty and a manhood rite." Secretly he still didn't like the taste. His real craving was for candy. But the madcap times were so intoxicating. He discovered that whether together or apart, men drank to celebrate good fortune and to forget bad fortune. They drank if they were in love or were jilted. If they have too much to do they drink, but they also drink if they have nothing to do at all. For every occasion—happy or sad, social or alone—men become the devotees of John Barleycorn.

As his heavy drinking increased, his extraordinarily strong constitution enabled him to continue this way of life. Also, the healthy life at sea guaranteed periods of sobriety. But all the while his drunken exploits got more dramatic and outrageous. And then John Barleycorn played on him a "magical trick." On a drunk he decided his life was meaningless. "This was the trick of John Barleycorn, laying me by the heels of my imagination and in a drug-dream dragging me to death."[11] Had he not seen all and lived everything in his wild escapades? Suddenly, he felt the melancholy tears and the sweet sadness of the weeping drunk. He would give it all up and go out with the tide and die the "hero's" death. Now, bidding a sentimental farewell to the distant wharf lights, he swam on in a drunken daze.

> The water was delicious. It was a man's way to die. John Barleycorn changed the tune he played in my drink-maddened brain. Away with tears and regret. It was a hero's death, and by the hero's own hand and will. So I struck up my death-chant and was singing it lustily, when the gurgle and splash of the current-riffles in my ears reminded me of my more immediate situation.[12]

But time and the cold waters sobered him up and put fear in his heart. He realized he didn't really want to die. Luckily he stayed afloat until a fishing boat came by and he was saved.

Tricked by John Barleycorn into these suicidal thoughts and deeds, now he realized he had to try to move away from the devilish clutches.

> But what gave immediacy to my decision to move on, was a trick John Barleycorn played me—a monstrous, incredible trick that showed abysses of intoxication hitherto undreamed. . . . And in passing, let me note that this maniacal trick John Barleycorn played me is nothing uncommon. An absolute statistic of the percentage of suicides due to John Barleycorn would be appalling. In my case, healthy, normal, young, full of the joy of life, the suggestion to kill myself was unusual; but it must be taken into account that it came on the heels of a long carouse, when my nerves and brain were fearfully poisoned, and that the dramatic, romantic side of my imagination, drink-maddened to lunacy, was delighted with the suggestion. And yet, the older, more morbid drinkers, more jaded with life and more disillusioned, who kill themselves, do so usually after a long debauch, when their nerves and brains are thoroughly poison-soaked.[13]

With these reflections, he continued on his way. But because John Barleycorn's power over men could bring immediate geniality, warmth, and fellowship to strangers, he continued to frequent saloons to self-destruction. For one of the tricks of John Barleycorn is that

> It is these good fellows that he gets—the fellows with the fire and the go in them, who have bigness and warmness, and the best of the human weaknesses. And John Barleycorn puts out the fire, and soddens the agility, and, when he does not more immediately kill them or make maniacs of them, he coarsens and grossens them, twists and malforms them out of the original goodness and fineness of their natures.[14]

Just this was happening to him all the while. He returned to Oakland and hung around the saloons, drinking daily, often to excess. Insidiously John Barleycorn was gaining power over him in an even deadlier way than when he sent him into the deeps of the sea. For now he was becoming dull and blunt. Life seemed to be "a rather cheap and ordinary affair."[15] His youthful search for spirit and meaning soddened as did his mind and body. And as he woke up shaky in the morning he reached for that stiff drink to brace him up. Such is the devilish trickery of John Barleycorn—to keep the victim coming back for more.

> (Oh! John Barleycorn is a wizard dopester. Brain and body, scorched and jangled and poisoned, return to be tuned up by the very poison that caused the damage.)[16]

Now seventeen and afraid of his disillusioned life, he signed up to go to sea again, this time to the Orient. But though the voyage started out with fifty-one days of glorious drink-free sailing, in the end he saw only the port saloons. Even though he was thirsting to see the exotic unknown world with his friends, "John Barleycorn reached out and tucked my arm in his."[17] So he stayed in the bars drinking with the men. When they returned all swore to save their money and not spend it on drink, but the bars beckoned to most as they stepped ashore and the good intentions were lost to jovial rounds of drinks.

Surviving this adventure tramp, he set down again to study. Since he didn't drink while studying, he was sure he was not an alcoholic. But now he was intoxicated with ideas, and this intoxication had its own mental tricks. Whatever he did, he did to excess, and now he studied nineteen hours a day. When the exams were over, he discovered he wanted one thing—to escape brain fag by getting drunk. For the first time he *consciously* desired to drink—a new manifestation of John Barleycorn's power. Because he had become used to alcohol, his brain cried out for a "drunk." At this time one binge was enough, and he went back to studying and writing.

When he took a laundry job to earn money, his studying suffered and his inactive mind craved something. So for the second time he consciously sought out the dreams of power and fancy and forgetfulness that the protean shapeshifter, John Barleycorn, could give him. Whether he yielded to drink or whether he refrained, now the seeds of desire for alcohol were germinating in his brain.

> John Barleycorn makes his appeal to weakness and failure, to weariness and exhaustion. He is the easy way out. And he is lying all the time. He offers false strength to the body, false elevation to the spirit, making things seem what they are not and vastly fairer than what they are. But it must not be forgotten that John Barleycorn is protean. As well as to weakness and exhaustion, does he appeal to too much strength, to superabundant vitality, to the ennui of idleness. He can tuck in his arm the arm of any man in any mood. He can throw the net of his lure over all men. He exchanges new lamps for old, the spangles of illusion for the drabs of reality, and in the end cheats all who traffic with him.[18]

At twenty-two he set out for more adventure—this time in the Klondike. Then his father died, and to earn money he devoted himself to writing. Always an extremist, he wrote a thousand words a day, slept only five hours a night, and pawned whatever he could to keep writing. Never, in the beginning of his writing, did he think of drink. But as he succeeded, his standard of living climbed. He wrote and lectured and attended parties where he was invited to drink. Since his hosts drank temperately so did he to be sociable, certain that he was merely a social drinker. "Besides, I no longer feared John Barleycorn. Mine was that most dangerous stage when a man believes himself John Barleycorn's master."[19]

As his success grew so did his pessimism—again his thoughts turned to suicide. But he did not turn to whiskey for escape. This time "the people" and his belief in socialism got him through. But he found the actual people boring. Social intercourse had lost its glamour. Once more the ever-patient John Barleycorn came to the rescue. A cocktail helped to liven things up. With some predinner drinks he could laugh once more with his company. Now a drink keyed him up and always made him feel better. Soon he found himself drinking alone regularly after he had done his morning's writing. But why not? He deserved it. Had he not proved that he was the master of John Barleycorn? Soon it took three cocktails to give him the effect of the first. So he began to steal an extra drink to every one that he offered his guests. And John Barleycorn provided a good excuse for every extra drink. More and more he *wanted* alcohol.

He had one unbreakable rule—never to drink until his day's writing was done. Then he could have a drink, which helped him not to think about his work until the next morning. In this way, he reasoned, John Barleycorn actually conserved his energy—one of the increasing good turns he now provided. Even so, sometimes he wondered why he drank, for he was happy. He had a wife he loved, and he was a successful writer. Sometimes he wondered if he was becoming an alcoholic through too many years of familiar contact with booze. But John Barleycorn was able to silence his uncomfortable thoughts by suggesting another drink.

The drinking game was growing in its clever moves. For example, when he sailed to the tropics aboard his ship, *The Snark*, there was no liquor on board. He wasn't bothered. After all, he was the master of John Barleycorn: he could drink whenever he wanted. So for the rest of the voyage he made sure there was plenty of liquor aboard, and he kept a pleasant, discreet, and canny hum in his head just like hundreds of thousands of other men who believe they are beating the game.

Slowly and imperceptibly the time came when cocktails were not enough. Their jolt was not as quick as straight shots. Sleep, too, began to be a problem: he found that on awakening in the night a drink put him back to sleep. Soon he needed a drink upon awakening, too, to quell the heavy head and nervous palpitations. Finally, his body was never free from alcohol, and he was sure to have some with him all the time.

The one rule never to be broken not to drink before finishing writing—took second place now to John Barleycorn.

> The gravity of this I realized too well. I made new rules. Resolutely I would refrain from drinking until my work was done. But a new and most diabolical complication arose. The work refused to be done without drinking. It just couldn't be done. I had to drink in order to do it. I was beginning to fight now. I had the craving at last and it was mastering me. I would sit at my desk and dally with pad and pen, but words refused to flow. My brain could not think the proper thoughts because continually it was obsessed with the one thought that across the room in the liquor cabinet stood John Barleycorn. When, in despair, I took my drink, at once my brain loosened up and began to roll off the thousand words . . . —if John Barleycorn could get such sway over me, a non-alcoholic, what must be the sufferings of the true alcoholic, battling against the organic demands of his chemistry while those closest to him sympathize little, understand less, and despise and deride him![20]

Now John Barleycorn began to collect his due from the mind, even more than from the body. The old sickness reappeared, as cynicism seeped into his happiness, and with it old ghosts arose, now armed with the White Logic of John Barleycorn. To quell this deadly pessimism, John Barleycorn offered yet another drink, with undelivered promises. How can one describe the land of the White Logic, to which John Barleycorn leads? "For there are fatal intuitions of truth that reside in alcohol. . . . Alcohol tells truth but its truth is not normal. What is normal is healthful. What is healthful tends toward life."[21] But the man who has come to see with the eyes of John Barleycorn sees the oppressive cosmic sadness that is the heritage of man world-sick from the White Logic; he learns to sneer at life's dreams. With jocose grin he acknowledges transiency and the skeleton within his disintegrating body.

> And now comes John Barleycorn with the curse he lays upon the imaginative man who is lusty with life and desire to live. John Barleycorn sends his White Logic, the argent messenger of truth beyond truth, the antithesis of life, cruel and bleak as interstellar space, pulseless and frozen as absolute zero, dazzling with the frost of irrefragable logic and unforgettable fact. John Barleycorn will not let the dreamer dream, the liver live. He

> destroys birth and death, and dissipates to mist the paradox of being, until his victim cries out, as in "The City of Dreadful Night": "Our life's a cheat, our death a black abyss."[22]

So does John Barleycorn finally infect the mind of the drinker who once innocently sought adventure and wild romance.

At the end of the novel, the protagonist reflects on his life as a drinker. He has success, a beloved soul mate, money, power, and land. Yet, John Barleycorn, now his ever-present companion, whispers in White Logic:

> Let the doctors of all the schools condemn me. . . . What of it? I am truth. You know it. You cannot combat me. They say I make for death. What of it? It is truth. Life lies in order to live. Life is a perpetual lie-telling process. Life is a mad dance in the domain of flux, wherein appearances in mighty tides ebb and flow, chained to the wheels of moons beyond our ken. . . . Life is ghost land . . .[23]

Thus John Barleycorn beckons him to fill his empty glass and forget.

London has not, he concludes, told the tale of a reformed drunkard. "I was never a drunkard, and I have not reformed."[24] Hardly one man in ten thousand is a chemical dipsomaniac, he argues. Rather, drinking is a habit of mind caused by availability, fostered by social pressure and the desire for fellowship. It is also a matter of mental association. For example, when he remembers Venice, he thinks of the sidewalk cafés. And if it is the city, London, he remembers the pubs. If one mentions the fine cooking of wild duck in a San Francisco restaurant, his memory turns to the long-stem wine glasses.

> And so I pondered my problem. I should not care to revisit all these fair places of the world except in the fashion I visited them before. *Glass in Hand!* There is a magic in the phrase. It means more than all the words in the dictionary can be made to mean. It is a habit of mind to which I have been trained all my life. It is now part of the stuff that composes me. I like the bubbling play of wit, the chesty laughs, the resonant voices of men, when, glass in hand, they shut the gray world outside and prod their brains with the fun and folly of an accelerated pulse.[25]

He concludes that he will take his drink "on occasion." With the aid of his books, he will know how to decide when to drink or not; he will learn to moderate his drinking; how to drink "more skillfully, more discreetly, than ever before."[26] He will bury the White Logic. Still under the sway of the Trickster, of John Barleycorn, he again denies he is an alcoholic, and absolving himself of responsibility, he ends:

> And yet, . . . I can well say that I wish my forefathers had banished John Barleycorn before my time. I regret that John Barleycorn flourished

> everywhere in the system of society in which I was born, else I should not have made his acquaintance, and I was long trained in his acquaintance.[27]

The novel *John Barleycorn* closely parallels London's own life, in which many of the patterns of the addict and the struggle between the Demon Lover and the Creative Daimon are reflected. In addition to drink and painkillers, London was addicted to being in debt, to control, and to work. He was an illegitimate child who never knew his personal father, reputed to be a vagabond moving through various professions—astrologer, sailor, editor, attorney, and politician. His emotionally remote mother, who dominated the home with her temper tantrums and hysteria, gave music lessons and held seances. Although she was not able to give London warmth and security, she taught him to read and had great ambitions for him. He did receive love from his stable stepfather and from his older sister.

One biographer says that London was always hungry for the missing mother love and this manifested in his hunger for food, especially meat and candy.[28] He was also ashamed of being a bastard, trying to hide that fact for most of his life. As a young boy, he was an avid reader and dreamer, living in an imaginary world of romantic adventures. But his outer life was full of work and the threat of poverty. All his earnings were claimed by his mother. He resented the grueling work denied of all pleasure, a pattern that seemed to recur in his life. But loneliness made him observe and be perceptive, a preparation and ground for his life as a writer.

In his teens he rebelled, roistering around the waterfront saloons, fighting and drinking, pirating the oyster reserves of big companies. Finally, at seventeen he sailed for Japan as a seaman on a schooner, searching for romance and adventure. He was wild, full of fierce desires and frustrations, and hungry for instant gratification.

The rough life at sea suited his temperament; he thrilled to the power at the wheel of the surging schooner. In the ports he drank and caroused, proud to be a sailor. Back at home, he decided to write his experiences for a newspaper competition and won first prize. For the first time he found that his ambitious mother approved of him. He went back to hard labor to try to rescue the family from debt, and in an orgy of dirty work shoveled coal so hard that he worked with swollen wrists. He was pushing himself beyond all sorts of limits, and his body was beginning to show it. Disgusted, he escaped by joining a traveling militia of protesting working men and was subsequently jailed. Soon he discovered that he was a socialist and returned home to study in "a frantic pursuit of knowledge."

While on his adventures, he drank and caroused. When he studied, he didn't drink. He finished his high school education, older, shy, shabbily kempt, and feeling out of place, but he continued writing and diligently prepared for the university examinations. A student of Marx, Darwin, and Spencer, he was thrown into a conflict between the notion of the individual's irrelevance in face of inevitable social revolution and his own personal desire for fame and success. Still, he believed in his own destiny as a writer. Yet he developed a pessimistic view of the struggle of the human spirit against unreasonable forces and the necessity of the survival of the fittest. During all this time of study he indulged in drunkenness only once. Mostly, he studied furiously, and he wrote, typing until his fingers blistered. Unable to sell his writing, he returned to the factory, where he felt like a work beast. The hope of escape lured him to the Gold Rush of the Klondike, where again he worked like a pack animal. Here London learned that survival was everything. He suffered from scurvy, swollen joints, and lost most of his teeth. The body's tortures, he learned, provided the trials for the spirit's growth. During the long, cold winter he visited the saloons, but he also read Milton and Dante. He came face-to-face with the Luciferian pride which, defying all creation, descended into the horrors of hell. Though he returned from the Klondike penniless, his experience became a literary gold mine—the source for his Alaska stories, among them *The Call of the Wild*.

When he returned from the Klondike, he set to work to write. He was willing to do hackwork to survive, but finally the *Atlantic Monthly* and Houghton Mifflin offered to publish some of his stories. He began to experience success, and he married a woman who could make him a home, type his manuscripts, and leave him alone to write. His marriage was part of his attempt to control his wildness. But the price he had to pay was the loss of his adventurer's life. Still, he drank and reveled with the smart bohemian set in the Bay Area while his wife stayed home with the children. When he was not partying with his friends, he studied and wrote. His life-style became more prosperous and he supported two households, his mother's and his own.

Like Dostoevsky, he became permanently in debt. Overspending, he took contracts under pressure, which kept him writing at his desk. Under the threats of creditors, he accepted in 1902 a total of $2,000 for *Call of the Wild,* which later sold millions of copies. In his lifetime of compulsive overspending, and in struggling with his debts, he seemed to find the excitement that he always craved. Meanwhile his marriage bored him and he started to break out. Eventually he divorced and remarried Charmian, who was both a playmate and a soul mate for the romantic and adventurous London.

London's novels seem to have come from great depths within his psyche, reflecting the interior oppositions that he experienced so intensely and which are inherent in all human beings. For example, *The People of the Abyss,* a novel about the grueling poverty and homelessness of workers, may be an expression of the abyss that London himself was experiencing—the abyss between his reason and emotions, between his workside and his wildness. *Call of the Wild* symbolizes the struggle of London's own suppressed beast side which, overworked, becomes chief of the work beasts and eventually turns against the men whose greed causes his death. London thought of his work as adventure stories. But many of London's novels are really human allegories, and their appeal to millions of readers is that they reach into the deepest recesses of the soul, laying bare the conflicts raging within the human psyche—conflicts that if untended can lead to the basis of addiction.

A typical addict, London "wanted it all now." His desire to devour existence all at once eventually cost him his life. He wanted to be the Romantic and the Adventurer, to be the famous creative writer, the great socialist liberator, and the California landowner who gave back to the land. He was both an idealist buoyed by a vision of a new life on earth for humankind and a fatalist oppressed by monstrous disillusions, which, in *John Barleycorn,* he attributed to the growing influence of alcohol in his body.

His body was beginning to show the ravages of his alcohol and drug use and of his hard life. He was in a great deal of pain, and he began to fear mental collapse. In a vain attempt to establish his mental and physical power as godlike, he undertook a sea voyage on his cruiser, *The Snark,* which endangered the lives of all aboard. Persisting in this image of "master," he insisted the cruise continue despite the storms that assaulted the vessel and the diseases that threatened the lives of those aboard. By this time, it seemed, he was addicted not only to alcohol, painkillers, and work, but also to power. He wanted to match himself against the greatest force of nature—the ocean. But the cruise ended in his physical collapse: he suffered from ulcers, piles, yaws, malaria, yellow fever, nervous attacks, and skin afflictions. He drank heavily to deaden the pain. Finally his physical condition deteriorated so much he had to return. Although he also had hoped to escape from his financial pressures, which were escalating due to the mounting debts of his land purchases, he came back to find himself in even greater financial disaster.

London's hunger for mastery and control gave him the illusion of access to superhuman powers that would enable him to exceed the limits of normal men. But along with the alcohol and drugs, this hunger was devouring him. His addiction now seemed not only to be the poison of alcohol, but also the poison of power.

Upon his return, London's health began deteriorating rapidly. Only thirty-five, he felt extremely anxious about his physical condition, which caused him to drink even more. "Cures" using arsenic and salvarsan only produced uncontrollable rages and mood changes, periods of manic-depression, and a terrible fear of going mad. He was afflicted with insomnia and nightmares. He felt guilty about his drinking and feared that his youthful drunken whoring had led to gonorrhea, which, combined with the poison in his system, might have caused Charmian's miscarriage.

In 1911 he wrote *John Barleycorn,* denouncing the trickery of alcohol and describing the "white logic" with which alcohol tortures the soul. Yet, he could not give up drink totally, for it assuaged his physical pain and stimulated him intellectually. *John Barleycorn* is a classic study of the drinker in denial. As it ends he contends he is not an "alcoholic," and that all the ills brought on by the trickery of John Barleycorn are due only to the physical availability of the substance. Arguing for Prohibition, he asserts that if society had not allowed this seductive substance to be available, he would not be suffering from its afflictions. A typical addict, he projects the responsibility for his suffering outward upon the substance and society, denying his own part in the process of this disease. For example, after a five-month period of abstinence during a cruise around the Horn, when no booze was aboard the clipper, he wrote: "I have learned to my absolute satisfaction that *I am not an alcoholic* in any sense of the word."[29] It was during this period of abstinence that he regained a sense of wonder and innocence—relief from the cynicism of the white logic—and wrote *Valley of the Moon,* which he described as a confession of his suppressed romanticism. But there soon followed a new period of heavy drinking and disgust. His urge to mastery reasserted itself as he began to work with his land and build Wolf House. He expressed it as follows:

> I am trying to master this soil and the crops and animals that spring from it, as I strove to master the sea, and men, and women, and the books, and all the face of life, that I could stamp with my 'will to do' . . .[30]

But he was not the ultimate master, for, despite his efforts, in 1913 Wolf House burned down.

That same year, London was warned by a physician that he would die of kidney failure if he did not stop drinking and give up his excessive eating of raw meat: to drink meant to die, and now even a little was too much. About this time he also was given prescriptions for morphine, heroin, strychnine, belladonna, and other opiates for various afflictions. The opiates helped him cut down on drinking, which softened the White Logic and helped control his mood swings. Just as he had had a high tolerance for alcohol (a signal of the disease), so now he developed a high tolerance for opium and morphine.

London began to get in touch with his dreams and became aware of the revelations of the unconscious that had always inspired his work. He wrote *The Star Rover,* a novel about the spirit's survival over the agonies of the body. Even though his drinking bouts continued and his opiate usage increased, he was gaining a new spiritual awareness. His discovery, in 1916, of the works of Freud and Jung helped him see that his writing told the archetypal truths of the collective unconscious. About his discovery of Jung he announced to Charmian: "I am standing on the edge of a world so new, so terrible, so wonderful, that I am almost afraid to look over into it."[31] From Jung he discovered that even his darkest nightmares could be revelations of spiritual meaning. In one dream he saw a strangely human imperial figure descending down a cascade of staircases. Looking up at it, he knew he must yield himself to it, even though it never reached him. He understood the dream to symbolize the surrender of his ego to a mysterious power greater than his materialism.[32]

With his new spiritual awareness he planned to rewrite *John Barleycorn* and to write an autobiography in which he would emphasize the thrill to universal life and the importance of the struggle toward human progress. He also tried to come to terms with his lifelong feelings of rejection by his parents and his resulting rejection of his daughters, whom he now tried to reconcile to him. Feeling the meaning of his own suffering, through his writing he wanted to expose the hypocrisy of materialism and the importance of living according to something higher. Now, instead of his youthful egoistic ideal of the romantic hero and adventurer, he began to identify with the shaman.

London's last Alaskan tale, "Like Argus of the Ancient Times," expresses the ancient myth of the "nightsea journey," in which the sun is devoured by the sea each night and must endure the darkness before it is reborn. In another story written late in his life, *The Red One*, an explorer is dying in the presence of an old shaman in Melanesia. Both have given up the desires and appetites of the body. As the explorer waits for his death, knowing his body will be eaten by cannibals, he yields himself up to the shaman. He sees the mystery at the source and delivers himself over to the great devourer, "The Red One." It seems that London saw his death approaching and understood surrender as part of the spiritual process of physical death. Thus, he was able to affirm that

> after having come through all of the game of life, and of youth, at my present mature age of thirty-nine years I am firmly and solemnly convinced that the game is worth the candle. . . . while I have suffered much, I have lived much, and felt much that has been denied to the average man. Yes, indeed, the game is worth the candle.[33]

As London was writing these final stories, he knew he was dying. His kidneys were diseased. He was still overworking and eating raw meat. He wasn't drinking as much, but he was taking increasing dosages of painkillers. Shortly before dawn one night in November, 1916, London injected himself with morphine mixed with other drugs, which he took daily to quell extreme physical pain. In a coma, he died the next evening. Whether the overdose was intentional is not known: there were no last letters or wills. The death certificate indicated uremic poisoning as the cause of death.

London's self-destruction had been taking place for years. His hunger for immediate gratification of opposing desires was typical of the addict. He was not able to live in the tension of his conflicting desires in a way that could enable him to reconcile them to a greater whole. Nevertheless, at the end of his life he seemed to experience spiritual growth. London is an example of someone who was possessed by the Creative Daimon and who, through his writing, gave much to his fellow man. But because he was also taken hostage by the Demon Lover, his physical life ended early, cutting short the creative work that might have come.

In contrast to the denial described in *John Barleycorn,* in a letter written toward the end of his life London acknowledged clearly that his creativity was not due to his drinking:

> No, please believe me, whatever I have accomplished in this world has been in spite of John Barleycorn, and not because of John Barleycorn. John Barleycorn never helped me to do anything. This is straight and flat and right out from the shoulder.[34]

It is a mistake to reduce the life and work of the creative person to his disease. But it is also a mistake to ignore a disease such as addiction and romanticize its relation to creativity. Perhaps what Jung says of the alcoholic is exemplified in the life and work of Jack London, who was both a creative writer and an addict:

> His craving for alcohol was the equivalent, on a low level, of the spiritual thirst of our being for wholeness; expressed in medieval language: the union with God. . . . You see, "alcohol" in Latin is *spiritus,* and you use the same word for the highest religious experiences as well as for the most depraving poison. The helpful formula therefore is: *spiritus contra spiritum.*[35]

Transforming the Trickster in addiction requires *trust.* For the creative aspect of the Trickster serves the individuation process, a spontaneous centering process arising from and returning toward the health and wholeness of the greater Self. Jung calls that direction of the psyche toward wholeness "the way of the transcendent function." But to follow this way presupposes grappling with the forces of good and evil in the world and in the greater psyche. It involves no longer projecting evil onto outer figures. This allows one to look at the evil within. For when one projects the Trickster figure outward, either on another person (as the co-addict tends to do) or on a substance, as London did in *John Barleycorn,* without acknowledging the figure in oneself, the way to creativity is barred.

Toward the end of his life, Jack London opened to the healing vision of a new humanity and accepted the validity of the ancient wisdom of the shaman. Perhaps, in his psyche, the Trickster was turning to this creative spirit.

Jung describes the relation between the trickster and the shaman as follows:

> Ability to change his shape seems also to be one of his [the Trickster's] characteristics, as there are not a few reports of his appearance in animal

> form. Since he has on occasion described himself as a soul in hell, the motif of subjective suffering would seem not to be lacking either. His universality is co-extensive, so to speak, with that of shamanism, to which, as we know, the whole phenomenology of spiritualism belongs. There is something of the trickster in the character of the shaman and medicine-man, for he, too, often plays malicious jokes on people, only to fall victim in his turn to the vengeance of those whom he has injured. For this reason, his profession sometimes puts him in peril of his life. Besides that, the shamanistic techniques in themselves often cause the medicine-man a good deal of discomfort, if not actual pain. At all events the "making of a medicine-man" involves, in many parts of the world, so much agony of body and soul that permanent psychic injuries may result. His "approximation to the saviour" is an obvious consequence of this, in confirmation of the mythological truth that the wounded wounder is the agent of healing, and that the sufferer takes away suffering.[36]

Sometimes the Trickster is even a manifestation of the divine energy itself. One example is the Hindu god of love, Krishna, who plays his flute in such a haunting way that he steals the hearts of the *gopis* (herdswomen) and lures them from their ordinary lives. For the promise of the special love with Krishna the *gopi* must first be ready to give up everything. Even then, she has Krishna's love only for a night, and is left by him in a community of others who long for his love. In one of the stories about Krishna, the *gopi* girls are bathing naked one winter morning as part of a vow of self-mortification and sacrifice, hoping to be granted a lover. Krishna comes by and tricks the *gopis* by stealing their saris while they are in the water, spreading the beautiful saris on the branches of a nearby tree. Only if they come out of the water naked will he give them back their garments. Krishna's skill disarms mortals by revealing them in the nakedness of their being by stealing their favorite possessions. He does not use force to do his work; his skill is in catching people off guard. Even his mother cannot hide Krishna's favorite food, butter, from him when he wants it. When Krishna steals the love of mortals through his tricks, he throws their lives into disorder. As the god of love, he does not like barriers or confinements or entanglements that want to possess love, for love is something that cannot be possessed. Krishna's tricks and thievery may rob us of our penchant for order and possession, but in that loss we may discover the mystery of our being and be opened to experience the divine. Krishna tricks us out of our reason, robs us of our control and leaves a space for revelation and new knowledge to enter. We are tricked out of our answers and opened to ourselves and God as questions.[37]

So it is with our addictions. When we lose everything through addiction, we are opened to face the truth of who we are as humans. Tricked out of the power, control, and order we think we have, in humility we must face our powerlessness and turn toward the question at the bottom of our being. Perhaps our addictions are similar to Rilke's dragons which can turn into princesses: if we turn and face them, there lies the surprise of the divine.

PART TWO: THE FALL

Once, if I remember well, my life was a feast where all hearts opened and all wines flowed.

One evening I seated Beauty on my knees. And I found her bitter. And I cursed her.

I armed myself against justice.

I fled. O Witches, O Misery, O Hate, to you has my treasure been entrusted!

I contrived to purge my mind of all human hope. On all joy,to strangle it, I pounced with the stealth of a wild beast.

I called to the executioners that I might gnaw their rifle-butts while dying. I called to the plagues to smother me in blood, in sand. Misfortune was my God. I laid myself down in the mud. I dried myself in the air of crime. I played sly tricks on madness.

And spring brought me the idiot's frightful laughter.

Now, only recently, being on the point of giving my last squawk, I thought of looking for the key to the ancient feast where I might find my appetite again.

Charity is that key—This inspiration proves that I have dreamed!

"You will always be a hyena . . ." etc., protests the devil who crowned me with such pleasant poppies. "Attain death with all your appetites, your selfishness and all the capital sins!"

Ah! I'm fed up:—But, dear Satan, a less fiery eye I beg you! And while awaiting a few small infamies in arrears, you who love the absence of the instructive or descriptive faculty in a writer, for you let me tear out these few, hideous pages from my notebook of one of the damned.

—Arthur Rimbaud, *A Season in Hell*

8: THE MADWOMAN

> Never mind . . . One day, quite suddenly, when you're not expecting it, I'll take a hammer from the folds of my dark cloak and crack your little skull like an egg-shell. Crack it will go, the egg-shell; out they will stream, the blood, the brains. One day, one day . . . One day the fierce wolf that walks by my side will spring on you and rip your abominable guts out. One day, one day . . .
>
> —Jean Rhys, *Good Morning, Midnight*

THE MADWOMAN IS at the very heart of addiction. Her energy can be destructive, leading eventually to insanity. But she is also the womb's center, the birthing connection to creativity. Madness and addiction have been linked through the ages, for ultimately, every addiction leads to madness. Yet in that madness there is a source of creativity. Because we fear madness and addiction, we tend to want to relegate addicts to dark corners. The addict lives out the craziness we fear, acting out of bounds, so we reject him. In turn, addicts come to reject the society that rejects them, often taking secret delight every time they have a chance to trick the collective conventions of normalcy. Instead of the creative connection that is possible between the culture and The Madwoman, a vicious circle of blame and retribution frequently results. When society rejects the "crazy feminine," this energy is rejected in individuals who embody it—like addicts—and in the culture at large. Because we refuse to accept the energy of The Madwoman, we are unable to see the creative wisdom inherent in her madness. Other cultures honor the creativity of dark goddesses like Kali, Hecate, Ereshkigal, Oya—and find exotic colors in the chaos. The challenge is to learn to recognize The Madwoman and to integrate and value the dark, chaotic creative energies that she represents. Through doing so, we can transform the energy of The Madwoman into that of The Priestess who has the intoxicating gift of divine prophecy and the intuitive knowledge of the dark moon mysteries that inspire cosmic renewal.

In addiction, The Madwoman is the raving, suspicious figure that drives the addict into the locked ward of loneliness and alienation. Sometimes The Madwoman explodes outwardly from her feeling of being unloved; she refuses love and ends up in a painful prison of paranoia. The anger and suspicion of The Madwoman is an expression of paranoia combined with denial. In love addiction The Madwoman can be the hurt, rejected, and embittered victim who turns her anger inward in self-destruction through her use of alcohol, drugs, or food. Or she can be the aggressor who devours people through demands, control, and anger in her insatiable craving for love or power.

Some madwomen turn their anger against men. They may do this by being the co-addict who plays the martyred wife, devouring the partner through control, guilt, and judgments and putting the partner down as weak willed. Or they may play the role of the wily seductress. In the same way, The Madwoman can function inside men in the form of misogyny. Some madwomen reject the other sex altogether. Still others live alone with The Madwoman in themselves, isolating themselves through anger, suspicion, and paranoia.

Cultural projections on women feed The Madwoman. Woman's role traditionally is to be loved by a man. In this role she is there to serve as his pure, angelic, feminine soul-image, the one who inspires him to love, beauty, and a better life. Or, as mother, her role is to be the ever-present nurturer and caretaker. If a woman happens to violate these projections by being alone, or being without a man, or by suffering from "unfeminine" afflictions—if, for example, she is an alcoholic or overweight or a love and sex addict—she disturbs these ideal projections and elicits projections of primitive feminine darkness. She may find herself labeled "whore," "tramp," or "bag lady." Women who buy into our cultural feminine ideal will have the same difficulty with the dark, chaotic form of the feminine, not daring to look at that side of themselves. Statistics seem to confirm this cultural projection. For example, the chances of a woman alcoholic being abandoned by her male partner are much greater than for an alcoholic man to be abandoned by his female partner. It is no wonder that in our society The Madwoman raves on.

While The Madwoman rages in the addict, the addict is frequently misdiagnosed as pathological, neurotic, and/or insane. The addiction is not understood to be the *disease* it is. Psychiatrists and psychotherapists often make the mistake of thinking that addiction is due to a "complex" stemming from developmental factors, such as inadequate mothering or fathering, and that through adequate depth analysis and therapeutic intervention the person under the sway of alcohol or drugs *should* be able to overcome the affliction through insight, ego strength, adaptation, and moral fortitude. Unfortunately, such an attitude on the part of the therapist makes it harder for the client to deal with an addiction. It adds an undue moral pressure and gives the addict the illusion that he or she could "do it all alone." Addiction is then misjudged as a psychological malady to be controlled or cured by psychotherapy and is not seen as a physical, emotional, and spiritual disease. And most important, the *spiritual transformation* that is essential for its healing is not acknowledged.

Thus many alcoholics and addicts are actually institutionalized as mad. Their addictive symptoms are often objectified and diagnosed in psychiatric classifications as antisocial personality disorders, borderline personality disorders, paranoid schizophrenia, or manic-depressive disorders because a careful history is not taken and/or the addictive syndrome is not recognized. Of course, the disease of addiction may coexist with any of these disorders. But even then, if the addiction is not treated as such, neither can the coexisting disorder be treated adequately. This state of affairs was particularly true in earlier years, when addiction was not understood, even by the medical profession, as a unique disease.

For example, in the early 1950s, the police had to come to our house many times in the middle of the night when my father was drunk and disorderly and haul him off to jail. Finally, they insisted he be confined in the sprawling general city hospital for the poor and indigent. There he was put in the locked ward, diagnosed as a paranoid schizophrenic, and given electroshock treatment, which broke not only several of his ribs but, worst of all, his spirit. When, as a young adolescent, I visited him there, he was in such a humiliated state that even today the horror and hopelessness of his condition overwhelm me. His hospital pants were falling off; he was not allowed a belt, nor shoes, not even a pencil with which to write. Alcoholism as a disease was not mentioned to him then, although every one of his offenses was due to drunkeness. Nor was AA recommended to him by the doctors in the hospital. He was dismissed as a hopeless madman. Today, with the increasing education about addiction, circumstances are better. But even so, many people, particularly co-addicts in denial, are still under the illusion that addiction is a matter of control. Beneath the careful persona of such people, deep within, lurks a strong fear of the archetypal image of The Madwoman—the energy of the dark feminine.

One co-addict who had not come to terms with the dark feminine within himself was continually drawn to alcoholic women who personified this side of his personality. He was simultaneously first attracted, then repelled, by these women on whom he projected various forms of the dark anima. Denying his own devouring, maddening side so he could live in the light of a conservatively correct, professional persona, he eventually would be embarrassed by the disturbing addictive behavior of his lovers. Then he became entangled with a "madwoman" who actually pursued him, imagining delusionally that he wanted to be her lover. In reality, this woman needed treatment for her own sickness. But, for him, she was symbolic of an inner Madwoman, who mirrored the inner torment resulting from his own addictions to love and control. This event drove him into treatment. Years later, when he saw the film *Fatal Attraction*, he understood from his own experience the disasters that can happen when the feminine is split into dark and light within the soul of man, and the dark feminine is not given its due.

In mythology, the maenads were such madwomen. Devotees of Dionysus, they would drink his wine and dance in frenzied abandon to his music. The maenads also nursed Dionysus and suckled wild animals with "the magic of a motherliness which has no bounds."[1] But, when the limits of measure were completely drowned, the maenads could turn, in bloodthirsty madness, upon the very babes they were suckling at their breasts and tear them to pieces. The mythic poet Orpheus fell victim to the maenads' rage. One day, while he was singing, a wild band of madwomen descended upon him, decapitating him and throwing his head in the river, where it floated to the isle of Lesbos. These stories symbolize the destruction of love and creativity that takes place when the maenad—the inner Madwoman—attacks the soul. From The Madwoman, then, comes the incomprehensible paradox of creation and destruction. This madness is the essence of Dionysus, god of intoxication, and is essential to creativity:

> The divine essence of Dionysus, the basic characteristic of his nature . . . is madness. . . . The madness which is called Dionysus is no sickness, no debility in life, but a companion of life at its healthiest. It is the tumult which erupts from its innermost recesses when they mature and force their way to the surface. It is the madness inherent in the womb of the mother. This attends all moments of creation, constantly changes ordered existence into chaos, and ushers in primal salvation and primal pain—and in both, the primal wildness of being. . . . The deep emotion with which this madness announces itself finds its expression in music and dance. What these mean to the followers of Dionysus can be seen in innumerable works of art.[2]

Shrieking sounds, melancholic silence, standing still as stone, or whirling madly—all were forms of possession that overtook the maenads as they became captivated by the sound of Dionysus's flute. Looking within, the addict can see these postures of The Madwoman—the wild hysterical devouring frenzy that eats up heart and soul, or the inert, melancholic, frozen stare and silence that petrifies both the addict and those around him. But inside also is the intoxicating Dionysian ecstasy, which can create and inspire. The transforming paradox of craziness and creativity takes us down into the abyss. From those elemental depths comes madness that threatens to destroy all sanity through loss of control and/or death. From the primeval wilderness within arises also the strange and uncanny, which breaks through the security of ordinary life and brings inspiration, ecstasy, and the prophecy of the new life. Dionysus is the divinity who contains these contradictions:

> Thus all earthly powers are united in the god: the generating, nourishing, intoxicating rapture; the life-giving inexhaustibility; and the tearing pain, the deathly pallor, the speechless night of having been. He is the mad ecstasy which hovers over every conception and birth and whose wildness is always ready to move on to destruction and death. He is life which, when it overflows, grows mad and in its profoundest passion is intimately associated with death. This unfathomable world of Dionysus is called mad with good reason. It is the world of . . . "self-destroying madness" which "still remains at the heart of all things. Controlled only by the light of a higher intelligence and calmed by it, as it were, it is the true power of nature and everything she produces."[3]

When the time to write about The Madwoman approached, I had a dream in which I awoke alone to find a woman in my room, hovering above me. She was beautiful, holding in her hand a dagger of jagged colored glass cut from the stained-glass window of an ancient cathedral. The dagger dazzled with rays of color, almost blinding me with its magical light. When the woman raised the dagger to plunge it into my heart, I knew this was The Madwoman who wanted to kill me *if I did not transform her*. The colored glass was a spiritual symbol of the imagination, which, if used addictively, would kill me. To transform The Madwoman's energy, I had to take that dazzling dagger and carve out a new creation.

The British writer Jean Rhys encountered the inner figure of The Madwoman as she wrote and rewrote the story of her love addiction. By looking at her writing we can see more clearly how the figure of The Madwoman functions in ourselves. Rhys writes of the romantic young girl at first addicted to being the fragile beauty who can capture a man's heart and soul forever (the "anima woman"), but then eventually becoming embittered by being rejected. As she ages and her external beauty wanes, her rage at her rejection and failure in "love" turns to revenge and paranoia. The women Rhys writes about want to be taken care of by men but end up lonely, isolated, and homeless instead. Their search for happiness through romance, glamour, and luxury leads to a mental prison of cynicism and embitterment, self-hatred and contempt. The female protagonist that Rhys describes is the "romantic madwoman" whose devouring cruelty to self and others eventually tears up the heart and soul in paranoid revenge. Possessed by love and addiction herself, Rhys was able to raise up this figure from her unconscious to mirror The Madwoman in her novels so later generations of women could see this figure in themselves. This is why feminists regard her as important.

Good Morning, Midnight was written when Rhys was in her forties. She was aging, facing disillusionment, and resorting heavily to drink for escape and to write. Through the character Sasha the novel portrays the decline into madness, in which Rhys explores her own "worst fears and her real demons: age and ugliness, drunkenness and paranoia."[4] Sasha is an imaginative, intelligent, sensitive, lonely woman who is aging and has taken to drink and is angry at her abandonment by men and the scorn she feels from women. A victim of her addiction to love and to drink, she encounters the contempt of society and the cruel Madwoman inside herself. Sasha is a prototype of the woman who, through her disease and woundedness, has disturbed the angelic, romantic projection upon women by men and the patriarchy. Her suffering and her madness are the embodiment of the dark feminine. Hers is a tragedy common to many women trapped in a culture that does not value the feminine. *Good Morning, Midnight* shows the madness of mistrust between men and women, the insanity of the addictive individual, and the craziness of a culture addicted to youth, glamour, and public appearance.

Sasha is a woman at an impasse. A foreigner living alone in a bleak Parisian hotel room, no longer young, her only goal in life is to get through the day. She is in Paris because "the drink is better there." Disillusioned with love and life, she hides in her dark room from the "wolves" outside who devour her with contempt in their eyes. Even the look of one of her friends says to Sasha: "She's getting to look old. She drinks."[5] When Sasha encounters people, she hears them saying: "What is she doing here, the stranger, the alien, the old one?"[6]—echoing the alienation she has felt all her life, even as a young and beautiful woman. But instead of working to create a place for herself in life, she has given herself over to the passive victim within and ultimately to the madness of addiction.

She says: "In the middle of the night you wake up. You start to cry. What's happening to me? Oh, my life, oh my youth . . . There's some wine left in the bottle. You drink it. The clock ticks. Sleep . . ."[7] To get through the day, Sasha tries to have a plan to pass the time, to eat and to drink just enough to make her mind fuzzy in order to forget her torments for a while. She tries very hard not to take that extra drink that leads to public crying and hostile outrage. Her life is spent avoiding the many cafés where she has become a nuisance and the dangerous streets where her loneliness and drunkenness render her vulnerable. While she projects the contemptuous stares of hungry wolves on others, she comes to learn that the "raving other" is really within herself.

Inside the hotel it is no better. Her room is dark; the walls are dirty; there are bugs. Next door is a man who never goes out and who parades madly about in his white dressing gown—"like the ghost of the landing." When he passes her in the hall, he looks at her in an ingratiating, knowing way, as though they understand each other. Once he even enters her room. The image of that madman in her doorway haunts her like a nightmare.

In the stares and whispers of others she has heard herself decribed as "a mad old Englishwoman, wandering around Montparnasse."[8] She has given up. No longer does she wish to be loved, to be beautiful or happy or successful. She only wants to be left alone. Five years ago Sasha was at the same impasse and considered drowning herself in the Seine. Now she chooses to drown herself in drink. For she has no pride or identity left. Reflecting on her past she thinks:

> It was then that I had the bright idea of drinking myself to death. . . . I did try it, too. I've had enough of these streets that sweat a cold, yellow slime, of hostile people, of crying myself to sleep every night. I've had enough of thinking, enough of remembering. Now whisky, rum, gin, sherry, vermouth, wine . . . I have no pride—no pride, no name, no face, no country. I don't belong anywhere. Too sad, too sad . . . It doesn't matter, there I am, like one of those straws which floats around the edge of a whirlpool and is gradually sucked into the center, the dead center, where everything is stagnant, everything is calm.[9]

Although Sasha has not succeeded in killing herself physically, her heart and soul feel quite dead. The traces of her "drowning" are noticeable in her sarcasm and in her desperate attempt to control life. She has been

> Saved, rescued, fished-up, half-drowned, out of the deep, dark river, dry clothes, hair shampooed and set. Nobody would know I had ever been in

> it. Except, of course, that there always remains something. Yes, there always remains something. . . . Never mind, here I am, sane and dry, with my place to hide in. What more do I want? . . . I'm a bit of an automaton, but sane, surely—dry, cold and sane. Now I have forgotten about dark streets, dark rivers, the pain, the struggle and the drowning. . . . Mind you, I'm not talking about the struggle when you are strong and a good swimmer and there are willing and eager friends on the bank waiting to pull you out at the first sign of distress . . . I mean the real thing. You jump in with no willing and eager friends around, and when you sink you sink to the accompaniment of loud laughter.[10]

Sasha is living in an agony of self-consciousness, isolation, and self-hatred. But she puts the blame for her loneliness on others. In this embittered state, one night, when two men try to pick her up and ask her why she's so sad, she thinks to herself:

> Yes, I am sad, sad as a circus-lioness, sad as an eagle without wings, sad as a violin with only one string and that one broken, sad as a woman who is growing old. Sad, sad, sad . . . Or perhaps if I just said "merde" it would do as well.[11]

But to the men she pretends all is okay and arranges to meet them the next day. What has she to lose? The next day, she begins to think about her appearance. Perhaps she'll dye her hair. In the meantime she must eat. The only restaurant close by has unpleasant memories. Inevitably, in her alienated state, she makes the wrong decisions—goes to the places where she has had bad experiences. In one such restaurant she overhears the proprietor talking about her to young girls who stare and laugh at her. As she eats, looking downward in self-conscious shame, her panic grows. What she anticipated has happened. To avoid crying, she thinks about what color to have her hair dyed. She manages to leave, wishing she had the courage to confront the girls, but she is too humiliated. She is seething and thinks:

> Never mind . . . One day, quite suddenly, when you're not expecting it, I'll take a hammer from the folds of my dark cloak and crack your little skull like an egg-shell. Crack it will go, the egg-shell; out they will stream, the blood, the brains. One day, one day . . . One day the fierce wolf that walks by my side will spring on you and rip your abominable guts out. One day, one day . . .[12]

With The Madwoman raging inside, her life continues. She cannot meet the Russian men looking like this—her hair undyed, deep hollows under her eyes. Perhaps a hat will help. In the milliner's she sees a woman with dishevelled hair, half dyed, half gray. This woman, like herself, hopes that a hat will help. But the mirror glares back painfully. As the woman tries on hat after hat, finally, "Her expression is terrible—hungry, despairing, hopeful, quite crazy. At any moment you expect her to start laughing the laugh of the mad."[13]

Sasha sees herself in the madwoman in the hat shop. Will she be like this in five years? The woman selling the hats is even worse—cold, smug, judgmental, mocking. "It's like watching the devil with a damned soul."[14] Of the two, Sasha thinks, she'd prefer to end up like the hag. But both these outer figures are figures in herself. Finally, she gets to another hat shop, where she buys a hat from a salesgirl who seems kinder. That night Sasha goes out.

After a drink at the Dôme, a young man, Rene, tries to pick her up. She thinks he is a gigolo fooled by the fur coat she is wearing. Suddenly his interest seems a chance to avenge herself on all the men who have been using her all her life. She thinks:

> Shall I tell him to go to hell? But, after all, I think, this is where I might be able to get some of my own back. You talk to them, you pretend to sympathize; then, just at the moment when they're not expecting it, you say, 'Go to hell."[15]

She agrees to go for a brandy but returns to her room alone, refusing to sleep with René.

In the next days, she encounters more men, more bars, more lonely times. It is hard to be an aging woman alone in a big city, especially one who longs for love and drink. She must try to look as if she has somewhere to go, as if going into a bar for a drink is normal. But once she has entered a bar and ordered the second Pernod, she is considered a drunk. After one such occasion, she reflects:

> Now the feeling of the room is different. They all know what I am. I'm a woman come in here to get drunk. That happens sometimes. They have a drink, these women, and then they have another and then they start crying silently. And then they go into the lavabo and then they come out—powdered, but with hollow eyes—and, head down, slink into the street.[16]

Sasha is a woman who wants to get drunk in order to forget her failure in life—that she cannot live well and that she cannot love. As she says: "I have an irresistible longing for a long, strong drink to make me forget that once again I have given damnable human beings the right to pity me and laugh at me."[17] For her "all the faces are masks" and "you can almost see the strings that are pulling the puppets. Close up of human nature—isn't it worth something?"[18]

Even so, she still has some moments of hope. One of the Russians who had tried to pick her up introduces her to a painter-friend. She is attracted to the painter and decides to buy one of his paintings. In her is a small flicker of hope. They agree to meet so she can pay for the picture, but instead of the painter, the Russian comes. He tells her the painter is mad. This experience is just one more of a series of humiliations. The picture she has bought—a mocking madman standing in a gutter playing a banjo—is a reflection of her own madness from the gutter.

She is flooded by memories of the marriage of her youth. Enno, a French journalist, promises an escape from dreary London to the good life in Paris. They will have fun, money, champagne, dancing, good food. But the money runs out before they even get to Paris. Once in Paris Enno meets a man with money. They go to eat and drink.

> I've never been so happy in my life. I'm alive, eating ravioli and drinking wine. I've escaped. A door has opened and let me out into the sun. What more do I want? Anything might happen.[19]

But the money doesn't last, and even in the city of romance, love can fade. Enno becomes cruel, criticizes her lovemaking, tells her that she bores him, and walks out, just as she realizes she is pregnant. She wonders what will happen. Enno returns with wine and money. She is too weak to tell him: "I won't be treated like this." So she continues with him, putting up with his well-timed cruelty, still hooked into his unpredictable kindnesses. She gets a job teaching English to foreigners and waits for the baby to come. But when the baby comes, he dies. Unable to stand her suffering, Enno leaves her again, alone in the dark, red, dirty room thinking: "God is very cruel, very cruel. A devil of course. That accounts for everything—the only possible explanation."[20]

She knew her marriage was finished, questioning: "Did I love Enno at the end? Did he ever love me? I don't know."[21] From then on life was a series of days when she tried to borrow money, sometimes ate with the destitute, sometimes had money for wine, which still sometimes filled her with gaiety. "But they never last, the golden days. And it can be sad, the sun in the afternoon, can't it? Yes, it can be sad, the afternoon sun, sad and frightening."[22] And so, gradually, she started to retreat. She tried to find a place to creep into and hide. For tomorrow might be a better day, when she could go out. "And when I have had a couple of drinks I shan't know whether it's yesterday, today or tomorrow."[23]

One day René comes to her room and asks her out for an aperitif. She begins to feel excited but then tells herself not to grimace and posture before men again. She eats little, but drinks a lot. She and René talk, drink more, go out to the exhibition, and stop again for more drinks. She goes to the lavabo to freshen up, to try to look youthful. But when he asks her why she goes so often she says cynically it's because she's growing old. Frowning, he tells her it's not that she's old. Rather, she's afraid to be young. She wants another drink. He asks to go back to her hotel room with her. She says no, she's afraid. What is she afraid of, he asks? Of men, of love? She muses about the mad black abyss into which she has fallen.

> You are walking along a road peacefully. You trip. You fall into blackness. That's the past—or perhaps the future. And you know that there is no past, no future, there is only this blackness, changing faintly, slowly, but always the same.
>
> "You want to know what I'm afraid of? All right, I'll tell you . . . I'm afraid of men—yes, I'm very much afraid of men. And I'm even more afraid of women. And I'm very much afraid of the whole bloody human race . . . Afraid of them?" I say. "Of course I'm afraid of them. Who wouldn't be afraid of a pack of damned hyenas?"
>
> Thinking: "Oh, shut up. Stop it. What's the use?" But I can't stop. I go on raving.
>
> "And when I say afraid—that's just a word I use. What I really mean is that I hate them. I hate their voices, I hate their eyes, I hate the way they laugh. . . . I hate the whole bloody business. It's cruel, it's idiotic, it's unspeakably horrible. I never had the guts to kill myself or I'd have got out of it long ago. So much the worse for me. let's leave it at that."
>
> . . . I know all about myself now, I know. You've told me so often. You haven't left me one rag of illusion to clothe myself in. But by God, I know what you are too, and I wouldn't change places . . . Everything spoiled, all spoiled. Well, don't cry about it. No, I won't cry about it . . . But may you tear each other to bits, you damned hyenas, and the quicker the better. . . . Let it be destroyed. Let it happen. Let it end, this cold insanity. Let it happen.
>
> Only five minutes ago I was in the Deux Magots, dressed in that damned cheap black dress of mine, giggling and talking about Antibes, and now I am lying in a misery of utter darkness. Quite alone. No voice, no touch, no hand . . . How long must I lie here? For ever? No, only for a couple of hundred years this time, miss . . .
>
> I heave myself out of the darkness slowly, painfully.[24]

René says sadly: "I have wounds." But Sasha cannot be sympathetic or compassionate, for she has never had the pity of others. She can only reply that she also has wounds. René understands. What awful thing has happened to make her so cynical and untrusting? He wants to make love with her. But the "little grimacing devil" in her head sings a sentimental song about faded roses and lilies in the dust. She refuses his offer.

Back in the hotel, René waits on the landing. Suddenly Sasha is happy. She takes him in her arms and invites him in: perhaps now she has a chance for the love and spring and happiness she thought she had lost forever. They kiss fervently, but immediately paranoia intrudes; half of her is someplace else. Has anyone in the hotel heard them? Maybe a whiskey will dull her suspicion. Even though it tastes bad, nervously, she takes more. The extra whiskey inflames her anger and resentment. René asks her not to take another drink, but she pushes him away. Her paranoia rises. Has she been such a fool, so free and easy to ridicule and to torture? Cynically, she asks him to go. He persists and tries to force himself on her. But finally she tells him that the money he wants is on her table. He won't have to waste his time making love to her. He leaves. Once more betrayed in love, Sasha cries, overwhelmed by all that has happened in recent days. She remembers the picture of the slightly mad banjo player—a mirror image of herself. She goes to the table to see how much money the gigolo has taken, but the money is not gone. Suddenly she realized that René was natural and sincere—intuitively, she had always known this. *He* did not steal her chance for love—she stole it from herself. Seeing that her suffering comes from her own rage and distrust, she cries out for René to come back. But it is too late. By this time she is very drunk. The door opens. She puts her arms out to the man who enters, but it is not Rene. It is the man in the white dressing gown, the madman with the flickering mean eyes whose image is as frightening as a nightmare. Welcoming him with open arms, she beckons him to make love to her, saying: "I look straight into his eyes and despise another poor devil of a human being for the last time. For the last time . . ."[25] With Sasha's gesture welcoming the madman, the novel ends. In accepting the madman as her own lover, she finally acknowledges in herself all of the rage and contempt which she has been projecting onto others.[26]

Jean Rhys wrote novels to try to understand why she was so unhappy, to try to exorcise her suffering and find out what her life was all about. From childhood onward, wherever she was, she had the feeling she didn't belong. Born in 1890 as Ella Gwendolyn Rees Williams she grew up in

Dominica, a white foreigner on a black island ruled at the time by England. Her father was a Welsh country doctor, loving but not often at home. She wrote that she probably romanticized him because he was away so much. Her mother was English, strong and practical, emotionally distant and increasingly indifferent to Jean after the birth of her little sister. But the scourge of Jean's life was her black nurse, Meta, who was bad tempered and mean, frightening Jean with stories of zombies and cockroaches that would fly into your mouth at night when you were sleeping. Meta continually played tricks on her, showing her a world of fear and distrust—so much so that even at the end of her life she still felt in that world.

Although she felt alien in the world of her childhood, she had great hopes that she would find in England the romance and excitement in life for which she yearned. But when in her teens she was sent to a girls school there, she was still the shy outsider. Her romantic, intuitive mind was dismissed as flippant and exaggerated by her more conservative teachers and fellow students. Their disapproval fed her tendency later in life to feel defeated at any rejection or insult. In England, as in Dominica, her fear that she would always be lonely hounded her. She was drawn to the theater and signed on as a chorus girl, hoping the excitement of the stage would provide the romance for which she yearned. In reality, life on the road was boring and lonely, so she ran away to London.

There she met the first and only passionate love of her life—Lancelot Hugh Smith, a wealthy upper-class man twenty years her senior. For her he seemed to be everything—father, lover, and friend. He teased her and listened to her, bringing her out of her shyness. And he bought her beautiful clothes. But Smith, her first love, was to remain a Ghostly Lover for the rest of her life, for, in the end, he was unobtainable. What she wanted was, perhaps, an impossible dream—a man who would be totally safe and secure, yet sensitive and exciting; someone who could understand her shy and rebellious nature, yet provide her with respectability and a firm anchor in life. And while Lancelot did have many of these qualities, he was too sensitive to bear her pain and loneliness. Nor did she meet his need for respectability. Twenty when she met him, twenty-two when it was over, for the rest of her life she suffered over this relationship, unable to let go of her dream, "addicted" to her longing for this lost love, feeling that her life was over, that she was one of the living dead. She felt helpless at his abandonment; betrayed, as it were, by life. Even so, for the next several years she lived on the allowance he sent her every week. Thus began a pattern of emotional and financial dependence on men that began to rule her life, leading to a growing feeling of failure, uselessness, and self-hatred.

But, from the intensity of her suffering and loneliness, Rhys also began her writing. In 1914, living in a depressing room in Chelsea, she bought some colorful quill pens and some exercise books to color up her bare table, and suddenly she began to write. Every day and long into the night she recorded her feelings of lost love and rejection in those exercise books, which became her diary. After more than a week of this constant writing, she felt the worst of the heavy blackness lifting. From then on she wrote whenever her intense feelings began to overwhelm her—her creativity became a source to transform the hopelessness of her addiction.

For the rest of her life, Rhys wrote about these feelings—of what would now be called a love addiction—trying to resolve them in herself. Her tendency to drink colluded with her love addiction, helping her forget the pain and assuage the unbearable loneliness of her unlived life. Many of her protagonists suffer agonies from both of those addictions. Rhys describes with brilliant accuracy how the increasing dependence on alcohol and love intermesh and lead to fear, isolation, debilitating self-consciousness, a consuming sense of rejection, and finally, a hatred for humanity. The result of this progression of feelings becomes so unbearable that they end in revenge, paranoia, and madness.

In 1917 she met Jean Lenglet, a man whom she eventually married. He was romantic and reckless, a gambler with life as well as with money, and although she was not in love with him, she liked him: he offered hope for escape from her depressing life. She wrote to Lancelot that she would no longer need his money since she was getting married and went with Lenglet to Paris, the city of romance, where her dreams could come true. For a while, she was happy. In Paris she became pregnant and gave birth to a boy, but the infant became sick and was taken to the hospital. To forget their fears, she and Lenglet drank champagne, unaware that the baby had died that very evening. Ever afterward, she felt guilty for drinking at the very time her little boy was dying.

The couple moved to Vienna and then to Budapest. Suddenly, Lenglet had money, which they spent madly. Now she had all the beautiful clothes, jewelry, and champagne she craved. But their luck changed: Lenglet had been gambling with other people's money on the exchange and he had lost. They moved all over Europe to escape the law. During this time she gave birth to a daughter, whom she did not raise. Living in near poverty, Lenglet wrote articles to sell to English journals, and she translated them. Her style of translation so impressed the woman who saw it that she asked to see Rhys's writing. The diaries Rhys submitted eventually ended up in the office of Ford Madox Ford who, recognizing her underlying talent, encouraged her to read good writers and write about her own experiences. With Ford as a powerful patron, she began to think of herself as a writer. Ford changed her married name, Ella Lenglet, to Jean Rhys.

Eventually, Lenglet was arrested and sent to prison. Afraid and lonely, Rhys turned to Ford for help and protection. Attracted to her helpless, submissive girlishness, he had an affair with her. Out of fear and loneliness, Rhys betrayed her husband. She was devastated by the strange triangle that she formed with Ford and his common-law wife, who acquiesced to his frequent affairs with young women in order not to lose him. Eventually the experience led to the loss of both Ford and her husband, who could not tolerate her betrayal. Her obsession with her need for Ford and her hatred of his wife became the substance for her novel *Quartet*. In writing it she poured out her feelings of bitterness and anger, trying to make some sense of things. Now she was not only a young, helpless girl tormented, rejected, and confused by life; she was also a writer who wanted to understand what was happening to her. In 1927 she went to England to try to sell the book.

In London, Rhys sought out a literary agent, Leslie Tilden Smith, who helped her publish *Quartet* (under its original title, *Postures*). From 1928 on she dedicated herself to writing, withdrawing more and more from the fast-moving life she'd previously sought. In the next decade she wrote and published most of her work—numerous short stories, three novels, including *Good Morning, Midnight*, and the first version of the novel that finally brought her so much acclaim, *Wide Sargasso Sea*. During this time she divorced Lenglet and married Leslie Tilden Smith, who was kind and chivalrous. He looked after her business, which relieved her enormously, for money and business threw her into a panic. He also took care of their domestic routines, which left her free for writing. He even typed and edited her manuscripts, taking them away from her when he thought they were fininshed. They weren't "in love," but they liked each other. Finally she had someone to take care of her, to take the edge off the external burdens so she could work to understand her life. Still tormented by her past, she continued to write about women suffering from love affairs. Though in her first novels she blamed men, in these later works she started to look within the women characters to find what was wrong in her own lifelong quest for the love that remained unfulfilled in her life. As she struggled with these longings in her writing, and as her writing matured, she started to probe the sources of her own unhappiness, her painful anger, and her penchant for self-destruction, which she took to the limit in her last two novels, *Good Morning, Midnight* and *Wide Sargasso Sea*.

In 1936, after she and Leslie were married, they went on a holiday to Dominica. Jean was excited about her first trip back to the island in thirty years. She found it changed. Her father's grave had been neglected; and as one of the old whites, she was an outsider to the black community. Again she was homeless; she didn't belong. While on her way home to New York, she indulged in a buying and drinking spree and had a terrible fight with one of her best friends. With all their money spent, Leslie was forced to borrow from his sister. This was a dark period for Jean, who was also trying to exorcise her inner demons through her writing.

In order to write and to live through the pain, she drank. While she was writing *Voyage in the Dark* she felt so much horror that she sometimes drank two bottles of wine a day. Eventually her drinking led to quarrels and drunken rages, affecting her relationship with Leslie. A typical co-addict, he started hiding bottles from her. When she was drunk she would attack him in a mad rage, sometimes hitting him, sometimes tearing up the work he had typed. Once she even threw his typewriter out the window. In these times, when he looked at her, she said, it was with "the hanging judge's face."[27] Too passive to fight back, he withdrew in icy silence, and eventually spent most of his time away from home.

Good Morning, Midnight was published in 1939, to good reviews. But never having received much notice as it was, now, during wartime, Rhys disappeared completely from the literary world. For many years people even supposed her to be dead. She had moved with Leslie to Norfolk, where he was based with the Royal Air Force. He was away much of the time and she was alone. Although she had tried to exorcise her paranoia by creating the character of Sasha, nevertheless she still felt shy, wary of others, laughed at, lied about, and pushed "into the limbo of the forgotten."[28] During the forties and most of the fifties, Rhys lived in this limbo, miserable, but still writing (mostly short stories) about The

Madwoman—about her demons, self-pity and paranoia. They moved back to London, where illness, irritability, despair, and depression overwhelmed her. After Leslie died of a heart attack in 1945, she wrote to his daughter:

> I grew *frightened* of my own loneliness, the not knowing. I did not *know* anything you see . . . I shall not ever forgive myself that I didn't stand up to things better—not ever. But at the end I was ill and the strain smashed me up sometimes. Especially as I was trying to write. I did love him though and knew all his generosity and gentleness—very well.[29]

After Leslie's death, Jean moved back to the country. Earlier she had begun writing what was to become *Wide Sargasso Sea,* which had sprung from her reading of *Jane Eyre.* Now, she wanted to finish it. She felt haunted by the figure of the mad wife, Mrs. Rochester. Meanwhile, another man stepped in to rescue her. Leslie's cousin Max Hammer was sixty-three and Jean was fifty-five when they met. He soon divorced his wife and they were married. This was her third marrriage, and as she later said, her happiest. But it, too, was full of disaster. Alone and depressed most of the time, Jean drank heavily, quarreled angrily with Max, and eventually suffered a nervous breakdown. When a neighbor was rude to her, she slapped him, and he charged her with assault. Found guilty, she was sent to the prison's hospital wing, where she was detained five days and given two years' probation. (Afterward, Jean wrote a story about this experience, as she did about most of the events of her life.) During the early fifties she was eating poorly and drinking so much that her hands trembled, and she slept to escape. At the same time, Max, a sweet, naive optimist with get-rich-quick schemes, tangled with some crooks and was imprisoned for fraud. By now, Jean was almost a complete dropout, writing to a few of her friends, living in isolation. Two of her three husbands had been "gamblers," ending up in jail. Worst of all, she suffered a writer's curse: she was unable to write to help herself out of the abyss into which she had fallen. But finally, she began a journal called "At the Ropemaker's Arms," which was eventually included in her unfinished autobiography, *Smile Please.* This diary was written in the form of a criminal trial—the trial of Jean Rhys. It is here that she confesses: "I am tired. I learnt everything too late. Everything was always one jump ahead of me."[30]

Miraculously, in the late fifties, Jean Rhys was rediscovered when an advertisement appeared asking for her or anyone who knew of her whereabouts to contact the BBC, which wanted to produce a performance of *Good Morning, Midnight.* Rhys responded. This led to her meeting Francis Wyndham, an editor who had long admired her novels but had believed her to be dead. When he learned she was at work on another novel, he contracted it, and in 1966 Rhys completed *Wide Sargasso Sea,* which finally won her the literary recognition she deserved.[31]

Rhys described the writing of *Wide Sargasso Sea* to Francis Wyndham as follows: "Indeed it is a *demon* of a book—and it never leaves me. Sometimes I am sure that it needs a demon to write it. Or a fraud. Well—I am not a fraud—and not yet a demon. Sometimes I have great hopes."[32] In *Wide Sargasso Sea,* Rhys was writing again about The Madwoman, and to do that she needed to write it "madly." But she also knew that, in the end, she had to be able to tell the same story from the man's point of view. Finally she told the story in three parts. The first part is told by Antoinette, a young Creole heiress who has been emotionally abandoned by her mad mother and is hated by most of the black society, which has recently been freed from slavery. Feeling the malevolence, menace, fear, and hopelessness of her situation, nevertheless she falls in love with an English suitor who is after her dowry. After their marriage, they stay on the beautiful island that bears outsiders either hate or indifference. The second part was written from the point of view of the Englishman's confused experience. He came to the West Indies to marry Antoinette but grew to hate her and the madness that accompanies her family. The last part was written from the mad mind of Antoinette, imprisoned in the attic of an English manor house.

Rhys drank to get into the mad mood of this book: "Then had to get back into the mood with the help of very bad drink. One day drunk, two days hangover regular as clockwork."[33] During most of this time she had to take care of Max, now in his seventies and suffering from a series of strokes, who did not understand the vicissitudes of writing a book. Through all of this she wrote with the "aid" of drink and pep pills, often ill and often drunk, lonely, and in frequent black moods, herself aging. Finally, Parts I and II were finished. When she went to London to work with her editor, Diana Athill, she had a heart attack. She survived but was so debilitated that the writing was extremely difficult, especially for such a perfectionist as Jean. When Max died in March 1966, she had a dream through which she realized that it was time to let the novel be published. About this, she wrote in a letter to Athill:

I feel that I've been walking a tightrope for a long, long time and have finally fallen off. I can't believe that I am so alone, and that there is no Max. I've dreamt several times that I was going to have a baby—then I woke with relief. Finally I dreamt that I was looking at the baby in a cradle—such a puny weak thing. So the book must be finished, and that must be what I think about it really. I don't dream about it any more. I am sorry for a sad letter and I send you my love.

Jean

It's so *cold*[34]

In the trial in "At the Ropemaker's Arms" she had spoken with the questioner about her own Creative Daimon: she felt bound to write what she had witnessed of life.

The trouble is I have plenty to say. Not only that, but I am bound to say it.

Bound?

I must.

Why? Why? Why?

I must write. If I stop writing my life will have been an abject failure. It is that already to other people. But it could be an abject failure to myself. I will not have earned death.

Earned death?

Sometimes, not often, a phrase will sound in my ear clearly, as if spoken aloud by someone else. That was one phrase. You must earn death.[35]

There, too, unflinchingly, she took a "moral inventory" similar to that of the fourth step. With honest clarity, she confesses to her possession by the Demon Lover, i.e., of her own "mortal sins": "Pride, anger, lust, drunkenness??, despair, presumption (hubris), sloth, selfishness, vanity, there's no end to them, coolness of heart. But I'm not guilty of the last. All the others."[36] In her quest for self-knowledge, she owns up to both the best and the worst in her, even though it is dangerous:

. . . all I can force myself to do is to write, to write. I must trust that out of that will come the pattern, the clue that can be followed.

Why is all this dangerous?

Because I have been accused of madness. But if everything is in me, good, evil and so on, so must strength be in me if I know how to get at it.[37]

Rhys was pursued most of her life by demons—not only by the Demon Lover of her addictions to love, drunkenness, and anger, but also by the Creative Daimon of her writing. Through her writing she expresses these afflictions of the human condition, and in doing so offers a gift to humankind. This gift is not an easy promise. Rather, it is a stunning and chilling description of madness, of the dark, demonic side of hatred at war with love, and of revenge. That monster of madness lurking in the mysterious heart of Nature—sometimes experienced as a dream of paradise and sometimes as a nightmare—is one we all must face. Probing deep into the heart of evil, Rhys does not give us answers. Instead she leaves us with haunting questions that reveal our own urge toward madness and revenge when the hunger for love is unfulfilled. We are left with the question of Antoinette, the heroine of *Wide Sargasso Sea*, who, after the death of her mad mother, asks her spiritual teacher the following question:

> "Such terrible things happen," I said. "Why? Why?" "You must not concern yourself with that mystery," said Sister Maria Augustine. "We do not know why the devil must have his little day. Not yet."[38]

Rhys could write about The Madwoman, but she could not transform it in herself. As she grew older, her drunkenness, her anger, her paranoia, her isolation, increased. Even her desire to be the beautiful young, gay romantic girl remained an illusory wish; she still preferred the company of men to that of women. She held onto her tragic and pessimistic view of life.[39] She dove into the abyss of the absurd, but she could not take the leap of faith toward the divine shining through the dark. Finally, her drinking completely eclipsed her writing. At the end, she was left alone with only drink and demons. She suffered a number of falls and other accidents until, at eighty-eight, slowly losing consciousness, refusing to eat or speak, she died in a hospital.

Jean Rhys was a creative person who was also an addict. She split these two sides of her life into what might be called parallel lives. As a writer, she was able to mirror, for us, the archetypal Madwoman trapped in the attic of addiction. She was able to give us the chance to see this figure clearly enough to transform it in ourselves. But she could not do that for herself.

Many creative artists are called to express their own personal suffering before their peers are aware of the same suffering in themselves. They are ahead of their time in order to give to that time. Jean Rhys was such an artist. In trying to understand the addictions that possessed her, she was able to raise up from the unconscious the figure of The Madwoman so that later generations of women could see this figure in themselves.

And to see The Madwoman is to begin to understand a part of feminine nature that we must accept in order to be whole. Writing about The Madwoman gave Jean Rhys hope for moving toward her own center, even though the process was agonizing. When she wrote, her ego-self was being directed by a higher power, the Creative Daimon. When she was able to bear the tension between the personal and the universal, her own ego became integrated with the transcending creative force. But when she returned to her private ego wishes and desires, she seemed to lose the very insight for herself that she had won for others.

As long as Jean Rhys drank to drown her rage and tears over the lost hopes she had for love and romance, she was unable to integrate The Madwoman, since the conscious faculty of judgment was then submerged in the fire water. And the leap of faith required for loving was burnt out by bitter pessimism. If only Jean Rhys, or her heroine, Sasha, could have heard the following words of an alcoholic woman who had faced the madness of her addiction but finally emerged through faith and recovery to find love all around her.

> There is no more "aloneness" with that awful ache, so deep in the heart of every alcoholic that nothing, before, could ever reach it. That ache is gone and never need return again. Now there is a sense of belonging, of being wanted and needed and loved. In return for a bottle and a hangover, we have been given the Keys of the Kingdom.[40]

Jean Rhys had the conscious courage to take the risk to jump into that "black hole in space"—to enter the chaos of the underworld to return with creativity. But she did not reap the fruits of her own labor due to her addictions. Perhaps the ancient Sumerian myth of the goddess Inanna, who descended into the underworld, confronted the split between the light and dark feminine energies, and returned with the creative power of the dark goddess, can give us a glimpse of the transformation of The Madwoman.

One day Inanna, Queen of the upperworld, decided to journey to meet the underworld queen, Ereshkigal, her dark sister. But Inanna made conscious preparations. She told a female aide to seek help if she did not return in three days. When Inanna descended into the underworld, Ereshkigal was furious that she had dared to enter her realm. Ereshkigal declared that Inanna would be stripped of everything, taken naked and bowed low. At each of the seven gates to the underworld, a piece of Inanna's beautiful jewelry and clothing was removed. Naked,

Inanna was then judged, and Ereshkigal, staring at her with the eyes of death, hung her corpse upon a peg until it became a piece of rotting meat. When Inanna did not return after three days, her aide sought help from the father gods. But most of the father gods were angry that Inanna had craved the power of the underworld and refused to help her, saying: "She who goes to the Dark City stays there."[41] Only Enki, god of the waters, was grieved and responded. From the dirt underneath his fingernail he created two small asexual creatures who slipped into the underworld unnoticed and grieved with Ereshkigal, who was "moaning with the cries of a woman about to give birth."[42] Ereshkigal was grateful for their empathy, and gave to them Inanna's corpse, which they revived with the food and water of life given to them by Enki. But Inanna was told: "No one ascends from the underworld unmarked."[43] Demons from the underworld clung to her side, and she was required to send back a substitute to take her place. Refusing to send her faithful feminine aide, she chose instead her husband, Dumuzi, who had been basking on high on his throne. Dumuzi tried to escape the demons, but they found him and beat him, stripped him naked, and took him to the underworld. Finally his sister agreed to share his fate, and each spent half the year in the underworld.

After her descent to the underworld, Inanna returned with knowledge of its power. Hearing the "call" and consciously choosing to meet Ereshkigal, her demon sister, Queen of the Underworld, she encountered madness. Ereshkigal, who is suffering labor pains, symbolically gives birth to the re-newed Inanna, who now knows humiliation—the deep wounds of the underworld and the chaotic raging created by rejection and knowledge of mortality. With the knowledge of both realms, she is reborn: the redeemed "madwoman" sends her husband, who has forgotten her and basks in his role as highest judge of all, to journey also to meet The Madwoman—whose realm of creative chaos can help energize and integrate the light and the dark.

But this meeting did not merely "happen" to Inanna. She prepared for it and opened a way for her return. Inanna's journey into the realm of the dark goddess shows a possibility for the woman or the man who is an addict to transform the inner Madwoman into the goddess who knows both realms.

Everyone who has been in the grips of addiction has felt the death of Inanna in themselves. Through alcohol, drugs, overeating, promiscuity, or through hunger for power or love, both soul and body become like "rotting meat" hung on the peg of humiliation. The addict becomes mad, judged severely, stripped bare of refinements and a proper persona. Both body and soul have been devouring and devoured. But the challenge is consciously to accept this journey, which can unite the mysteries of the light and the dark, to transform humiliation into humility, and to return with the creative knowledge and energy to transform not only the Madwoman of the matriarchy but the Judge of the patriarchy.

The Madwoman and The Judge are archetypal energies in a time and culture dangerously out of balance. On the surface the patriarchal judge values linear rationality and calculative thinking, which can lead to addictions to power and perfection. While the discriminating awareness of judgment is essential to creativity, it becomes static, rigid, and inflexible when it relegates the dynamic energy of the dark feminine to the shadows. In compensation, this rejected Madwoman energy then rises up from the depths, threatening to throw the world into total chaos. (Nazism can be seen from this perspective as such a distortion, born of the destructive collusion of the unintegrated Madwoman and Judge.)

The discriminating awareness of judgment, wedded to the dark chaotic visions of the Madwoman, is required for creative expression. When these two archetypal energies are out of balance, addiction—whether to love or to power, to substances or to activities— fills the gap and obscures the danger. This way of denying the feared energy leads further to dangerous polarities. Only by facing what we fear and letting it arise, can we find a balance. Only by consciously confronting and transforming these inner addictive figures—The Madwoman and The Judge—can we unite their energies to create a whole and healthy world.

9: THE JUDGE

> People hasten to judge in order not to judge themselves. What do you expect? The idea that comes most naturally to man, as if from his very nature, is the idea of his innocence. . . . We are all exceptional cases. We all want to appeal against something! Each of us insists on being innocent at all cost, even if he has to accuse the whole human race and heaven itself.
>
> —Albert Camus, *The Fall*

THE PATRIARCHAL JUDGE sets for both women and men the standards of linear rational thought, and can be an obstacle to creativity. It tends to split off The Judge from the "judged," separating the innocent from the guilty as if perfection were a possibility on this earth. In this respect it posits a dualism that denies the finitude of the human condition. In addition, it splits off the dark from the light, denying the cyclical rhythms of Mother Earth and nature. This destructive dualism is enacted when the unintegrated figures of The Madwoman and The Judge—inner characters who are not gender related—enter into an unhealthy collusion. This can be seen in women who are enraged at the patriarchal Judge and who project their madness outward, failing to face the inner Judge that keeps them victims; or in those who retreat to the interior Madwoman and lose themselves in chaos. Men who are afraid of their own devouring hunger for feeling and love and project it on the external woman by judging the feminine as the Madwoman fail to face their inner vulnerability. The Judge succeeds in severing these men and women from the feminine heart.

Whether The Judge's debilitating criticism is directed externally against others or internally toward oneself, whenever the focus is on perfection, one's inherent wholeness is obscured. This leads inevitably to addiction instead of creative human life. The Judge is the one who says "You cannot do it," or "It *should* be done *only* in this way." It is the self-righteous figure who seeks perfection and dominance. The Judge has an answer to everything; self-justification is his ploy; control and power are his goal. The Judge operates in the psyche of every addict, whatever form the addiction takes.

At the crossroads between addiction and creativity, when we are confronted with the choice to accept or reject the unknown leap of faith that the creative process requires, The Judge often tells us what we do is not good enough or that we are not perfect. As compensation, it may then offer us a drink or a drug or an escapist romance or ploy for power.

The Judge then plays upon the shadow—the inferior undeveloped side of the individual, the family, or the culture. As the figure who leads us to our fallen state, the undeveloped side of our humanity, it persecutes us in our unconscious relationship to evil. The Judge refuses to let us face our own humanity, and hence our creativity.

On the outer level, The Judge is a pivotal figure in the societal drama of addiction. The addict often is judged by others as the bad one and tends to judge himself severely. Through this projection of the shadow—the capacity for destruction—the addict becomes a handy scapegoat for those who need to see themselves as superior. In the addictive family, the role of The Judge is often enacted by the co-addict, the partner who stays with the addict and suffers from the addict's excesses. Instead of living their own lives, co-addicts martyr themselves in bondage to the addict, living "around" the unpredictability of their partners. In comparison to the excesses of the addict-partner, the co-addict's life appears to be virtuous; he or she appears to be in control. From their higher place of controlling dominance in the family structure, the co-addict falls easily into the role of The Judge. Often unconsciously resentful of the addict's seemingly uninhibited and libertine life, the co-addictive partner may judge the addict as weak-willed and/or immoral. The children in the family, formed into adults before their time, are usually judged as well—"bad" if they resemble the addict-partner and "good" if they support the martyred co-addict.

While the role of Judge is detrimental to all concerned, it is probably the worst for the co-addict. The Judge provides the co-addict the *illusion* of control, dominance, and moral superiority, covering up an enormous shadow of unmanageability, dependence, and unowned guilt lurking underneath the armored ego. Although the person acting out the Judge role appears to be "on high," in actuality, to be the Judge of others is a "fallen" state; the co-addict experiences intense loneliness, alienation, and the hidden chaos of The Madwoman, which is intensified by the armor of self-justification. While the co-addictive partners often long for intimacy, they cut off themselves from love by the need to be superior. A recovering co-addict whose mother and husband are alcoholics in recovery, clearly articulates the denial of the co-addict as, "There's nothing wrong with me. I'm not sick—it's them."

On the inner level, The Judge is a major archetype operating in the psyche of the addict. This archetype often surfaces as an "addiction to perfection" that can obstruct the creative process.[1] The workaholic syndrome may stem from a reaction to or a repetition of the perfectionistic standards of a patriarchal judge that devalues the work and way of life that flows spontaneously from the inner center of the feminine heart. For example, a musician was plagued with inner accusations that she wasn't working hard enough to learn and practice this new art form—a challenge which she had taken up at midlife. Her Judge began to tell her she must work all the time, harder and harder, until finally she had little time left for a love relationship or for friends or other activities that she enjoyed. Although she was totally committed to her music, she began to feel her life was being narrowed radically. The critical judges also assailed her in the form of anxiety attacks, which she suffered constantly between performances. She feared that other musicians would judge her as untalented or accuse her of not working hard enough. Above all else, she was obsessed with controlling all situations so she wouldn't be judged "the fool."

In Anna's family history, many patterns had fostered this fear of judgment. Both of her parents were "wealthy, white judges." They expected her to live up to the collective values of WASP society and to assume the appearance of perfection. By nature artistic and introverted, she did not fit in with her parents' expectations, particularly their wish that she should be a social star. Although she went her own way as an artist when she left home, the inner judgmental voices still possessed her—particularly the voice of her mother, who valued control and perfect appearance above all else. This inner voice criticized her public performances and threatened persecution if she should do anything imperfectly or appear to be a fool. In reaction to this judgmental maternal voice, Anna tried to be the opposite of her mother. She projected this inner voice unconsciously in the form of her fears and expectations of how she would be judged by others—as if they were as inflexible, strict, and snobbish as her mother. To allay these fears she became obsessed with being perfect at whatever she did and tried to control every aspect of her life so that she would not be judged. Her obsesssion with perfection and control was beginning to destroy her capacity to enjoy and to live in the moment. She was overwhelmed by anxiety coupled with obsessive thoughts that fixated on any imperfection. She set herself up for failure at every turn. Like Kafka, who was never able to satisfy his perfectionistic father and who spent his life writing about this patriarchal judge, she felt she was constantly "on trial." When The Judge archetype dominates, some people become judges of others while others turn The Judge against themselves. This latter form was Anna's primary mode, although in some performance situations she became the critical one. In everyone, while one mode of the Judge tends to be dominant, the other mode is always lurking in the unconscious.

She hit bottom when she realized the control-perfection syndrome had narrowed down her life so much that spontaneity had almost disappeared. Yet, the very playing of her music required spontaneity, as did enjoying her life. Control was so dominant at this point that there was hardly any space for romance. Her life felt tight and dry to her, and although she was not addicted to drugs or drink, her situation resembled the paradox the alcoholic is caught in, described by Bill W., cofounder of AA. Trapped in the narrow abyss of her reduced existence, she was able to identify her addiction to control and perfection and to focus on the inner figure of The Judge.

As she looked at The Judge inside herself, Anna began to distinguish its different voices and its different guises. She saw how she had first incorporated, then projected The Judge onto her mother, then her brother, then her teacher and her fellow musicians. She realized that her real "work" was to give up control and to live in the moment and be present in the music of her life. She learned to distinguish the constricting voice of criticism, from the discriminating voice that enhances her creativity.

> Before, The Judge was my mother or someone else outside of me. The Judge was saying, "You aren't any good," and was judging me in terms of a goal outside of myself that I wasn't achieving and that wasn't coming from within myself. So even if I reached that goal, it was never good enough and I was never "there"; I never reached "success." The patriarchal ideas of perfection and competition were toxic for me. I felt under a spell as though my creativity was bewitched by judgments that betrayed process—i.e., the mystery of experience. I see now that The Judge was any figure in my mind that was trying to hold me hostage and inferior against some other critical figure in my mind. Now I'm more in tune with the *process* and there is a kind Judge helping me to discriminate what I really value. Now The Judge reflects my own values. And I'm accepting myself and my process as valuable. Now I can value what I do well along with my growth.

Dominated by the super-ego Judge that had developed from her parents, Anna had grown used to reducing and objectifying her own process, which prevented the spontaneous flow of her creativity. Yet, in her heart of hearts she knew she had to let go and stand in the paradox of the life process. She was particularly moved by a filmed interview with the director Andrey Tarkovsky (*The Sacrifice*), who said that the history of the creative process was the history of the soul's struggle between the forces of good and evil. The artist's task was to endure the creative tension by trying to give expression to affirmative and creative energies. His words expressed what she experienced while she was playing music. She reflected:

> When you're playing, you are being your soul over and over. Playing music is the soul's struggle to be in the fullest way, to keep learning new things and to have that show in the musical expression. When you play you have to face yourself over and over again in your limitations. You're on the line from minute to minute.

These insights allowed her to accept herself and others. She became more open and risked letting her vulnerability show. She even allowed herself to fall in love and live with a very spontaneous man who was not afraid to let his feelings and his inner "holy fool" show.

As I wrote this book, I knew The Judge was a powerful inner figure that I would have to encounter. As an alcoholic, I had felt judged severely by those who could control their drinking. As the daughter of an alcoholic father, I had felt the shame and guilt of not belonging to a family respected by society. On the one hand, I tried to compensate by working hard; on the other, I rebelled against societal standards. Both reactions stemmed from an addictive background. But both also contributed to my creativity: I developed the capacity to work and adapt to society, but as an "outsider" I could often feel what was missing and what was needed in the established order.

When I first conceived of writing this book, which coincided with my early recovery, I also found within myself the co-addict, the side that tended to judge. Thus, I suffered all the painful desires for control and self-justification that the co-addict experiences. I felt trapped in this tension of the opposites, unable to see how to break through the dualism of addict and co-addict. Finally, I decided to begin this chapter on The Judge. A friend suggested I look at Camus's novel *The Fall*, for not only did it delve deeply into the problem of evil; its very theme was judgment. What I discovered after living intensely with this novel was that I, like many others, was susceptible to "bad faith" by wanting to be "above" it all. The fatal flaw of The Judge is wanting to be *above* the disease of addiction, and at the deepest level, to be above the finite human condition, to want to be so special that one does not deserve the "unjust" treatment of having a disease. The addict says: "I'm sick and it's not fair," while the co-addict says: "I'm not sick; it's you that's causing all this trouble." Camus's novel shows the complex self-deception inherent in addiction.

In *The Fall*, Camus paints a portrait of the archetypal figure of The Judge, showing the predicament of people who wish to be innocent and immune to judgment, yet at the same time want to control and judge others. More than just the story of an individual, the novel mirrors the downfall of an entire age addicted to victory, dominance, and judgment. Through his protagonist, Camus shows how the twentieth-century penchant for control, power, and self-justification proceeds from an outer image of proper appearance, security, societal approbation, and self-justification to the discovery of the capacity for evil within. The facets of The Judge that Camus reveals are familiar to all addicts, whether they identify with the one who judges or the penitent who is judged.

Once a successful, sophisticated lawyer in Paris, Jean-Baptiste Clamence now sits in a shadowy bar in the sailors' quarters in Amsterdam. Over drinks he tells a stranger his story, a confession calculated to seduce and shock the listener. Thrown into awareness of his own dark side, he has come to Amsterdam as a "judge-penitent," and he now holds court every evening in this bar. Clamence wants to tell this stranger about the bourgeois hell in which most of us pass our time. In the bar, he explains, they are now in the last dark circle of hell, where the comforts of alcohol can shield them from the cold and foggy night outside.

> Fortunately there is gin, the sole glimmer of light in this darkness. Do you feel the golden, copper-colored light it kindles in you? I like walking through the city of an evening in the warmth of gin. I walk for nights on end, I dream or talk to myself interminably, Yes, like this evening—and I fear making your head swim somewhat.[2]

Clamence describes his former life: his persona was proper—the right emotional tone, a good physical appearance, persuasiveness and warmth, impeccable manners, and the pride of self-esteem. He was adept at defending victims. Satisfied that he was always in the right, he scorned judges. According to Clamence, the criminal emerges when the feeling of self-righteousness is lost. That is why so many crimes occur: "their authors could not endure being wrong!"[3] For example, one man, who had deceived his virtuous wife, was so furious at his own deception and wrong action that all he could think to do was to kill her; his vexation at that perfect wife was intolerable. (Remember the same reaction—murdering the wronged wife—that Hickey had in *The Iceman Cometh.)* Always above reproach himself, Clamence defended only noble murderers. He never resorted to bribery or flattery and often worked for low fees or for free, enjoying the image of the rescuer; his generosity was well known. From the mastery of goodness he took the utmost pleasure. Above the masses, he lived in a kind of Eden. To be atop the supreme summit—to live a lofty existence—was his aim, which was fulfilled by the legal profession.

> It cleansed me of all bitterness toward my neighbor, whom I always obligated without ever owing him anything. It set me above the judge whom I judged in turn, above the defendant whom I forced to gratitude. . . . I lived with impunity. . . . The judges punished and the defendants expiated, while I, free of any duty, shielded from judgment as from penalty, I freely held sway bathed in a light as of Eden. . . . Such was my life. I never had to learn how to live.[4]

Popular and successful, Clamence fit in wherever he went, feeling personally chosen for this success, singled out by some higher decree, even though he had no religious beliefs. For many years he soared in his success, but ironically was satisfied with nothing.

> Each joy made me desire another. I went from festivity to festivity. . . . I ran on like that, always heaped with favors, never satiated, without knowing where to stop, until the day—until the evening rather when the music stopped and the lights went out.[5]

One evening, high on success, he went atop the Pont des Arts, where he could look out over the river. Here he felt a vast sense of power and completion—on top of the world so to speak. In that moment of immense satisfaction he celebrated his feeling of control by lighting a cigarette. But he was interrupted in this ritual by a laugh that seemed to break out behind him. When he looked, he saw no one about. Suddenly, he had trouble breathing; his heart beat rapidly; he felt dazed. His feeling of power vanished, and he hurried home. Then he heard laughter outside his window, but no one was outside. When he looked in the mirror, the smile he saw seemed double. He tried to forget about this unsettling night, but several times he heard a laugh inside himself. About this time he stopped walking around the Paris quays. Life in general became less easy; he suffered some health problems, a slight depression, some difficulty breathing. To relieve his depression he took stimulants, and after that he alternated beween stimulation and depression. Up until that evening he had always been able to forget, particularly any resolutions or commitments he had made. Now he began to remember some truths about himself. Just as the mirror had reflected a double smile that troublesome night, so now he began to realize he had a double face. Outside, to the public, he showed a face of generosity, modesty, goodness, and altruism. But to the inner viewer his face burst with vanity and he felt special—I, I, I was the refrain of his life. Experiencing his dark side had thrown Clamence into bitterness about the human condition. To his listener he explained: "That's the way man is . . . He has two faces: he can't love without self-love."[6]

What brought Clamence to these realizations about himself? What brought him to hear the laughter at himself? A few years before, late on a drizzly November night, he was crossing a bridge over the Seine. He passed a young woman in black leaning over the railing and staring at the water. He hesitated for a moment but didn't stop. Then he heard something fall into the water, and several cries that seemed to be going downstream. Struck with fear and trembling, he wanted to run but was paralyzed with indecision. Finally, thinking, "Too late, too far . . .," he went on and told no one.[7] In the following days he avoided reading the newspapers, so he never knew what happened to the woman.

After that night he tried to elude judgment by forgetting. He became more adverse to others; from the moment he realized he was not as admirable as he had thought, he became increasingly distrustful, fearing he would be devoured by judgments. Although no one knew about this event, he felt vulnerable. The disorder he now felt in himself opened him up to public accusation.

> In my eyes my fellows ceased to be the respectful public to which I was accustomed. The circle of which I was the center broke and they lined up in a row as on the judge's bench. In short, the moment I grasped that there was something to judge in me, I realized that there was in them an irresistible vocation for judgment. Yes, they were there as before, but they were laughing.[8]

The hidden smiles he saw in people's eyes caused him to stumble, even fall, in public places. He began to realize he had enemies, both socially and professionally. He felt the hostility of strangers. Now he felt condemned for past successes. Having lived before in the illusion of innocence, now he saw the mockeries and judgments in the eyes of all around him. Alerted by the laughter, he became lucid, feeling all his wounds and losing all his strength in the same moment. His innocence had been lost.

> People hasten to judge in order not to be judged themselves. What do you expect? The idea that comes most naturally to man, as if from his very nature, is the idea of his innocence. . . . We are all exceptional cases. We all want to appeal against something! Each of us insists on being innocent at all cost, even if he has to accuse the whole human race and heaven itself.[9]

Now he understood why wealth and power are so sought after: they shield one from immediate judgment. Humans do not want to be guilty, yet they do not make the effort to change—that would require facing up to judgment. Both evil and good take energy. So, humans try to settle for "Limbo."

From the evening Clamence heard the laughter, he had to find an answer. Finding he was not simple, he discovered the duplicity of human beings. The only excuse he could dig up for this wretched state of being was that he had never taken human concerns seriously. Those people with passionate convictions or great loves, or those who sacrificed themselves to something higher, he could never understand. Rather, he found them tiresome. Although he lived among humans, he did not share their involvements. Excelling both in scorn and self-pity, he lived under a double code.

Prior to these discoveries, he had taken his natural sense of superiority and ease in life for granted. Unconsciously condescending, he regarded himself as a better lover than others—more sensitive, intelligent, and skillful. His persona, his public appearance of righteousness, dominated his life. To be respected and to dominate in all things had been his goal.

As he began to see his life more clearly, he realized that he, the defense lawyer, was on the side of the accused only if he was not a victim of their crime. When threatened, he became hard, mean, a judge who wanted to humiliate the offender. Thus, he became cynical about his vocation for justice as well as his reputation as defender of the bereft. Again his "double face" intruded on his noble image of himself. Now he, the godlike one, was looking into his own inner hell: "Yes, hell must be like that: . . . One is classified once and for all. . . . [My sign would be a] double face, a charming Janus, and above it the motto of the house: 'Don't rely on it.' On my cards: 'Jean-Baptiste Clamence, play actor.' "[10]

In relationships with women, he also needed to remain "on high." He was charming, and he got what he wanted without having to ask for it. Because he was not romantic he intrigued any woman who believed that she might be the special one who could succeed. With women he loved to gamble, to play games. The play always involved the "mysterious something," the "incomprehensible attraction," and the allure that it was "too late" for love for him. This kept the woman who wanted to be special on the hook. While he was never in love with these women, he wanted them to swear they would not belong to another man. Only then could he break up with them, for then he was the one in power. Once, on learning that he had been criticized by a woman who was not the passive victim he had judged her to be, he charmed her back into love with him and then got his revenge by giving her up and taking her back until they were bound together as "the jailer is bound to his prisoner."[11] He needed always to be in control in love. Now, with these new perceptions of himself, he began to laugh cynically—at his speeches to women and even more at his speeches in court.

Still, his life went on as if nothing had changed. People even began to praise him more, and this made him feel much worse. At that point the idea of death broke into his daily life. Obsessed by the fact that he might die before accomplishing his "task," he doubted even having a task. He was also tortured by the thought of dying without confessing all the lies he had lived, not to God, for he was above that, but to another human being. Death was with him every morning when he awoke. And the false life he was living grew unbearable.

Rage was his first reaction. He was in a rage at the very word "justice." Despite what he had learned about himself after walking away from the drowning woman, he still wanted to dodge judgment. What better way was there to dodge judgment than to judge others? So he became a judge. In his speeches he started to ridicule the humanitarian spirit. And he punctured the esteem with which he was regarded; for now his flattering public reputation particularly enraged him.

In the foggy state of his consciousness, he then sought to escape condemnation through the company of women, even though he looked down upon them in contempt. For women

> don't really condemn any weakness; they would be more inclined to try to humiliate or disarm our strength. This is why woman is the reward, not of the warrior, but of the criminal. She is his harbor, his haven; it is in a woman's bed that he is generally arrested. Is she not all that remains to us of earthly paradise?[12]

So he turned to the refuge of women, particularly those who were so thoroughly convinced by "true love" stories that they spoke of such love to him. But once these women became his mistresses he judged them severely, continuing to have simultaneous loves, which resulted in more misfortune. Finally, he began to loathe love and tried to give up women. But neither was chastity his forte. His cynicism about love and women increased.

> After all, their friendship ought to satisfy me. But this was tantamount to giving up gambling. Without desire, women bored me beyond all expectation, and obviously I bored them too. No more gambling and no more theatre—I was probably in the realm of truth. But truth, *cher ami,* is a colossal bore.[13]

Debauchery was next for him. He drank every night and slept with whores. This gave him a degree of "lucid intoxication." In debauchery there is no obligation. It even gives the illusion of being immortal.

> Alcohol and women provided me, I admit, the only solace of which I was worthy. I'll reveal this secret to you, *cher ami,* don't fear to make use of it. Then you'll see that true debauchery is liberating because it creates no obligations. In it you possess only yourself; hence it remains the favorite pastime of the great lovers of their own person.[14]

But finally, debauchery didn't work: his liver failed, and then he was overcome with fatigue, which dulled his vitality but also dulled his pain. The fog from those nights of orgy finally began to muffle the laughter that had been plaguing him. He became more indifferent, more resigned to boredom. He allowed himself to grow older and fatter. Of course, his professional practice had already decreased, in large part from the excesses of his court speeches and his chaotic life.

As he slowed down, the crisis seemed to pass. But one day, aboard a cruise ship on a trip he was taking to celebrate his cure, he spotted what seemed to be a drowning body. When he forced himself to look at it he saw that it was just some scrap left on the sea. But he realized that the cry he'd heard years ago from the Seine had never ceased and "would continue to await me on seas and rivers, everywhere, in short, where lies the bitter water of my baptism."[15] That was the day he realized that he was not "cured," nor would he ever be. Thus, "Ended the glorious life, but ended also the frenzy and the convulsions. I had to submit and admit my guilt. I had to live in the little-ease."[16] The "little-ease" was a dungeon cell of the Middle Ages that was too short and too narrow for a prisoner to stand up or lie down. As the body stiffened, "the cond man learned that he was guilty and that innocence consists in stretching joyously."[17] Hence, for the person who wants to live atop the summit, like himself, yet is condemned to the "little-ease," there is no innocence.

Set upon this course of thinking, Clamence came to the following conclusion:

> God is not needed to create guilt or to punish. Our fellow men suffice, aided by ourselves. You were speaking of the Last Judgment. Allow me to laugh respectfully. I shall wait for it resolutely, for I have known what is worse, the judgment of men. For them, no extenuating circumstances; even the good intention is ascribed to crime.[18]

Just as in the "spitting cell," where the prisoner must endure the spit that every jailer who passes by inflicts on him through an opening at face level, so we are spit upon by our accusers.

> . . . our faces are dirty, and we wipe one another's noses. All dunces, all punished, let's all spit on one another and—hurry! to the little-ease! Each tries to spit first, that's all. I'll tell you a big secret, *mon cher*. Don't wait for the Last Judgment. It takes place every day.[19]

Even our redeemer, Christ, must have known he was not totally innocent, for the slaughter of the children of Judea occurred while he was being rushed to safety. So many of today's martyrs are all too ready to trample over Jesus to climb higher upon the cross themselves and set him upon The Judge's bench, so that they can judge in his name. And yet Christ himself was no judge, saying "Neither do I condemn thee!"[20] But people now are eager to condemn without absolution, "with pardon on their lips and the sentence in their hearts."[21] In contrast, Christ "didn't expect so much. He simply wanted to be loved, nothing more."[22]

When fatigued and in a fog, Clamence calls himself

> an empty prophet for shabby times, Elijah without a messiah, choked with fever and alcohol, my back up against this moldly door, my finger raised toward a threatening sky, showering imprecations on lawless men who cannot endure any judgment. For they can't endure it, *très cher*, and that's the whole question. He who clings to a law does not fear the judgment that reinstates him in an order he believes in. But the keenest of human torments is to be judged without a law. Yet, we are in that torment. Deprived of their natural curb, the judges, loosed at random, are racing through their job. Hence we have to try to go faster than they, don't we? And it's a real madhouse. Prophets and quacks multiply; they hasten to

> get there with a good law or a flawless organization before the world is deserted. Fortunately, *I* arrived! I am the end and the beginning; I annouce the law. In short, I am a judge-penitent.[23]

Clamence invites his listener to visit him at home the next day, when he will reveal exactly what it means to be a "judge-penitent." When his visitor arrives, Clamence is in bed, sick with a fever that he is treating with a dose of gin. Suddenly he asks his visitor to check that the door is locked and bolted. He is not afraid for his safety, he is worried about his presence of mind—hence, his obsession with locks and bolts. He is eager to "block the door of the closed little universe of which I am the king, the pope, and the judge."[24]

Now Clamence shows his visitor a painting that he keeps hidden and secret. It is *The Just Judges*, a panel from the famous Van Eyck altarpiece, *The Adoration of the Lamb*. The painting, which depicts the judges coming to adore the sacred lamb, was sold by a thief for a drink one night at the bar where Clamence now holds court, and for some time there it hung, the devout judges unrecognized. But finally, when Clamence explained that the painting was famous, the bar's owner asked him to keep it locked up and hidden in his cupboard. With this painting in his possession, Clamence now has a chance to dominate. For while the world admires the false judges, it is he alone who knows the true ones. Since Clamence believes there is nothing sacred, he claims that the thief unknowingly put matters in their own peculiar harmony: for now justice is "separated from innocence—the latter on the cross and the former in the cupboard."[25]

Returning the painting to his cupboard, Clamence explains more precisely what it means to be "judge-penitent." Of course, we are "the first to condemn ourselves."[26] But we can dilute this condemnation by extending it to all others. As judge-penitent, Clamence refuses to grant humans either innocence or guilt. He now concludes that the sweet-smelling freedom he used to extol naively is a chore too heavy for humans. Like Dostoevsky's Grand Inquisitor, he has become an "enlightened advocate of slavery." Freedom is

> a long-distance race, quite solitary and very exhausting. No champagne, no friends raising their glasses as they look at you affectionately. Alone in a forbidding room, alone in the prisoner's box before the judges, and alone to decide in the face of oneself or in the face of others' judgment. At the end of all freedom is a court sentence; that's why freedom is too heavy to bear, especially when you're down with a fever, or are distressed, or love

> nobody. Ah, *mon cher,* for anyone who is alone, without God and without a master, the weight of days is dreadful. Hence one must choose a master, God being out of style. Besides, that word has lost its meaning.[27]

When Clamence turned away from the drowning woman, he discovered he was afraid to risk freedom. He learned it is easier "to cease being free and to obey, in repentance, a greater rogue than oneself."[28] Slavery makes us all comfortable in our guilt; the collective makes each of us like the other. In this way we avoid facing death alone. Thus, his aim became to avoid the burdens of freedom and judgment. One way to do that is to extend judgment to all, so that it is lighter for oneself to bear. If everyone were to be accused, he could sit more comfortably on the outside ring of judgment. Clamence found an ingenious solution—to be both penitent and judge.

So he left Paris, closed his law practice, and traveled for a while, intending to practice under a new name. By chance, he ended up in this crowded capital of foggy waters, a port town frequented by humans from all corners of this worldly life. And now he practices his profession in this very bar, preying especially upon the straying bourgeoisie. His profession is to indulge in public confession, accusing himself, but skillfully, so his listener is drawn to identify with the portrait drawn and to see himself in the mirror, perhaps with an even uglier face.

> The Prosecutor's charge is finished. But at the same time the portrait I hold out to my contemporaries becomes a mirror. Covered with ashes, tearing my hair, my face scored by clawing, but with piercing eyes, I stand before all humanity recapitulating my shames without losing sight of the effect I am producing, and saying: "I was the lowest of the low." Then imperceptibly I pass from the "I" to the "we." When I get to "This is what we are," the trick has been played and I can tell them off. I am like them, to be sure; we are in the soup together. However, I have a superiority in that I know it and this gives me the right to speak. You see the advantage, I am sure. The more I accuse myself, the more I have a right to judge you. Even better, I provoke you into judging yourself, and this relieves me of that much of the burden. Ah, *mon cher,* we are odd, wretched creatures, and if we merely look back over our lives, there's no lack of occasions to amaze and horrify ourselves.[29]

Clamence then asks his listener if, by now, he feels less good about himself than he did prior to their conversation. As for himself, he is quite comfortable as judge-penitent: he has found the perfect niche for his duplicity. Instead of struggling, he now permits himself everything. Of course, he must continue to confess his crimes, but this ironically makes things lighter and allows him to enjoy not only his self-loving nature but also the charm of his repentance. Relieved of the burden of change, Clamence has found a way to be the highest judge. He describes to his listener the details of his technique—the way he can be the supreme judge of all, the dominant master of control.

> I haven't changed my way of life; I continue to love myself and to make use of others. . . . Since finding my solution I yield to everything, to women, to pride, to boredom, to resentment, and even to the fever that I feel delightfully rising at this moment. I dominate at last, but forever. Once more I have found a height to which I am the only one to climb and from which I can judge everybody. At long intervals, on a really beautiful night I occasionally hear a distant laugh and again I doubt. But quickly I crush everything, people and things, under the weight of my own infirmity, and at once I perk up. . . . You will see me teaching them night after night that they are vile. This very evening, moreover, I shall resume. I can't do without it or deny myself those moments when one of them collapses, with the help of alcohol, and beats his breast. Then I grow taller, *très cher,* I grow taller, I breathe freely, I am on the mountain, the plain stretches before my eyes. How intoxicating to feel like God the Father and to hand out definitive testimonials of bad character and habits. I sit enthroned among my bad angels at the summit of the Dutch heaven and I watch ascending toward me, as they issue from the fogs and the water, the multitude of the Last Judgment. They rise slowly; I already see the first of them arriving. On his bewildered face, half hidden by his hand, I read the melancholy of the common condition and the despair of not being able to escape it. And as for me, I pity without absolving, I understand without forgiving, and above all, I feel at last that I am being adored![30]

Enthroned in his role as false prophet, intoxicated by his evil words, Jean-Baptiste Clamence admits that at times he has his doubts. But what other choice is there?

> To be sure, my solution is not the ideal. But when you don't like your own life, when you know that you must change lives, you don't have any choice, do you? What can one do to become another? Impossible. One would have to cease being anyone, forget oneself for someone else, at least once. But how? . . . Yes, we have lost track of the light, the mornings, the holy innocence of those who forgive themselves.[31]

Suppose, Clamence continues, there really was redemption. Suppose one had that second chance—the chance to take the risk of sacrifice—to save the drowning woman and with her to save oneself. What would one do? A second chance—the chance to change—is indeed a "risky suggestion!" For if taken literally, we humans would have to act. And just think how cold and deep that water would be, Clamence reminds us. And so, with the ingenious rationalization of the addict, Clamence concludes: "But, let's not worry! It's too late now. It will always be too late. Fortunately!"[32]

In *The Fall* Camus describes The Judge who wants to look good and be above. The "perfect persona"—a proper appearance, a charming manner, and a guise of nobility—hides his shadow, a libertine life, and an arrogance that judges others as inferior, particularly women. After he fails to help a drowning woman, symbolic of his own rejected suicidal feminine side, he becomes conscious of his failure. Yet he still hopes to escape judgment by denial, trying to forget his action. However, the recurring laughter he hears breaks through his denial to call him to look at himself honestly. Still evasive, he attempts to find external causes for the laughter and fails until he is forced to acknowledge that the laughter comes from within, mocking his perfect image and revealing his arrogant egoism. Cunningly, he continues to avoid judgment by judging others first: this way he can try to avoid his own guilt while making the other feel even guiltier. The co-addict inside every person knows about this trick and unconsciously does this with their inner and/or outer addict partner. Camus's protagonist goes one step further. Conscious of what he is doing, he holds hands with the devil. He sits in a bar as "judge-penitent" and confesses his own vices, seducing his drinking addict listeners to confess their crimes and to feel guiltier than himself. Here one can see, within the figure of the Demon Lover, the progression from The Moneylender to The Trickster to The Judge. For with his confession Clamence first offers others the illusion that it is only he who is the "bad one." But in the mirror he holds up to them, they see themselves as even lower in the hierarchy of hell. Then he sits enthroned above those around him, still in control. By maintaining the position of the highest judge, he attempts to rise above all judgment, even that of God. Since he believes in neither love nor forgiveness, there is no transformation or redemption. Instead, having lost his humility, he plays at being "God" himself. Like Dostoevsky's Grand Inquisitor who, as pope and highest Judge, sacrifices Christ and with Him all love and forgiveness in order to relieve humankind of the burden of their freedom and the judgments that attend that freedom, Clamence neither respects nor trusts human beings. But Camus's protagonist is even more ingenious because he makes his destructive judgments from his deceptive confessions in the foggy haze of alcohol, similar to the fog in which Dracula, the Demon

Lover, appears. And, just as Dracula seduces his willing victims who, in unconsciousness, lift up their necks to be bitten, so does Camus's judge-penitent seduce with his own confessions, the confessions of those addicted ones who would rather be judged destructively by another than risk taking a second chance in order to change and make the sacrifice to redeem their lives.

The name, Jean-Baptiste Clamence is significant. John the Baptist was the prophet who heralded the coming of the redeemed Christ. Despite his own overwhelming charisma, he announced the coming of an even greater one, higher than himself. John the Baptist also baptised Christ, and he resisted the seductress Salome. This resistance to seduction was a sacrifice, for he was imprisoned, and Salome, in revenge, demanded his head be cut off. Symbolically, John the Baptist is the one who resists not only the seduction of sexual addiction but also the ultimate seduction of being the highest and the most beloved of all, for he "makes way" for the Lord. The "Fall" of Clamence is that consciously he begins to understand his inflation after he fails to respond to the drowning woman. This event forces him to confront himself. Still he tries to dodge the confrontation and all judgment by manipulating himself into the position of highest judge. Thus, he refuses the honor of his name. His negative attitude toward women reflects his negation of the feminine in himself. Not only does he seduce them, he denigrates women as weak. He sees them as reward and refuge, not of the hero, but rather of the criminal. He does not value women as friends, for they bore him. All this suggests the attitudes of love addiction where the relationship is one of exploiter-exploited. Rather than resist it, Clamence embraces it. In ignoring the drowning "woman in black" he rejects the suffering and depth of his own feminine vulnerable side and thus refuses the voice of transformation.

His last name, Clamence, suggests *clémance*, the French word for clemency, mercy, and forgiveness—a possibility for redemption that he also rejects. As the novel ends, Clamence suggests to his listener that perhaps indeed there is a second chance to choose to act differently. But the redemptive nature of that second chance, he intimates, is too risky, for it requires a possible sacrifice of one's life—a sacrifice that Clamence does not want to make. When he hides from others the sacred image of the stolen painting *The Just Judges*, he hides with it the "sacred sacrifice." The picture symbolizes a justice that believes in Christ's reality, the gift of true sacrifice in love and forgiveness for the redemption of others, a sacrifice that John the Baptist made for Christ. Clamence refuses to face the finality of the Last Judgment, trying instead to set himself up as the highest Judge of all. In this way he abnegates Justice with its concommitant acceptance of existential guilt. His experience brings him to acknowledge humankind's "duplicity," that human beings are neither simple nor innocent creatures of a paradise. But he does not want to bear the cross of tension of the opposites that human duality requires, the knowledge of good and evil and the opposing poles of innocence and guilt. Instead, like the addict who is hostage to the devil, he denies the choice to endure the existential guilt that life requires. He splits off the possibility of innocence from justice. And like the devil, he manipulates the confessions of penitence to allow himself the highest place of judge. He seduces, tricks, and holds his listeners hostage in a cell of guilt so constructed that it allows no space for the weighing and balancing of these opposites. Instead of integrating the judge and the penitent in service of creativity, he combines them in a model of destruction. Thus, with full knowledge that it is possible to sacrifice and change one's life, he mocks the redeeming view of Justice and chooses himself to be the highest judge instead.

In contrast to the inflated protagonist in *The Fall,* the judge in Tolstoy's *The Death of Ivan Illych* undergoes transformation. He learns that human wholeness, not perfection, gives meaning to life. Ivan Illych shares many of the qualities of Clamence—the pleasant and proper persona, the judicial position of power, the low estimation of the feminine, the avoidance of personal feelings, the life of superficial ease. He is able to control his feelings and master events. The change for Ivan Illych begins when he falls and injures himself. At first he ignores the injury, but as his physical discomfort increases, he becomes irritable, blaming external events, never looking inward. Finally his bursts of temper disturb his family life. His wife and daughter resent his illness, since it intrudes upon their own desires for comfort, pleasure, and security, so they try to ignore the encroaching disease. For as long as he can Ivan Illych tries to control the course of this disease. He consults many doctors, receiving different diagnoses and methods of cure. The doctors treat Ivan, indifferently and impersonally, just as he, a judge, had treated the accused in the courtroom. Finally, Ivan is forced to look at himself:

> There was no deceiving himself: something terrible, new, and more important than anything before in his life, was taking place within him of

> which he alone was aware. Those about him did not understand or would not understand it, but thought everything in the world was going on as usual. . . . Ivan Illych was left alone with the consciousness that his life was poisoned and was poisoning the life of others, and that this poison did not weaken but penetrated more and more deeply into his whole being. With this consciousness and with physical pain besides the terror, he must go to bed, often to lie awake the greater part of the night. Next morning he had to get up again, dress, go to the law courts, speak, and write; or if he did not go out, spend at home those twenty-four hours a day each of which was a torture. And he had to live thus all alone on the brink of an abyss with no one who understood or pitied him.[33]

Ivan Illych saw that he was dying, but he simply could not accept the fact that this universal event, *death*, could end was happening to him. In his position as Judge he had always upheld the abstract, logical, and impersonal approach in deciding men's fates. But privately he always regarded himself as different, as unique, and as a special exception. He, Ivan Illych, could not be that "universal man" of the logical proposition: "Caius is a man, men are mortal, therefore Caius is mortal."[34] This universal proposition of human fate might apply to the abstract "Caius," but it certainly did not apply to him—the Ivan who had once been a little boy, played as a child, fallen in love, and been a good judge. Surely, the mortality that confronted all men could not apply to him.

In desperation, he goes back to the law courts, hoping that his old routines and duties will banish the dreaded thought of death. But even there on the bench he feels recurring pain, so death looks him in the eyes, drawing him down in confusion. Not even his judgmental duties can deliver him from death, which

> drew his attention to itself not in order to make him take some action but only that he should look at *It*, look it straight in the face: look at it and without doing anything, suffer inexpressibly.[35]

Even though Ivan tries to hide from death's terrible stare by obsessively searching for causes of his fall, none of these subterfuges work: Death would always reappear and ask him: " 'What is it all for?' . . . alone with *It*: face to face with *It*. And nothing could be done with *It* except to look at it and shudder."[36]

Finally it becomes apparent to him that everyone is waiting for him to die so that all can be released from his suffering. He had to eat special foods; others had to remove his excrement. Unseemly as this was, in this way he came to know the young peasant, Gerasim, who carried out these tasks. Gerasim was always good-natured and did easily and simply whatever was required. His very presence began to make Ivan Illych feel better. Recognizing that Ivan Illych was ill and dying, Gerasim accepted this fact with compassion, saying: "We shall all of us die, so why should I grudge a little trouble?"[37]

What had been tormenting Ivan Illych most was the denial of his condition by his family and friends. The deception that he was only ill was a lie in which they wanted him to participate. This was the agony Ivan Illych felt.

> The awful, terrible act of his dying was, he could see, reduced by those about him to the level of a casual, unpleasant, and almost indecorous incident (as if someone entered a drawing-room diffusing an unpleasant odour) and this was done by that very decorum which he had served all his life long.[38]

The other thing that tormented Ivan was that secretly he wanted to be pitied as a sick child—to be able to weep and be cried over. But, except with Gerasim, he assumed his habitual air of the serious official Judge. "This falsity around him and within him did more than anything else to poison his last days."[39]

One evening, toward the end of his illness, Ivan Illych fell into a deep black hole. In the course of that day his doctor and his family had visited as usual, trying to keep up the conventional deception. By now his wife had adopted an attitude of loving reproach that he was somehow to blame for his distress, as if he were not following instructions properly. And instead of addressing the real issue of life and death that faced his patient, the doctor debated the relative position of the kidney and the appendix that might be the cause. His daughter, who was young and impatient for life, resented his suffering. Each tried to keep up the deception. On this day, however, Ivan Illych suddenly became silent, which frightened them all. When they left his room the falsity left with them, but the pain continued. That night, he had the following experience:

> It seemed to him that he and his pain were being thrust into a narrow, deep black sack, but though they were pushed further and further in, they could not be pushed to the bottom. And this, terrible enough in itself, was accompanied by suffering. He was frightened yet wanted to fall through the sack, he struggled but yet cooperated. And suddenly he broke through, fell, and regained consciousness.[40]

When he awoke, he finally

> restrained himself no longer but wept like a child. He wept on account of his helplessness, his terrible loneliness, the cruelty of man, the cruelty of God, and the absence of God.[41]

He asked God why He had forsaken him and what he had done to deserve this fate. Suddenly, in silence, he heard a new voice—"the voice of his soul"—which asked him: "What is it you want?" "To live and not to suffer," was Ivan's reply. The inner voice questioned: "To live? How?"[42] Ivan replied that he wanted to live as before, well and pleasantly. But when he tried to recall what that pleasant life had been like, he could only remember some early memories of childhood; that child seemed to exist no longer. As he began to go through his life, what before had seemed to be joys now appeared as trivialities. Except for a few memories of love, the further he proceeded in his life, the worse it all seemed to him.

It suddenly occurred to Ivan Illych that perhaps he had not lived as he should have done. Yet, he had always lived so properly! Then he simply dismissed the question of how he had led his life ("this, the sole solution of all the riddles of life and death") and returned to his wish to live as he had formerly, as The Judge, crying out in self-justified anger "But I am not guilty!"[43]

In his final weeks, forsaken and lonely, Ivan Illych lay in his bed facing the wall. His memories went back to childhood, the place in his life where he could see light and life. Memories of his adult years were black. Still, he could not understand or accept his agony and was unable to surrender the idea that he had lived as one ought to live; he could not give up the justification of the "legality, correctitude, and propriety of his life."[44] Ivan Illych was struggling to defend his former life.

Then, one night, as he lay awake looking at the good-natured face of the dozing Gerasim, he thought: "What if my whole life has really been wrong?"[45] Now he reviewed his life in quite a different way. All the correctness and social propriety seemed false. When he looked at his wife and daughter, who were living by these very values, he saw in their evasion of both death and life a reflection of his own denial. Awaking to the fact that he had been hiding from life and death, he hated this truth about himself and his family. After this realization, he screamed for three days and nights. He was struggling in the black abyss, resisting it.

> For three whole days, during which time did not exist for him, he struggled in that black sack into which he was being thrust by an invisible, resistless force. He struggled as a man condemned to death struggles in the hands

> of the executioner, knowing that he cannot save himself. And every moment he felt that despite all his efforts he was drawing nearer and nearer to what terrified him. He felt that his agony was due to his being thrust into that black hole and still more to his not being able to get right into it. He was hindered from getting into it by a conviction that his life had been a good one. That very justification of his life held him fast and prevented his moving forward, and it caused him the most torment of all. Suddenly some force struck him in the chest and side, making it still harder to breathe, and he fell through the hole and there at the bottom was a light.[46]

At this moment, when Ivan Illych admitted that the way he had lived life was not all right, his hand fell upon the head of his young son, who was crying by his bedside, kissing his father's hand. Suddenly awake, Ivan Illych felt sorry for his son, and seeing his wife, her face wet with tears, he felt sorry for her too. He realized that he had been making them all wretched. Ivan showed that he was sorry for them and although he could not speak quite correctly, he tried to say "forgive me," waving his hand, "knowing that He whose understanding mattered would understand."[47] As Ivan Illych uttered his plea for forgiveness the agony and pain suddenly dropped away. He was now able to say "Let the pain be."[48] The death that Ivan Illych feared was no longer there; now light was in its place. Accepting death, he gained the light of life and cried out loud "What joy!" For others who attended him, Ivan's agony lasted for two more hours, until his body twitched and his gasping decreased. But for Ivan Illych all this

> happened in a single instant, and the meaning of that instant did not change. . . . "It is finished!" said someone near him. He heard those words and repeated them in his soul. "Death is finished," he said to himself, "It is no more!" He drew in a breath, stopped in the midst of a sigh, stretched out, and died.[49]

The story of Ivan Illych, who represents the rigid, self-justified, patriarchal judge, shows the way of transformation. After denying and protesting his disease as unjust, he accepts "the fall," descends into the abyss, and feels at bottom his own powerlessness and vulnerability. The receptivity and acceptance of the nurturing peasant, Gerasim, who has integrated the feminine, shows Ivan another way and helps him let go of his rigid self-righteousness. He lets go of The Judge. Surrendering to the whole mystery of dark and light, before him, Ivan sees and affirms both the pain and the joy of the human journey of death and rebirth.

In making judgments that serve creativity, feminine energy is necessary for the transformation to occur. We need only to note that in mythology Justice is shown in feminine form as Athene, the Greek goddess of justice and wisdom, and Maat, the Egyptian goddess of justice, truth, and law. And in the Tarot, an ancient game of divination reflecting the archetypal journey of the individuation process, the Justice card also reveals a woman seated on a throne. We can see the same image in "Halls of Justice"—a statue of a seated woman. In her right hand Justice holds an upright sword tip pointing to the heavens, emphasizing the vertical axis to the spiritual realm. In her left hand she holds the scales, two pans connected by a horizontal rod, emphasizing the earthly axis. This imagery shows the duality of the human condition and also suggests that, although The Judge is often imagined to be masculine and patriarchal, its original source may spring from the feminine, which holds the discriminations of feeling.

Viewing justice as related to addiction, the sword pointing toward heaven symbolizes the ability to discriminate—to "cut through" denial, false images, and the confusion of addiction—to the higher truth of our creative being. It is a weapon of courage to meet the responsibility of this creative challenge: its ritual meaning is sacrifice. For recovery, the addict must sacrifice dependence on the enslaving substance or activity, just as the creative person must make many sacrifices in the act of creation. Both must sacrifice unconscious innocence and bear the burden of judgment, which requires the assumption of responsibility for the knowledge of good and evil that one has learned in life's process. This means accepting the human burden of existential guilt. Individuation requires sacrificing our projections of outward judgment, i.e., blaming other people for our own guilt. Instead of seeing the devil in others (the addicted parent, partner, etc.), one must face that Demon Lover within. This means sacrificing the image of oneself as victim.

The upright sword symbolizes the central truth of the addict's life—the necessity to put sobriety first. The artist or writer needs to make a similar sacrifice of the less important things in his or her life in order to serve the call of the Creative Daimon. The sword of justice pointing toward the heavens symbolizes dedication to a purpose higher than any individual ego impulse or desire.

Just as the sword symbolizes the unwavering yang energies of discrimination and sacrifice, so the scales symbolize the yin energies of receptivity and flexibility. The cups of the scale are there to receive and weigh life's experience and events, to balance the opposites and create the equilibrium necessary for recovery from addiction and for the creation of any new being. Both the feminine and the masculine—the yin and yang energies—are needed to make illuminating judgments. The function of Justice in this image is to mediate and create a harmony between opposing energies.

The task for humans is to relate to this archetypal force but not to identify with it as did Clamence in *The Fall.* Clamence was neither open nor receptive. He rejectd his feminine side, symbolized by the suicidal "madwoman," and he rigidified into the Judge. In his desire to be the highest judge and dominate, he suffered inflation. By wanting to be the highest—even higher than God—he sold his soul to the devil. This inflation is the temptation that The Moneylender offers us in the beginning of any addiction; the result is possession by the Demon Lover.

The philosopher Hannah Arendt, who lived through the Holocaust, devoted her life to trying to illuminate this dark event and to understanding the meaning of judgment in human thought and action. For her, the function of judgment is to reveal meaning and is necessary to prevent oneself from supporting evil, for it is essential to be able to live in peace with oneself. Judgment, she said, requires internal dialogue and listening, an inner harmony. It presupposes a time of withdrawing from the world: "Once you are empty," she said, "then, in a way which is difficult to say, you are prepared to judge."[50] Detachment is needed for judging, which is the "political" activity of the mind and enables one to live day to day. In its original Greek sense, a critic was a judge or interpreter who could make distinctions, thereby separating things from one another and giving meanings. For Arendt, judgments need to be made not from on high, according to a book of rules, but individually, from the space of internal harmony. Thus, the individual must be responsible for his or her choices and actions, and this requires a clear, serene interior space, which addictive life destroys.

At the heart of creation and of recovery we meet this burden of judgment, which requires the acceptance of existential guilt. In order to create, we must continually make discriminating judgments: what to include, what to throw away, when to stop, when to continue, what fits, what can best express our vision? These judgments require us to endure the burden of finitude. A work, whether it be the work of one's life or one's art, cannot be perfect. The vision of what we can create is always far greater than what can be expressed concretely in any given work of art or in any life. Thus there is a "guilt" inherent in the process of creation, for the creator always knows that he has been unable to give complete and perfect expression to his vision. The artist must be able to stand in the tension between the potentiality of the vision and the finite limits of the embodiment, just as a genuine work of art always contains creative tension and offers it to the recipient. This conflict—essential to the creative process—keeps many people from daring to create or to risk putting their creation out into the world. The same issue arises in the recreating of one's life.

In order to live creatively we must learn to discriminate between two types of judgments: those that help us honor the mystery of creation and celebrate recovery, learning to bear its tension flexibly as it leads toward growth and wholeness; and those delivered from "on high" by the inflated Judge who would rather lock us up in the "little-ease" of addictive stagnation. Some of the toxic tendencies upon which the voice of the destructive Judge plays are the following: fear of failure and/or success, self-pity, scorn, envy, resentment, jealousy, perfectionism, lack of commitment, ambivalence, low self-esteem, grandiosity, unwillingness to make necessary sacrifices, inability to balance and/or establish priorities, procrastination, and lack of discipline to follow through to the embodiment of the creative vision.[51] The patriarchal Judge emphasizes comparing and competing, as well as results (fame and fortune) rather than process. This impedes creativity. All of these proclamations from The Judge, who wants to be "highest," are toxic to the creative process. In contrast, creativity requires judgments that have unconditional respect for the unique voice and style of each person and that celebrate the creative process.

One mistake those of us plagued with harsh inner critics often make is to want to get rid of The Judge entirely. And that is precisely "the Fall" of Camus's protagonist—to try to control by avoiding judgment. Failing that, he tried to manipulate others in order to become the highest Judge himself. But humans are neither entirely innocent nor entirely guilty. We are finite beings who stand between Heaven and Earth, who bear within ourselves the duality between spirit and matter, the cross of earthly finitude and spiritual striving.

10: THE KILLER

> Did I murder the old woman? I murdered myself, not her! I crushed myself once for all, for ever. . . . But it was the devil that killed that old woman, not I.
>
> —Fyodor Dostoevsky, *Crime and Punishment*

DREAMS SHOW ME the way when I write a book. One night I asked for a dream to illumine the meaning of addiction and creativity, and awoke, frightened and shocked, from the following nightmare:

> My editor had come to California to work with me on the two chapters I had written to date. As we were working together we heard reports that a pathological killer who had murdered four men was on the loose. He intended to murder more people, and both of us knew that he was angry about this book. We knew he would be aiming for us.

After this dream, I asked myself: "Who or what is The Killer in addiction and how does this relate to creativity?" Immediately, several people came to mind: Truman Capote wrote about murder in his "nonfiction novel" *In Cold Blood* and later died from his addiction to drugs and alcohol. Eugene O'Neill, an alcoholic who finally was able to choose to stop drinking so he could continue writing, portrayed the way addiction becomes a cold killer in *The Iceman Cometh*. And Dostoevsky, both a gambling addict and a creative writer, portrayed the underworld killer in novels such as *Crime and Punishment*, *The Idiot*, *The Possessed*, and *The Brothers Karamazov*. But Dostoevsky was able to transform his gambling addiction and to affirm the meaning of life in his last work, *The Brothers Karamazov*, through the character Alyosha, who embraced childlike faith.

Addiction—The Killer—kills love and creativity within the addict. It also kills the inner child. Whatever its form—chemicals, gambling, control, shopping, romance, or co-dependency—it devours the heart of creativity with its insatiable hunger and drains it of vitality like the vampire that lives off the life blood of its victims. The addict's ability to be spontaneous, vulnerable, receptive, or intimate is severely wounded, as are the hope and faith in life and love.

One woman recorded over forty dreams with The Killer motif, showing the multifaceted character of The Killer and its connection with love. In some of these dreams it is clear that if she does not kill The Killer she will be killed herself. But in other dreams, particularly the later dreams when she grew to be able to love herself, we see that The Killer is transformed through love.

Adrienne's primary relation to addiction was as an adult child of an alcoholic, and she developed into a co-addict who was also out of control in her use of diet pills and her consumption of sugar. As a co-addict, she tolerated her husband's addiction for the first fifteen years of their marriage. After he stopped using drugs and started going to Narcotics Anonymous, she was left to face her own addictive patterns, which had previously been obscured by his more obviously destructive behavior. It was about this time that she started to record her dreams.

As a child she felt abandoned, rejected, and unloved by her parents. She said: "My mother sold us (children) out for all of her men. Although she gave us hugs and kisses, she was unavailable, verbally abusive, and withheld her love. And when I entered my teens and fell in love for the first time, my mother brutally insisted I give up my love and told me this love was wrong. I resisted for over a year, but my mother's cold, brutal attacks were stronger, so I finally gave in and gave up love and covered it up and withdrew." During Adrienne's childhood her mother had three husbands, all addicted to alcohol. Her natal father had abandoned the family for another woman when she was two and a half years old. She remembered him as being charming but cold. As an adult she experienced him as being cold and rejecting. Soon after her father left, her mother married a man who was warm and creative, but manic-depressive. Although in his healthy periods he composed music and loved her, the love was unpredictable because of sudden nervous breakdowns during which he was unavailable for her. When she was twelve he died of a stroke, and thus she was abandoned again. She referred to the third man her mother married as an "alcoholic asshole." He got drunk often and would come home and beat up her mother. Although she wasn't afraid of him, neither did she respect him. His son, her stepbrother, whom she met at fourteen, was the love with which her mother interfered and finally destroyed through her overpowering dominance and the daughter's submission.

Although she withdrew from this first love, she did not withdraw from relationships altogether. She had a series of boyfriends, but she did not give herself totally to these men. Her hopes for love had been injured, and someone inside herself was hesitant and cynical about love: "I never had it as a kid; I don't expect to get it now, and I don't ask for it." So for love she substituted addictive relationships, and the cynic in her sought out men who couldn't give her the love she needed and didn't dare want or ask for. Finally she fell in love again and married a warm, spontaneous, and loving man who gave her a lot of attention. But, like her second father, he suffered from an illness: drug addiction. He too was unavailable and unable to meet her need for listening, fidelity, and intimacy.

Despite the difficulties of this relationship, she stayed in it, and the destructive patterns in the relationship confirmed the cynic's words: "I never had love as a kid. I don't expect to get it now. I don't ask for it." Somewhere along the way the cynic in her became The Killer, who appeared to torment her in so many different forms in her dreams. But the threats from The Killer carried a message for her: "Wake up, Adrienne. Your life is unmanageable. If you don't change your life you will die."

The Killer in her dreams assumed many forms—Mafia men, tough-looking youths, Oriental women, armed robbers, Secret Service men, sexual harassers, a vampire, an armed couple, drug addicts, sinister hands without a body, group sex murderers, mean-looking men, a crazy love zapper, a misshapen hatchet murderer, a giant, a POW commandant, tricksters, and tough women. In some of the dreams she herself was the killer. After studying the dreams in depth as a series, she discerned several major motifs—motifs that illuminated her personal life and also pointed to some of the universal issues in addiction.

One of the most frequent images in her killer dreams was "covering up." In the first of the dreams, she covered up the identity of a Secret Service man who was out to kill her. She lied about his identity because she was afraid if she revealed it he would not only kill her but also would blow up the world. Covering up or denial was part of her patterning, resulting from growing up in an alcoholic family, a pattern she continued in her marriage. Typical of children in alcoholic families, she learned to cover up her feelings and pretend things were OK. For, as the dream suggested, if she stopped covering and named The Killer, his anger might blow up the world. This pretense grew into a rigid armor that denied the family was sick, an armor of strength and control that covered up her vulnerability and her need for intimacy, which kept herself emotionally unavailable and other people at a distance. In her marriage she denied her pain and resentment over her husband's addiction to other women and drugs, and she also denied her own addiction to trying to save him. For in denying she was powerless to change him, she did not have to think about changing herself. Nor did she have to take the risk of becoming vulnerable by opening up. The self-destructive result of continually denying her feelings was shown in the next few dreams. A strong muscleman was trying to kill her; she escaped to the ladies room, where the toilets were filled up with paper and urine. The toilets were an image of the rejected feelings, which she had regarded as trash and stuffed up in herself. In a following dream a woman kills herself in the toilet, also a dream that presents another image of Adrienne's lack of self-esteem. It was in this dream that the denial pattern was shown to be linked with her mother: after the toilet scene the dreamer was on a bed with her mother and realized it was her time to die, but she was unable to express it to her mother, who ignored her daughter's fear by busily chatting.

These dreams and the many others that revealed the covering-up motif and linked it to The Killer preceded an event that broke through some of her defenses. At a meeting of Al-Anon Adult Children of Alcoholics (ACA), she was listening to the heart-rending story of another woman who had hidden her feelings for many years. Adrienne's own tears poured out and with them the emotional realization of her pattern of denial—the denial of the pain from her childhood wounds and the current pain over the facade she was maintaining by denying her needs for love, intimacy, and self-acceptance, as well as her need to be vulnerable and receptive to love from herself and others. Her pattern had always been to deny the fear, anxiety, shame, and guilt she felt about her family in the pretense of being normal like other people. One typical way for the children of alcoholics to do this is to focus on others, to try and fix everything, and not to experience or trust personal feelings because they are so fearsome and unmanageable. Trying to keep the family disease a secret becomes all-important because in addition to the shame and fear of social judgment, the child does not want to face his or her fear, anger, powerlessness, and helplessness. To deny, to doubt the facts, to withdraw, to live in fantasy, and to pretend even to oneself that everything is OK—these were the ways Adrienne took to protect herself, and they are common for those who grow up in alcoholic families. Adrienne's mother had also taken the route of denial, as shown in the dream where she chats mindlessly while her daughter thinks she is dying.

In another recurring dream her mother is unconcerned when Adrienne, fearing some tough-looking youths will break in and try to kill her, asks if the door is locked at night. Each time Adrienne struggles to lock the door she finds there is still another door unlocked or broken into, and her mother always ignores her fear. Finally Adrienne gives up and walks away feeling it is "useless to try." This recurring dream showed the patterns of denial and withdrawal and hopelessness that Adrienne had learned from her mother's denial and lack of love and protection for her daughter. The following dream revealed how threatened she felt by facing her problems.

> I am talking to a woman from the sex institute about alcoholism. Then a man asks me long and involved questions about alcoholism and co-alcoholism. As I talk a dwarf comes in. He is misshapen and has the body of an eight year old but the strength of five men. He tries to kill me, and we scuffle. He says he likes to kill women with a hatchet and chop them up. Some people try to help in subduing him with an injection, but I know it won't work. He comes at me again, and we scuffle. Finally, in desperation, I take a cymbal and throw it at him like a Frisbee. The cymbal slices his neck.

This dream revealed the inner terrorist who would try to kill her if she tried to break out of the addict/co-addict pattern. It also linked the addictive issues with sexuality. The dream showed that the threat of the terrorist cannot be subdued with a quick fix (the injection). And while other people may be of help, they are not enough. She herself must meet the terrorist head on. Her most effective weapon is the "cymbal," an image which for her evoked the depth and power of music. The cymbal's roundness reminded her of the tai chi movement of letting go, and of the universal symbol of centering, the mandala. At the similarity of the sound of the word *cymbal* to the word *symbol* she said: "I love the cymbal deeply. It is like a deep chord that gets played in my soul. Perhaps the cymbal is the 'symbol' that can transform The Killer." Adrienne believed in the power of symbolic transformation. She knew she had within her a cynic that killed her love and faith; the dwarf represented the psychopathic manifestation of The Killer. The dwarf, she felt, was her own cynical lack of respect and the resulting severe, condemning judgment about her mother, her husband, and ultimately herself. No matter what she did it wasn't good enough. She couldn't seem to love herself. In contrast, the cymbal was a transforming symbol of centering love.

She associated the dwarf's age of eight years old, which belied his enormous strength, with her own arrested emotional development at the same age. Up until then she had been a sickly child whose weakness her mother could respond to in the way she responded to the weakness she seemed to look for in a husband. But, at eight, when Adrienne's health improved and her strength began to show, her mother withdrew. Now Adrienne sees that this set the pattern for the dichotomy she felt between "strength" and "weakness," which had seemed to her to be irreconcilable opposites. Either she was "strong" and unable emotionally to ask for help or for what she wanted because her mother didn't listen, or she was "weak," "vulnerable," and sickly. This dichotomy corresponded to the addict/co-addict dichotomy within herself and within her marriage. As a co-addict, she was seen as strong; she felt that people didn't like her for it. But inwardly she felt too weak to follow her own feelings.

An archetypal trio of Killers in the psyche of addicts consists of the terrorist, the martyr, and the victim. Developmentally, this reflects a typical pattern in an alcoholic family. The alcoholic parent is like an unpredictable terrorist, and from the child's perspective may be a persecutor who operates by provoking fear. The other parent often falls into the role of judgmental martyr, trying to control the alcoholic and usually others in the family by provoking guilt. Instead of giving spontaneous love, the martyr-caretaker parent often talks of love as duty. The child usually grows up feeling unloved and helpless, playing the role of victim even as an adult. But more than likely the child also internalizes the other two figures. So, the terrorist continues to internally torture the victim through fear, and The Judge continues to severely condemn through guilt. Adrienne was secretly afraid of the unpredictability of her angry and vulnerable feelings and a hostage of the guilt-provoking, cold Killer-Judge within.

The dwarf dream portrayed her arrested emotional development, the disparity between her strength and her vulnerability, and the threat to her life that this perverse patterning posed. It suggested the addict/co-addict patterning in her life. As horrible as the figure of the dwarf was, however, it showed that she, Adrienne, did not have to be a victim, for she had the power of the cymbal to protect herself.

The dwarf dream showed her that in order to face The Killer she had to look at The Killer in herself. It showed that if she faced The Killer head on instead of covering up the threat with a fix, she had the power of the cymbal (symbol) to fight back. This takes both strength and supportive love. At the time of this dream she had both love and strength from the twelve-step program of Al-Anon/ACA and also was doing the inner work of intensive therapy. The following dream vividly showed that *she* herself was The Killer. Although the external history of her childhood had led to the killing of love, The Killer was now internalized.

> I am in a hotel with several other women. We're killing people—the first is a woman in an empty tub. I grab her hair and bang her head and knock her out. Then I go to another room to kill someone. I'm doing the killing and the other women are my accomplices. They lure the people in and hide in another room while I do the killing. I see a naked man with an erection. First I have a sexual encounter with him and then go to kill the last man. To murder him I feed him candy and then try to kill him as he swallows it. But he is tough and fights back, taking out a pen knife. Now I have on white kid gloves and finally knife him in the throat. But when I close the door to the room and look back I see him sitting and smoking a cigarette. I throw a box of cornflakes down the incinerator and go to the lobby to escape gracefully. But as I look up the staircase there he is smiling with vampire teeth as he throws me a flattened top hat. I smile, and I, too, have vampire teeth.

In this dream the connection between sexual seduction and the vampire is startling: she has vampire teeth herself. She associated the vampire to the Demon Lover that was present in her marriage: "We sucked the life out of each other as people do in an addict/co-addict relationship. Vampires are the 'living dead,' and this is what I felt our life was like, neither of us really feeling for ourselves or for the other. My feelings were sucked dry. Like the woman in the empty tub, there was no flow in my life." Adrienne said she could identify with the vampire in her own addiction to men—that she needed men to affirm her as a person. As she put it, "When I'm upset and depressed I want sweets and men. Then everything seems OK for a while." In the vampire dream she tried to kill the man by seducing him with candy, but he was tough and didn't fall for it. But after the seduction attempt he turns into a killer, cool and detached. In looking at the dream she could see in herself the vampire syndrome—both as victim whose life blood is sucked out and as killer-vampire with the cold toothy leer.

Now that she could see The Killer in her dreams as part of herself, that it was *she* who was participating in the addictive relationship patterns and that it was *she* who was killing her feelings with the cold defense that she had learned from childhood, she had a chance to transform The Killer. Her dreams reflected this possibility: around the time she had the vampire dream she also had several dreams in which The Killer was connected with love addiction.

In one of these dreams The Killer was a crazy man who gave her a "love zap" in the back of the head over and over again, which felt great. She and The Killer sat in the same chair, he with an erection and she wanting a sexual encounter. But in the dream, encountering this man was linked to losing his car, then her keys, and finally happening on a drug deal, which she reported to the police. Losing her car (a frequent theme in her dreams) symbolized the loss of her personal freedom of movement, and losing the keys symbolized the loss of her choice to open and close herself, to know when to say yes and when to say no. The drug deal linked this loss to addiction.

One of the chief characteristics of an alcoholic family is unpredictability—the child of an alcoholic never knows what to expect, or when the frightening event will happen, or what causes the parent to drink. The child tries to control the crazy, uncontrollable domestic scene through externals—by placating or rescuing others, by withdrawing and becoming a helpless lost child, or by becoming the scapegoat. Love seems crazy and unpredictable because they never know when they'll be loved and when they'll be hated, or when they'll be sexually harassed or abused. Many children of alcoholics are sexually abused, and many more are emotionally threatened by the possibility of physical abuse. Adrienne couldn't remember any physical sexual violation, but she could remember hearing sex and violence when her parents were drinking. The theme of sexual harassment, which continually came up in her dreams, showed there was a disturbance, at least emotionally, in this area. One of the "sexual harassment–Killer dreams" was connected to a film scene of a group murder of Marilyn Monroe, who, like the romantic longing for the "love zap," finally killed love by killing herself. For Adrienne, the danger of the love zap was the danger of her crazy relation to love. In the dream the love zap came from behind, where she could not see what was happening and had no control at all, and it connected her sexually with a crazy killer. Nevertheless, the allure of the love zap was great. She knew that she herself went crazy in this unpredictable, unconscious area.

This dream connected with other dreams in which The Killer was trying to kill her lover and her love. But then her dreams started to show a transformation as she started to confront The Killer. Instead of running and hiding from The Killer, or denying his existence, or letting him zap her from behind, she started to look him in the eyes and fight back.

> My house was being remodeled, and I noticed a lump under the rug in the bedroom. As I stepped on it a burglar emerged. I tried to placate him, but

> he pulled out a weapon. I ran away, feeling very vulnerable. Then a group of women came by, and I joined them for protection. When more burglars came again, no one helped me. I fought back, strangling one of them. Then I looked the other straight in the eye and told him, "The more I'm with you the more I love you," and I kissed his cheek. He looked back at me and said he loved me too.

In this dream she actively uncovered The Killer, faced him, and in doing so was able to transform The Killer into someone who could express his love.

One of the ways of uncovering The Killer is to understand how the theme of sexual harassment was connected with it. She felt sexual harassment in her married life as an intrusion upon her personal space to be a woman without having to perform sexually. Her inner harasser kept her trying to please men sexually so they would love and be true to her. But pleasing and seduction became a substitute for intimacy. She did this in her marriage, but the result was to deny herself the private space she needed for developing and nurturing her true self. During the period of her husband's addiction she felt that she couldn't satisfy his continual sexual hunger. She could never give him enough to make him happy. Never knowing when he wanted sex, never knowing where the boundaries were and whether she could even walk around the house nude and naturally without having to perform, reflected the unpredictability of her childhood. Finally she felt reduced to a sex object like Marilyn Monroe. All addicts have to learn to honor and nurture their true self—not the identity of ego desires but the process of inner growth. As Adrienne came to recognize this her dreams emphasized that she now had a second chance to deal with the patterns in her life that were killing her.

> I am talking to druggies in a house from my past. I wonder why there aren't more windows so there is a view, and ask my husband to put in a window in the corner. But he says he can't do it. The neighbor's house has been remodeled, and I admire it.
>
> Next I am walking on the street in spike heels. They are very uncomfortable and keep falling off. I go into a store run by young men whom I have encountered sometime in my past. They are Jews for Jesus, and they want to kill me as they once had done before in a past life.
>
> Through some fast and clever moves I escape through a crowd of customers. But I go into a van and there they are again, trying to kill me. I have long scissors but hesitate to use them because I'll kill them, so I start to stab them, hoping that will change their minds. But they still want to kill me, so I stab harder. They are weakened, so I escape, but they are still after me and are joined by strangers, and I realize that these men

> killed me the last time I dealt with them and I don't know what went wrong. As I wake up I know these are The Killers and this is my last chance!

The first scene of this dream brought up her dissatisfaction with her past and her addiction-dominated relationship. In the dream she wants more vision and perspective in their relationship. She asks her husband to do the work, but he can't do it for her. However, the remodeling of the neighbor's house shows that such work can be done and that she likes it. The next scene brings up two of the things that needed to be changed. She had been wearing spike heels, symbols of the uncomfortable and constricting feminine sexual role that she had been living. Then she encountered The Killers—"Jews for Jesus," which symbolized for her, a Jew, the spiritual contradiction and basic self-betrayal that she had been living by focusing not on herself but rather on her husband. At the time of this dream her husband was already three years into his own recovery, so she could no longer assume that his drug addiction as such was the problem. Rather, the addictive form of the relationship itself and the addictive patterns in her own life were at issue. Several months earlier she dreamed of a little bird in a cage who repeatedly sung out, "I'm an addict. I'm unhappy." The caged bird, the spike heels, the sexual harassment, and the murder of Marilyn Monroe were all dream images of her own co-addiction to a false cultural, sexual feminine role to which she had given over herself. This role was part of her own self-betrayal and kept her trapped in the negative patterns of her marriage and her life. In the "caged bird" dream she had given away the caged bird to a couple who had just remodeled their house. She knew that remodeling meant changing the structure of the patterns that were killing their relationship and her life.

The "second chance" dream showed she had a new chance to deal with these killing patterns. In this dream it was clear she must kill these particular Killers if she was to live, for they represented the same murderous patterns of self-betrayal that had killed her life in the past. Her tendency, in the dream, still was to avoid this brutal but necessary act and try to escape instead. But she also knew it was her last chance, and that now she had the consciousness and strength to do what she needed to do to change her life.

Killing the inner Killers of her self-betrayal was the prelude to her inner wedding. By confronting the Demon Lover that was killing her own creativity she would be free to meet her inner spiritual bridegroom.

This possibility was shown to her in a "wedding" dream about a month later.

> I am camping out in a tent with others and the men and women pair off. I'm with a guy, and it's very wet and uncomfortable. Then I'm driving in a car, then a motorcycle, and encounter roadblocks. I walk on foot to go around the roadblocks. I am angry at myself that I've been eating shitty food all day. Finally, I get myself a cup of soup.
>
> Suddenly I realize that I am on the way to my wedding, so I ask the man who's with me for support. When I get there it's like a surreal play—the people, many of whom are blacks, are wearing makeup and are in a huge auditorium, and all is in slow motion. When I get past the slow-motion people to the wedding area, there are people dancing and laughing, and it's fun.
>
> Now I am walking down the aisle to the altar. There I meet a man, *not* the groom, and I can feel his penis through his clothes as we hug and kiss. But I realize the groom is not coming here to this loose affair. So I leave to find him.
>
> Then I find myself in a house that has been built recently and that has workmanship of the highest quality. As I go through the rooms, I encounter a female guest from the wedding. She is just now dressing. I enter a room, and there to my surprise are art books, exquisite knickknacks, and a window with a view. At first I wonder why there is only one window, but then I see there are many more windows, carefully constructed so the afternoon sun will be deflected and not too strong. When I find some magic tools and a book about the magic of love, I also realize that the owner of this house knows about magic.
>
> Encouraged and amazed I enter the next room and see a man in a bed and another person totally covered. When I pull back the covers, I know I've found the groom. He is older than I am, half white and half black, and very happy that I've uncovered him and finally found him. We kiss, and I tell him the house is wonderful. There is more, he says. He has asked the contractors to build it especially for me. I worry about the cost, but he is happy and continues to talk with the other man, a scientist friend. I realize the groom is a wonderful blend.

She said that the first scene of the dream mirrored the way she felt when she lived by negative addictive patterns. Transitory, uncomfortable, and alone, she encountered obstacles and felt angry at herself for her behavior. But when she decides to get on her own two feet and eat something nutritious, the scene changes and she is on the way to her wedding. Though the groom is not yet there, the atmosphere is fun and imaginative, and she has a male companion to call on for support. She can flow in this relaxed atmosphere, which is opposite from the controlled way she was leading her life. On the way to the altar she meets another man, and they embrace. It is an enjoyable sexual encounter. Contact through the clothes meant to her that although sexual intimacy was beginning, emotional intimacy was not yet present. This was an important transitional place, but she was not yet ready for the groom. In her outer life this corresponded to a period of separation from her husband when she lived alone. She found she could handle sexual intimacy but not yet emotional commitment.

Finally, in her search for the groom she had to leave the loose social scene and enter a new house in which she encountered the feminine side that was getting ready for the wedding (the female guest). Only then did she discover the wonders of the new home she was building within herself and uncover the inner bridegroom who was now there as a result of the inner work she was doing.

The new house built by the groom symbolized the house of her recovery from a life of addiction. The groom was the inner figure who could integrate the mystical and the practical, who could live in the tension of these two worlds. Adrienne had split off these two worlds from each other. In the outer world she was extremely practical, adept at control and getting things done. But her inner world was magical and mystical. She loved to be with her dreams and dwell in the numinous world of symbols and shamanistic visions. In her marriage she had projected her own romantic side upon her husband while she took on the burdens of the practical world. This made her angry, and she became the martyred Judge constantly criticizing her husband's romantic tendencies. In doing so she cut off herself from her own romantic, magical side. The bridegroom in her dream was the *inner* figure who could dwell in mystery and be practical at the same time. Not only did he have a book that expressed the magic of their love; he had the magic tools to build a house with many windows to the outer world so these two realms could flow into each other. Half white and half black, the inner bridegroom knew the dark realm of the lower depths of addiction and could acknowledge suffering and pain, anger and grief. But he also knew the joy of the light world of hope and faith, the realm of recovery.

What were some of the steps of her transformation from a life of addictive control into creativity? What was her path of recovery? Initially she went to a therapist to work through some of the feelings of pain and anger about her husband's addiction. At this time her husband was still using and she had not yet heard of Al-Anon, nor was she aware of her own addictive issues. But this initial therapy helped her realize that she had to stop focusing on the relationship and work on herself. So she went back to school to finish her degree so she could work and become more independent. Dreams had always fascinated and inspired her, so she went into Jungian analysis and started to record them. As she did so the above patterns began to emerge; now she was able to face her own darkness. The dreams were part of the process that helped her see her own denial. She was not just the *victim* of The Killer, addiction, as the child of an alcoholic and the wife of an addict. The Killer was also within herself, as the vampire dream showed. As she said, "Control, power, and ultimately possession by demonic pride are The Killer for me; they prevent intimacy, love, openness." In the process of facing her own darkness she was brought before her own death—the death of her ego desire for power and control. She was brought to admit she was powerless over alcohol and drugs, powerless over people, places, and things, and that her life had become unmanageable. To do this, which is the first of the twelve steps (though she did not know it at the time) was for her most important and difficult. The twelve-step Al-Anon/ACA program which she later joined, along with the practice of Tibetan Buddhist meditation, became the focal spiritual practice of her creative recovery process.

Soon after the dream about the bridegroom with magical powers, she had another dream that prepared her for the practice of Tibetan Buddhism to which she is presently committed. In that dream a man was preparing her with love for the spiritual teacher who was to empower her. In the dream, instead of feeling the suspicion, control, and lack of trust that had formed her co-addictive pattern, she relaxed. She awoke feeling enveloped in love. Shortly after this dream she went to a Tibetan Buddhist ritual of empowerment and teaching and began a daily practice of meditation and visualization. Through meditation she learned to turn over her fears of betrayal, rejection, and abandonment. She began to learn to accept life as a gift and be grateful for every experience, even the painful ones, as ways to learn. Through visualization she learned to relate to the transcendental energies, within and without, that empower and guide human life. This practice helped her to cut through disillusionment and embrace with gratitude the life that was hers through the creative powers. Instead of escaping into transient and impermanent "people, places or things," she took refuge in "the three jewels"—the Buddhas (the deities), the Dharma (the teachings), and the Sangha (the community of practitioners). Her spiritual work helped her to realize the importance of Karma (cause and effect). Instead of wasting time while she had the gift of life on earth, her creative challenge was to become mindful of her thoughts, speech, and actions. Her spiritual practice is a process leading to enlightenment and loving-kindness—for herself and for all other sentient beings. Sitting meditation helped her to see what her mind was clinging to, to let it go, and recognize her own Buddha ("awake") nature. Instead of the endless clutter of controlling and manipulative thoughts, she began to experience—through meditation—the open and sacred spaces of her being.

Ironically, it was her addiction that led her to this new way of being, for it caused her to face her powerlessness and reach out for help, to make a "leap of faith." In the process she learned the ways of the twelve steps and the Tibetan Buddhist practices. In the course of this process she was graced with the following dream showing how she had transformed The Killer of addiction into her new spiritual life.

> I am driving up the road to the Buddhist temple. I get out of the car and begin to walk. Suddenly a rainbow comes from the top roof of the temple and enters the top of my head.

Instead of the addictive love zap from the crazy Killer of her dreams several years ago, now she was given the colorful rainbow of blessings coming from the Tibetan temple. She was learning to follow the path of loving-kindness, which cultivates joy, serenity, love, and compassion for all sentient beings.

The Killer in addiction is pride—whether in an individual, in a family system, or in a nation. The Killer thinks he is above all laws, beyond all boundaries, exempt from the human condition. In the Big Book this attitude is described as "self-will run riot." A person in the grips of such arrogance usually feels "higher" than others, whom he wants to control. When this attitude dominates, neither openness nor receptivity are possible. The addict feels self-justified—exempt from the finitude of the human condition. This Luciferian pride puts one "above" good and evil even though the individual may see himself as doing good. Humility is denied, and with it the possibility for transformation. Genuine love is murdered. At its worst, The Killer is exemplified by the demonic possession of Hitler, who felt justified in killing off the Jews and whoever else got in his way.

Pride is behind the "denial" in addiction. The person who feels "above" or superior to obvious addicts looks outward and judges the other to avoid looking at their own addictive patterns. At twelve-step meetings one often hears that an individual may have gone once or twice to a meeting and thought they were better than the people there. I'm not one of "those," the person thinks and leaves. Years later, when the addiction has progressed and the bottom has been hit, the same person returns in humility. The denial has been broken and with it the arrogant pride, and in its place is humble compassion for others. The redemption of The Killer comes through love and forgiveness.

In *Crime and Punishment* Dostoevsky shows the inner workings of The Killer's mind and points a way toward transformation. Two killers are portrayed in *Crime and Punishment.* One of these killers seems incapable of transformation while there is possibility for the other. In Dostoevsky's analysis the irredeemable killer, Svidrigailov, has become frozen, all love objectified into indifference. There is no forgiveness in him. He is possessed, no longer bearing the tension of good and evil within himself. Having given himself over totally to the demonic destructive force that seeks annihilation, he finally commits suicide. The other killer, Raskolnikov, suffers from his crime and also has within him the hope for spiritual rebirth. In the psyche of the addict The Killer has this dual aspect—the part that like Dracula must be named and held accountable for its self-destructiveness and the part that can be forgiven and transformed.

Dostoevsky wrote this novel during the period of his own debt and gambling addictions. When he conceived this novel he was, like Raskolnikov, in "exile" in a cramped and lonely room, deprived of money, food, and light, yet "burning with some kind of inner fever." He had just lost all of his money on a five-day gambling binge in Wiesbaden, where he had fled to avoid debtor's prison. Previously, Dostoevsky had planned to write a novel called *The Drunkards,* which later had to be abandoned when he could not find a publisher. Eventually *The Drunkards* became incorporated via the story of the drunken Marmeladov and his family in this novel about a killer.

The murderer, as Dostoevsky originally conceived him, was a young student expelled from the university who was living in poverty and disconcerted by the nihilistic ideas of the time. In Dostoevsky's original conception, Raskolnikov decides to murder an old woman, a greedy moneylender who is vile, mean, of no use to anyone, and even harrasses her younger sister. After killing her, he plans to rob her of her money, which will enable him to support his mother and save his sister as well as finish his own studies and help him break out of poverty. Dostoevsky's original plan for this character was that he lead, after this one crime, an honorable humanitarian life, which would redeem his crime. By accident, he is able to commit the crime, and he is not suspected. But inwardly he is tormented by his conscience and finally turns himself over to the police. One of Dostoevsky's intentions was to expose nihilism—the theory that the end justifies the means. But as the novel finally was written the central drama lay in the conflict between good and evil within The Killer's soul. Raskolnikov's theory—that there are powerful superior individuals who are above the law and have the right to murder—is contradicted by the unexpected feelings of guilt and remorse that rise up in his heart.

Raskolnikov's dreams reveal this inner conflict. For example, before the murder he has a nightmare in which he wakes up in terror from a frenzied brutal scream. In another dream a drunken cart driver brutally beats to death an old nag who is so overloaded it cannot pull the cart. Only a child of seven in the dream, Raskolnikov cries out in horror. In tears, he rushes to protect the horse and kisses the dead and bloody mare on its eyes and lips; he cannot endure the murderer's cruelty. Both the sadistic killer driver and the horrified child can be seen as two opposing sides in Raskolnikov's character. Consciously, he thinks he is superior and has the right to murder the old moneylender-hag just as the cart driver unmercifully beats the old nag to death. But the dream shows that the child in Raskolnikov cannot bear this brutality. After this dream his childhood faith is restored for a while. His better Self, through the voice of his dreams, shows him the poison of murder. For a brief time he feels freedom from the fascination with crime. But eventually he is drawn back into his philosophy of murder. Later, just as in the dream the drunken driver took an iron crowbar and struck the mare to death, so in actuality Raskolnikov took an axe and split the moneylender's skull.

The setting for the crime is the Haymarket—place of drunkards, prostitutes, and poverty. Wandering there by chance Raskolnikov learns that the old moneylender will be alone at a certain time on a certain day. Mechanically, he visits the moneylender on that day, killing her and also her sister by accident, and fails to steal the bulk of the money. After the murder, he returns to his "coffin" of a room and falls ill with a nervous fever. Close to madness, he wants to kill himself. His ideas of murder have been disembodied. He has been possessed by a kind of perverse dreamy romanticism about murder. His theory is that the superior individual can commit a crime without remorse. Above good and evil, the superior one can remain in control. Having performed the actual deed, Raskolnikov cannot endure the conflict between good and evil in his soul.

After the murder, the conflict Raskolnikov feels between romantic idealism and atheistic nihilism begins to drive him close to madness. He feels intensely alienated from humankind. During the three days of illness he suffers after the crime, dream and reality become confused. When he regains his memory, the proud, strong-willed person in him surfaces again and expounds the idea of the exceptional personality who has the right to go beyond all limits, even to shed blood. The Killer Raskolnikov is the archetypal symbol of "self-will run riot" in the addict. By now, he is addicted to his power, intoxicated with a diabolical pride. Even so, he cannot sustain this position. A mysterious stranger calls him "murderer." This upsets Raskolnikov again and he doubts himself. He resents the moneylender and feels like a louse rather than the superior "bronze man." That night he dreams that he tries again to kill the old moneylender, but she only laughs at him. She seems immortal and impossible to kill. Her mocking laughter reminds him of his impotency. Struggling for self-knowledge through the terrible path he has chosen, Raskolnikov realizes he has committed the murder to see whether he was just like everyone else, or whether he was different. "Would I be able to step beyond or not?" Was he merely a member of the human herd, or could he dare to have the power of a desot, of a Napoleon? But, his self-doubt only proves to himself that he is just contemptible and cowardly. Still his pride returns. If he gives himself up, it will not be out of humble repentance but only because of his cowardice.

The investigator, Porfiry, analyses the crime as the result of a troubled heart "exasperated by theories." Finally, Raskolnikov confesses. But he cannot "bow down" humbly and kiss the ground in repentence, as the loving Sonia had told him to do. Raskolnikov is sent to Siberia. Sonia, who loves him, follows him there, but he is rude to her and contemptuous of her loving faith. What he understands is not redemption. Rather he feels that he is the weak victim of a blind and tragic fate. Raskolnikov allows his "self-will run riot" to follow to its end. Thus, his pride—the demonic pride and self-deification that solidifies into The Killer—continues to control his life. Raskolnikov demonstrates none of the humility that leads to conversion. In the novel's epilogue, however, there is a suggestion that Raskolnikov finally begins to love Sonia, representing a possibility for new life and resurrection.

In *Crime and Punishment* there are many inner figures of addiction. It is a moneylender whom Raskolnikov chooses to kill. His ostensible reason for the murder is to help his family get out of debt. But the underlying motive is to prove to himself that he is above the mass of ordinary people. Thus he plans to commit a murder to prove his superiority. He gambles with life to see if he dares to risk going beyond all moral limits.

Raskolnikov is not a simple character. There is in him a cold, inhuman figure, detached, who intellectually tries to justify the murder and to prove the superiority of his self-will to power. This side cuts him off from human love and makes him an alienated outsider to a world that he experiences as hostile. Thus, Raskolnikov is an extension of the Underground Man and his resentment. In its extreme, the Underground Man, denying love, becomes a Killer. But Raskolnikov has in himself also a compassionate side capable of love and charitable action. Once he commits the actual murder his soul is torn apart by tormenting conflict. Although his cold intellectual side can justify the killing, his loving heart cannot endure the reality of murder.

In order to magnify the two opposing sides of Raskolnikov's personality, Dostoevsky created other characters symbolizing these extremes. There is the cold and calculating killer, Svidrigailov, who feels no remorse. There is also the humble gentle Sonia, who offers Raskolnikov the redemptive possibility of self-forgiveness and love for others. The duality in Raskolnikov's nature is shown by his disgust for Sonia's meekness and his repulsion for Svidrigailov's proud indifference.

Killing the moneylender has isolated Raskolnikov from the rest of humanity. Sonia's father, the drunkard Marmeladov, symbolizes the hopeless agony Raskolnikov feels when he "hits bottom" in this way. In the novel, Raskolnikov frequently is compared to a drunkard. He lives in disorder, dresses in a disheveled fashion, is in debt, and mutters to himself on the street so that passersby think he is drunk. Just like an addict, "He was in the condition that overtakes some monomaniacs entirely concentrated upon one thing."[1] In his heart there is such accumulated bitterness and contempt that he is contemplating murder. After his first visit to the old moneylender to size up the possibility for murder, he feels so repulsed and disgusted that to escape his wretchedness, confusion, and agitation, he stops in a tavern to have a drink.

Although he is not alcoholic, his feelings resemble those that cause an addict to drink.

> Till that moment he had never been into a tavern, but now he felt giddy and was tormented by a burning thirst. He longed for a drink of cold beer, and attributed his sudden weakness to the want of food. He sat down at a sticky little table in a dark and dirty corner; ordered some beer, and eagerly drank off the first glassful. At once he felt easier; and his thoughts became clear. "All that's nonsense," he said hopefully, "and there is nothing in it all to worry about! It's simply physical derangement. Just a glass of beer, a piece of dry bread—and in one moment the brain is stronger, the mind is clearer and the will is firm! Phew, how utterly petty it all is!" But in spite of this scornful reflection, he was by now looking cheerful as though he were suddenly set free from a terrible burden: and he gazed round in a friendly way at the people in the room. But even at that moment he had a dim forboding that this happier frame of mind was also not normal.[2]

In the tavern he meets Marmeladov, who tells him the story of his life. He had lost his job in government service due to alcoholism. His daughter, Sonia, had been forced to support the family by prostitution because he would not quit drinking. Recently he had been given another chance; he was reinstated as a clerk. However, five days ago he stole his wife's savings and went on a five-day binge. Now he was plunged back into a drunken morass of tears and tribulation. As he now says to Raskolnikov, "I drink so that I may suffer twice as much."[3] Marmeladov confronts Raskolnikov with the question: "Do you understand, sir, do you understand what it means when you have absolutely nowhere to turn? No, that you don't understand yet."[4]

Feeling sympathy for the drunken man, Raskolnikov helps him to his home, where the scene is one that most adult children of alcoholics know too well. His angry wife berates Marmeladov for stealing the family's money, searches his pockets, and in a fury screams and drags him by the hair.

> The child asleep on the floor woke up, and began to cry. The boy in the corner losing all control began trembling and screaming and rushed to his sister in violent terror almost in a fit. The eldest girl was shaking like a leaf. "He's drunk it! He's drunk it all," the poor woman screamed in despair—"and his clothes are gone! And they are hungry, hungry!"—and wringing her hands she pointed to the children. "Oh, accursed life!"[5]

In a moment of pity, Raskolnikov leaves some money for the poor family—an act of compassion which his Killer side later regrets. Hastily, he departs. The meeting with Marmeladov mirrors the hopelessness of his own condition. While Marmeladov's feelings of disgust, unworthiness, and low self-esteem lead him to drink, Raskolnikov's similar feelings lead him to thoughts of murder. Although he drinks, Marmeladov has a simple faith. In the tavern he cries out his drunken despair, but he also cries out his credo.

> And He will judge and will forgive all, the good and the evil, the wise and the meek. . . . And when He has done with all of them, then He will summon us. "You, too come forth," He will say. "Come forth ye drunkards, come forth, ye weak ones, come forth, ye children of shame!" And we shall all come forth, without shame and shall stand before Him. And He will say unto us, "Ye are swine made in the Image of the Beast and with his mark; but come ye also!" And the wise ones and those of understanding will say, "Oh Lord, why dost thou receive these men?" And He will say, "This is why I receive them, oh ye wise, this is why I receive them, oh ye of understanding, that not one of them believed himself to be worthy of this." And He will hold out His hands to us and we shall fall down before Him. . . . and we shall weep. . . . and we shall understand all things! Then we shall understand all! . . . and all will understand, Katerina Ivanova even . . . she will understand . . . Lord, Thy kingdom come![6]

Marmeladov in his drunken tears is caught in the despair of weakness while Raskolnikov, in his bitter pride and cynicism, is caught in the despair of defiance. Each is but the shadow of the other. Kierkegaard analyzes these forms of despair in *Sickness Unto Death.* According to Kierkegaard, the human condition is a continual movement between the opposing poles of possibility and limitation, of spirit and matter. Being human requires a conscious and freely chosen affirmation of this paradox as well as an affirmation of the relation to the Creator. Without this consciously chosen affirmation of the creation and its Creator, humans will suffer from despair. Most of humankind try to escape this human fate and choice through distractions, remaining unconscious that they are in despair. Addictions are an example of such unconsciousness. At some point boredom, frustration, resentment, anxiety, depression, fear, or anger break into the unconscious despair and announce the fragmented nature of such a life. Such feelings crop up in the course of addiction, announcing to the addict that something is not right. It is then that despair becomes conscious.

First one usually becomes conscious of one's weakness. At this point a person realizes he or she is out of relationship with the higher Self and despairs over the weakness and inability to choose and affirm a better way of life. It is into the despair of weakness that Marmeladov has fallen. Conscious of his weakness, he despairs, unable to move out of his addiction. This is a stage that many addicts will recognize in themselves, particularly when they feel caught in self-pity. But the addiction can also serve to bring humans to the consciousness that they are out of relationship to the higher powers of creation.

At this stage, if they can make a leap of faith, they can meet the challenge and meaning of human creative life. Such a leap is absurd; it goes beyond all logic and reason. But this leap of faith is demanded by the higher powers of creation. It corresponds to the second step. If at this stage the leap of faith is not made, Kierkegaard says that a person may remain in the despair of weakness. This is a state of mind in which suicides often occur. Or, becoming conscious of the bitterness and resentment at such a condition, the person may become defiant.

In the despair of defiance, one is consciously angry at God and feels rebellious. Even if God were to come and offer salvation, at this point an individual is likely to rebel and refuse the better life merely out of resentment and bitter pride. This, too, is a state of mind that causes suicide. But suicide, like Svidrigailov's, takes place from pride and contempt for creation. Raskolnikov, caught in the despair of defiance, contemplates murder, but at the same time he is really killing himself. He recognizes this after the murder when he confesses to Sonia in a spasm of agony:

> Did I murder the old woman? I murdered myself, not her! I crushed myself once for all, for ever. . . . But it was the devil that killed that old woman, not I.[7]

Like Raskolnikov, many addicts are caught in this despair of defiance, drinking themselves to death; murdering love out of jealousy, control, or addiction to power.

According to Kierkegaard it takes humility to take a leap of faith, for the leap is beyond rational control. Thus, the leap of faith requires turning the will over to a higher power, the Creator. Turning over his will to something higher is contradictory to Raskolnikov's theory that the extraordinary individual can do whatever serves his own ends. If he is superior, Raskolnikov reasons he should be in control and be able "to keep all one's will power and reason"[8] and thus commit the crime. But when he actually commits murder, fear takes over and his mind becomes confused. Afterward he vacillates between the need to confess and the desire to be superior, above it all.

Svidrigailov symbolizes such a "superior individual" possessed by demonic pride. He kills himself in the "despair of defiance." Raskolnikov is attracted to this character, but he is also repulsed. Simultaneously he is attracted to Marmeladov's suffering. After the murder, like the drunkard, he hits bottom and swings between the two poles of despair. His hope lies in the figure of Sonia, who symbolizes for him the suffering of all humanity. Through her humility, Sonia is able to make the "leap of faith," and symbolizes the possibility of redemption for The Killer.

Like the addict hiding the evidence of his addiction, Raskolnikov is overcome with the compulsion to hide the evidence of his crime. After regaining consciousness, he frantically stuffs all the things he has taken from the moneylender into the hole under the peeling wallpaper in his room. But when he sees the bulging wallpaper, "Suddenly he shuddered all over with horror; 'My God!' he whispered in despair, 'What's the matter with me? Is that hidden? Is that the way to hide things?' "[9] Again and again, he suspects a search and, mastered by his terror, hurries to hide things. Finally he finds a stone under which to hide the remaining trinkets. In great relief he says: "I have buried my tracks!"[10] But the next moment he is overwhelmed by a fit of fury. "Damn it all! . . . If it has begun, then it has begun. Hang the new life! Good Lord, how stupid it is! . . . And what lies I told today! How despicably I fawned upon that wretched Ilya Petrovich!"[11]

When he is called to the police department, on the landlady's summons, ordering him to pay his rent, he faints as he hears the murder being discussed. In continual torment and terror, he begins to hear things. He thinks that Ilya Petrovich, the assistant police superintendent, has been beating the landlady. But the maid tells him: "No one has been here. That's the blood crying in your ears. When there's no outlet for it and it gets clotted, you begin fancying things."[12] He fears everyone knows he has committed the crime and are all only mocking him for the moment. He feels he has cut himself off from all human contact. His suffering conflicts with his theory that the superior person does not need help. Again he is much like the person hiding an addiction—tormented by this hiding yet unable to reach out.

Like the addict who gambles with his nemesis, Raskolnikov meets a policeman and converses with him about the murder. He even gives his own explanation of the perfect way to commit such a crime, describing in detail exactly what he has done. The policeman thinks he is mad but becomes suspicious. Later, Raskolnikov returns to the scene of the crime. At this point he decides to confess the crime and end his inner torture. But by chance, he sees the drunken Marmeladov, who has been run over by a carriage. He helps him to his home, where the dying man asks forgiveness of Sonia, whom Raskolnikov sees for the first time. Overcome with compassion for the suffering family, Raskolnikov gives Marmeladov's widow his last twenty ruples, money he has just received from his mother.

After Raskolnikov leaves, he feels new life. The dead man's blood is splattered on him from helping, not from killing. Just then, Marmeladov's daughter Polenka rushes out to thank him and to take his name. Raskolnikov consoles the little girl and asks her to love him and to pray for him. After this he feels reborn.

> "Enough," he pronounced resolutely and triumphantly. "I've done with fancies, imaginary terrors, and phantoms! Life is real! Haven't I lived just now? My life has not yet died with that old woman!"[13]

Raskolnikov feels strong, as though he was "challenging some powers of darkness" with growing pride and confidence. This was his first encounter with the loving and forgiving Sonia, and he felt inspired to help. Just as every recovering addict experiences that helping others heals himself as well, so Raskolnikov began to feel redemption through giving help. This is the principle of the twelfth step of recovery. Hence Raskolnikov is now drawn to the forgiving love of Sonia.

Feeling new life does not last, however. For Raskolnikov's inner torment throws him between the side of his being that believes in the superman's will to power and the side that wants to confess and be forgiven. When he sees his mother and his sister, who have just arrived in St. Petersburg, these two sides of his character show. First, he opposes an arranged marriage for his sister with a petty government official because he feels his sister, encouraged by his mother, is sacrificing everything for him. In a letter announcing the proposed marriage his mother had written: "You know how I love you; you are all we have to look to, Dounia and I, you are our all, our one hope, our one stay."[14] Many adult children of dysfunctional/addicted families will recognize this projection. Upset at his mother's statement, Raskolnikov also feels the proposed practical marriage is a kind of "legal prostitution," a sacrifice not unlike Sonia's. So when he sees his mother and sister in person he says, "I won't accept the sacrifice." But later he becomes indifferent and tells Dounia to do what she wants. He also feels impatient with his mother and thinks he seems to love them more in their absence than when they are actually present. Aware suddenly that his family seems afraid of him in his change of personality, a cold chill goes through him.

> Again that awful sensation he had known of late passed with deadly chill over his soul. Again it became suddenly plain and perceptible to him that he had just told a fearful lie—that he would never now be able to speak freely of everything—that he would never again be able to *speak* of anything to anyone. The anguish of this thought was such that for a moment he almost forgot himself.[15]

The crime Raskolnikov is hiding makes him seem mad. The murder is like the bottle of booze that the drunkard needs to hide—this hiding nearly drives him crazy. At the same time, Raskolnikov is drawn to the police—especially Porfiry—to find out what they know. Porfiry tries to trap him by asking for details that only the murderer would know. After one encounter, Raskolnikov feels sure Porfiry suspects him and returns again to his room to see if he has forgotten to hide any of the evidence. He resents the old moneylender but feels no remorse for the crime. As he leaves his room a stranger appears and says "Murderer!" Raskolnikov sinks into confusion, then falls into an exhausted sleep in which he has the dream about trying to kill the moneylender, who only laughs at him. Upon awakening he sees Svidrigailov standing in his doorway. This was the very man who had insulted his sister when she worked for him. Although Raskolnikov felt the man was evil, he felt a strange affinity to him as well. Svidrigailov even said they were "birds of a feather." He told Raskolnikov he hoped to see his sister once more and also wanted to pay her ten thousand ruples so that she won't have to marry the petty Luzhin.

Soon after Svidrigailov's visit, Raskolnikov visited Sonia. He told her of his meeting with her father and he pointed out her desperate situation—the poverty of the family, the consumptive disease of her stepmother, the plight of the children. But Sonia cried out: "God will not let it be."[16] Raskolnikov then taunted her by suggesting that there may not be a God. Seeing that she had been tormented by the shame of her condition, he asked: "how this shame and degradation can exist in you side by side with other, opposite, holy feelings?"[17] To drown herself in the canal, to end in the madhouse, or to sink into depravity was all the skeptical Raskolnikov could imagine as her end. Since Raskolnikov was an "angry young man," living by abstractions rather than by his heart, this last end, that of a depraved heart turned to stone, seemed to him the most likely. Yet, thus far she had still preserved her purity of spirit. Perhaps she was mad, a religious fanatic, he thought, who could not believe in life without God. He asked her to read the story of Lazarus, and as she read it he saw how difficult it was for her to unveil her "secret treasure." For the story was of Christ's miracle—the raising of a criminal like himself from the dead. Sonia read with soulful passion, but Raskolnikov's response was from the demonic side. After she had finished he told her she had betrayed herself through prostitution, that she was mad and had destroyed her own life. They were on the same journey, he said, and should take it together. Then he tormented her with the following words, which unveiled his pride.

> What's to be done? Break what must be broken, once for all, that's all, and take the suffering on oneself. What, you don't understand? You'll understand later. . . . Freedom and power, and above all, power! Over all trembling creation and all the antheap! . . . That's the goal, remember that! That's my farewell message.[18]

Abruptly, Raskolnikov leaves, saying he would tell her later the name of the murderer. Unknown to them, Svidrigailov was listening by the wall next door. Meanwhile, Sonia was confused and feverish. For in the midst of all this Raskolnikov, like a madman, had stared into her eyes, then bowed down before her and kissed her foot, saying that through this act he was bowing down to the whole of suffering humanity. Raskolnikov had finally reached out to another suffering human being. But The Killer in him was trying to negate it.

On the following day Raskolnikov finally asked Porfiry directly if he was suspected. Porfiry hinted that he had secret information and that he liked Raskolnikov and wanted to help him. Just then a man opened the door and confessed to the murder. Porfiry and Raskolnikov were dumbfounded. Raskolnikov felt perhaps he had another chance to escape confessing. Still, he had promised to tell Sonia the identity of the murderer, a confession he knew was essential.

When Raskolnikov went to talk to Sonia, he began by asking the following hypothetical question: If she had to decide who would die—her poor half-crazed stepmother or the mean Luzhin, who had insulted and humiliated Sonia by tricking her—who would she choose? To this Sonia answered clearly:

> But I can't know the Divine Providence. . . . And why do you ask what can't be answered? What's the use of such foolish questions? How could it happen that it should depend on my decision—who has made me a judge to decide who is to live and who is not to live?[19]

Despite the shame and humiliation she had suffered, Sonia's faith in God remained unshaken. It was to this gentle and forgiving feminine energy that Raskolnikov was drawn. Her ability to accept suffering and her capacity for self-sacrifice was what he needed to affirm in himself for his redemption. She symbolized the part in himself that opposed his nihilism—the loving and compassionate side that surpassed his "superior individual" theory, the feminine spirit of compassion that could redeem The Killer in him. This is the forgiving feminine spirit that addicts need to embrace in themselves.

Raskolnikov tried to tell Sonia that he was the murderer, but he could hardly say a word. Sonia, in terror at how he was suffering, finally understood that the murderer stood before her. Falling on her knees, she threw her arms around him, sharing with him his unhappy burden. Tears came into his eyes and suddenly his heart softened. He asked that she never leave him, and Sonia replied that she would stay with him forever, follow him even to Siberia. At the mention of Siberia, he recoiled and a hostile haughty smile came upon his face. Seeing the murderer before her, Sonia asked him how he could have done such a thing. None of the answers he spewed out seemd quite right to him. Finally, he tried to explain to her his gloomy credo:

> . . . that power is only vouchsafed to the man who dares to stoop and pick it up. There is only one thing, one thing needful: one has only to dare! Then for the first time in my life an idea took shape in my mind which no one had ever thought of before me, no one! I saw clear as daylight how strange it is that not a single person living in this mad world had had the daring to go straight for it all and send it flying to the devil! I wanted *to have the daring* . . . and I killed her. I only wanted to have the daring, Sonia! That was the whole cause of it![20]

Sonia cried out, "You turned away from God and God has smitten you, given you over to the devil!"[21] Raskolnikov replied that although the devil had led him on, he found the devil was merely mocking him. To his self-disgust he discovered that he was a louse just like all the rest. It was himself he killed, through the temptation of the devil. "Did I murder the old woman? I murdered myself not her. I crushed myself once for all, for ever. . . . But it was the devil that killed that old woman, not I."[22]

In desperation, Raskolnikov asked Sonia what he should do now. Sonia, her eyes full of fire, said:

> Stand up! . . . Go at once, this very minute, stand at the cross-roads, bow down, first kiss the earth which you have defiled and then bow down to all the world and say to all men aloud, 'I am a murderer!' Then God will send you life again. Will you go, will you go?[23]

Raskolnikov could not make this confession or go to Siberia. People would only laugh at him and consider him a coward and a fool. He was not yet ready to confess or make amends. So when Sonia gave him a little wooden cross, offering to share his suffering and go to Siberia with him, Raskolnikov said: "Not now, Sonia. Better later."[24] Sonia replied that he should put the cross on only when he was ready.

Soon after this encounter, Sonia's stepmother died. Svidrigailov appeared, offering a large sum of money for the children and for Sonia. To Raskolnikov he then revealed that he had overheard his confession. " 'I told you we should become friends,' he smirked. From this moment Raskolnikov's mind seemed to break down. It was as though a fog had fallen upon him and wrapped him in a dreary solitude from which there was no escape."[25] Morbid agony and panic often alternated with apathy, as is sometimes seen in a person who is dying. "He seemed to be trying in that latter stage to escape from a full and clear understanding of his position."[26] He saw that he needed to come to terms with the menacing Svidrigailov, for whom he felt such a rush of hate that he could kill him. He felt the same toward Porfiry, who just then came to his door.

Porfiry had come to confront Raskolnikov with the murder. Up until then, the investigator had been challenging Raskolnikov's theories and was trying to trick him to confess. He admired Raskolnikov, for he saw his potential, the human behind the murderer-theoretician's mask. Raskolnikov's intellect, he knew, could be a powerful force for the betterment of humanity. The murder, Porfiry said, was

> a fantastic, gloomy business, a modern case, an incident of today when the heart of man is troubled, when the phrase is quoted that blood "renews," when comfort is preached as the aim of life. Here we have bookish dreams, a heart unhinged by theories.[27]

For Porfiry, the murder symbolized the nihilistic attitude that could destroy the heart of humanity. He told Raskolnikov he would wait a day or two before arresting him to give him time to confess on his own, knowing that if Raskolnikov could acknowledge his errors, confess freely, and take the suffering on himself, he could be transformed. An intellectual complement to Sonia's eros, Porfiry symbolizes the positive Trickster and the thinking side of Raskolnikov that could be used for the good of self-transformation. In the addict, Porfiry is the positive logos that can recognize the inner Killer, name the addiction, and collect the facts and evidence; the side that can cut through the denial yet also have the patience to wait for the proper timing so that self-knowledge and transformation can occur. He knew that Raskolnikov would not run away, for having ceased to believe in his own theories, he had nowhere left to turn or hide.

After Porfiry left, Raskolnikov rushed to find Svidrigailov, who he knew had "hidden power" over him. He felt followed by him. He was also afraid of Sonia, whose admonition to expiate his sins and take on his suffering was a sentence to confess his guilt. But with Svidrigailov he had something in common even though his own crime, he felt, was different than the evil doing of the depraved, cunning, deceitful, and perhaps malignant Svidrigailov. Now he feared that Svidrigailov had evil designs on his sister. When they met, Svidrigailov told Raskolnikov about his attraction to young women and also quizzed him about the murder. Raskolnikov became repulsed and left. Just then Dounia arrived in response to Svidrigailov's letter. He lured her to his room and told her about her brother's confession, implying that she could save Raskolnikov if she would be his. Dounia refused and wanted to leave, but Svidrigailov had locked her in. She took his revolver, and he taunted her to shoot him. But she couldn't do it. Secretly, Svidrigailov hoped she could love him. To this request, she cried: "Never!" He let her go. That dark, rainy night Svidrigailov went from one low haunt to another. He went to give some money to Sonia and then to the parents of a young girl to whom he was engaged. He told them all he was leaving for America. Then he took a room in a bleak hotel. Dozing off, he had a series of frightening nightmares.

In one he saw a coffin in which lay the body of a young girl who had drowned herself. Crushed by an insult to her purity, she had destroyed herself. Svidrigailov recognized the girl as one whom he had abused. Awakening for a moment, images of the river overflowing with cellar rats swirled in his brain. Then he had another dream. In a dark corner he saw a five-year-old girl who was crying and shivering from the wet and cold. He took her home, undressed her, and put her in bed. "What folly to trouble myself," he said, suddenly annoyed at his own foolishness.[28]

When he went back to see how the child was sleeping, she looked at him with the shameless grin of a French harlot. She had turned into a prostitute, laughing at him hideously and inviting him to bed. Shocked from this night of horrors, he shot himself in the head.

Svidrigailov is a man whose self-will has run riot, which leaves him utterly alone. Although he has committed evil, he has not been punished externally. But, having crossed all human boundaries, there is no pleasure left in life for him. Having failed to win the human love of Dounia, having isolated himself from humanity, he finally realized that the only will to power left was to kill himself. Svidrigailov symbolizes the "self-will run riot" in the addict. At its extreme this will to power leads to the destruction of oneself and/or others.

In Raskolnikov's personality, Svidrigailov represents the cold and calculating Killer possessed by demonic pride that puts his will above all else. It is this cold Killer that Raskolnikov feels has been following him around. Svidrigailov embodies Raskolnikov's theory of the superior man who can murder without remorse. (Rumor has it that Svidrigailov had poisoned his own wife, abused a servant who then killed himself, and raped a mute thirteen-year-old girl who hanged herself in shame.) Self-will brings him to isolation and suicide.

In the meantime Raskolnikov still could not accept the idea that suffering is healing and regenerative. Nevertheless, when his sister confronted him with what she had learned about the murder and, like Sonia, told him to face the suffering, he agreed to confess even though his pride prevented him from seeing the evil in his deed. But he wept in the arms of his suffering mother, told her he loved her, and asked her to pray for him. Still he asked why must he be the one to suffer and be humbled, when all the others around him are criminals and guilty too. And reproaching the love of his mother and his sister, he cried:

> Oh, if only I were alone and no one loved me and I too had never loved any one! *Nothing of all this would have happened.*[29]

Sonia was waiting for Raskolnikov with dreadful anxiety—would he confess or would he kill himself? She was anxious because "she knew his vanity, his pride and his lack of faith."[30] Just then he came into her room and asked her for the cross. In anguish, she saw the mask that concealed his anger. "A poignant and rebellious doubt surged in his heart."[31] Bitterly he went to the crossroads, but then he remembered Sonia's words to bow down and ask forgiveness. For a moment his heart softened and, with tears in his eyes, he bowed down and kissed the earth in bliss. He heard around him a roar of laughter; the people in the crowd thought that he was drunk. The words, "I am a murderer" dropped away as he heard the jeering crowd. But seeing Sonia, he knew she would follow him forever. So he went to the police office to confess. However, when there he heard that Svidrigailov had killed himself, he decided to leave without confessing. Near the entrance he saw Sonia looking at him wildly in poignant agony and despair. Opposing Svidrigailov, Sonia was the better part of himself that was also following him. The simplicity of her loving and humble presence promised the self-forgiveness and the redemption that comes from accepting suffering and making amends. Seeing her, Raskolnikov turned around and confessed that he was the murderer.

Raskolnikov was sentenced to a reduced term of eight years in Siberia. After nine months there, his heart remained closed and sullen. He held himself aloof, contemptuous of Sonia, whom the other prisoners loved for her simple, loving presence. His pride still kept him from repenting of his crime, and he felt ashamed and ill.

> But it was not his shaven head and his fetters he was ashamed of: his pride had been stung to the quick. It was wounded pride that made him ill. Oh, how happy he would have been if he could have blamed himself! He could have borne anything then, even shame and disgrace. But he judged himself severely, and his exasperated conscience found no particularly terrible fault in his past except a simple *blunder* which might happen to anyone. He was ashamed because he, Raskolnikov, had so hopelessly, stupidly come to grief through some decree of blind fate, and must humble himself and submit to the "idiocy" of a sentence, if he were anyhow to be at peace.[32]

The only crime he recognized was that he had been unsuccessful in the murder. Now he wondered why he had not killed himself as Svidrigailov had done. What had he to live for? He could not understand how his fellow prisoners could prize life the way they did. What he did not realize was that

> at the very time he had been standing looking into the river, he had perhaps been dimly conscious of the fundamental falsity in himself and his convictions. He didn't understand that the consciousness might be the promise of a future crisis, of a new view of life and of his future resurrection.[33]

Just before Easter Raskolnikov was sick in the hospital. There he was tormented with dreams of destruction—of a plague in which people killed one another and could not judge between good and evil; of killings by men who could not agree and who abandoned their work upon the land. After his release from the hospital, he saw Sonia once again. Now he wept and flung himself at her feet. Finally, she knew he loved her and that the promise of the future, of the new life of resurrection, had arrived: ". . . renewed by love; the heart of each held infinite sources of life for the heart of the other."[34] Seven years of waiting lay before them until he was released from prison, but both felt the new life that had risen in his being. Even the fellow prisoners looked different to him now and were friendly. This was the beginning of the renewal of Raskolnikov, the beginning of a new and unknown life.

> He was simply feeling. Life had stepped into the place of theory and something quite different would work itself out in his mind. . . . He did not know that the new life would not be given him for nothing, that he would have to pay dearly for it, that it would cost him great striving, great suffering.[35]

Crime and Punishment shows with chilling accuracy how the feminine is abused and murdered in addictive life when "self-will run riot" rules. In addictions the nurturing feminine is abused and finally killed through indifference and the monomania of wanting what one wants when one wants it. The extreme form of this demonic attitude of calculating power and indifference is characterized by Svidrigailov, The Killer who feels no remorse. This is the most frightening figure in the psyche of the addict. In the novel there is no transformation for this character. Alienated from human caring, his end is murder of self and others. In contrast, there is hope for Raskolnikov, who experiences the suffering resulting from having killed. His vacillations between the theory of the superior man who has the right to murder and his attraction to the loving, forgiving Sonia show the crazy swings between the defiance that keeps one in denial and addiction and the leap of faith that can redeem. The machinations of control and hiding that drive Raskolnikov crazy are the very ones that torture addicts who know the devastation of their addictions yet feel driven to the denial that finally isolates them from the loving care of other humans. They, like Raskolnikov, experience the overwhelming anxiety resulting from the inner addictive killer. The hope that lies in Sonia requires forgiveness, confession, and suffering. It requires bowing down in humility through a leap of faith. But it also promises redemption for the loving feminine side that honors life.

All addictions are killers; each in its own way kills living in the moment, kills creativity, love, and the trusting faith of the inner child. Archetypally The Killer is the inner character who decides against life. Like Svidrigailov, who has no heart commitment and coldly withdraws from participation in life, The Killer doesn't care. This can take the form of icy perfectionism, inflated self-justification, or the passive victim.

Inwardly, The Killer in addiction is not one simple thing. Like the complex interplay of psychic forces that confused Raskolnikov, so The Killer can use the various archetypal energies at play in the drama of addiction—The Moneylender's lure of euphoria and the "quick fix," The Romantic's longing for the infinite, The Gambler's desire to exceed limits, The Underground Man's alienation and resentment, The Madwoman's devouring hunger, rage and paranoia, The Judge's control and superiority, The Outlaw's rebelliousness, and The Trickster's cunning and unpredictability—to confuse us and cover up the authentic call to creative life. The Killer wants to obstruct our basic goodness; addictions do this by deadening consciousness through self-deception and reducing human growth to a monomania instead of honoring the mystery of life's cyclical process. The Killer is the inner character who gives up the struggle of life. None of us are exempt from the necessity to be conscious of these energies, to experience the inner cross of human freedom, to bear witness, and to make daily the creative choices that affirm and nurture human growth. To do this we need to acknowledge the fact of our propensity to addiction in order to transform it.

Although it is a Killer, the addiction itself, when transformed, can be a source for developing the power to create a new life. As one recovering addict said, "If the pain doesn't kill you, it serves to make you stronger!" In *Platoon*, a film about the ravages and addictions of war, the protagonist, in order to return and try to rebuild on the earth, had to kill the evil soldier who thrived on war and killed goodness. Taken symbolically, this means that every addict must look within, encounter The Killer rage inside, and identify it in order to be able to turn it over. If one blames others—projects The Killer outside—then the inner Killer can run free. Part of the paradox of addiction is that the interior Killer energy of destruction must be "killed"—confronted, let go, and turned over to the Creative Daimon for transformation to occur. In the creative act the new idea "kills" the old stale and rigid expressions that have lost their vital energy. Ultimately, The Killer forces all of us to face death, giving us the possibility to consciously choose a creative life.

11: THE WORLD'S NIGHT

> . . . you must remain your own witness, marking well everything that happens in this world, never shutting your eyes to reality. You must come to grips with these terrible times, and try to find answers to the many questions they pose. And perhaps the answers will help not only yourself but also others.
>
> —Etty Hillesum, *An Interrupted Life*

> . . . even in the darkest times we have a right to expect some illumination. . . . [This] may well come less from theories and concepts than from the uncertain, flickering and often weak light that some men and women, in their lives and works, will kindle under most all circumstances and shed over the time span that was given them on earth.
>
> —Hannah Arendt, *Men in Dark Times*

JUST AS AN individual can be hostage in the abyss of addiction, so can an entire epoch or culture. This is true for our epoch, which is plunged into the World's Night. Western civilization is experiencing a Dark Night of the Soul due to our self-asserting will to control, epitomized by the technology that we expect to provide us with a secure, happy, and comfortable life. What is described here in cultural terms is exactly the primary description of the addict to be found in the Big Book: "self-will run riot."

The central addiction here is a monomaniacal will to control life for the purposes of power, security, comfort, and victory. Everything that threatens that control—death, love, pain, and the indwelling space of the heart's mystery—is warded off and objectified. For example, as Heidegger describes, we try to deny death through obituary statistics or with funeral parlors that try to make death palatable by covering up the horror of death and the relationship of the living to the dark rites of dying. We try to control love and human relationships through noisy small talk and gossip, which escalates through alcohol, rather than opening up ourselves to the surprise of genuine conversation, when we listen with awe to each other and to the silence of creation. To maintain the status quo, we often dismiss the disclosure of meaning as revealed in art, song, dance, and poetry as "mere play" with words or paints or notes or body—something to entertain us—rather than that which essentially confronts us with the meaning of life and death. Instead of honoring the sacred silence revealed in the poetic image, we prefer the clear concepts of logical, rational thought. We want easy answers and "how to do it" solutions rather than insights that leave us with a new reverence for the questions of human life. Even with the horror and atrocity of world war and impending holocaust, we try to objectify the threat of death and evil by projecting it on our enemies and/or the atom bomb, rather than looking at its source within human nature. In the addiction to control, we deliver ourselves over and reduce our lives to only one part of the whole mystery we are. Heidegger has described our addictive tendencies to "self-will run riot" in this way:

> What is deadly is not the much-discussed atom bomb as this particular death-dealing machine. What has long since been threatening man with death, and indeed with the death of his own nature, is the unconditional character of mere willing in the sense of purposeful self-assertion in everything. . . . the undisturbed continuing relentlessness of the fury of self-assertion which is resolutely self-reliant. . . . What threatens man in his very nature is the view that technological production puts the world in order, while in fact this ordering is precisely what levels every *ordo*, every rank, down to the uniformity of production, and thus from the onset destroys the realm from which any rank and recognition could possibly arise.[1]

So, we lose our genuine awe before the mysterious world in which we dwell. We lose the living spirit of presence in the relentless fury of our will to control. As Martin Buber said, we reduce the living relationship with everyone and everything around us to an "I-It" relationship, which treats all beings as objects, losing the relationship to the "Thou," the mysterious Other. In this way we lose our relationship to the holy. Our addiction to control, objectified through our adoration of technology, brings us before the World's Night. The history of Western civilization has been a descent into the "Dark Night of the Soul" as described by St. John of the Cross. But it has been, in large part, an unconscious descent that has been explained away or forgotten. By objectifying the world through technology humans oppose openness and block their own path. Heidegger describes the approach of the world's night as follows:

> The man of the age of technology, by this parting, opposes himself to the Open. . . . The essence of technology comes to the light of day only slowly. This day is the world's night, rearranged into merely technological day. This day is the shortest day. It threatens a single endless winter. Not only does protection now withhold itself from man, but the integralness of the whole of what is remains now in darkness. The wholesome and sound withdraws. The world becomes without healing, unholy. Not only does the holy, as the track to the godhead, thereby remain concealed; even the track to the holy, the hale and whole, seems to be effaced. That is, unless

> there are still some mortals capable of seeing the threat of the unhealable, the unholy, *as* such. They would have to discern the danger that is assailing man. The danger consists in the threat that assaults man's nature in relation to Being itself, and not in accidental perils. This danger is *the* danger. It conceals itself in the abyss that underlies all beings. To see this danger and point it out, there must be mortals who reach sooner into the abyss.[2]

To address the issue of the World's Night and The Abyss, Heidegger enters into dialogue with the poets. The time is destitute, he writes, as he comments upon Hölderlin's elegiac poem "Bread and Wine." It is marked by the "god's failure to arrive." This does not deny the relationship with the divine that lives on in individuals and in churches. Nor does it discount this experience. But it does point to the phenomena of an era.

> The default of God means that no god any longer gathers men and things unto himself, visibly and unequivocally, and by such gathering disposes the world's history and man's sojourn in it. The default of God forbodes something even grimmer, however. Not only have the gods and the god fled, but the divine radiance has become extinguished in the world's history. The time of the world's night is the destitute time because it becomes ever more destitute. It has already grown so destitute, it can no longer discern the default of God as a default.[3]

This is The Abyss—the abyss not only of the individual soul but of the world's soul in its historical addictive decline. We do not even know we have fallen into it. In this context, the denial experienced by the individual addict is a microcosm of the denial experienced by our addictive age. In commenting upon The Abyss from this perspective, Heidegger points out that the German word for abyss, *Abgrund,* means originally the soil and ground that is undermost. As such it is the ground toward which a thing tends in its downward course of growth. For there in the ground, in the soil, it is possible to "strike root and to stand."[4] In our age, Heidegger says, the ground is absent. And thus our entire age hangs in The Abyss. In order for a fundamental turn to take place in our time, in order for a spiritual transformation to occur, there must be those who venture into The Abyss and encounter it. Otherwise, who will be there to receive the revelation? The ground must be prepared for the divine radiance to shine and be seen. Heidegger writes:

> In the age of the world's night, the abyss of the world must be experienced and endured. But for this it is necessary that there be those who reach into

> the abyss. The turning of the age does not take place by some new god, or the old one renewed, bursting into the world from ambush at some time or other. Where would he turn on his return if men had not first prepared an abode for him? How could there ever be for the god an abode fit for a god, if a divine radiance did not first begin to shine in everything that is? The gods who "were once there," "return" only at the "right time"—that is, when there has been a turn among men in the right place in the right way.[5]

The Abyss must be entered, and we must be prepared to receive the divine. Addicts who have reached the bottom and who, whether in the despair of quiet or in wailing, have cried out in humility to be released from the depths to which their addiction has taken them know this truth of the turning point. The first three steps say it clearly:

1. We admitted we were powerless over alcohol—that our lives had become unmanageable.
2. Came to believe that a Power greater than ourselves could restore us to sanity.
3. Made a decision to turn over our will and our lives to the care of God *as we understood Him.*

The poet Hölderin, who lived in The Abyss during periods of his madness, expressed this insight in his unfinished hymn "Mnemosyne."

> . . . The heavenly powers
> Cannot do all things. It is the mortals
> Who reach sooner into the abyss. So the turn is
> With these. Long is
> The time, but the true comes into
> Its own.[6]

Etty Hillesum was a person who "reached sooner" into the abyss. A young Jew in Nazi-occupied Holland, she was the child of an addictive age. The Demon Lover, in the form of Hitler's rabid addiction to power, was poisoning human life on earth. Etty, however, had found silent sacred spaces deep within herself. Even in the abyss of Nazi demonic power, she felt the divine radiance. Although her health was failing and she suffered from splitting headaches and terrible fatigue, and although she was marked by the star of David on her arm, she did not internalize the negative projections upon her. Instead, she knew she had within her vast resources of spiritual strength. She was developing her relation to "God," ". . . that deepest and richest part (of myself) in which I repose."[7] Her spiritual guides and companions were Rilke, Dostoevsky, and Jung. When she went to the concentration camp she hoped to be able to pack in her small rucksack the Bible, Rilke's *Book of Hours* and *Letters to a Young Poet, The Idiot,* and *Symbols of Transformation.*

Etty, who was fully aware of the demonic nature of the Holocaust, felt that personal resentment and bitterness were childish and inappropriate responses to the catastrophic events and course of destruction that was happening around her. Instead of trying to go into hiding or to escape, she felt her task was to give to others even in the concentration camps. Thus, voluntarily, she chose to go to Westerbork, a transit camp for the trapped Jews in Holland. She wanted to share the fate of her people and help them. She felt her path was to suffer

> what all the others have to suffer. And whether or not I am a valuable human being will only become clear from my behaviour in more arduous circumstances. And if I should not survive, how I die will show me who I really am.[8]

Her love of life was not diminished: "I am not bitter or rebellious, or in any way discouraged. I continue to grow from day to day, even with the likelihood of destruction staring me in the face."[9] Etty felt that by squarely facing the evil around her she could make the world a better place. Instead of freezing in denial, she continued to affirm meaning *in spite of* the world's dark night. At times she suffered from intense despair, but instead of succumbing to the destructive course of events, she took refuge in her leap of faith. She realized that life was a whole, both good and evil, contained within every human being. Thus the work against the forces of destruction had first to be done within. She said:

> Yes, we carry everything within us. God and Heaven and Hell and Earth and Life and Death and all of history. The externals are simply so many props; everything we need is within us. And we have to take everything that comes: the bad with the good, which does not mean we cannot devote our life to curing the bad. But we must know what motives inspire our struggle and we must begin with ourselves, every day anew.[10]

Etty hoped to pass on the spiritual work she had done in her own life to future generations so that others need not start all over again. She wanted her life to be a good example, and she hoped to make a contribution through her writing. She prayed that her life and her writing would be a worthy gift for other humans on this earth.

> Very well then, this new certainty, that what they are after is our total destruction, I accept it. I know it now and I shall not burden others with my fears. I shall not be bitter if others fail to grasp what is happening to

us Jews. I work and continue to live with the same conviction and I find life meaningful—yes, meaningful. . . . Living and dying, sorrow and joy, the blisters on my feet and the jasmine behind the house, the persecution, the unspeakable horrors—it is all as one in me and I accept it all as one mighty whole and begin to grasp it better if only for myself, without being able to explain to anyone else how it all hangs together. I wish I could live for a long time so that one day I may know how to explain it, and if I am not granted that wish, well, then somebody else will perhaps do it, carry on from where my life has been cut short. And that is why I must try to live a good and faithful life to my last breath: so that those who come after me do not have to start all over again, need not face the same difficulties. Isn't that doing something for future generations?[11]

Etty knew that what mattered most in this dreadful time was to love one another. The demonism of the Nazi addiction to power was that it reduced human beings to mere objects, to the "I-it" mode. In the last analysis, any addiction makes of the addict and those around him an "it," because it reduces the human being by objectifying the soul and spirit. In contrast, creativity fosters the I-thou relationship because it honors the mystery of the Other. Etty knew that what mattered most in this desperate situation was to honor human life creatively with love. "All that matters now is to be kind to each other with all the goodness that is in us."[12] And, at the same time, despite the imminent threat of death, to honor meaning, knowing that one has lived and died well.

. . . the main thing is that even as we die a terrible death we are able to feel right up to the very last moment that life has meaning and beauty, that we have realized our potential and lived a good life.[13]

In order to come to terms with life, Etty found she had to come to terms with death—to look it directly in the eye by accepting it and by going on. Faced with imminent death she wrote:

By "coming to terms with life" I mean: the reality of death has become a definite part of my life; my life has, so to speak, been extended by death, by my looking death in the eye and accepting it, by accepting destruction as part of life and no longer wasting my energies on fear of death or the refusal to acknowledge its inevitability. It sounds paradoxical: by excluding death from our life we cannot live a full life, and by admitting death into our life we enlarge and enrich it. This has been my first real confrontation with death.[14]

In this way, by "reaching sooner" into the abyss, Etty was able to clear a space for the dwelling place of the divine, to house eternity in her daily life. Thus, she said, the feeling grew much stronger in her that "a hint of eternity steals through my smallest daily activities and perceptions."[15]

Etty had not been an ascetic free of cravings. Rather, she had lived sensually and erotically; she had been hungry for life and wanted to own it. Through her spiritual search she realized that this longing could never be satisfied. At the time that she was writing her diaries she met an older man, a mentor and spiritual guide, whom she learned gradually to love in a nonpossessive way. Reflecting on this love and her romantic longing, she wrote:

> Whenever I saw a beautiful flower, what I longed to do with it was press it to my heart, or eat it all up. It was more difficult with a piece of beautiful scenery, but the feeling was the same. I was too sensual, I might almost write too greedy. I yearned physically for all I thought was beautiful, wanted to own it. Hence, that painful longing that could never be satisfied, the pining for something I thought unattainable, which I called my creative urge.[16]

Previously, even through her writing, she said she had wanted to hoard experience so she could have it all to herself. Through her spiritual work—learning to accept the whole of life—she was able to stop grasping and instead be open and grateful for what was there. Paradoxically, in letting go of things, she found a wealth of inner riches. As she wrote:

> And this grasping attitude, which is the best way I have of describing it, suddenly fell away from me. A thousand tyrannical chains were broken and I breathed freely again and felt strong and looked about with shining eyes. And now that I don't want to own anything any more and am free, now I suddenly own everything, now my inner riches are immeasurable.[17]

Similarly, she had always lived in chaotic anticipation of the future rather than in the moment, a step at a time. But time, too, she learned was a whole to be lived in its totality. Thus she wrote:

> And now, now that every minute is so full, so chock-full of life and experience and struggle and victory and defeat and more struggle and sometimes peace, now I no longer think of the future, that is, I no longer care whether or not I shall "make it," because I now have the inner certainty that everything will be taken care of. Before, I always lived in anticipation, I had the feeling that nothing I did was the "real thing," that it was all a preparation for something else, something "greater," more "genuine." But that feeling has dropped away from me completely. I live here-and-now, this minute, this day, to the full, and life is worth living.[18]

Etty talked of a "creative unease" which she experienced, "a strange, infernal agitation." She knew this unease could be a source for generosity if she could learn to channel it. And so she prayed: "Oh God, take me into Your great hands and turn me into Your instrument, let me write."[19] She knew she had to turn over the great chaos raging in her to something higher and to reclaim some solid ground for discipline to wrest some form and order from the "sacred unease" within. In her struggles to open herself up as a channel, Etty saw the dilemma of the creative person. She realized the necessity of looking into The Abyss of suffering and discovered in herself an urge to lose herself in it. She knew that to see the angels of creation she had to wrestle with the demons too. And she knew that this took discipline, wresting form from the chaos.

> There are moments in which it is suddenly brought home to me why creative artists take to drink, become dissipated, lose their way, etc. The artist really needs a very strong character if he is not to go to pieces morally, not to lose his bearings. I don't quite know how to put it properly, but I feel it very strongly in myself at certain moments. All my tenderness, all my emotions, this whole swirling soul-lake, soul-sea, soul-ocean, or whatever you want to call it, wants to pour out then, to be allowed to flow forth into just one short poem, but I also feel, if only I could, like flinging myself headlong into an abyss, losing myself in drink. After each creative act one has to be sustained by one's strength of character, by a moral sense, by I don't know what, lest one tumble, God knows how far. And pushed by what dark impulse? I sense it inside me; even in my most fruitful and most creative inner moments, there are raging demons and self-destructive forces. Still, I feel that I am learning to control myself, even in those moments. That is when I suddenly have the urge to kneel down in some quiet corner, to rein myself in and to make sure that my energies are not wildly dissipated.[20]

The image of a vast interior empty plain, an inner clearing where "God" and "Love" could enter the soul, came to Etty. This image expressed for her the aim of meditation, a practice that could open up inner spaces for love and creativity.

> So let this be the aim of the meditation: to turn one's innermost being into a vast, empty plain, with none of that treacherous undergrowth to impede the view. So that something of "God" can enter you, and something of "Love" too. Not the kind of love–de-luxe that you revel in deliciously for half an hour, taking pride in how sublime you feel, but the love you can apply to small, everyday things.[21]

Etty knew that by coming to grips with herself in the here and now, in this very place and time in which she lived, she could perhaps help others. Thus she saw her soul as ground for the struggles of good and evil, and the way she lived her life as the way to help heal the wounds of humankind. She wrote:

> I feel like a small battlefield, in which the problems, or some of the problems, of our time are being fought out. All one can hope to do is to keep oneself humbly available, to allow oneself to be a battlefield. After all, the problems must be accommodated, have somewhere to struggle and come to rest and we, poor little humans, must put our inner space at their service and not run away.[22]

Her duty in these catastrophic times, she felt, was to bear witness to what she saw—the evil and the good in creation, "the gaping chasms which swallow up man's creative powers and *joie de vivre*."[23] Evil, she felt strongly, had first to be eradicated within the individual. The mistake was to eradicate other humans instead. She wrote "only if deep inside, we rebel against every kind of evil will we be able to put a stop to it."[24] In the worst of times she prayed not to dissipate her strength on hating the German soldiers for:

> The rottenness of others is in us too. . . . I really see no other solution than to turn inwards and to root out all the rottenness there. I no longer believe that we can change anything in the world until we have first changed ourselves. And that seems to me the only lesson to be learned from this war. That we must look into ourselves and nowhere else.[25]

In the face of the horror around her Etty had many moments of rebellion, sadness, and despair. But she did not cling to them, nor did she prolong the agony. Rather she learned to let them pass through her "like life itself, as a broad, eternal stream, they become part of that stream, and life continues. And as a result all my strength is preserved, does not become tagged on to futile sorrow or rebelliousness."[26]

To deal with the toxicity and terrors surrounding her, Etty turned to the protective circle of prayer. Here she describes the rhythm of her interior journey and her return to the outer path:

> The threat grows ever greater, and terror increases from day to day. I draw prayer round me like a dark protective wall, withdraw inside it as one might into a convent cell and then step outside again, calmer and stronger and more collected again. I can imagine times to come when I shall stay on my knees for days on end waiting until the protective walls are strong enough to prevent my going to pieces altogether, my being lost and utterly devastated.[27]

Eradicating evil within and preserving the strength of peace, clearing a space for it to flourish and to pass on to others in the form of love—this became her goal.

> True peace will come only when every individual finds peace within himself; when we have all vanquished and transformed our hatred for our fellow beings of whatever race—even into love one day.[28]

This was no easy task, she knew. Although earlier in her life she had many romantic inclinations, now, in the face of "the world's night," she clearly saw the only way was to face them and bear witness.

> . . . but I am no fanciful visionary, God, no school girl with a "beautiful soul." I try to face up to Your world, God, not to escape from reality into beautiful dreams—though I believe that beautiful dreams can exist beside the most horrible reality—and I continue to praise Your creation, God, despite everything.[29]

Organically, as she felt a new spiritual life within, she opened to this holy presence and allowed it to flourish in herself. Her life became an increasing continual conversation with this deepest center of serenity, which she called "God." Through this inner dialogue she hoped, with her life and writing, to channel creativity for others.

> All that matters now is the "deep inner serenity for the sake of creation." Though whether I shall ever "create" is something I can't really tell. But I do believe that it is possible to create, even without ever writing a word or painting a picture, by simply moulding one's inner life. And that too is a deed.[30]

Ultimately, Etty's response to life held the paradoxical opposites. At the same time it was mystical and political. Mysticism for her was not an escape from reality but rather an active path enlightened by the clear vision of what is. As she wrote: "Mysticism must rest on crystal-clear honesty, can only come after things have been stripped down to their naked reality."[31] She chose not to escape from the horrors of the world but to face them squarely and affirm life there in the concentration camps by sharing her love and courage with others. From an Eastern perspective, one might say Etty chose the bodhisattva way of loving-kindness. The person on this path tries to peel away the veils of self-deception and addiction in his or her own self so the serene center of the Buddha nature can emerge. Then, from that serene center, the renewed person returns to the earth to try to help others discover their own Buddha nature and make the earth a better place to live for others. It is this same path that grounds the twelve steps of recovery for addicts. And so it was for Etty Hillesum, who was the child of an addictive age. In 1942 she volunteered to accompany the first group of Jews that were sent to Westerbork camp and remained there for a year working at the local hospital. With a special permit from the Jewish council she was allowed to travel back and forth to Amsterdam, delivering messages and bringing back medicine.

Although her friends tried to convince her to hide, once even attempting to kidnap her, she refused, for she wanted to understand with others what was happening. Security and comfort were not her goal. Rather, she wanted to bear witness to the catastrophe in order to help her own and future generations understand in order to transform human life on earth. Thus she wrote:

> I want to be sent to every one of the camps that lie scattered all over Europe, I want to be at every front, I don't ever want to be what they call "safe," I want to be there, I want to fraternize with all my so-called enemies. I want to understand what is happening and share my knowledge with as many as I can possibly reach. . . .[32]

Given the historical moment into which she had been thrown, Etty wanted to be the "thinking heart of the barracks," the poet who could experience life there and sing about it, the bard who could "find the words that bear witness where witness needs to be borne."[33] She felt that God had chosen her to experience so much and had given her the strength to bear it and the words to express it. Her last diary entry states: "We should be willing to act as a balm for all wounds."[34]

After she was interred in Westerbork, the few letters that reached the outside world bore witness to the devastating cruelty, horror, and outrage she saw and experienced there. Her descriptions of the hellish abysses of misery in the camps are vivid. But her philosophy did not waver. In one letter she wrote: "Against every new outrage and every fresh horror we shall put up one more piece of love and goodness, drawing strength from within ourselves. We may suffer, but we must not succumb."[35] Despite all of the atrocities she saw, just three weeks before she was sent to her death at Auschwitz, Etty wrote:

> . . . things come and go in a deeper rhythm and people must be taught to listen to it, it is the most important thing we have to learn in this life. I am not challenging You, oh God, my life is one great dialogue with You. . . . And all my creative powers are translated into inner dialogues with You; the beat of my heart has grown deeper, more active and yet more peaceful, and it is as if I were all the time storing up inner riches.[36]

To reclaim peace in ourselves and to reflect that serenity toward others, Etty believed, is the moral duty of human life on earth. Only this task of reclamation can spread peace in our troubled world. But discovering inner peace and serenity is a labor of love and prayer—digging out the divinity buried within us:

> There is a really deep well inside me. And in it dwells God. Sometimes I am there too. But more often stones and grit block the well, and God is buried beneath. Then He must be dug out again. I imagine that there are people who pray with their eyes turned heavenwards. They seek God outside themselves. And there are those who bow their head and bury it in their hands. I think that these seek God inside.[37]

With the great battle raging around her, in the midst of the devastation of human life and value by the demonic addiction to power, Etty wrote that God needed human help. Humans, she said, needed to prepare a dwelling place within them for the divinity.

> But one thing is becoming increasingly clear to me: that You cannot help us, that we must help You to help ourselves. And that is all we can manage these days and also all that really matters: that we safeguard that little piece of You, God, in ourselves. And perhaps in others as well. Alas, there doesn't seem to be much You Yourself can do about our circumstances, about our lives. Neither do I hold You responsible. You cannot help us but we must help You and defend Your dwelling place inside us to the last.[38]

Etty Hillesum felt that the greatest cause of suffering was a lack of inner preparation, which made humans give up hope even before they had set foot in a concentration camp. The World's Night needed first to be met with an inner preparation of the soul. St. John of the Cross has discussed the soul's preparation in his description of the Dark Night of the Soul. St. John described the way of the "secret stair" in the abyss to the divine. Theodore Roethke also described it in his poem "The Abyss." Rilke and Dostoevsky have pointed the way as well. Every individual who follows this path is a link in the chain of the world's conversion. In this respect, the recovering addict is among those who have made the journey into the abyss. Bill W.'s description of the chain of hope and help that became the twelve-step programs also provides an image for the turning point in the abyss, which engenders both a spiritual and social revolution. One thinks of Mother Theresa, Etty Hillesum, Rosa Luxembourg, Karl Marx, Friedrich Nietzsche, Søren Kierkegaard, Carl Jung, Sigmund Freud, Marc Chagall, Rainer Maria Rilke, Martin Heidegger, Hölderlin, Käthe Kollwitz, Joan of Arc, Albert Camus, Dostoevsky, Solzhenitsyn, Simone Weil, Albert Schweitzer, Martin Buber, Elie Wiesel—all those who have dared, in whatever way and on whatever level, to venture into the absurdities of The Abyss and to return with the gift of hope for humanity. The hope need not be an answer that would save us from The Abyss forever. As Elie Wiesel has said:

> Does this mean that hope constitutes an answer to tragedy? No. There is no answer to the tragedy my generation has lived through. It remains a mystery. And hope is part of that mystery.[39]

PART THREE: THE CREATION

In a dark time, the eye begins to see,
I meet my shadow in the deepening shade;
I hear my echo in the echoing wood—
A lord of nature weeping to a tree.
I live between the heron and the wren,
Beasts of the hill and serpents of the den.

What's madness but nobility of soul
At odds with circumstance? The day's on fire!
I know the purity of pure despair,
My shadow pinned against a sweating wall.
That place among the rocks—is it a cave
Or winding path? The edge is what I have.

A steady storm of correspondences!
A night flowing with birds, a ragged moon,
And in broad day the midnight come again!
A man goes far to find out what he is—
Death of the self in a long, tearless night,
All natural shapes blazing unnatural light.

Dark, dark my light, and darker my desire.
My soul, like some heat-maddened summer fly,
Keeps buzzing at the sill. Which I is *I*?
A fallen man, I climb out of my fear.
The mind enters itself, and God the mind,
And one is One, free in the tearing wind.

—Theodore Roethke, "In a Dark Time"

12: THE ABYSS

> In that abyss I saw how love held bound
> Into one volume all the leaves whose flight
> Is scattered through the universe around. . . .
> —Dante

THE JOURNEY OF the addict takes him inexorably into The Abyss of darkness, the depths of despair, where he reaches bottom and asks for help. It is in that long journey into night's despair that he is forced to face his powerlessness. The first step in any process of recovery is to admit that one is powerless over one's addiction and that one's life has become unmanageable. These admissions of powerlessness can turn the intense humiliation and helplessness one feels in The Abyss to humility and hope. The pivotal point in transforming an addiction is letting go—surrender.

We are fearful of, yet fascinated by The Abyss, and our fascination often draws us down to its depths. It is also the place where we can creatively transform our lives, a place whose image has been evoked in philosophy, psychology, literature, art, and religion. Nietzsche's concept of "creative chaos," Heidegger's notion of "No-thingness," the other side of Being, the existentialist image of "the absurd," Rilke's notion of "the Whole," which encompasses both life and death, Jung's notion of the "Collective Unconscious," the "Ungrund" of Berdyaev, the Buddhist notion of the Blue Dragon Cave, the mystic's image of the abyss of the "divine darkness," the physicist's concept of chaos and the black hole—all are expressions of The Abyss, which can change our rational, orderly, controlled lives into dark chaos and turn them upside down.

In "What are Poets For?" Heidegger points to The Abyss as the most significant place for human transformation. He writes:

> It may be that any other salvation than that which comes from *where* the danger is, is still within the unholy. Any salvation by makeshift, however well intentioned, remains for the duration of his destiny an insubstantial illusion for man, who is endangered in his nature. The salvation must come from where there is a turn with mortals in their nature. Are there mortals who reach sooner into the abyss of the destitute and its destituteness? These, the most mortal among mortals, would be the most daring, the most ventured.[1]

For Heidegger, whose writings challenged the rational, logical, and empirical modes of being and thinking in the twentieth-century Western world, human existence is a constant call to creativity. As humans, our very existence is the place where revelation and meaning occurs. This requires us, if we choose to be authentic in our lives, to open ourselves to listen to the revelations of Being, the process of creation, which paradoxically conceals as it reveals. We are, ourselves, beings of paradox. For example, we could not survive without using the rational thought process to control our environment. Survival requires us to be practical. But, at the same time, we are much more than our practical selves, much more than the goals we set for ourselves, or the personas we envision, or the answers we seek. Our very being is to question what it means to be. And the questions that we ourselves live are part of the creative process of Being.

The creative process is chaotic. There is in it an unfathomable void. Nietzsche says the creative challenge is to live in this chaos, to learn to walk the tightrope of the tension of the opposites within ourselves and in the cosmos. Thomas Wolfe also described the creative process:

> It was a progress that began in a whirling vortex and a creative chaos and that proceeded slowly at the expense of infinite confusion, toil, and error toward clarification and the articulation of an ordered and formal structure. My editor, who worked and strove and suffered with me through the greater part of this period, shrewdly and humorously likened the making of these books to the creation of the world as described in Genesis: "In the beginning God created the heaven and the earth. And the earth was without form, and void; and darkness *was* upon the face of the deep. And the Spirit of God moved upon the face of the waters."[2]

For Jakob Boehme, a visionary gnostic writer of the sixteenth and seventeenth centuries, The Abyss is an expression for God, the Being of all Beings, who is neither good nor evil but the source of both. In The Abyss humans are plunged into the conflict between good and evil in order to create love out of chaos. In one of his visions, Boehme wrote:

> In my inward man I saw it [The Abyss] well, as in a great deep; for I saw right through as into a chaos, where everything lay wrapped, but I could not unfold it. Yet from time to time it opened itself within me like a growing plant. For twelve years I carried it alone within me, before I could bring it forth in any external form; till afterwards it fell upon me like a bursting shower that kills where it lands, as it will. Whatever I could bring into outwardness I wrote down. The work is none of mine; I am but the Lord's instrument, with which He does what He wills.[3]

If we must enter chaos to create ourselves and our world, we must be prepared to accept discomfort, uneasiness, anxiety, restlessness, frustration, boredom, loneliness, fear, panic, depression, tears, laughter, hunger, desire, brooding, silence, and finally the expression of the new being when it emerges in exterior form.[4] These are all experiences that most of us try to avoid through our addictions. Paradoxically, the addictions through which we try to escape the revelations from The Abyss are the very experiences that force us down there to confront the mysteries of existence. Once we admit our addictions and acknowledge our powerlessness over them, we must face our time and place in The Abyss, with all of its anxiety and terror. Facing that anxiety is a feature of the creative process:

> Creative people, as I see them, are distinguished by the fact that they can live with anxiety, even though a high price may be paid in terms of insecurity, sensitivity, and defenselessness for the gift of "divine madness," to borrow the term used by the classical Greeks. They do not run away from non-being, but by encountering and wrestling with it, force it to produce being. They knock on silence for an answering music; they pursue meaninglessness until they can force it to mean.[5]

The following story of an artist whose drinking came close to ruining his life and career attests to the creative necessity of facing the chaos in the abyss consciously, by choice, without the artificial aid of alcohol. Since his recovery sixteen years ago he feels his work has become more honest, more profoundly expressive of his unique vision of reality. Since his recovery his work has also received national attention, and he is proud of it. But in the last days of his drinking he knew that both his life and his art were becoming watered down, mechanistic, false, and artificial. Paintings bursting with energy had degenerated into self-conscious, illustrational, artificial forms.

Always a shy and lonely child, Joseph felt insecure and unwanted. He spent much of his time drawing and painting, which became his major source of joy from junior high school on. Except for one uncle who drank to excess, there was no known history of alcoholism in his family. But there was a history of interest in the arts—his father was a successful commercial artist. Even though he followed in his father's footsteps, Joseph felt his father preferred his older brother to him. When he entered college in the sixties he began to drink, and suddenly became popular. Miraculously and instantaneously, drinking made him a star. He was "instantly hooked." "Getting drunk became a regular part of my life. From a shy, lonely introvert, I became a dramatic artistic personality and a 'wild hippie.' " Initially he felt the drinking freed up his painting, bringing out a series of strong and powerful sexual images. But inwardly he felt like a buffoon and a monster, and he expressed this negative view of himself in a series of self-portraits. At first his friends and colleagues covered for him because he was so gutsy and talented. But finally his drinking became disastrous.

Although during the first five years of his drinking Joseph had felt a bold and free release, in the final five years his path descended steeply downward. He was arrested many times as a "public drunk" and was also arrested for drunken driving. He started teaching his college classes drunk and missing work. He didn't pay his bills, and he couldn't organize his life. Worst of all, his painting suffered from his egoistic and artificial life. On a wild drinking binge he felt grandiose and all-powerful, and in the hangover that followed, he would work out of a sense of terrible guilt. He knew his work was becoming affected and slick, autobiographical and erotic, influenced more by pop artists than by the abstract expressionists whose work he so admired. In the last year of his drinking he lived in total chaos, drank in scuzzy bars, wrecked his car, and was jailed on his fourth DUI charge. It was the most painful, lonely, distressing, and distraught time he had ever experienced, a living hell. Finally he reached out for help to a friend and colleague he knew was in AA. He started going to meetings and working the twelve steps.

Two years after he became sober, his work was chosen for exhibit at the Whitney Museum in New York. As his recovery grew, so did the honesty of his work. The energy that formerly had been diverted into drinking was now freed up for painting, and he was able to give first priority to his art.

After he stopped drinking, his paintings became more abstract and expressionistic. He began to see how they were interconnected, how certain images would reappear in painting after painting—for example, void spaces. When his father died, his paintings took a new turn and became dark. Now his work is like a dark field with effusions of light shining through. It expresses the mystical feeling of formless flying, a feeling he often experiences in his dreams. (He is now in therapy, where he works with his dreams, though he does not as yet consciously paint from them.)

The way he works seems to fit Jung's description of the visionary process. The void spaces, flying forms, and dark fields with flying light suggest the mystic's abyss of "divine darkness." This is how he describes his creative process:

> What I love the most is the work. When I'm painting it's like praying. It's a religious, mystical experience. The Higher Power seems to come through in the process of painting and that's my connection with it. Conceptually I have a hard time with God because I had an overload of religion as a child. But the process of creating is mystical for me. That doesn't mean it's easy. Often I get scared and shaky when creating. Particularly before I start a painting I get spurts of anxiety, and I may try to avoid getting started. But if I do this I feel guilty for not working. Yes, you might say I feel possessed by the Creative Daimon. I feel the call to create. Maybe I'm addicted to creativity. Now I go to teach my classes with a hangover from painting instead of alcohol. And I know now that I'll never get rid of the pain and anxiety—that it's part of the process of life and creativity. So I make efforts to start the work that I love to do, but before which I am anxious. I wander around my studio puttering here and there. I may do collages. I may sweep the floor. Sometimes I don't sleep for thirty hours. Then a different energy takes over. Suddenly I get hooked into the process and I begin. Once in the work I'm lost. I'm just doing it. When I'm in it I'm totally immersed to look at it and look at it. I create from chaos. I like the disorder and I need the chaos to create, and there is some other order in all that. But when I create and paint, it's like praying.

The descent into The Abyss can *happen* to one, as in the case of the addict. But once the addict has fallen into The Abyss he must find the meaning of his time there and a way to return. Or, one can consciously choose to go, as frequently happens in the process of creativity. In mythology there are parallels to both ways. The innocent maiden, Persephone, is pulled into The Abyss by Pluto, Lord of the Underworld. In some versions she is entranced by a narcissus flower; in others by a poppy, from which comes opium. Icarus falls into the sea when he flies too high and the sun melts the wax that holds the wings to his body. Both figures symbolize the youthful flight of intoxication and the fall into the unconscious, representing the first unconscious part of the addict's journey. In contrast, the Sumerian goddess Inanna consciously chose to leave her place as Queen of Heaven to descend into the Netherworld. She prepared for her journey. Orpheus also consciously chose to descend to the underworld to bring back his beloved wife, Eurydice. These latter two figures symbolize the conscious descent required in the creative process and show the way the addict can turn the unconscious fall into meaningful creative transformation.

As the poet who dared to descend into the underworld, Orpheus is a fitting symbol of the creative process. If Orpheus could descend into the depths and there, even in the most frightening realm, sing, so perhaps can we. Orpheus was a poet so gifted that he could charm even the birds and the beasts. He lost his wife, Eurydice, to the realm of the dead. Descending into The Abyss, he so enchanted the powers of the underworld with his lyre that he was allowed to lead her back to the realm of the living on the condition that he not look back to see if she was following him. At the last moment of his journey out of the underworld, he looked back. Eurydice was taken back to Hades, and Orpheus had to return alone, in deep despair, to the world of the living. But he continued to sing and play the lyre. One day in the woods a tribe of mad women, the maenads, descended upon him and in a frenzy tore him to bits. A mystery religion formed around Orpheus, worshipping him as a god of rebirth and a mediator between the realms of life and death.

In his film *Orphée,* Jean Cocteau, who was an opium addict, presents his version of the Orpheus myth. Here Orpheus is a well-known poet whose creative inspiration has dried up. He is no longer popular. As he sits glumly in a café, a royal, elegant dark woman enters. Orpheus is fascinated by her. She seems to be connected to a younger poet who has replaced Orpheus in popularity but who is suddenly killed in an accident by two speeding motorcyclists ominously dressed in black. Investigating, Orpheus is pulled into the limousine of the Dark Lady, who turns out to be the Lady of Death, Queen of the Underworld. All this while, absorbed in his own anger, depression, and cynicism at his blocked creativity and lost success, Orpheus has been neglecting his wife, Eurydice.

At the Dark Lady's mansion, he finds she has many powers—she holds the power of death. Her car radio emits fragments of verse which Orpheus is irresistibly drawn to copy, believing they have been sent to him as his own future work that will restore his former position to him. Orpheus is so engrossed with these verses that he continues to neglect Eurydice. He doesn't notice she is pregnant, nor how near she is to death. But when she dies, he descends into the underworld to retrieve her. Although he is entranced by the mysterious Lady of Death—perhaps the "Lady" opium—nevertheless he leads Eurydice back to life, under the condition he shall never again look at her. Driving home, however, he again becomes so captivated by the radio emissions that he absent-mindedly looks into the rear-view mirror and sees Eurydice behind him, whereupon she is returned immediately to the realm of death. Shortly afterward, the masses, led by a group of mad women, finally desert the still unproductive Orpheus and, going berserk, murder him.

Cocteau's version is interesting because it shows the poet with a spurious relation to the archetypal powers of death and creativity. Orpheus has lost his relationship to the creative principle, due perhaps to his ambitious desire for public acclaim. Drawn to the creative powers of the underworld, he becomes a hostage to them. He hopes to copy his poems from the radio, without working on them himself. As a result of his captivation by the easy way to creativity, he forgets and loses Eurydice, the earthly feminine inspiration that gives body to his creativity. Although he succeeds in his descent to the underworld to save her, he forgets what he has learned. Again he loses faith in his own earthly human power and turns to the radio, symbolic of an artificial inspiration separated from the conscious work of forming the material. In doing so, he absent-mindedly sees Eurydice in the mirror, and they are separated forever.

Hence, forgetting his task to save Eurydice, his earthly inspiration, he loses her. In the end he is destroyed by the irrational and chaotic masses—symbolizing dysdaimonic possession by the Demon Lover—who turn against the creative individual when he fails their expectations. Cocteau's view of Orpheus suggests what will happen to the poet and anyone else who becomes so entranced by the archetypal powers that they neglect their earthly aspect. This is very common among addicts, particularly those who try to create while on drugs or alcohol. Often they are torn apart by the maenadic forces of either their own unconscious chaos or of the external crowd, which projects its own inner chaos and unlived creative expectations on them. There are many examples of addicted artists finally torn apart and devoured by the maenadic projections of the masses: Marilyn Monroe, Judy Garland, Lenny Bruce, Elvis Presley, Montgomery Clift . . . to name just a few.

In contrast to Cocteau's *Orphée,* Rilke's Orpheus is the poet who has consciously dared to descend into The Abyss without succumbing to the fascination with death or drugs and who is at last at home in The Abyss and on the earth as well. Although in his last act of nonacceptance he looks back and loses Eurydice, perhaps symbolic of the ever-present human temptation to control and require proof, he nevertheless goes on singing. Overcoming the last temptation of possessiveness, he thus enters into relationship with the whole. In Rilke's view even the maenads, mad at his betrayal of the earthly feminine, ultimately could not destroy Orpheus. For, accepting the sacrifice of his life, he becomes a part of the whole and reappears in Nature's singing. This paradox is expressed in "Sonnet 13," which Rilke has said was for him the nearest and perhaps the most valid:

> Be—and at the same time know the condition
> of not-being, the infinite ground of your deep vibration,
> that you may fully fulfill it this single time.
>
> To the used as well as the muffled and mute
> store of full Nature, the uncountable sums,
> jubilant add yourself and cancel the count.[6]

Rilke—who his whole life felt the call of the Creative Daimon—spent many years in The Abyss, waiting for the poetic inspiration to write a cycle of poems that he believed would be the reason for his being on this earth. He described his time of doubt and despair in his letters and in *The Notebooks of Malte Laurids Brigge,* hoping to work through the chaos in himself so he could be open to the creative revelations. And all the time he worked at the craft of writing, growing more capable in expressing what might come forth. Toward the end of his life, graced with the poetic song, he expressed the creative visions he finally received in the *Duino Elegies* and the *Sonnets to Orpheus.* Rilke came to see The Abyss as the essential dwelling place for humans in their creative and spiritual transformation:

> The strong, inwardly quivering bridge of the Mediator has sense only where the abyss is granted between God and us—, but this very abyss is full of the darkness of God, and where one experiences it, let him climb down and howl in it (that is more necessary than to cross over it). Only to him for whom the abyss too has been a dwelling place do the heavens before him turn about and everything deeply and profoundly of this world that the Church embezzeled for the Beyond, comes back; all the angels decide, singing praises, in favor of earth![7]

The creative process demands a descent into darkness in order to bring something forth into being. The addict has fallen into the abyss, unconsciously hung on the peg of humiliation, and trembled in terror before the chaos in his soul. Yet, all of these experiences are part of meeting the creative challenge. In describing the creative process, Nietzsche says it is just in the chaos where creative potentialities come to be. To be lost in the chaos throws us into a fertile disorder. It is there that the creative can break through and put everything into a new perspective. At this point clinging to either substance addiction or to control addiction (e.g., rational linear thought) prevents us from being creative.

It is creative consciousness "which performs the psychic alchemy necessary to transform nihilism into the 'arrow of longing' which posits meaning and value."[8] In this vein, the psychological reductionism and philosophical rationalism which tries to simplify the dynamic interplay of the many parts of ourselves into a character so clear, logical, and orderly that ultimately it becomes boring and ends in nihilism is itself a self-destructive addiction to control. Rather, it is living in the polarity, the multiplicity of different perceptions, and allowing the paradox of tension in our being, that opens up the creative. Philosopher Phyllis Kenevan writes:

> . . . if one resists the "intellectual corruption" stemming from the need to simplify and attends to the polarity, the result is not simply chaos, but a fertile sort of disorder; for it becomes closed off through systematic limiting beliefs. Even though there may be a vertigo of multiplicity and especially of contradictions, yet it is precisely in this situation that new and better beliefs can emerge. The creative potential is activated out of these open possibilities.[9]

This awakened consciousness is the hallmark of what Nietzsche calls the Synthetic Man, the person who embodies the Dionysian openness of a creative consciousness that can accept the ambiguity of the many in oneself. According to Nietzsche, creative geniuses such as Beethoven or Goethe are "virtuosos through and through, with uncanny access to everything that seduces, allures, compels, overthrows; born enemies of logic and straight lives, lusting after the foreign, the exotic, the tremendous, the crooked, the self-contradictory."[10] Here we have a description of many characteristics of the addict. Yet there is a difference. In the end the addict succumbs to the temptation to escape the tension of multiplicities by reducing himself to monomaniacal possession by the one thing to which he is addicted, losing all creative openness and withdrawing from life. In contrast, the creative person embraces life, much in the way Nietzsche describes Goethe in *The Twilight of the Idols:*

> . . . he did not retire from life but put himself into the midst of it; he was not fainthearted but took as much as possible upon himself, over himself, into himself. What he wanted was *totality:* he fought the mutual extraneousness of reason, senses, feeling, and will . . . he disciplined himself to wholeness he *created* himself.[11]

Jung, too, sees the journey into The Abyss as the deepest and most original facet of the creative process. It is in the abyss of the unconscious that "visionary" works of art are born. As he describes it, visionary art brings up from the depths primordial experiences which

> . . . rend from top to bottom the curtain upon which is painted the picture of an ordered world, and allow a glimpse into the unfathomable abyss of the unborn and of things yet to be.[12]

The source of such art, according to Jung, comes from "the sphere of unconscious mythology whose primordial images are the common heritage of mankind," which Jung calls the collective unconscious. Because they come from such a strange dimension, such works often confuse, frighten, even disgust us, reminding us of nothing or little of our daily life, "but rather of dreams, night-time fears, and the dark recesses of the human mind."[13] Works created in this way arise not from preplanned ego consciousness and control; they cannot be willed. Rather, they arise spontaneously from the depths in a sudden moment of inspiration, overtaking the conscious plans of the poet, almost writing themselves. Thomas Wolfe describes that he wrote his novels in just this way.

> It was exactly as if this great black storm cloud I have spoken of had opened up and, 'mid flashes of lightning, was pouring from its depth a torrential and ungovernable flood. Upon that flood everything was swept and borne along like a great river in the South in its flood tide of the spring, and I was borne along with it. I wrote because this floodtide power of writing had flowed through me and swept me with it, and I could not do otherwise. During that first period all that I can now say is that the writing wrote itself.[14]

In such a process the poet is a vessel through which the inspiration is formed. If the poet is not to be completely overcome by such a revelation, then he or she must be open enough to receive these revelations and strong enough to give them form. This requires a sacrifice of ego and a readiness to die which enables one to be open for transformation. The same is true for the recipient, who must be willing to die to the ordinary way of looking at things in order to receive the art work. For as Erich Neumann wrote: ". . . our time and our destiny, and often our art as well, strike us in the face, perhaps also in order to fling us into the void of the center, which is the center of transformation and birth."[15] Facing The Abyss, the "void of the center," facing death, is inherent in creative transformation. Neumann points out that death means being overwhelmed by human finitude and also by the perilous and the terrible. "It is everything that strikes the ego as suffering and ruin. In praising death as the prerequisite of every transformation that merges life and death, the poet allies himself with the creative God himself, the God of transformation who bestows and *is* life and death."[16] Sooner or later in the creative process all of us encounter death. The artist knows this and chooses to face death continually as he creates. The addict is forced to face death through his disease, and in this way is brought to the edge of creativity.

The necessity of facing death and going into a dark night of the soul is, according to Jung, essential to human development. This dark night may be forced upon one, as in the case of the addict, or it may be freely chosen, as in the case of the creator. But, in any case, it is the way of the transformation process. And, as is the paradoxical nature of humankind, the way down is at the same time the way up. Jung explains:

> When the libido leaves the bright upper world, whether from choice, or from inertia, or from fate, it sinks back into its own depths, into the source from which it originally flowed, and returns to the point of cleavage, the navel, where it first entered the body. This point of cleavage is called the mother, because from her the current of life reached us. Whenever some great work is to be accomplished, before which a man recoils, doubtful of his strength, his libido streams back to the fountainhead—and that is the dangerous moment when the issue hangs between annihilation and new life. For if the libido gets stuck in the wonderland of this inner world, then for the upper world man is nothing but a shadow, he is already moribund or at least seriously ill. But if the libido manages to tear itself loose and force its way up again, something like a miracle happens: the journey to the underworld was a plunge into the fountain of youth, and the libido, apparently dead, wakes to renewed fruitfulness.[17]

This describes the challenge for the addict who has fallen into The Abyss—to turn that addictive underworld journey into the fruitful return to life and creativity.

The poet takes the turn of transformation in The Abyss by giving expression to what he finds there. In this respect, poetry is a call to all of us to embark upon the nightsea journey. It calls us forth, if we respond, into the dark unknown by jolting us from the ordinary with its unusual and powerful images. Yet it is also an attempt, while in the depths, to articulate the numinous unknown—a primordial beginning to name that which emerges toward us from the depths. Poetry invites us to accept momentarily the death of our ordinary ego world so that we may enter into a strange, often terrifying new vision, and from this extra-ordinary experience to return renewed (as did the mythical poet Orpheus) to a higher, more differentiated level of human existence—one that can accept and dwell more consciously in mystery. It beckons us to a death that leads to the power of renewal. Jung describes the poet's call from The Abyss as follows:

> Whoever speaks in primordial images speaks with a thousand voices; he enthralls and overpowers, while at the same time he lifts the idea he is seeking to express out of the occasional and the transitory into the realm of the ever-enduring. He transmutes our personal destiny into the destiny of mankind, and evokes in us all those beneficent forces that ever and anon have enabled humanity to find a refuge from every peril and to outlive the longest night. That is the secret of great art and its effect upon us. The creative process, so far as we are able to follow it at all, consists in the unconscious activation of an archetypal image, and in elaborating and shaping this image into the finished work. By giving it shape, the artist translates it into the language of the present, and so makes it possible for us to find our way back to the deepest springs of life.[18]

Revolting against the one-sidedness that has far too long rationalized existence, the artist of the twentieth century must confront those opposite unconscious chaotic forces that have too long been repressed. Hence in the art of our time we are confronted with the grotesque and the demonic, with the surreal, with the horror of chaos and death. Consider the works of Miró, de Chirico, Picasso, Kafka, Frida Kahlo, Käthe Kollwitz, and James Joyce.

The history of Western civilization, with its materialistic values, has been precisely to try to ward off death and chaos with control and rationality lest the tenuous security that has been won, those "half-filled masks," to use an image from Rilke, be torn off. The creative task that faces all of us in our rationalistic, power-driven society is to face death and the chaos in ourselves that we have tried to suppress. This task requires descending into The Abyss. In this respect, the addict who is recovering can be a leader: he has suffered the hell of descent and has learned how to create a new life from the darkness.

One woman, a recovering alcoholic with many years of sobriety, expressed the experience of The Abyss and its turning potential for creativity this way:

> We've all been through our own individual hell and that is why we have a common bond. We are united through our experience of pain and the fact that we had a fatal illness and were just playing "Russian Roulette" through our drinking. But we have faced that pain and death and that is why we have the compassion and courage to deal with suffering—with our own

wounds and the wounds of others. AA has given me that freedom of and the possibility to help others along the way. And sobriety has me the experience of creativity. Before, when I was drinking, I know I could paint. But since sobriety I've found that I can be creative. We all have these untapped resources. Creativity is one of the most vital elements of my new life of joy.

One of the dangers of descending into The Abyss is precisely to be torn apart by the wild chaotic forces that rant and rave there. But if one doesn't take this risk, one risks losing all creative potentialities. Rilke emphasizes that courage before all aspects of existence, even the "unheard-of," is essential to the creative journey. He writes:

> We must assume our existence as *broadly* as we in any way can; everything, even the unheard-of must be possible in it. That is at bottom the only courage that is demanded of us: to have courage for the most strange, the most singular and the most inexplicable that we may encounter. That mankind has in this sense been cowardly has done life endless harm; the experiences that are called "visions," the whole so-called "spirit-world," death, all those things that are so closely akin to us, have by daily parrying been so crowded out of life that the senses with which we could have grasped them are atrophied. To say nothing of God. But fear of the inexplicable has not alone impoverished the existence of the individual; the relation between one human being and another has also been cramped by it . . . only someone who is ready for everything, who excludes nothing, not even the most enigmatical, will live the relation to another as something alive and will draw himself exhaustively from his own existence.[19]

Only if we confront the chaotic irrational powers at the very depths of our being will be be able to transform them into something meaningful. And, perhaps more important, only then will we be able to face them in another person. Facing the chaos in the abyss of our being is requisite for creative relationship. Rilke, in his personal transformation, dared to descend into The Abyss, and he waited there, in the night, for the poetic voice to speak. He dared to face the chaotic forces of creativity and tried to give them form. Although he believed in his destiny as a poet, he was tempted many times to flee it. But his "daimon," his "inner call," was too strong. Even in one of his most despairing periods, when he was overwhelmed with suicidal fantasies, he bore the tremendous conflict in his soul, and made the commitment to the creative call:

> If I look into my conscience I see but one law, relentlessly commanding: to lock myself into myself and in one stretch to end this task that was dictated to me at the very center of my heart. I am obeying.—For you

> know that being here I have wanted only that, and I have no right whatever to change the direction of my will before I have ended that act of my sacrifice and my obedience.[20]

Both creativity and recovery require sacrifice and surrender. They require a readiness to die for the birth of the new creative being—whether it is an artwork or the new person one can be.

What Joseph Campbell has said of the inward journeys of the shaman, the mystic, the mythological hero, and the schizophrenic is true for the addict and artist as well: all plunge into the same deep waters and must learn to swim if they are to survive. And the return is experienced as rebirth of a new and greater creative self with the wisdom and strength to serve others.

> The new ego is in accord with all this, in harmony, at peace; and as those who have returned from the journey tell, life is then richer, stronger, and more joyous.[21]

This readiness for the creative journey requires giving up possessiveness and expectation, dying to old ways of perceiving, daring to leap into the unknown, and being ready to be open and receive what comes, be it something or nothing. This is what is required of the recovering addict from step one through step three, the steps of surrender, hope, and receptivity.

This was Rilke's way. He waited in that monstrous abyss, trying to endure, trying not to be overcome by the horrors of a meaningless world war or by the cold absurdities and cruelty he saw around him every day, trying not to be defeated by the vacuum within, which prevented his creative vision from taking form. He tried, rather, to affirm that very abyss, believing that out of it could eventually come the treasure, believing that the "dragons" could after all be "princesses in disguise."

In *Letters to a Young Poet,* written during his descent into The Abyss, he said:

> We have no reason to mistrust our world, for it is not against us. Has it terrors, they are *our* terrors; has it abysses, those abysses belong to us; are dangers at hand, we must try to love them. And if only we arrange our life according to that principle which counsels us that we must always hold to the difficult, then that which now still seems to us the most alien will become what we most trust and find most faithful. How should we be able to forget those ancient myths that are at the beginning of all peoples, the myths about dragons that at the last moment turn into princesses; perhaps all the dragons of our lives are princesses who are only waiting to see us once beautiful and brave. Perhaps everything terrible is in its deepest being something helpless that wants help from us.[22]

13: THE DARK NIGHT OF THE SOUL

> Terrified, I sent out the
> greatest shriek, saying: "O
> mother where are you? I would
> suffer pain more lightly if I
> had not felt the deep pleasure
> of your presence earlier. . . . Where
> is your help now?
>
> —Hildegaard of Bingen

THE COFOUNDER OF Alcoholics Anonymous, Bill W., described his time in The Abyss as one of utter despair and hopelessness. After years of drinking he had run the gamut of his alcoholism. His doctor finally had given up on him, pronouncing his case hopeless from the point of view of medical treatment. For Bill W., this was a shattering blow, for it meant that he would have to be committed to a mental institution. Just at this time, a drinking friend, Edwin T., another "hopeless case," heard of Bill W.'s plight and came to see him. It was 1934, and so far there was no known cure or hope for this dreadful affliction. Much of society still judged alcoholics as being weak willed or downright immoral profligates. But on this visit, miraculously, Edwin T. was not drinking and was in a very evident state of "release," which was convincing to Bill W., to whom he described the following experience. Edwin T., too, had been in a hopeless situation due to his drinking and had been threatened with commitment to an institution. From out of nowhere he was visited in the hospital by two men who were also alcoholics but who had been released from their drinking by a conversion experience. One of them, Roland H., had originally consulted Jung for help and thinking he was cured, went back to his former life. But then he had a relapse. He returned to Jung who, accepting his limitations as a doctor and as a psychotherapist, told him that further medical or psychiatric treatment would be to no avail. From the medical point of view, Jung said, his case was hopeless. But Jung added that a genuine spiritual experience might remotivate him. To put himself in a religious atmosphere and hope for the best would be his only chance. This advice led Roland H. to seek out and join the Oxford group, an evangelical movement that emphasized the principles of self-survey, confession, restitution, and giving oneself in service to others. It also emphasized the importance of meditation and prayer. In this atmosphere he experienced a conversion that released him from the compulsion to drink. Having experienced such a powerful conversion and release, Roland H., in the company of some other alcoholics who had found similar release, personally went to hospitals and homes to help others who were also afflicted. This chain of help began to grow until it reached Bill W. When he heard Edwin T.'s story of release from his addiction, Bill W. believed him. "Because he was a kindred sufferer, he could unquestionably communicate with me at great depth. I knew at once I must find an experience like his or die," Bill W. wrote in a letter of thanks to Jung.[1] At once Bill W. returned to the care of his doctor to sober up so he could get a clearer view of Edwin T.'s release. But, although clear of alcohol, he found himself in a deep depression, unable to find the simplest faith. Edwin T. visited again, repeating his story and the simple truths of the Oxford group. But when he left, Bill W. became even more depressed. He writes:

> In utter despair, I cried out, "If there be a God, will He show Himself." There immediately came to me an illumination of enormous impact and dimension, something which I have since tried to describe in the *Alcoholics Anonymous*. . . . My release from the alcohol obsession was immediate. At once, I knew I was a free man.[2]

Following this experience Edwin T. came back to the hospital to visit Bill W., bringing him a copy of William James's *Varieties of Religious Experience*. From this book Bill W. realized that most conversion experiences have a common denominator—"ego collapse at depth." Bill W. writes:

> The individual faces an impossible dilemma. In my case the dilemma had been created by my compulsive drinking, and the deep feeling of hopelessness had been vastly deepened by my doctor. It was deepened still more by my alcoholic friend when he acquainted me with your verdict of hopelessness respecting Roland H. In the wake of my spiritual experience, there came a vision of a society of alcoholics, each identifying with and transmitting his experience to the next—chain style. If each sufferer were to carry the news of the scientific hopelessness of alcoholism to each new prospect, he might be able to lay every newcomer wide open to a transforming spiritual experience. This concept proved to be the foundation of such success as Alcoholics Anonymous has since achieved.[3]

Thus, from out of The Abyss of hopelessness and the deep collapse of the ego that Bill W. suffered as a result of his addiction, came a powerfully creative vision of communal healing—a vision that has helped re-create the lives of over one million members in AA alone throughout the world and that has led to the formation of the twelve-step programs focused toward healing many other addictions. The impossible dilemma that Bill W. faced through his addiction, the deep ego collapse faced by addicts at the bottom of The Abyss, is fundamental to spiritual conversion and to the re-creation of one's life.

The Abyss was the place of transformation for the mystics. In its depths shone the illumination of the "divine dark," where divinity revealed itself. Dionysius the Areopagite even speaks of God as the "Divine Darkness" and sees darkness as the secret dwelling place of God. In his imagery there is a "divine progression," a ladder or chain that links ordinary mortals with the divine. Another of the great mystics, St. John of the Cross, speaks of the "secret stair" by which one descends in the dark night to meet the Beloved—the way the soul journeys into union with God. But prior to that union of ecstatic rapture with the Beloved comes the Dark Night of the Soul, that painful period of privation when one feels imprisoned in The Abyss.

Just as the chaos of The Abyss is an essential aspect of the creative process, so is it essential to spiritual growth. The chaos the addict experiences in the abyss of his addiction is similar to the chaos experienced by the creative person, and to the Dark Night of the Soul experienced by the mystic. Evelyn Underhill, in her classic study of mysticism, describes this as follows:

> Psychologically, then, the "Dark Night of the Soul" is due to the double fact of the exhaustion of an old state, and the growth toward a new state of consciousness. It is a "growing pain" in the organic process of the self's attainment of the Absolute. The great mystics, creative geniuses in the realm of character, have known instinctively how to turn these psychic disturbances to spiritual profit. Parallel with mental oscillations, upheavals, and readjustments, through which an unstable psycho-physical type moves to new centres of consciousness, run the spiritual oscillations of a striving and ascending spiritual type.[4]

The growth process requires a period of chaos that intervenes between the old state breaking down and the formation of the new state of being. We see such a state dramatically manifested in adolescence, the transition between childhood and adult life. For the great mystics, such periods of chaos and misery often lasted months or even years before the new and higher state of spirituality is reached; often the dark side is experienced before the possibility of the new is apprehended. Underhill, describing this experience, writes: "The self is tossed back from its hard won point of vantage. Impotence, blankness, solitude, are the epithets by which those immersed in this dark fire of purification describe their pains."[5] Yet this very period of blackness is precisely that which contributes to the re-creation of character. This great period of negation in The Abyss is "the sorting-house of the spiritual life," just as it is the agonizing effort for the artist who gropes in the dark before the creative outburst. The descent experienced by the mystic and the artist is also experienced by the addict who, having reached the bottom of the soul's abyss, is faced with the inner trial by fire and the decision to accept his powerlessness, surrender his addiction, and move on toward recovery. Underhill describes this "dark night" as a threshold to a higher state. Heroism is required to endure and not succumb to the danger and the pain. The mystical journey is neither rational nor linear.

> Those who go on are the great and strong spirits, who do not seek to *know*, but are driven to be. . . . The states of darkness and illumination coexist over a long period, alternating sharply and rapidly. Many seers and artists pay in this way, by agonizing periods of impotence and depression, for each violent outburst of creative energy.[6]

Feelings of impotence and aridity, torments of temptation by old demonically possessed states, deception of both self and others, bitterness, anger, even hatred and denial of the Divinity, madness, and the propensity toward self-destruction—all can be experiences of the mystic and the creative person in this darkness. As the mystic Suso said of this state, "It seemed at this time as if God had given permission both to men and demons to torment the Servitor."[7] And just as the mystic and the artist must face these experiences, so too must the addict.

The Dark Night of the Soul refers to the common experience of the mystics whereby, after a period of great illumination, one swings back to emptiness, to pain and desolation, to impotence and helplessness, in preparation for the total self-surrender to the Divine. Having had an intense intuitive experience of God in the period of illumination, i.e., having had a spiritual awakening, the mystics describe this as a testing time, a time when one agonizes over feeling abandoned by God. It is a time of "privation worse than hell," according to Angela of Foligno. But it is also an essential time in which there is a dying to self, the necessary precondition to eternal life and union.

St. John of the Cross distinguishes between two phases of the Dark Night—the Night of the Senses in which the emotions, the imagination, the bodily senses, the lower part of the soul, are purged; and the Night of the Spirit, which entails the purgation of the intellect and will, the higher part of the soul. This latter period brings one down in the most drastic and often humiliating way before one's own disharmony and deprivation to face death, which clears the ground for humility and surrender to what is: the whole. Underhill describes it as the "naughting of the soul," directed to utter humility. The mystic Tauler described this abyss as follows: everything depends on "a fathomless sinking in a fathomless nothingness," necessary because "the Godhead really has no place to work in, but ground where all has been annihilated."[8] Thus, the whole process of transformation for the mystic requires "entering even further in, ever nearer, so as to sink the deeper in an unknown and an unnamed abyss; and, above all ways, images and forms, and above all powers, to lose thyself, deny thyself, and ever unform thyself."[9]

In the Dark Night, the soul is emptied and dried up. Just as the earthly lover fears abandonment and rejection by the beloved and can be possessed by jealousy and hatred, so the soul, in its intense thirst for love, feels forsaken and as dried up as is the lost wanderer in a desert wasteland. (Recall the imagery in the film *Paris, Texas,* in which the abandoned lover wanders dazed and lost in the desert prior to his transformation from an addictive relation to love.)[10]

In his description of this state of utter desolation, St. John cites the agony of Job, who was suddenly undone. For a time he hoped only for relief in death. He reminds us also of the hell of Jonas, swallowed by a beast of the sea and devoured in the darkness of its belly. He remembers the humiliation and imprisonment of Jeremiah, who experienced the indignation of a God whom he felt had turned against him.[11]

The deepest poverty and wretchedness are felt in the Dark Night. But through all this, the soul is being purged, and annihilated, purified in the fire. ". . .The soul is purified in this furnace like gold in a crucible," writes St. John, so that it is "conscious of this complete undoing of itself in its very substance, together with the direst poverty" and at times the consciousness of the experience is "so keen that the soul seems to be seeing hell and perdition opened."[12] The purpose of all this is that the soul may be humbled so that it may afterward be greatly exalted. "This dark night is an inflowing of God into the soul, which purges it from its ignorances and imperfections, habitual, natural and spiritual, and which is called by contemplatives infused contemplation, or mystical theology. Herein God secretly teaches the soul and instructs it in perfection of love, without its doing anything, or understanding of what manner is this infused contemplation."[13]

St. John continues, "the soul is as powerless in this case as one who has been imprisoned in a dark dungeon, and is bound hand and foot, and can neither move nor see, nor feel any favour whether from above or from below, until the spirit is humbled, softened, and purified, and grows so keen and delicate and pure that it can become one with the Spirit of God, according to the degree of union of love which His mercy is pleased to grant it; in proportion to this the purgation is of greater or less severity and of greater or less duration."[14]

The purgations of the soul may seem to blind the spirit and bind it into darkness. But they do so only to illuminate it, enabling soul to see the dazzling light behind. Just as a burning log is fully transformed into the fire itself, so it is with the soul immersed in the "Divine fire of contemplative love," writes St. John. First the log loses its moisture in the heat of the fire. Then it blackens and begins to smell. Slowly, the dark and ugly elements of the log are driven out as are all those aspects that are contrary to the fire's nature, until at last the purified log is transformed into the blazing beauty of the fire itself. And so it is with the soul on fire, burning in the flames of divine love. Slowly, gradually, it is purged of its evils and impurities, all those elements accidental to its being. As with the burning log, there is a stage in which the soul seems uglier, more abominable, worse than ever before, because the "Divine purgation is removing all the evils and vicious humours which the soul has never perceived because they have been so deeply rooted and grounded in it; it has never realized, in fact, that it has had so much evil within itself. But now that they are to be driven forth and annihilated, these humours reveal themselves, and become visible to the soul because it is so brightly illumined by this dark light of Divine contemplation."[15] This process happens in stages; there are periods of relief in which one can find respite and see the work that has been done. But the fire of love attacks again; the soul is increasingly refined. Burning, blackening, the soul is assailed by bitterness at the evil it sees in itself. But as purification progresses, joy increases as well. Finally, moving toward union in the divine fire, the soul consents and sings its passion for God, the ecstatic song of the divine wedding. And so St. John sings out his soul's surrender to the Beloved:

STANZAS OF THE SOUL

1. On a dark night, Kindled in love with yearnings—oh, happy chance!—
I went forth without being observed, My house being now at rest.
2. In darkness and secure, By the secret ladder, disguised—oh, happy chance!—
In darkness and concealment, My house being now at rest.
3. In the happy night, In secret, when none saw me,
Nor I beheld aught, Without light or guide, save that which burned in my heart.
4. This light guided me More surely than the light of noonday
To the place where he (well I knew who!) was awaiting me—
A place where none appeared.
5. Oh, night that guided me, Oh, night more lovely than the dawn,
Oh, night that joined Beloved with lover, Lover transformed in the Beloved!
6. Upon my flowery breast, Kept wholly for himself alone,
There he stayed sleeping, and I caressed him, And the fanning of the cedars made a breeze.
7. The breeze blew from the turret As I parted his locks;
With his gentle hand he wounded my neck And caused all my senses to be suspended.
8. I remained, lost in oblivion; My face I reclined on the Beloved.
All ceased and I abandoned myself, Leaving my cares forgotten among the lilies.[16]

In The Abyss of the Dark Night one is plunged into paradox. The stress, deprivation, trials, and tribulations are part of the process of this unfathomable transformation. But there is no redemption without the cross, say the Christians. Nor, according to the alchemists, is there the transmutation of lead into gold without going through the fire. This is also the paradox of the alcoholic's "Firewater." In this very image of opposites is the paradox that can poison or redeem. Consider the alchemist's signs for the elements for Fire, (△) which is over our heads, and Water (▽) which is under our feet. The synthesis of fire and water gives (✡), a sign not only for alcohol ("burnt water"), but also for the divinity in Kabbalistic mysticism, as the combination of the Hebrew consonants for fire and water gives the word for Heaven.[17] In nature, fire and water also combine to give us the radiant rainbow.

The great paradox of The Abyss is described by Maeterlinck as follows:

> Here we stand suddenly at the confines of human thought, and far beyond the Polar circle of the mind. It is intensely cold here; it is intensely dark; and yet you will find nothing but flames and light. But to those who come without having trained their souls to these new perceptions, this light and these flames are as dark and as cold as if they were painted. Here we are concerned with the most exact of sciences: with the exploration of the harshest and most uninhabitable headlands of the divine "Know Thyself": and the midnight sun reigns over that rolling sea where the psychology of man mingles with the psychology of God.[18]

In The Abyss is the paradox of all existence: joy mingled with terror, one's greatest loss as one's greatest possession, ignorance and knowledge, light and dark, ice and fire, life and death as One. Ultimately, though we dare to speak of this strange and uncanny space, it is ineffable. The mystic Tauler describes the paradox as follows:

> The great wastes to be found in this divine ground have neither image nor form nor condition, for they are neither here nor there. They are like unto a fathomless Abyss, bottomless and floating in itself. Even as water ebbs and flows, up and down, now sinking into a hollow so that it looks as if there were no water there, and then again in a little while rising forth as if it would engulf everything, so does it come to pass in this Abyss. This, truly, is much more God's dwelling-place than heaven or man. A man who verily desires to enter will surely find God here, and himself simply in God; for God never separates himself from this ground. God will be present with him, and he will find and enjoy Eternity here. There is no past nor present here, and no created light can reach into or shine into this divine Ground; for here only is the dwelling-place of God and His sanctuary. Now this Divine Abyss can be fathomed by no creatures; it can be filled by none, and it satisfies none; God only can fill it in his Infinity. For this abyss belongs only to the Divine Abyss.[19]

What The Abyss asks of us, ultimately, is surrender, a Dionysian abandonment that is precisely not into the pleasures of our addictions, but rather into what some of the mystics call the "God-intoxication." This is the movement of the whole person, freely and unfettered, into the whole heart of the great "Mysterium tremendum et fascinans." From the descent into The Abyss can come the gift of the humble surrendering of Love. The Sufi poet Rumi expresses this as follows:

> This is Love: to fly heavenward
> To rend, every instant, a hundred veils,
> The first moment, to renounce life;
> The last step, to fare without feet.
> To regard this world as invisible,
> Not to see what appears to oneself.[20]

Theodore Roethke lived at the edge of The Abyss. Threatened by madness from manic-depression complicated by excessive drinking and spending during the phases of his mania, Roethke wrote poetry from the depths of personal suffering. His images arose spontaneously from the soul's abyss, revealing truths of the creation. The creative act seemed to be the integrating force that held him together. From his own "dark time," he gave expression to the alienation of humans and the loss of personal communion with the divine. But in The Abyss Roethke came to see the divine light of the creative. As he said in his poem "The Pure Fury":

> I live near the abyss, I hope to stay
> Until my eyes look at a brighter sun
> As the thick shade of the long night comes on.[21]

In his poem "The Abyss" Roethke describes the journey of the soul that descends into darkness and conflict to find serenity and divine light. This poem "dramatizes, for an age that has lost its faith, an individual's hard and dark mystic way to God, whose essence he best perceives when he descends into and experiences the true nature of the Divine Abyss."[22] From the poem we can learn about the process of re-creation and recovery.

In the first stanza of "The Abyss," the speaker stands at the edge in crisis, questioning the downward path.[23]

> Is the stair here?
> Where's the stair?
> 'The stair's right there,
> But it goes nowhere.'
>
> And the abyss? the abyss?
> 'The abyss you can't miss;
> It's right where you are—
> A step down the stair.'

Clearly, the way is the way down into darkness and failure through a "cloud of unknowing." Any addict knows this way well. But the very failures resulting from addiction, if acknowledged and accepted, can be the fertile ground for growth. The fall can be an awakening for the addict, just as it is for the mystic. The slowing of the wind in the next verse suggests an image of the quiet time before the storm, the hush of anticipated revelation, the awakening to the voice of the greater Self.

Each time ever
There always is
Noon of failure,
Part of a house.

In the middle of,
Around a cloud,
On top a thistle
The wind's slowing.

Awakening to the call of something higher in us requires that we look at ourselves and recognize the unlived lives we have led when we have lived in denial and were unable to hear the call of the creative. In The Abyss, the addict must face the pain of knowing that his life blood was sucked away by the vampirism of his addiction. This requires the purgative way of intense introspection. Roethke expresses this as follows in the next section of the poem:

I have been spoken to variously
But heard little.
My inward witness is dismayed
By my unguarded mouth.
I have taken, too often, the dangerous path,
The vague, the arid,
Neither in nor out of this life.

Among us, who is holy?
What speech abides?
I hear the noise of the wall.
They have declared themselves,
Those who despise the dove.

Acknowledging the false and superficial existence we have led and naming the ones in us who "despise the dove"—those who would destroy through addiction the love and peace of the Holy Spirit—is central to the addict's recovery. It is expressed in the first and second steps, when the addict acknowledges that his life has become unmanageable and that he needs to be restored to sanity. The parallel to this on the mystic's journey is the step of Purification, which requires mortification and humiliation to break through the defenses of the ego. In order to purify himself, the mystic consciously chooses this path. This requires facing one's painful and humiliating cravings. Roethke expresses this as he calls upon the spirit of his mentor, Walt Whitman, who bears witness to love and transcendental faith.

> Be with me, Whitman, maker of catalogues:
> For the world invades me again,
> And once more the tongues begin babbling.
> And the terrible hunger for objects quails me:
> The sill trembles,
> And there on the blind
> A furred caterpillar crawls down a string.
> My symbol!
> For I have moved closer to death, lived with death;
> Like a nurse he sat with me for weeks, a sly surly attendant,
> Watching my hands, wary.
> Who sent him away?
> I'm no longer a bird dipping a beak into rippling water
> But a mole winding through earth,
> A night-fishing otter.

Here Roethke calls upon the higher power of the Creative Daimon, embodied by Whitman, to help him fend off his craving for material objects, which threaten to disrupt his new relation to the creative Self. But the caterpillar is there in the abyss; the creature who transforms ultimately into a beautiful butterfly, symbol of the psyche. The string upon which the caterpillar crawls represents the thread of connection that can reconcile the depths and the heights. Now Roethke has named the demons, called upon the Creative Daimon, faced death, seen the symbol of his transformation, and accepted his descent into The Abyss, identifying with the subterranean mole and the otter, who can fish for its nurturing needs in the dark night. His ability to give up his flight and identification with the bird and affirm the crawling creatures of the dark ground shows a humility requisite for the purification of the self and for its creative transformation.

With this experience, a new vision is possible, one that can be blinding if one is not prepared: the illumination that The Abyss itself is divine. For how can one explain that the most humiliating and painful experience of all—the fall into The Abyss—is itself the terrible fire of creation?

Roethke expresses this paradox, before which every addict who has come to the point where addiction turns into recovery and creativity stands in continual awe.

> Too much reality can be a dazzle, a surfeit;
> Too close immediacy an exhaustion:
> As when the door swings open in a florist's storeroom—
> The rush of smells strikes like a cold fire, the throat freezes,
> And we turn back to the heat of August,
> Chastened.
>
> So the abyss—
> The slippery cold heights,
> After the blinding misery,
> The climbing, the endless turning,
> Strike like a fire,
> A terrible violence of creation,
> A flash into the burning heart of the abominable;
> Yet if we wait, unafraid, beyond the fearful instant,
> The burning lake turns into a forest pool,
> The fire subsides into rings of water,
> A sunlit silence.

Here is the place where the fire becomes water, where the burning lake becomes the forest pool, the place where the opposites turn into each other. But to experience this great mystery we must be able to endure beyond the fearful instant. We must be able to wait. From the fire of the abominable comes the sunlit silence. From the misery of addiction comes serenity. From the opposition of the "Firewater" comes creation. The journey is a journey of the mystery of the opposites ("mysteriosum oppositorum," as Jung calls it). There is the cold height of the burning abyss, the "burning lake," the "cold fire." (The titles of two works in the literature of addiction, *The Iceman Cometh* and *Under the Volcano*, reflect these opposites.) Creation itself is a violence that "strikes like a fire" and unites these mysterious contraries; the fire imagery is used by many of the mystics to express the transcendent state. It is the imagery of poets from time immemorium for the fire of the creative process. And, it is the burning, searing experience of addiction.

Having passed through the fire of the opposites to the place of "sunlit silence" at the bottom of the abyss, one arrives at a new place of questioning. Having faced one's limits, one encounters new possibilities. But by now one has learned that it is by "being" and by resting rather than by striving that one finally comes to "know." Meister Eckhardt expresses this: "He must be in a stillness and silence, where the Word may be heard. One cannot draw near to the Word better than by stillness and silence. And when we simply keep ourselves receptive, we are more perfect than when at work."[24] The recovering addict knows this truth. In step three he turns his will and his life over to God and waits and listens for the Word of the Higher Power. In the same way the poet opens to receive the Word and transmit it to others. Thus, Roethke asks these questions from The Abyss:

> How can I dream except beyond this life?
> Can I outleap the sea—
> The edge of all the land, the final sea?
> I envy the tendrils, their eyeless seeking,
> The child's hand reaching into the coiled smilax,
> And I obey the wind at my back
> Bringing me home from the twilight fishing.
>
> In this, my half-rest,
> Knowing slows for a moment,
> And not-knowing enters, silent,
> Bearing being itself.
> And the fire dances
> To the stream's
> Flowing.
>
> Do we move toward God, or merely another condition?
> By the salt waves I hear a river's undersong,
> In a place of mottled clouds, a thin mist morning and evening.
> I rock between dark and dark,
> My soul nearly my own,
> My dead selves singing.
> And I embrace this calm—
> Such quiet under the small leaves!—
> Near the stem, whiter at root,
> A luminous stillness.
> The shade speaks slowly:
> 'Adore and draw near.
> Who knows this—
> Knows all.'

Here Roethke seeks a new beginning, symbolized by the child's hand reaching out and by the tendrils which seek, reach out, and naturally take hold of the new life. He asks if humans can leap over the "edge" as Kierkegaard's man of faith leaps over the abyss of despair. He has learned to obey the wind, following the spiritual forces of nature in order to bring home what he has brought up from The Abyss in the twilight fishing.

Only at this place of "half-rest," where knowing slows, can Being enter. Here the opposites dance in harmony, "the fire dances to the stream's flowing." Finally one has begun to retrieve the soul from the devil of addiction; it is almost one's own to devote to God. Finally one can draw near to the luminous being of love and adoration one has found and come to know in The Abyss. Thus Roethke unveils the secret of The Abyss. Like the stem that is lighter at the root, so at the bottom of The Abyss shines the light. The misty condition, the cloud of unknowing, the rocking between the dark opposites, are accepted, the undersong of death is heard. The shade says it clearly: "'Adore and draw near./ Who knows this—/Knows all.'" This is the truth that is revealed if one dares to enter The Abyss and honor the Dark Night of the Soul.

The descent into The Abyss culminates in the ecstasy of union, the mystical marriage, the mystic's goal, the raison d'être of the journey. This divine wedding is also the gift the addict receives if he sees his addiction as the dark part of an individuation journey toward wholeness. If accepted and transformed, the addict is purged of neurotic guilt and the humiliation of failure and opened to the grace of the transcendent power that was always within. In the final section of "The Abyss," Roethke praises the divine wedding he has found—that for which, like the addict, he was always thirsting.

> I thirst by day. I watch by night.
> I receive! I have been received!
> I hear the flowers drinking in their light,
> I have taken counsel of the crab and the sea-urchin,
> I recall the falling of small waters,
> The stream slipping beneath the mossy logs,
> Winding down to the stretch of irregular sand,
> The great logs piled like matchsticks.
>
> I am most immoderately married:
> The Lord God has taken my heaviness away;
> I have merged, like the bird, with the bright air,
> And my thought flies to the place by the bo-tree.
>
> Being, not doing, is my first joy.

The ecstasy of union which Roethke expresses here is an intoxicating merge of the soul with the Creator. The imagery of thirst and drinking is also used by the mystics to express their longing for the infinite, with intoxication a symbol of the utter delivery of oneself over to the divine, the devotion of the soul to God. The secret of the mystic union is to be "drunk with God." Rumi wrote: "God is the Sake and the Wine," and:

> With Thy Sweet Soul, this soul of mine
> Hath mixed as Water doth with Wine.
> Who can the Wine and Water part,
> Or me and Thee when we combine?
> Thou art become my greater self;
> Small bounds no more can me confine.
> Thou hast my being taken on,
> And shall not I now take on Thine?
> Me Thou for ever hast affirmed,
> That I may ever know Thee mine.
> Thy Love has pierced me through and through,
> Its thrill with Bone and Nerve entwine.
> I rest a Flute laid on Thy lips;
> A lute, on Thy breast recline.
> Breathe deep in me that I may sigh;
> Yet strike my strings and tears shall shine.[25]

To be drunk with God is to be intoxicated with the wine of Love, a spiritual experience that supplants one's worldly addictions. The addiction is no longer to a material substance, but to the divine wine of pure Love, God. For the Sufis, just as wine is symbolic of a spiritual reality that escapes all earthly limitations, so drunkenness is symbolic of the ecstasy that breaks through the confines of the ego and opens the soul to the radiant energy of the divine spirit. The mystic Nabuluai says: "Wine signifies the drink of divine Love that results from contemplating the traces of His beautiful Names. For this love begets drunkenness and the complete forgetfulness of all that exists in the world."[26]

As Sufi scholar Victor Danner points out: "The process of being addicted to the wine of Allah begins only when one perceives that it is absolutely different from worldly wine."[27] (The same symbolic meaning applies to erotic love.) While addiction to worldly things and activities blots out the ability to discern the real from the unreal and the transcendent from the transient, addiction to the divine opens up the soul for the celestial encounter. Thus, addiction to the worldly manifestations of "wine, women, and song" covers up the true thirst of the soul for transcendence.

Jung's letter to Bill W., cofounder of Alcoholics Anonymous, expresses this same insight. Jung wrote of a former patient who was an addict:

> His craving for alcohol was the equivalent, on a low level, of the spiritual thirst of our being for wholeness; expressed in medieval language: the union with God. . . . You see, "alcohol" in Latin is *spiritus*, and you use the same word for the highest religious experience as well as for the most depressing poison. The helpful formula therefore is: *spiritus contra spiritum*.[28]

This is the intoxicating truth of creation that the addict learns by falling into The Abyss, that the mystics learn by stepping down the "secret stairs" in the Dark Night of the Soul, and that the poet experiences by descending into the dark well of creativity.

14: THE BATTLEGROUND

> The awful thing is that beauty is mysterious as well as terrible. God and the devil are fighting there and the battlefield is the heart of man.
>
> —Fyodor Dostoyevsky, *The Brothers Karamazov*

> If you realize what the real problem is—losing yourself, giving yourself to some higher end, or to another—you realize that this itself is the ultimate trial. When we quit thinking primarily about ourselves and our own self-preservation, we undergo a truly heroic transformation of consciousness.
>
> —Joseph Campbell, *The Power of Myth*

IN THE ACT of creation, we wrestle with the elements. To bring the new creation into being requires our standing in the struggle between that which shelters and conceals and self-disclosing openness.[1] The artist is a gentle warrior who must stand between these opposing elements to allow and bring forth the new. What is true of the artist struggling to create a painting or a poem is true of the addict struggling to create a new being. The act of creation requires fighting the battle and knowing the battleground. Addicts who survive the deadly battle with addiction go through a process similar to the creative process. They must wrest their new being from the grips of the Demon Lover and put themselves in the service of the creative spirit that contributes to the well-being of themselves and others.

In order to create a new being, recovering addicts must review their entire lives and repair their relation to the Eros (loving energy) that was damaged through their addictive behavior. This means confronting all the dark feelings of pain that were repressed through their addictions and allowing them to resurface. Then one must sort out the painful experiences and assess one's own part and assume responsibility for it. In the twelve-step program, the work of digging down into oneself, looking at one's shadow, taking responsibility for one's own feelings, and making amends for addictive behavior are encompassed in steps four through ten.[2] These steps can be done only after the first three steps, which accept the descent into the dark abyss, acknowledge the fall to the bottom through addiction, and surrender to the greater powers that be. In these steps, the addict admits to powerlessness, recognizes a power higher than the ego, and surrenders in faith by turning the will over to that higher power.

Creative artists experience numerous parallels to this process of recreating one's life—this work phase of individuation. Thomas Wolfe, for example, wrote of the struggle, the intense suffering, and the inordinate amount of work involved in the writing of a novel, acknowledging the black abyss and his Herculean struggle with its demons. After the success of *Look Homeward, Angel,* Wolfe spent anguished years of arduous labor to bring up—he knew not what. He only knew that he must create. But after describing this experience, Wolfe concludes that he emerged not only with several novels but also with a restored faith and belief in the fortitude of the human soul. He wrote:

> It was a black, a bitter, and a brutal time, and I suppose that this huge chronicle of injustice, ugliness and suffering, gained an added darkness, a heightened anguish from the anguish and frustration of my own spirit at that time, but it is also true that I have never lived so intensely and so richly or shared with such a passionate and sympathetic understanding in man's common life as I did during those three years. That blind, kaleidoscope of night, that century of tormented living when I strove with my own demons and wrought upon the making of a book. And from it all, curiously and marvelously, there has come as the final deposit, the soul, the essence of all that period of defeat and torment and black suffering, a glorious memory, a certain evidence of the fortitude of man, his ability to suffer and endure, not to complain, and somehow to survive. And it is for this reason now that I think I shall always remember this black period with a kind of joy, with a pride and faith and deep affection that I could not at that time have believed possible, for it was during this time that I somehow survived defeat and lived my life through to a first completion, and through the struggle, suffering, and labor of my own life came to share those qualities in the lives of people all around me. And that is another thing which the making of a book has done for me. It has given my life that kind of enlargement and growth which I think the labor and fulfillment of each work does give the artist's life, and insofar as I have known and experienced these things, I think that they have added to my stature.[3]

Jung talks about this stage of the individuation process, in which wrestling with the unconscious forces calls forth the creative powers. He says:

> . . . the fight against the paralysing grip of the unconscious calls forth man's creative powers. That is the source of all creativity, but it needs heroic courage to do battle with these forces and to wrest from them the treasure hard to attain. Whoever succeeds in this has triumphed indeed.[4]

As Jung sees it the divine force itself is transformed through this process. He mentions as an example Hiawatha who "wrestles with himself in order to create himself." In the legend, Hiawatha wrestles with the corn god, Mondamin, for a mythical three days. On the fourth day, when Hiawatha conquers him, he does as Mondamin had bidden, burying him in the mother earth which later yields new corn sprouts for the nourishment of humankind. Jung points out that if Hiawatha had not conquered Mondamin, he would have been killed by him and "possessed" by a demon. When Hiawatha took on the battle and won, the daimon was transformed from the demonic into the creative. But before the creative energy could be reborn, there had to be a battle: the hero had to wrestle with the daimonic energy in its hostile form.

Sometimes the bottom of The Abyss is like a battleground, where the soul struggles against possession by monsters of the deep. At this time one must be strong. The following story of an artist, also a recovering alcoholic, shows the terrors of The Abyss and the battle for recovery. Claude came into analysis during a period of intense crisis over the breakup of a love relationship. Although he had been in recovery for sixteen years, he had a disturbing dream that he had started to drink again. Consciously he had no desire for alcohol, but the end of his affair had thrown him so off center that he started to have thoughts of suicide. He felt abandoned, rejected, and humiliated, unloveable and incapable of love. He was possessed by a lifelong, insatiable hunger for love, which could be traced back to his childhood. His father was absent emotionally. His mother, an actress who was always playing center stage, seductively pulled for his attention, then rejected him. Claude could still remember the cold hatred in her eyes when he was in her way, a look that made him feel worth nothing. He later internalized his mother's hatred in the form of low self-esteem and self-loathing. The fears of abandonment and rejection that were sparked by his mother were transferred to the women he loved. So was his insatiable longing for love, which manifested in jealousy and an obsessively possessive attitude. At the slightest rebuff he would be hurt, angry, and withdrawn, driving the women he loved away. Eventually, he would be rejected. He was also attracted to women who were hurt and abused themselves and therefore possessed by the same pattern. Ironically, his very longing for love undermined love and ended in rejection. This humiliating pattern, over which he seemed to have no control, threw him into an abyss of bleak despair, shown in the following dream:

> In a deep abyss people are hanging perilously on ropes. Over the ropes and the people, multitudes of stinging scorpions are crawling. They glisten

> and look like vivid reddish-orange creatures. I observe this horrible scene with fright and fascination. Then I am in a room with a giant black scorpion that almost fills the room. I know I must kill it. An older man and a younger man put on masks and take up swords to fight the scorpion.

The Abyss symbolized the Dark Night of the Soul into which he was plunged as a result of his love addiction. While his dreams about drinking were a warning about the danger of relapse, which haunts every alcoholic, they also reflected his need for a deeper spirituality in his sobriety. For he was still an addict in his insatiable longing. Now the potion he must not touch was the milk of his mother's poisoned love. To the scorpions in his dreams he associated self-destructiveness: stinging oneself to death like a scorpion in a ring of fire. Any addiction, be it to love, alcohol, or control, is like an imprisoning ring of fire to an addict. The stinging self-destructiveness of this man was embodied in his low self-esteem: he felt that he was no good, he was unloveable, he didn't deserve anything, and if he did get something, he deserved to be punished. These feelings, internalized due to his mother's rejection, contributed not only to his sense of unworthiness in relationship, but also to his relation to his creativity. A talented and successful artist and sculptor, he was unable to value his creative gifts.

In the abyss dream there were two scenes. In the first the people were hanging helplessly, victims of the stinging scorpions on the rope. In the second the scorpions had become one giant scorpion. Two men who were not victims were heroically armed and actively engaged in battle with the monster. This image brought to mind the painting of St. George fighting the dragon, a religious symbol of the archetypal battle of the hero with the terrible monster.

Every creative person must be heroic. Some are required to take an active role and slay the dragon from without. Others must, like Jonah, first be swallowed by the monster, dwell inside it, wait there until the proper moment, and patiently cut their way out. In life, both of these heroic modes are needed at different times. The stages that Joseph Campbell describes for the hero's journey—the surrender to the call, the trials and the struggle with the "dragons," receiving the revelation of new insight and strength, and the return to contribute to society with the new child of creation—correspond to both the phases of the creative process and the twelve steps of recovery.

The major part of this man's battle was to cut the ties with the poisoned love of the rejecting women who held him in their power. At bottom this was an interior task, for the poisoned love and the rejecting feminine had been internalized in himself and had taken the form of love addiction. But even more important was the work of loving himself. Claude struggled with the monster of rejection on a variety of levels. In his therapy he worked to understand the ways in which the negative mother relationship had been internalized and had poisoned his relationship to himself and to others. He reviewed his past relationships with women to see the underlying patterns and dynamics operating in them, then tried to catch these patterns in potential relationship as he saw them starting in his fantasies. He realized he had to build a new relationship to the feminine and learn to be friends with women, more than just the longing lover. In the course of the analysis, he had a dream which promised this transformation—the crumbling of the old heavy structures of addiction and a new relation to the feminine.

> I was under a huge and heavy superstructure—like the area in which series of freeways cross. Some twelve-year-old boys were playing ball, and poking at the huge posts. Suddenly the superstructure crumbled, and I was out free in open green pastures with a little four-year-old girl. We were exploring together. We passed an old house filled with antiques and decided not to go in but to go on. Through the green fields we came to a village—a dwelling place where I recognized a woman who was my friend.

He also did some work on the imaginal level, asking for images of the poisoned umbilical cord—a cord he had to cut. Three images presented themselves to him. An image of the ties to his ex-wife and some former lovers was of strings, easily snipped. The image of the tie to the broken love that had brought him into analysis was pictured as a thick plant root. It was hard work to saw through it, but finally he was successful. The image of the tie to his mother was overwhelming, reducing him to tears and hopelessness. As he looked up toward her, he saw the giant black smothering wings of a vampire bat hovering above his head so close that he could not see how or where to cut the tie that held him in bondage. Here, clearly, the only resource against the vampire was the spiritual sword of his twelve-step work in AA.

The vampire Dracula is one of the striking archetypal images of the Demon Lover behind addiction. As in the novel about him, it takes the combined resources of the different characters working together to fight this monster, so within the psyche it takes the combined energies of many inner figures to fight this battle.[5] In the novel, ultimately the only protection against Dracula's power is the crucifix. Before this spiritual power, Dracula cannot advance. The analogue for the crucifix in recovery from an addiction is the spiritual power of the work of the twelve steps. And, it was to this spiritual work that this artist was called.

Once more Claude reviewed his life, this time with the focus on his love addiction. He got a new sponsor from the AA program, a guide to help him in this work. The first step—the acknowledgment of his powerlessness over the love addiction that had become unmanageable in his life—was to surrender. He had already acknowledged that he was in The Abyss of addiction when he came into therapy. The humiliation of repeating this pattern so many times was overwhelming. The second step, the belief that a Power greater than himself could restore him to sanity—the act of faith, was harder. Having already experienced this faith in his recovery from alcoholism helped. The third step—to turn his will and life over to God as he understood him—was the only viable hope at this point. The way he had experienced "God" was as the love he found at AA meetings—the miracle that happens when recovering addicts get together and share the serenity, courage, and wisdom that comes out of their struggle in The Abyss and their return to the world. These three steps—surrender, faith, and hope—were essential to ground the work that lay before him.

The next task was to tackle steps four through nine—the steps of detailed inventory of his life, this time focusing on his love addiction. He had to review meticulously all his love relationships and look at his own part in their failure—his anger, resentment, fear, guilt, and pride. For even though he had been attracted to sick and wounded women who themselves were resentful and rejecting, it was only with himself that he could do the work. This is the work of the fourth step. Once done, the fifth step is called up—the admission to God, oneself, and to another human being of the exact nature of these wrongs. This he did with his AA sponsor. Steps six and seven required an honest humility and a readiness to change: he had to become entirely ready to have God remove all these defects of character and humbly to ask God to remove these shortcomings. Then he was ready for step eight—to make a list of all the persons he had harmed through his love addiction and to be willing to make amends to all of them. Step nine followed: to make direct amends to these people wherever possible, except when it might injure them or others. After a lot of soul searching he was able to do this with the woman who had just broken his heart. He was able to admit to her his own hurt feelings, anger, and jealousy, which had played a role in the breakup of the relationship. After he made this amend to her sincerely and wished her success, he felt relieved and peaceful. Then he had the following dream:

> I see a girl who is badly bitten and whose skin is shredded by a giant spider whose babies are multiplying in a threatening way. I rescue the girl from the spider, take her into my arms, and climb to a safe place at the top of a mountain. On the way, Poseidon emerges from the ocean and angrily throws a tidal wave to kill us. But the wave misses us, and Poseidon goes back into the sea. I awake as I hold the injured girl safely in my arms atop the mountain.

The giant spider is a symbol of the terrible mother, who was devouring his love and relation to the feminine. Here he completes the hero's task of rescuing the feminine from the mutilation by the devouring mother and taking her to a safe place. The injured girl symbolized his own injured feminine and his relationship to love. The tidal wave, thrown by the angry Poseidon, was a reminder of the powerful energy of the unconscious, still waiting to be transformed through his creative work.

One great amend needed to be made—the amend to himself. In any addiction it is essential to make this amend so that one can love and forgive oneself for the suffering one has inflicted on oneself through addiction. The sickness of addiction needs to be acknowledged and the harm forgiven so it can become a creative source of love and healing. This was particularly true for Claude, who felt so unloved, unloveable, and unworthy. Now he had to learn to love himself. One of the pitfalls here is self-pity—the passive mode of the victim. For him, the heroic mode required the active effort to love himself. To this end he put aside a daily period for spiritual reflection and for reviewing his life, so that the fears, angers, resentments, and guilts did not build up further. He had done the great excavation work on the wreckage of his past, trying to rebuild his life to the present. Now he had the daily task of keeping it in order. This is step ten, and it is grounded by step eleven—establishing a daily period for prayer and meditation. During this period he also said "affirmations," reminding himself that he was a loveable human being just like others. Part of the amend to himself was to remember the good things he had done. He had loving relationships with his son and daughter. He had worked especially hard to transform the wounded father-daughter relationship to a loving and creative one—a huge task of re-creation. This relationship was his first actual loving and creative relationship with a woman, and was a preview of good relationships he could have with other women—be it as a friend or lover. The last step, step twelve, is one in which the recovering addict carries the message of his own spiritual awakening to other alcoholics and tries to practice these principles in all of his affairs. This step is essential, for it is a return to the world, this time to contribute creatively instead of destructively. He embodied this step by going to AA meetings, where he could help others, and he made commitments of service there. As a gifted artist and teacher, by learning to love and honor his creative gifts, he was able, like the firebird, to give transcendental beauty on this earth for others. But most important, as he expressed it, his task on the battleground was that of "creating a new person."

The courage the addict must have to change is similar to the courage it takes to create. The act of creation requires a leap into the unknown. To create means to "bring into being." This is tantamount to bringing something out of "nothing"; writers and artists will tell you that they frequently begin creating with only a simple idea or image or phrase and through a long and arduous process finally bring something out of nothing. This process requires the courage to leap into the unknown "abyss" of nothingness; the courage to dwell in the silence of the unknown to hear what can be heard; the courage to continue despite the despair and anxiety that nothing new will come; and the courage to work with what finally appears.

In the *Courage to Create* Rollo May points out that courage requires one to be centered, and this requires a commitment, a vow to stand in the center. The act of creating, he points out, is an encounter, an engagement with reality. Creativity requires the enactment of this encounter. Actualizing one's potentialities gives one the sense of joy, the heightened awareness, and the ecstasy one feels in the creative process. All this requires the courage to choose to create and stand in the center of this ongoing process.

The act of creation is a paradox. To create one must have the courage to stand in the tension of opposites. To create one must be alone and set aside a sacred time and space to listen to the deeper Self; one must achieve a certain distance to have perspective. But one must also be involved with others. Another paradox which the creative person must bear is the "failure" or the "error" of one's work: the work always falls short of the vision, the immensity of which it never can fully express. Then, too, there is the paradox of faith and doubt in every creative process. To create one must hold one's faith that one can create, that one will be spoken to and receive the inspiration. Yet, one must live with the doubt that one might be wrong, which counters inflation, grandiosity, and fanaticism. May puts it this way: "Commitment is healthiest when it is not without doubt, but in spite of doubt."[6] Perhaps the courage required for the ultimate paradox is the courage to stand in the tension of life and death—the death of the old and the birth of the new. For ultimately all acts of creation demand new attitudes on the part of oneself, others, and society; they disrupt the old rigid views. Creativity threatens the status quo. It requires clearing away the lifeless forms in oneself and society, and also forging something new.

When we create, the "old gods" must die in order for the new ones to be born. Nietzsche's dictum: "God is dead!" meant precisely this. Creation requires the death of the old rigid psychic rulers, the old beliefs, so that the new creative ones can break through. May describes this process as a battle, saying:

> What occurs in the breakthrough is not simply growth; it is much more dynamic. It is not a mere expansion of awareness; it is rather a kind of battle. A dynamic struggle goes on within a person between what he or she consciously thinks on the one hand, and, on the other, some insight, some perspective, that is struggling to be born. The insight is then born with anxiety, guilt, and the joy and gratification that is inseparable from the actualizing of a new idea or vision.[7]

He points out that the breakthrough usually comes in a paradoxical moment—the moment of transition between work and relaxation. One must struggle in a committed way with what is trying to be born. But one must also "let go" in order to leave a space in which the new being can emerge on its own, in the way it wants. The new insights, while requiring the ego's work, struggle, and attention, often come when one least expects it.

Jules Henri Poincaré says that the breakthrough of his contributions to mathematics came suddenly, but was preceded by intense work—the struggle on the battleground. Perhaps his words will be of help to the recovering addict, for whom struggle has been paramount yet who still has not experienced the breakthrough. The twelve steps themselves emphasize the paradox of letting go and struggle. Steps one through three emphasize surrender and letting go. Steps four through ten emphasize work and struggle. Step eleven emphasizes rest, prayer, and meditation before step twelve, the step of creative contribution. Poincaré writes:

> There is another remark to be made about the conditions of this unconscious work: it is possible, and of a certainty it is only fruitful, if it is on the one hand preceded and on the other hand followed by a period of conscious work. These sudden inspirations (and the examples already cited sufficiently prove this) never happen except after some days of voluntary effort which has appeared absolutely fruitless and whence nothing good seems to have come, where the way taken seems totally astray. These efforts then have not been as sterile as one thinks; they have set agoing the unconscious machine and without them it would not have moved and would have produced nothing.[3]

In mythology, there are many parallels to the struggle of re-creating a new being. The story of Psyche and Amor tells how Psyche must perform a number of tasks to restore her relation to Eros, tasks of the creative battle that happen within the psyche of all persons engaged in the creative process. These tasks reflect also part of the process any recovering addict must perform in going through the steps. Before each task Psyche is afraid she will be unable to do it and even thinks of suicide. These are feelings of frustration to which many addicts in the recovery process will attest. They are also experienced during the creative process, particularly at the points of "creative block." But Psyche also shows a way of hope. She completes the tasks and the journey to the underworld and upon her return she regains her relation to Eros.

Psyche was originally separated from her mysterious love, Eros, because she succumbed to the suspicion with which her jealous sisters tempted her—the suspicion that her lover was a monster. He had told her she could never know or see him fully in the light: she could be with him only in the dark. Psychologically, her relationship to him was one that was not yet conscious. When she lifted a lighted lantern to see him, the glowing light revealed him to be Eros, the god himself. But when a drop of oil from the lantern fell upon him, he awoke to catch Psyche disobeying the condition of their relationship. So Psyche was separated from Eros.

In despair Psyche thought to kill herself. Had she not destroyed the pure love between them? She begged Aphrodite, the goddess of love and Eros's mother, for another chance. Aphrodite had been jealous because Psyche's beauty on earth had rivaled her own. Indeed, it was Aphrodite who had demanded Psyche's father sacrifice his daughter on top of a mountain by leaving her to be devoured by a monster. But the kind West Wind had lifted Psyche from the mountain down to Eros's palace. Now Aphrodite gave Psyche four tasks to complete in order to return to Eros, tasks so difficult that they seemed impossible. Before each task, Psyche fell into despair. The only solution seemed to be to kill herself. But each time, help came from an unexpected source. When she accepted the aid given her and struggled through her anguish to do the task, step by step, Psyche slowly regained her relationship to Eros, now a conscious one, for she had battled the obstacles and done her work along the way.

Psyche's first task was to separate into different piles an infinite number of seeds. Alone, no human could accomplish this. But some worker ants came to help her; finally the seeds were separated into the appropriate piles. The task of sorting is essential to any creative process. For example, a writer must sort out which words to use and where, and a film director must sort out a myriad of images. In recovery, the addict must sort out the various emotions that have been standing in the way of growth, the negative feelings that led him or her to addiction in the first place. The addict must sort through everything in life that has been rooted in these negative feelings. This is what is required in step four—to make "a searching and fearless moral inventory of ourselves." The inventory requires going over what has happened in the course of the addiction. It involves the adage "know thyself," often bringing up the wounds of childhood, which the addiction has covered. Recovering addicts and persons feeling powerless to create need to sort out their fear, anger, guilt, resentment, procrastination, jealousy, dishonesty, self-justification, boredom, self-pity, complacency, impatience, intolerance, perfectionism, false pride, conning, inflation and self-hatred. All these can block both recovery and creativity. Anyone would stagger before this tremendous task of sorting out the shadow. But to help with this task there are "friends": the symbolic "worker ants" within the psyche, as well as other recovering addicts, who help in one's life. Most important is the help of the great Friend, the Higher Power.

Psyche's second task provides an image for a way to approach all the frightening energy uncovered through the sorting process. In this she must gather the fleece from the golden solar rams, who are so fierce that no mortal dares approach them. Just as Psyche is about to give up and throw herself in the river, a reed growing on the nearby bank whispers to her that the trick is not to approach the rams head on, but to wait until nightfall, when their energy is subdued. By then Psyche will be able to gather the fleece that has fallen on the bushes through which the rams have raged. The fleece of the rams symbolizes the intense energy raging within the soul in the form of addiction, which can be transformed into creative energy in the recovering addict. Psyche is advised by the reed not to face the rams' energy head on by herself alone, but to be patient and wait and gather the fleece a little at a time.

If a recovering addict were to face all the pain and guilt and negative feelings from the past by himself alone, all at once and head on, it would be overwhelming. Timing and accepting helpful counsel are suggested in this second task. One of the pitfalls of the addict's thinking is precisely this: "*I* can do it all by myself." Step five, like "the reed," suggests proper timing and the helpful presence and dialogue with another human being in order to look at the shadow energy. In step five one admits to God, to oneself, and to another human being the exact nature of one's wrongs. This step entails confession as a dialogue to contain the acknowledged darkness in oneself. In addition to the presence of another human being, there is also help from the holy presence (God) to contain these dark energies. The twelve-step programs emphasize the essential importance of the community of recovering addicts, who can help each other face and deal with the underworld energies that they all have experienced and must consciously confront and acknowledge.

The importance of seeking guidance from a sponsor, another addict who has already traveled consciously between the depths and the heights, is also stressed. The sponsor is like the eagle of vision that appears in Psyche's third task. Here she must fetch and contain the water from the river that flows between the deepest spot in the underworld and the top of a mountain encircled with dangerous serpents. Again, it seems impossible, and Psyche starts to give up. But an eagle comes to her aid and by flying is able to bring back the water in a crystal bowl. The water is the water of spiritual life for which any addict thirsts in the deflating depths of The Abyss and the heights of inflated desires. The crystal bowl is a symbol for containing the spiritual waters of the soul. The recovering addict needs to find this containment within the Self, and often first feels this "crystal bowl" in the containing love of the group of recovering addicts surrounding him or her at every meeting. Psyche's third task is a symbolic expression of the recovering addict's need to contain the creative waters of spiritual life and to accept the love and help of others in that process.

In the fourth and final task Psyche is told by Aphrodite she must journey to the Underworld where she is to face its queen, Persephone, and obtain a box containing the secret of Beauty. Psyche must then bring back the box unopened and give it to Aphrodite. Again, Psyche falls into despair. Those who go into the Underworld do not return. So how can she, a mere mortal, succeed in this most impossible of trials? She sees a tower and climbs to the top to jump to her death. But from the tower a voice speaks to her: this task is possible if she takes the necessary precautions. She must take with her coins for the ferryman to cross the river Styx, which must be traversed to reach Hades. And she must take cakes to feed the big black dogs that guard the gates to the Underworld. Above all, she must not take pity on beggars or anyone and give these items away. Otherwise she will not be able to complete her task. And one thing more—she must accept neither food nor drink, even if Persephone offers it to her. For no one who eats or drinks in the Underworld returns. This was indeed the error of Persephone herself, who while playfully sniffing the poppy flower, had been kidnapped and taken hostage by Pluto to be his bride. When her mother, Demeter, Goddess of Growth, demanded the return of her daughter, she was led by Pluto back to the Earth's domain. But just before Persephone was to leave Hades, Pluto tempted her with the taste of a delicious pomegranate. Forgetting the rule not to eat or drink while in the Underworld, Persephone took a bite of that most delicious pomegranate, whereupon she was taken back to Hades to rule as its queen. The analogy to the addict here is striking: like Persephone, he is taken down to the Underworld unconsciously and remains there in forgetfulness or denial of the addiction. Given the chance to return, if he forgets the fate of the addiction—that to "eat or drink" of it is fatal—and in relapse partakes of the addictive substance or activity, he is returned, hostage once again to the demonic forces that possess him.

Psyche is a symbol of the recovering addict who consciously makes the journey to the Underworld to retrieve the creative energy that was lost there. In this fourth and final task, she is told to face Persephone, symbolic of the addict self, but cautioned not to eat or drink, no matter what Persephone offers her. Facing Persephone is essential, for the recovering addict can never lose sight of the addict within himself. He must always balance his potential for recovery with the reality of his addiction. This is one of the dramas one witnesses in every AA meeting, where a recovering alcoholic tells his story—the "drunkalogue" of his past and the way he has come to recovery—holding the tension of these opposites in his psyche in "creative attention." The others present remember the same drama within themselves, thus joining together in a "creative consciousness" of their shared journey through the fire. Together, they are, like Psyche, facing Persephone. Like Psyche's tower, the twelve steps are a vertical force that reminds them of their goals of creative recovery and the discipline needed to achieve them. Were they to indulge the beggarly part of themselves in self-pity, or indulge one another's fears, they would lose sight of the sobriety necessary for survival. That is why the straightforward attention to the *work* of the steps is necessary. One must face the addictive underworld self and retrieve the energy lost in addiction in order to be able to return to the world and create.

On hearing the Tower's counsel, Psyche makes the journey to the Underworld successfully. She avoids the grasping hands of those who play on her pity and still has the coins and cakes when she needs them for the ferryman and the guard dogs. Once in the Underworld she faces Persephone, accepts neither food nor drink, takes the box, and returns to the Earth. But, she has yet to give the box back to Aphrodite.

The great danger following the descent to the underworld is spiritual inflation. Inflation occurs when one takes what belongs to the gods—when one sees oneself as "godlike" and loses touch with one's mortality. When Psyche opens the Beauty Box that belongs to Aphrodite and takes ointment for herself, she sinks into a deep sleep. In the specific context of love addiction, one might say that Psyche succumbed to the "anima addiction," wanting to be the most beautiful and ideal loved one. In the myth this is expressed when Psyche wants to possess the secret of beauty to enchant Eros. But Eros is a holy power that can never be possessed by a mere mortal. Thus Psyche's journey is marked by failure, which paradoxically reminds us of the very thing she forgot—our human path is one of "progress not perfection." Perfection is an inflated ideal against which the recovering addict must always be on guard. For there, in pride, lurks the Demon Lover. Recovering addicts are constantly reminded of this at their group meetings. In every meeting, after the twelve steps are read, comes the following statement:

> Many of us exclaimed, "What an order! I can't go through with it." Do not be discouraged. No one among us has been able to maintain anything like perfect adherence to these principles. We are not saints. The point is, that we are willing to grow along spiritual lines. The principles we have set down are guides to progress. We claim spiritual progress rather than spiritual perfection.[9]

Psyche's failure is a reminder to every recovering person that the goal is neither perfection nor possession. Rather, recovery is a cyclical day-by-day process, not aimed in a rational linear way at a completed end. In the twelve steps of recovery, as in the work of creation, the "battle" is not aimed at "victory," the possession of a power or an end goal to be won. As Rilke once wrote: "Who talks of victory; to endure is all."[10] The goal of victory and power is the temptation offered by the devil of addiction, who is "cunning, baffling, powerful. . . . Without help it is too much for us," we are reminded in the Big Book. "But there is One who has all power—that One is God."[11] For Psyche, this prophecy comes true. Even though at the end she falls into unconsciousness when she opens the Beauty Box, Eros comes to her rescue and raises her to the heavens to be his bride. From their union is born a daughter, Joy. If Eros is understood to be merely the erotic love of mortal man this ending denigrates the feminine. It even validates the addictive way. But, interpreted from the viewpoint of recovery, Eros, as the Higher Love of the Creator, is "the One who has all power—that One is God." Thus the myth suggests it is never too late for the human soul (Psyche) to be lifted to the heavenly plane, nor to enter into the divine wedding and give birth to Joy. However, it is only after Psyche's Dark Night of the Soul that this happens. As the mystic Mechtild of Magdeburg says of her own trials:

> There comes a time when both body and soul enters into such a vast darkness that one loses light and consciousness and knows nothing more of God's intimacy. At such a time when the light in the lantern burns out the beauty of the lantern can no longer be seen. With longing and distress we are reminded of our nothingness.[12]

But, like Psyche, Mechtild accepted her trials and the battleground of suffering and thus she could finally write:

> From suffering I have learned this: That whoever is sore wounded by love will never be made whole unless she embrace the very same love which wounded her.[13]

And Hildegaard of Bingen, one of the great celebratory mystics, says:

> Beaten down by many kinds of illnesses, I put my hand to writing. Once I did this, a deep and profound exposition of books came over me. I received the strength to rise up from my sick bed, and under that power I continued to carry out the work to the end, using all of ten years to do it.[14]

15: THE SOUL ON FIRE

> Without suffering, happiness cannot be understood. The ideal passes through suffering like gold through fire. The heavenly kingdom is attained through effort.
>
> —Fyodor Dostoevsky

THE STORY OF Dostoevsky's life—his flight and fall into addiction and the gift of his spiritual recovery and creativity—shows a soul on fire. Through the transformation of his own addictive patterns into creativity, Dostoevsky was, like all recovering addicts, a "witness to the fire." He was "possessed" by the energies of both the Demon Lover and the Creative Daimon. Many of the archetypal figures of addiction are portrayed in the various characters in his novels. From him, we can learn in depth not only the powerful machinations of the mind of the addict, but also the transforming and redemptive path of recovery and creativity.

Dostoevsky lived for literature. From the time he was born, his parents read aloud to each other and shared their love of literature with their children. The peasant wet nurses who frequented the home also influenced Dostoevsky, for they told Russian fairy tales that stirred his imagination. The legend of the firebird was one of his favorite stories. Russian folklore was his first experience of literature, and already at three years old he was creating his own fairy tales. He was also moved, when quite young, by the lives of the saints in Russian legend. One of Dostoevsky's most treasured childhood memories is a prayer he was taught by one of his peasant nurses: "I place all my hope in Thee, Mother of God, preserve me under Thy protection."[1] When he was four, his mother taught him to read and write.

Born October 30, 1821, in Moscow, Dostoevsky was the second son of seven children. His father was a doctor who worked at the Hospital for the Poor. The dark side of life—the hospital surroundings of suffering, sickness, poverty, and death—was a part of his early childhood. His father was a complicated and sensitive man, jealous and distrustful, given to bursts of temper and depression and despondency, who lived in fear of poverty. He loved his children, but his despotism and his angry outbursts were frightening for them. A wild child, Fyodor often got in trouble with his father. His mother—who died when Dostoevsky was in his teens—was very loving, gentle, and humble. After her death, his father turned to drink and debauchery, and is said to have been murdered by his own mistreated serfs.

As a child, Fyodor had been described by his mother as a playful "ball of fire." But at school, his contemplative, introspective, and dreamy nature predominated. He tended to be pensive and unsociable. The few friends he admired were intense, romantic, poetic, and mystical. Rather than engineering—which he and his older brother Mikhail were required to study—his passion was for literature: Homer, Hugo, E. T. A. Hoffmann, Schiller, Walter Scott, Pushkin, Shakespeare, Gogol, Goethe, and Balzac. The literature he read, he lived in his own being, and this was more "real" to him than outer events. He was always searching for the secret of human existence. At eighteen, certain of his vocation, he wrote:

> My soul is no longer susceptible to its former violent impulses. Everything in it is as quiet as in the heart of a man who conceals a deep secret. I am learning a good deal about "what is man and what is life;" I can study human characters from writers with whom I spend the best part of my life, freely and joyfully. This is all I can say about myself. I have confidence in myself. Man is a mystery. It must be unraveled, and if it takes a whole lifetime, don't say that it's a waste of time. I am preoccupied by this mystery because I want to be a human being.[2]

After graduation from the Academy of Engineers, Dostoevsky entered the military service. In addition to his salary he received every month his share of the inheritance from his father's estate. No matter how much money he had, it was never enough. He lived in disorder and wild extravagance. He was constantly at the pawnbroker's to borrow money, to be gambled away at once. But he continued to dedicate himself to literature. In 1844, he left the military service to devote himself to writing.

His debts now mounting, he felt poor, one of the cold and starving. It was at this time that he began to write his first novel, *Poor People,* in which he expressed how the power of money is used to humiliate those who don't have it. A perfectionist, he wrote at his desk day and night, constantly revising, never completely satisfied with the form of his work. Everything hung on the success of this first novel, and he agonized over it to such an extent that he even thought of suicide. Brief moments of ecstatic inspiration turned to agony as he tried to put his vision into words.

Poor People—a masterly psychological tale with the qualities of a social novel—was a resounding success, a brilliant portrayal of the internal feelings and external realities of the poor. One of the images Dostoevsky used in this book is the debtor and his bondage to the moneylender. The main character, in debt to his landlady, has sold his overcoat. Cold and humiliated, he is ridiculed by his fellow workers. All his hopes rest upon a loan, but when he visits the moneylender, he fails to get it and falls into despair. At the same time he suffers from an impossible love for a young girl who marries a wealthy man for security. Finally he takes to drink and dies. In *Poor People* Dostoevsky showed how poverty robs people of their self-respect, without which they cannot live a truly human life. In many ways this novel also showed the roots of The Underground Man who, when degraded, suffers, grows bitter, and rebels.

About this first novel—now seen as an event in the history of Russian literature—one critic wrote Dostoevsky:

> Truth has been revealed and proclaimed to you as an artist; it has been apportioned to you as a gift. So, value your gift and be faithful to it, and you will be a great writer.[3]

Ecstatic from this praise, Dostoevsky vowed to remain forever faithful to his destiny as a writer. He felt that something new had been born. This moment, he wrote later in *Diary of a Writer*, was the most blissful of his whole life, one that was to sustain him even during the prison sentence of hard labor that he was later to serve.

Suddenly fame catapulted Dostoevsky to the top. Previously he felt inferior to his wealthy relatives. Now the center of attention—especially in literary circles—he became inflated and arrogant, intoxicated with success. Shy and nervous, he did not know how to behave socially. Offended, the other young writers, led by Turgenev, began to ridicule him, both in the meetings of writers and in literary lampoons. Eventually, Dostoevsky was so humiliated that he literally ran out of one of the meetings. And so again, he became "the outsider." Like Icarus, after his flight to the heights of fame, he fell into the sea of humiliation. He began to suffer from depression, dizziness, and hallucinations, hemorrhaging of the heart, and nervous attacks later diagnosed as the early signs of epilepsy.

Many of the next works Dostoevsky wrote were criticized even by formerly favorable critics as romanticizing the unhealthy and the madhouse. Realism was now fashionable, and Dostoevsky's visionary mysticism was seen as a "step down." Scathingly, one critic wrote: ". . . we may have hit bottom with this genius." Many perceived the success of his first novel as merely the sign of a passing literary trend.

In addition to poor mental and physical health, and bad reviews,

Dostoevsky was also suffering great financial stress. Continually in debt to the editor of *Fatherland Notes* for the advances he received for unpublished works, he had to do proofreading and newspaper work to survive. This "slave work," as he called it, kept him from writing the deeper novels he envisioned. He lamented that this system of advances interfered with his hope, talent, and creative longing. Thus, later in his life Dostoevsky gave the following advice to young writers:

> Remember that you must never sell your soul. . . . Never accept payment in advance. All my life I have suffered from this— . . . Never give a work to the printer before it is finished. This is the worst thing you can do. . . . It constitutes the murder of your own ideas.[4]

Dostoevsky's financial excesses and his constant indebtedness were signs of addictive patterns. From his own life, he knew well the figure of The Moneylender—to whom one could sell one's soul, integrity, and creativity—be it a pawnbroker or unscrupulous publisher. In *Crime and Punishment,* it was a moneylender that the protagonist decided to murder. The victim of parricide in *The Brothers Karamazov* was also a moneylender.

In Dostoevsky's early works one can find portraits of archetypal addictive characters—The Moneylender, The Underground Man, The Romantic, the Demon Lover, and the Wounded Woman. In *The Double* one finds a characterization of an Underground Man who lives so resentfully that eventually he trusts no one, finally succumbing to a paranoid state of madness. The short story *Mister Prokharchin* probes the loneliness of the human soul in the guise of the miser Prokharchin. Addicted to being rich, he becomes an ascetic, starving himself in the process. In *The Landlady* we see an early portrayal of the Demon Lover's power. In *A Faint Heart* Dostoevsky describes The Romantic's desire to swim in the continual ecstasy for which his ardent heart longs. *White Nights* further develops the romantic archetype. In the unfinished *Netochka Nezvanovna,* Dostoevsky presents two sides of the feminine (the proud and the meek) wounded by dissolute fathers and a nihilistic patriarchy—a wound that Dostoevsky later ascribed to the loss of faith and the devaluation of Mother Earth.

Dostoevsky was a writer who lived with his characters. His writing was his individuation process. As one biographer described it:

> The hours of Dostoevsky's doubting and despair were transformed into the very tragedy of (his character's) life. It is in his creative work that the writer realized *the possibilities of his own spirit.* . . . This is the reason why

> there is so much "anguished torment" in Dostoevsky's psychological approach. He analyzed his own self not for the sake of dispassionate knowledge, but as a *therapy*.[5]

Each of Dostoevsky's characters is a facet of his own psyche which, through writing, he tries to understand and transform in order to reconcile the disparate parts of his personality. Embodied in his books, these inner figures develop their own uniqueness and meet their own respective fates.

While he was writing these early works, Dostoevsky was facing his own anxiety and deflation. His quick rise to public acclaim and his consequent fall, forced him to look at the dark sides of himself, at his own vanity, his romantic longing, his fearfulness, his resentment, and his terror of being. He wrote:

> . . . little by little with the first approach of twilight, I gradually begin to succumb to that state of soul which now comes to me so frequently at night, in my sickness, and which I call *mystical terror*. It is a most oppressive, tormenting fear of something I myself cannot define, of something that is not understood and that does not exist in the natural order of things, but that without fail, perhaps this very minute, will happen, as though in mockery of all the arguments of reason, and will come to me and stand before me as an undeniable fact, horrible, unseemly, and implacable. This fear usually grows more and more intense in spite of the arguments advanced by my intellect, so that finally the mind, in spite of the fact that at these times it assumes perhaps an even greater clarity, nonetheless is stripped of all power to resist these sensations. It goes unheeded. It becomes useless, and this inner split serves only to intensify that frightening anguish of anticipation. I guess that it is somewhat like the anguish of people who are afraid of the dead. But in the anguish that I experience, the uncertainty of the danger intensifies my suffering even more.[6]

Dostoevsky was experiencing The Abyss into which people fall when they face the awesome creative realm. It was this inexplicable darkness that Dostoevsky was probing in his work.

On the inner level Dostoevsky was confronting his inability to control life and his anxiety before the unknown. Synchronistically, he was soon to be faced with his own impending death when in 1849 he was arrested for subversive political activities and condemned to die.[7] On December 22, 1849, Dostoevsky, along with the other prisoners found guilty, was taken to the parade grounds where a huge scaffold covered with black cloth had been raised in the middle of the square. The death sentence was read, and each prisoner was given the cross to kiss. Swords were broken over their heads, and they were given white shirts, final dress to wear for the execution. Three by three they were led to the execution posts. Dostoevsky was in the second group, so he would have enough time to hear the first shots, yet would not have more than a minute to live. But, instead of the shots, at the last moment a retreat was sounded and a reprieve from death was read to the prisoners, after which an actual sentence was given. The Tsar had ordered a mock execution to shock the prisoners! The sentence given to Dostoevsky was four years of hard labor in Siberia and thereafter service as an ordinary soldier. His right to publish was taken away. Significantly, one of the people who implicated him as a revolutionary was someone from whom he had borrowed money—a dark, demonic moneylender to whom Dostoevsky felt he had sold his own soul, referring to him as "my own Mephistopheles."[8]

Directly facing his death affected Dostoevsky profoundly. Hours after his reprieve, he wrote his brother:

> Brother, I have not lost courage and I do not feel dispirited. Life is life everywhere, life is within ourselves and not in externals. There will be people around me, and to be a *man* among men, to remain so forever and not to lose hope and give up, however hard things may be—that is what life is, that is its purpose. I have come to realize this. This idea has now become part of my flesh and blood. . . . They will lacerate and torment me now, it is true! But I have, inside me, the same heart, the same flesh and blood that can still love and suffer and pity and remember—and this, after all, is life. . . . Never before have such rich and healthy reserves of spiritual life been seething in me as now. But will my body stand the ordeal?—that I do not know. I am setting out in poor health. . . . How many images to which I have given life and which are still alive will perish, will be snuffed out inside my head or will spread like poison in my blood! Yes, if I cannot write, I shall perish. Better fifteen years of confinement with a pen in my hand! . . . If anyone remembers me unkindly and if I have quarreled with anybody or left him with an unpleasant impression of me, ask him to forget about it, if you happen to come across him. There is no bile or malice in my soul, and I should like so much, at this instant, to love and to press to my heart any of these former acquaintances. It is a joy; I experienced it today as I was taking leave of those who were dear to me before I was to die. . . . When I turn back to look at the past, I think how much time has been wasted, how much of it has been lost in misdirected efforts, mistakes, and idleness, in living in the wrong way; and, however I treasured life, how much I sinned against my heart and spirit—my heart bleeds now as I think of it. Life is a gift, life is happiness, each minute could be an eternity of bliss. Si jeunesse savait! Now, at this

> turning point in my life I am being reborn in another form. Brother! I swear to you that I will not lose hope and will keep my spirit and my heart pure. I shall be reborn to something better. This is all my hope, my whole consolation![9]

Having faced death, and receiving the gratuitous gift of his life at the last moment, changed Dostoevsky's philosophy. The gift of life was an experience of the heart, greater than rational understanding could comprehend. Although it took him many years to fully realize the extent of its meaning and to express it in his novels, with this experience Dostoevsky was reborn.

In prison, Dostoevsky had to wear heavy shackles. The conditions were brutal—swarms of lice and fleas were everywhere; the room reeked from defecation pails; the prisoners were squeezed together; and the noise and clamor were unbearable. Many of the criminals resented Dostoevsky, who was from a noble class and whose taciturn temperament was offensive to them. Still worse he was never able to be alone. His health suffered, and he began to have fits. Dostoevsky's time in Siberia was a veritable hell, described later in *The House of the Dead.* But despite the degradation and misery, Dostoevsky learned much about the criminal mind and also about the Russian people, whom he began to believe were extraordinary. For under the rough hard shell of many of the convicts, Dostoevsky found the gold of deep, strong, and beautiful characters. These four years of suffering in prison were a turning point in his spiritual development. The isolation of imprisonment forced him to look at himself and his past, to make a conscious re-examination of himself:

> I remember that all that time, despite my hundreds of companions, I lived in terrible solitude. Alone in my heart I re-examined all my past life, sorted out everything to the last detail, carefully thought about my past, *judged myself* unyieldingly and sternly and even at some times blessed fate for having sent me this solitude without which neither this judgment of myself nor this stern re-examination of my previous life would have taken place. And with what hopes did my heart then start to beat! I thought, I resolved, I swore to myself that in my future life there would be neither those errors nor those falls which had previously been made. . . . I waited, I bade fate to hurry, I wanted to put myself to the test once again in a new battle. . . . Freedom, a new life, *resurrection from the dead.* What a glorious moment![10]

In taking his own "fourth step," Dostoevsky cleared away a space in his soul for hope, for the seeds of a new life. In the very misfortune and suffering that was thrust upon him, he found that "one thirsts for faith as 'the withered grass' thirsts for water, and one actually finds it, because in misfortune the truth shines through."[11] In prison, Dostoevsky encountered the presence of Christ among the criminals—not the Christ of the Church, but the human image of the radiant Christ, the most beautiful and loving of human beings.

In 1854 Dostoevsky was released from prison to serve the rest of his sentence in the military. By edict of the Tsar he was not allowed to publish, but at last he was free to read and write in the little time he had left over from his oppressive duties as a soldier. But, there, unexpectedly, in this forlorn outpost, Dostoevsky fell in love for the first time—a tragic and devastating love that sucked up much of his creative energy. Maria Dmitriyevna was about thirty, an attractive blonde with a capricious and passionate nature, well read, and cultured. She was married to a drunkard, living in poverty with her husband and a young son. Her wretched suffering attracted Dostoevsky. However, she never fell in love with him and even considered him a "man without a future."[12] When her husband was transferred to another town, she left with him, and Dostoevsky wept bitterly. Soon afterward, her husband died, and Dostoevsky sent her money (which he himself had to borrow), along with ecstatic and despairing love letters. But Maria was now toying with the proposals of two other men. Mad with love, Dostoevsky teetered on the brink of suicide and insanity: "I'm an unhappy madman! Love in such forms is a disease."[13] This was love fraught with hysteria, jealousy, dramatic outbursts, agony, and occasional moments of bliss. As Dostoevsky wrote in a letter to one of his friends:

> Ah, may God spare all men this terrible, this dreadful feeling. Great is the joy of love, but its sufferings are so intense that it is much better never to love. I swear I reached the bottom of despair.[14]

When, however, Dostoevsky was promoted, Maria agreed to marry him. To pay for the wedding, Dostoevsky went in debt. From the start the marriage was difficult. Immediately after the wedding, Dostoevsky had a fit which repulsed and frightened his new wife and threw him into a deep depression: his epilepsy was now diagnosed as certain. The couple was married for seven stormy years until Maria died from consumption. But in the last years they lived apart, and Dostoevsky fell passionately in love with another woman. Nevertheless, he spent the last days of Maria's life with her, at her bedside, in forgiveness and compassion.

During his first three years of exile, Dostoevsky's energy and passion were so devoured by his love for Maria that he could not write, even though his thirst to write tormented him continually. But finally he wrote some comic tales in which "the dreamer" is deromanticized. For after spending four years in prison, his romanticism had to crumble. In March 1859, Dostoevsky was allowed to return to Russia, although he was not permitted to live in the capital. He decided to settle in Tver, a city which he came to consider as one of the most hateful upon the earth. Then, after many letters of remorse and apology for the mistakes of his youth, he was permitted to publish and return to St. Petersburg, exactly ten years after the time when he had been exiled.

Finally, Dostoevsky felt free to work on *The House of the Dead*, in which he began to explore the nature of the prisoner and the philosophy of crime. Layered beneath his journalistic depiction is a profound psychological analysis of the personality of the prisoner and a metaphysical inquiry into the conflict of good and evil within the human soul. Dostoevsky's description of the prisoner corresponds to that of the person hostage to an addiction. The hallmark of the prisoner is to be without a will, *to lose one's freedom*. One can eventually become accustomed to the physical sufferings; the real torture is the psychological restraint. One of the prisoner's greatest passions is for money, because it gives the illusion of freedom. The prisoner will go through the greatest danger and toil for a single kopeck, save them up, and in one spree spend it all. Why? So he has the illusion of freedom, which he values more than money.

> What is more precious than money for the convict? Freedom or some sort of dream of freedom. . . . The word convict means nothing else but a man with no will of his own, and in spending money he is showing a will of his own. In spite of brands, fetters and the hateful prison fence which shuts him off from God's world and cages him in like a wild beast, he is able to obtain vodka, an article prohibited under terrible penalties, to get at women, . . . and even persuading himself, *if only for a time*, that he has infinitely more power and freedom than is supposed. He can in fact carouse and make an uproar, crush and insult others and prove to them that he *can* do all this. . . . Moreover all this disorderliness has its special risk, so it all has a semblance of life, and at least a far-off semblance of freedom. And what will one not give for freedom? What millionaire would not give all his millions for one breath of air if his neck were in the noose?[15]

The spree of the prisoner in *The House of the Dead* is akin to the spree of the addict who, in his or her wild indulgence, feels "freedom" but awakens to find an even greater imprisonment. The greatest torment to humans, Dostoevsky points out over and over again, is the loss of freedom. If a human being were to be given a palace but was never allowed to leave it, the palace would become a prison, and its inhabitant a sullen and resentful hostage. Dostoevsky writes:

> Try, build a palace. Furnish it with marble, pictures, gold, birds of paradise, hanging gardens, every sort of thing . . . and enter it. Why, perhaps you may never even have the desire to come out! Perhaps, as a matter of fact, you might not go out! Everything is to be had! The best is an enemy of the good. But suddenly a trifle! Your palace is enclosed by a fence, and you'll be told: everything is yours, delight in it! But only do not go one step away from here! And believe me at that same moment you'll want to be rid of your paradise and to step over beyond the fence. Moreover, all this magnificence, all this luxury will even foment your suffering. It will become offensive to you, precisely because of this splendor.[16]

Such a palace is a "gilded cage," recognizable by every addict who consciously has felt trapped by a romantic relationship, obsession for power, or money or sex, a glass of wine or a line of cocaine. The reason the prisoner, or addict, becomes so sullen and irritable, so morose and resentful, is because human dignity is lost when there is no freedom. Humiliated, the prisoner-addict becomes resentful like Dostoevsky's later character, The Underground Man, who would rather live by his own stupid will than in the "Crystal Palace" of dreams. But the resentment, although it is a manifestation of longing to be free, only increases the imprisonment to the point of frenzy.

There are two basic types of prisoner, Dostoevsky writes, those that are gentle-hearted and humble and those that are strong willed. The former is able to transform humiliation to a spiritual humility because he is able to love and to turn his will over to the good. But the latter, out of contempt, puts his will higher than all others, "as it were, considering himself better than all the rest."[17] Like Lucifer, he becomes inflated with the grandeur of evil, feels above *all judgment,* and believes that for him "everything is permitted." The encounter with this type of character, who feels neither repentance nor suffering from any inner anguish, and who feels above all other humans and all morality, deposed Dostoevsky's former dreamy romanticism, along with his humanistic utopianism. From this time on Dostoevsky was forced consciously to confront the problem of good and evil, a confrontation that engendered his spiritual transformation.

While Dostoevsky was writing *The House of the Dead* (1860–1862) he was also working on another novel, *The Insulted and the Injured* (1860–1861) in which he presented another Demon Lover figure, Prince Volonsky, who understands the perverse dynamic of victim and victimizer and capitalizes on it for his own powerful purposes. The victim's pleasure in being miserable and pride in being humiliated are intricate parts of the love addiction that Dostoevsky describes in so many of his novels and which he lived out dramatically in his own life. Love triangles abound in his novels, reflecting what happened in his own love with Maria—he pitied her humiliated state and his pity increased his passion. When she tormented him in his love by pitting him against a younger man and an elderly wealthy suitor, his passion increased even further. He wrote that he would die or go mad if he had to lose her. But once he finally had married her, his passion ceased, and he later described his married life as unhappy, hard, and bitter. But this experience was not enough to inhibit Dostoevsky's passion for unfulfilling love. In 1861 he met Polina Suslova, a young student of twenty, and fell madly in love with her. Flattered by the attention of a famous author and attracted by his opposition to oppression and serfdom, Polina, the daughter of a former serf, returned his admiration. In contrast to the pitiable Maria, Polina was proud, vain, independent, and beautiful. Yet she also had a childlike naiveté and enthusiasm. After their first sexual encounter, she became angry at the lustful way Dostoevsky treated her. Moreover, he excluded her from his literary creativity and wanted to keep her as his mistress. She refused to accept the subordinate position. Expecting the ideal love he had depicted in his novels, she found instead male chauvinism and lust. Her love turned to hate, and subtly she began to take revenge on him. Nevertheless, she continued to see Dostoevsky off and on and eventually met him in Europe in 1863.

On his way to meet Polina in Paris, Dostoevsky stopped off in Wiesbaden, a gambling center. Caught between his two great loves, gambling and Polina, the roulette wheel won out and Dostoevsky stayed until he lost most of his money. Meanwhile, Polina was having a passionate love affair in Paris with a young Spaniard. By the time Dostoevsky arrived, he was too late. Again he was plunged into despair—abandoned for a younger rival. Even so, they continued their journey together, traveling platonically.

Dostoevsky suffered under these traveling conditions with the unobtainable Polina, who enjoyed her dominant position. He spent most of his time in the casinos. For Dostoevsky, as for many addicts, the dynamics of his love addiction were meshed with those of his gambling. In each, he was the loser! Polina, like a co-addict, did not oppose his gambling: she knew his losses gave her all the more power over him. In her imagination, she was reveling in the struggle of her two rivals, and she continued to torture Dostoevsky by flirting with younger men. Alternately she was cold and loving with him. All this only increased Dostoevsky's passion for her, in typically addictive fashion, just as his losses increased his passion for gambling. In Baden-Baden he lost almost everything. There, too, he had an encounter with Turgenev that later seemed to increase the hostility between the two writers. During these gambling sprees and his tormenting travels with Polina he conceived the idea for *The Gambler*, in which he described both the destructive love relation as well as the hellish prison that the casinos came to embody for him. By this time, Dostoevsky knew that his tortured relationship with Polina was self-destructive, but he could not understand this fatal love. Several years later he expressed it in a letter to her sister as follows:

> Apollinaryia is a great egoist. Her egoism and vanity are colossal. She demands *the utmost* of people, all the perfections; she will not excuse a single failing out of respect for other good features, but she herself refuses to acknowledge even the slightest obligation toward others. She chides me, to this day, for having been unworthy of her love, she constantly complains and rebukes me. But it was she who, in 1863, met me in Paris with the words: "You have come a bit late," meaning that she had fallen in love with someone else, although two weeks earlier she had written me an ardent letter telling me she loved me. . . . I am still in love with her, very much in love, but now I do not want to love her any more. She *is unworthy* of that sort of love. . . . She has always treated me haughtily. She was offended because I, too, wanted at long last to speak up, complain, disagree with her. She will not countenance equality in our relations. All human feeling is absent in her relations with me. Why, she knows very well that to this day, I am still in love with her. So why does she have to torture me?[18]

In her diary, Polina had written down the feelings that were her response to Dostoevsky:

> When I recall what I was two years ago I start to hate D. He was the first to kill my faith. . . . Now I feel and see clearly that I cannot love, cannot find happiness in the delight of love, because a man's caresses will remind me of *abuse and suffering.*[19]

Nonetheless, Polina became a model for many of the women who inhabit Dostoevsky's novels, such as Grushenka and Katerina in *The Brothers*

Karamazov. And, toward the end of his life, he referred to Polina as his "eternal friend."

When Dostoevsky finally tore himself away from the roulette tables in Bad Homburg, it was because he heard his wife was dying. Upon his return to Russia to be with her, he wrote *Notes from Underground,* one of his darkest novels—an analysis of resentment and cynicism. Dostoevsky described writing *Notes* as follows:

> Sat down to work, to the tale. I am trying to get it off my shoulders as soon as possible. . . . In its tone it is too strange, and *the tone is bitter and savage,* could offend; consequently, it's necessary that poetry soften and support everything.[20]

One of his most brilliant works, *Notes from Underground* became the prologue to his great later novels. It was Dostoevsky's cynical rejection of romanticism and idealism and also of the socialistic utopianism based on rational principles. An analysis of The Underground Man's defiance and the resentment that is at the bottom of addiction can be found in Chapter 4 of this book. But in the context of Dostoevsky's life story, it is significant that he wrote about this archetypal figure immediately after his torturous European trip with Polina. Moreover, the suffering and imminent death of his wife, to whom he had been addicted formerly, haunted him all the time he was writing it. The Underground Man mocks romantic love and shows the demonic hatred for love and goodness that is often aroused in the soul of the sinner. This resentment arises because he feels rejected in love and his dream of brotherhood has been betrayed. Underneath is a yearning for something better, but it takes a descent into ugliness and horror to discover a deeper faith. (The novel contains passages about faith in God that were censored at the time.) In order to get to the real depths of the soul's transformation, Dostoevsky believed one had to face the malicious despair in oneself and be conscious of that ugliness. Thus, in his notebook, he wrote:

> The tragedy exists precisely in the ugliness. . . . I am the only one who has portrayed the tragedy of the underground, a tragedy that comes from suffering, from the recognition that there exists something better that cannot be reached.[21]

At the end of all his resentful cantations, The Underground Man paradoxically alludes to the need for faith when he admits:

> And so, hurrah for underground! . . . Ah, but even now I am lying! I am lying because I know myself that it is not underground that is better, *but*

something different, quite different, for which I am thirsting, but which I cannot find!'"

This passage shows that Dostoevsky understood very well, as do all recovering addicts, that the only way to achieve spiritual regeneration is to confront their resentment in order to clear the way for new light to shine forth.

In April 1864, his wife, Maria, finally died. Then, only three months later, his beloved brother, Mikhail, died of a liver infection. Overcome with grief and fear, Dostoevsky felt utterly alone. Moreover, Mikhail had left his family burdened with debts from the journal which the two brothers published, and the family blamed Dostoevsky for this misfortune. Dostoevsky offered to assume the debts to help out. Finally, he was himself in danger of being thrown into debtors' prison. At this time he signed over the rights to future works to the literary speculator, Stellovsky, as security for a 3,000-ruble advance on a future novel, which he committed himself to finish by November 1, 1886. If Dostoevsky did not deliver the completed work by that date, Stellovsky would own all of his future work for a number of years. The unscrupulous Stellovsky actually paid Dostoevsky only a small portion of the sum in cash for he also bought up promisory notes due on the journal and held Dostoevsky responsible for them.

In this situation of debt and threats from his creditors, Dostoevsky headed for the gambling halls of Wiesbaden with only 175 rubles. Within five days he had lost all his money, even gambling away his watch. He then tried to borrow money from friends—even from Polina, who was there briefly. The hotel manager denied him food and candles. Finally a Russian Orthodox priest came to his rescue and put him on the coach back to Russia. From this humiliating situation eventually emerged *Crime and Punishment*, which he began writing on his return. *Crime and Punishment* first appeared as installments in the journal *The Russian Messenger* and was an immediate success with the public. But the critics, with several exceptions, misunderstood the novel, and some even claimed he was attacking the younger generation. Interpreting it externally, they did not see that Dostoevsky was trying to penetrate to the heart of the battle of good and evil within the human soul.

Before Dostoevsky had finished *Crime and Punishment*, his November 1 deadline with the moneylender-publisher was looming, and he had not even begun the promised novel. Although he asked Stellovsky for a few months' grace, the publisher refused. He had speculated that Dostoevsky could not finish a novel by the deadline. In effect, this best-selling author would become his slave for the next years. Some of his friends offered to help him write the novel, but Dostoevsky could not honestly accept their offer. He did agree to try working with a secretary who would take dictation. Working with Dostoevsky was difficult. He dictated too quickly and he was often peevish and temperamental. But, the stenographer, Anna Grigoryevna Snitkina, had greatly admired Dostoevsky's novels—her nickname was "Netochka" after one of his heroines. Patient and diligent, she stuck to the task, and on October 30 she handed him the completed copy of *The Gambler*. When Dostoevsky went to deliver the completed manuscript, the unscrupulous publisher was not there, hoping to prevent the delivery. Dostoevsky went to the district police from whom he was able to obtain a receipt attesting to the date of delivery. In only twenty-six days, with Anna's help he had completed an entire novel—and the speed with which they worked together seemed to have heightened the novel's suspense. He asked Anna to continue to work with him to finish *Crime and Punishment*. He also told her of a recent dream in which he was sorting through his manuscripts, putting them in order, and there he saw a gleaming object, a tiny brilliant diamond. Knowing the "diamond" to be Anna, Dostoevsky proposed that very day. Accepting his proposal, Anna laughed and said she was not a gleaming diamond, but merely "a very ordinary little stone."[23] But Dostoevsky, whose creativity sparkled with diamonds, knew he needed that simple little stone to keep him grounded.

The love between Anna and Dostoevsky was not grandly romantic. Nor did it seem to have the same addictive pattern as his loves for Maria and Polina. Rather, it seemed to be a consciously chosen relationship. Dostoevsky was tired of his solitude and he also wanted children. Twenty-five years younger, Anna felt primarily compassion and admiration for this immensely gifted man. Through her practicality, her capacity for endurance, and her religious nature, she was able to give him the nurturing and stability he needed. As a woman who wanted to help people, she knew this was how she could also be of service to the history of Russian literature. She devoted herself to Dostoevsky all of her life.

One biographer describes her role as follows:

> . . . she was his devoted wife, self-denying collaborator, passionate admirer. Anna Grigoryevna comprehended little of her husband's ideas, did not share in his spiritual life, but stood as a faithful guardian at the door of his study. To her he owed the relative well-being of the final years

> of his life, the domestic comfort, the orderly existence. She quietly endured everything, forgave, comforted, worried, supervised, managed the household, raised the children, transcribed his novels, took care of the budget and correspondence, set aside money for a rainy day. She lived only by him and for him; after his death she devoted herself to the cult of his memory.[24]

Although Dostoevsky's family opposed their marriage, on February 15, 1867, the couple wed. After the celebration, as after his first, Dostoevsky was stricken with two severe epileptic attacks. Again, he was advised by his doctor to go abroad for treatment.

With some of the money Anna had prudently put away they were able to go abroad for their honeymoon and for his cure. Going abroad was also a way to escape the threat of debtors' prison, for Stellovsky still held a number of the writer's old promisory notes. For Anna, it was also a way to escape the hostility of Dostoevsky's relatives. Although the couple planned to be away for only three months, their stay abroad was to last four years.

In Europe they settled in Dresden. At first things were idyllic, but then Dostoevsky became moody and difficult, and the couple found themselves quarreling constantly. Jealousy also was an ugly problem between them. Anna was jealous of Dostoevsky's continued correspondence with Polina, and he was jealous when she went to a stenographer's conference in Germany. Abroad, Dostoevsky felt homesick; he felt he needed the inspiration of the Russian soil. Attempting to escape from his restlessness, he went to Bad Homburg to try his luck at gambling. Although he intended to stay only for a few days, instead he remained until he had lost all of his money.

In *The Gambler* Dostoevsky had compared the hell of the roulette table to the hell of prison in *The House of the Dead.* Even before his marriage to Anna, he knew that his gambling had to be countered by something greater. As Anna wrote in her memoirs:

> Once, when he was for some reason in a particularly anxious mood, he told me that he was standing at a crossroad at that moment and that three paths lay open before him: to go to the East—to Constantinople and Jerusalem—and remain there, perhaps forever; or to go abroad and play roulette and there to immolate himself in that game he found so utterly engrossing; or finally, to marry again and seek joy and happiness in family life.[25]

Despite the fact that Anna was an inordinate helpmate and a loyal and devoted wife, she seems for a while to have been a co-addict to his gambling. She even pawned her favorite jewelry to support his habit, even though she knew she would never see it again.

> I took off my earrings and brooch and looked at them. Perhaps this was the last time I would ever see them—it was so hard, so hard. I loved these things—I had after all been given them by Fedya, they were my dearest possessions. . . . Fedya said it was hard to look at me, hard to take these things from me. But what was he to do? We had known all along that it would turn out this way. In secret I said farewell to my things and kissed them.[26]

It may not have been merely from powerlessness that Anna stopped protesting his gambling, for this addiction was a way to bind him to her. In this drama, he was the villain—the victim of an obsessive passion—and she was the angel—the one who could make things right. She wrote:

> I had been asleep for quite a long time, and when I opened my eyes, I saw Fedya standing by the side of my bed. He was dreadfully perturbed. I understood at once that he had lost the ten gold pieces I had given him. I tried to calm him and asked him if he wanted more money, and he thanked me profusely, it was as if I had done him a great kindness, . . . He promised to come back as soon as possible. . . . But it was not until eleven o'clock that he returned, once again in a dreadfully perturbed state. He begged and implored for forgiveness, God knows for what—said that he was a villain and I an angel, and so on ad infinitum. It was almost impossible to make him quiet down.[27]

Finally Anna came to understand that her husband's gambling was not due to a weak will but rather that it was a disease over which he had no control.

> It seemed strange to me at first. How was it that Fyodor Mikhailovich, who had so courageously endured so many and such diverse sufferings in his life—imprisonment, the scaffold, banishment, the death of his beloved brother, of his wife—how was it that he did not have enough will power to keep himself in check, to stay inside a definite limit of losses, not to risk his last thaler? This seemed to me even rather degrading, unworthy of his lofty character! And I found it painful and wounding to acknowledge this weakness in my dear husband. But I soon understood that this was not a simple weakness of will but an all-consuming passion, an elemental force against which even a strong character could not struggle. One had to come to terms with it, to look at his gambling passion as a disease for which there was no cure. The only means of struggle was flight. But we could not flee Baden before receiving a considerable sum of money from Russia.
>
> In fairness to myself, I never reproached my husband for his losses and and I never quarreled with him over them (he prized this aspect of my

> character). I handed over the last of our money to him without a murmur even though I knew that my things would certainly be lost if they were not redeemed in time (which did indeed happen), and even though I had to suffer the unpleasantness of our landlady and our petty creditors.
>
> But it wounded me to the depths of my soul to see how Fyodor Mikhailovich was suffering. He would come back from the roulette tables (he never took me with him, considering a young, respectable woman out of place in a gambling hall) white, exhausted, barely able to stand on his feet. He would ask me for money (he had handed over all our funds to me), go away and come back again for more within a half hour, even more distraught. And this would go on until he had lost every penny we had. When there was nothing to go the roulette hall with, and nowhere to get money from, Fyodor Mikhailovich would be so crushed that he would start sobbing, fall on his knees before me and beg my forgiveness for torturing me with his behavior. He would fall into utter despair. And it cost me much effort, much convincing and exhortation to comfort him, to picture our position as not so hopeless, to think of ways out of it, to direct his attention, and his thoughts elsewhere.[28]

Dostoevsky was intoxicated with the risk of gambling. Anna thought he even looked like a drunkard in the gambling halls—he had a red face and bloodshot eyes—although Dostoevsky was generally very moderate in his drinking due to his epilepsy. Like all addicts, his tendency was to put blame for his gambling on externals. If he lost, it was because he was distracted by other gamblers. Often he became quarrelsome and offensive in the gaming rooms. If he had intended not to gamble, but instead found himself losing at the roulette table, again it was blamed on externals. In one case he said that "a scoundrel of a waiter" at his hotel had failed to wake him up in time to catch his train. With several hours left on his hands before the next train, what was left to do except to pass the time at roulette? Of course, he lost all of his money except for the fourteen-franc train fare.

With respect to his gambling, Dostoevsky's denial was enormous. In one breath, he justified his gambling with a plan for winning, and in the next he denounced the repulsiveness of this obsession. In a letter to Anna, he wrote:

> Yes, here one must be made of marble, *superhumanly* cold and cautious—then there is *no doubt* that one can win *as much as one wishes to*. One must merely have plenty of time, many days, and if one is not lucky, one must content himself with small winnings and not try too hard. One of my fellow-gamblers has held out for several days, always gambling with terrible, *inhuman* coldbloodedness and calculation. Now the bank is begin-

> ning to fear him: he rakes the money towards him in great piles and goes home each evening with at least one thousand gilders. In short, I shall do my utmost to gamble as carefully as possible. On the other hand I have not the strength to remain here very long. To be frank, Anna, all this is repellent. It is so foul that I would prefer to run away from myself, and when I think of you, I am drawn to you with the whole of my being. Oh, dear Anna, I know in advance how sorely I need you.[29]

Dostoevsky knew his passion for gambling was destructive and ultimately demonic, eating at him in much the same way that his love for Polina had devoured his soul. But he was caught in the whirlwind, in the dizzying atmosphere of gambling that he had described in *The Gambler*, in the intoxication of challenge. Yet, it was this urge to live intensely on the edge of The Abyss and to push beyond all limits that also drove him to surpass himself creatively. The very struggle with fate at the edge of the precipice that he experienced at the roulette table was the same force that fed his creativity. In a letter, describing his obsession with gambling, he had once written disparagingly about himself: "And the worst part of it is that I have a vile and overly passionate nature. Everywhere and in everything I drive myself to the ultimate limit, all my life I have been overstepping the line."[30] In his novels, too, his characters try to cross the frontiers and struggle to transgress the limits, just as Dostoevsky continually crossed and created new frontiers with his writing. A gambler and a love addict, he knew intimately the power of the Demon Lover and portrayed that figure brilliantly in his work. He also knew how to struggle with that energy and transform it creatively through his writing. He knew the greater power of the Creative Daimon. Instead of adding to the destructive and nihilistic forces in the cosmos, Dostoevsky wanted to give humankind a gift, and consciously he suffered and sacrificed himself to do this. Eventually, through his writings, he freed himself from most of his addictions.[31]

From the gambling center of Saxon-les-Bains, in November, 1867, Dostoevsky wrote his wife that he had hit bottom and would never gamble again. Work on the novel, he knew, was the only thing that could save him.

> Anya, my beloved, I have gambled everything away, everything! Oh, dear angel, don't be sad, don't be apprehensive! Rest assured that the day will soon come when I shall at last be worthy of you, when I shall no longer rob you like a coarse, filthy thief! Now the novel, the novel alone, must save us. Oh, if only you knew what hopes I have of it! Be sure that I shall reach my goal and earn your respect. I shall never gamble again, never.

> Exactly the same thing happened two years ago in Wiesbaden. The situation was desperate then, too, but my work saved me. I shall now take up my work with hope and love—and in two years' time you shall see![32]

Although this was not yet to be the end of Dostoevsky's gambling, it was the beginning of a novel about a new inner figure—a compassionate man with a pure and beautiful heart, "a wholly beautiful individual."

When Dostoevsky returned to Geneva, he wrote one hundred pages in three weeks time about a character who promised redemption from his own tragically addictive passions. Dostoevsky had been wrestling with many ideas about the hero for a new novel. His notebooks show sketches of a protagonist who is full of pride, one who is bored and becomes self-destructive. But the image of the "holy fool" won out. Again, Dostoevsky had taken an advance for the novel and had promised the first installment for January 1868. Writing *The Idiot* was for him like the risk he took at roulette. Dostoevsky himself makes this analogy:

> Then (since my entire future depended on it) I set about the painful task of inventing a *new novel*. . . . For a long time already, there was one idea that had been troubling me, but I was afraid to make a novel out of it because it was a very difficult idea, and I was not ready to tackle it, although it is a fascinating idea and one I am in love with. That idea is—*to portray a perfectly good man*. I believe there can be nothing more difficult than this, especially in our time. I am sure you will agree entirely with this. The idea used to flash through my head in a somewhat artistic form, but only *somewhat*, not in the full-blown form that was needed. It was only the desperate situation in which I found myself that made me embark upon an idea that had not yet reached full maturity. I took a chance, like at roulette. "Maybe it will develop as I write it!" That is a quite unforgivable thing to do. On the whole, a plan has taken shape. As I go along, various details crop up that I find fascinating and stimulating. But the whole? But the hero? Somehow the whole thing seems to turn on the figure of *the hero*. That is the way it has evolved. I must establish the character of the hero. Will it develop under my pen?[33]

Thus, the "beautiful individual" was born out of his desperate financial situation, and he risked letting this premature figure develop on the printed page. His character, Prince Myshkin, was an enigma who gradually created himself. It was not until the end of the novel that the author was at all clear about him. Just as the parents of a new baby do not know beforehand the person they bring forth, so it was in writing for Dostoevsky. All creation is a *risk!* The difference between the risk of an addiction and the risk of the creative process is that the former leads in the end only to slavery and self-destruction, while the latter opens up new worlds.

During the writing of *The Idiot,* Dostoevsky experienced both the miracle of birth and the tragedy of death. In the winter of 1868, Anna gave birth to a daughter, whom the couple named Sonya, after his niece and the heroine of *Crime and Punishment.* The birth of this "angelic soul" was a great delight and gift for Dostoevsky. But only three months later Sonya died of pneumonia, and Dostoevsky and Anna were left in despair. The death of his daughter brought forth the question that was formulated by a later character, Ivan Karamazov: How can the suffering of even one little child be allowed by a good God and how can it be forgiven? Shortly after Sonya's death, the couple moved, first to Vevey in Switzerland and then to Italy. Dostoevsky found it agonizing to continue writing *The Idiot.* He also learned he had been put under surveillance by the secret police in Russia. Under the stress his epileptic attacks increased and he feared he was going mad. The spiritual agony he was undergoing was infused in his novel, and there are many parallels between the author and his protagonist: the background of impoverished aristocracy, the disease of epilepsy, a four-year exile from society (Dostoevsky in prison; Myshkin in the sanitorium), and an intense mystical experience and religious perspective. Through Myshkin, Dostoevsky spoke about the ecstatic feeling a deadly disease could engender:

> "What if it is disease?" he decided at last. "What does it matter that it is an abnormal intensity, if the result, if the minute of sensation, resembled and analyzed afterwards in health, turns out to be the acme of harmony and beauty, and gives a feeling, unknown and undivined till then, of completeness, of proportion, of reconciliation, and of ecstatic devotional merging in the highest synthesis of life?" . . . It was not as though he saw abnormal and unreal visions of some sort at that moment, as from hashish, opium, or wine, destroying the reason and distorting the soul. He was quite capable of judging of that when the attack was over. These moments were only an extraordinary quickening of self-consciousness—if the condition was to be expressed in one word—and at the same time of the direct sensation of existence in the most intense degree. . . . "Yes, for this moment I seem somehow to understand the extraordinary saying that *there shall be no more time.*"[34]

Although Dostoevsky here is speaking as an epileptic, the recovering addict can experience the same sense of wholeness and reconciliation from having been in The Abyss.

In *The Idiot* the struggle of a "wholly beautiful individual" thrown into a "fallen world" is described. Prince Myshkin's physical appearance is similar to that of the Christ pictured in Russian icons. He, too, is a stranger to this world, a "holy fool," an innocent who believes in paradise on earth.[35] He embodies the principles of love, compassion, forgiveness. The baser passions of hatred, jealousy, and pride are foreign to him. Awkward, naive, and impractical, he lacks the proper persona for society; thus he is the object of laughter and ridicule. The society he enters is dominated by the passion for money; the other male characters are moneylenders or thieves. Money possesses them. Prince Myshkin's opposite, Rogozhin, is a millionaire and a murderer whose passion is not for money but for women. He wants to own the beautiful Nastasya Filippovna, who becomes the betrothed of Prince Myshkin. A wounded woman, Nastasya is both a "proud beauty" and one of the "humiliated heart." Orphaned at seven, she was raised by a rich landowner who made her his mistress when she was seventeen. After she moves to St. Petersburg she becomes possessed by hatred and revenge for the man who has wronged her. Suddenly both Rogozhin and Myshkin enter her life. She falls in love with the purity of the prince. When Rogozhin tries to buy her love for 100,000 rubles, Myshkin, who recognizes the essential beauty of her soul, offers to marry her to save her, even though he loves another woman. His is a love of pity and compassion. But Nastasya is so wounded in spirit, so bound by guilt for wanting revenge on men, so unable to forgive herself, that she cannot accept the innocent and forgiving love of Myshkin. Instead she runs away with Rogozhin who, as she has feared, finally kills her in a fit of passion. At the novel's end Myshkin and Rogozhin are joined at her death bed, mysterious accomplices to the crime. For their two loves, so opposite in nature, have joined in a love that kills the soul: opposing and unintegrated, the divided loves of pity and passion can only distort the psyche and kill the human heart.

In the end Prince Myshkin seems an ineffectual model for humankind. From a cynical perspective his ideal life of innocent love, forgiveness, and humility leads to the murder of Nastasya. But the "wholly beautiful being," the idiot prince and the holy fool, nevertheless remains an image of hope. Here this character is still split off from his shadow brother, who embodies the dark world. Dostoevsky had yet to integrate the ideal man of heart with the dark side in his own nature. It would take him ten more years of inner struggle, embodied in his later novels, to bring forth the figures of Alyosha and Zossima who, having experienced both the light and the dark, can affirm the whole of human existence. In *The Brothers Karamazov*, his last novel, Dostoevsky's characters finally meet and struggle with their angels and their devils, bearing witness to the fire of creation within the human soul.

The Idiot was not as big a success with the public as *Crime and Punishment.* After its publication, Dostoevsky was still in great financial difficulty. In September 1869, a second daughter, Lyubov—whose name means "love"—was born. The baby was a great source of joy to him, but having a child increased his desperation about money. He coped by gambling. However, within two years he experienced a transformation that ended his gambling forever.

From 1869 to 1871 Dostoevsky wrote *The Eternal Husband,* a novel about the jealous rivalry of two men bound to each other through their relation to the same woman. The Don Juan–type lover and the naive husband are distorted reflections of each other. Many considered this short novel to be his most successful work technically. About this time Dostoevsky envisioned a work called *The Life of a Great Sinner,* which would consist of five novellas. He wrote: "The main question which will run through all the parts of the novel is the question that has tormented me either consciously or unconsciously all my life—the existence of God."[36] Although Dostoevsky never wrote *The Life of a Great Sinner,* it was to become absorbed in his last novels, and the "majestic, *positive* holy figure" he envisioned in it was to become a model for Father Zossima in *The Brothers Karamazov.* This figure was based on the life of an actual monk, Tikhon Zadonsky, and to write the projected work about him Dostoevsky knew he had to return to Russia. Internally, he was in the process of making a firm decision to deal with his indebtedness, which was the reason he had left Russia and the only reason he had not yet returned—he feared debtors' prison. With his poor health, he knew that he might not survive it, much less be able to write. And writing, although it was his great torment, was also his creative destiny. Through it he realized that "Without suffering, happiness cannot be understood. The ideal passes through suffering like gold through fire. The heavenly kingdom is attained through effort."[37]

Before Dostoevsky could return to Russia to write the book about the holy monk, he had to confront the publisher Stellovsky, who had purchased all the writer's old IOUs and forced the author to sign a contract damaging to his interests by threatening to put him in debtors' prison. In March 1871, he told his friend Maikov to obtain the services of a good lawyer and "start a case in court."[38] On the outer level, Dostoevsky needed to take action against Stellovsky, who continued to harass him by threatening to take all his money and put him in debtors' prison. But Stellovsky also corresponded to an interior figure in Dostoevsky's psyche—The Trickster–Moneylender—which the writer needed to exorcise. These were two tasks Dostoevsky had to undertake before he would be free from his addiction. (To recover, addicts have to make changes both externally and internally.)

Dostoevsky's way to transform himself was to write. He had already written about the addiction to gambling in *The Gambler*, to money in *The Idiot*, and to jealousy in *The Eternal Husband*. Now Dostoevsky confronted an even more universal, tragic, and sinister character who was holding him hostage: in *The Possessed* he wrote about a nihilist who becomes possessed by the Demon Lover. This was the inner figure that Dostoevsky needed to exorcise personally and which he felt on the universal level was a threat to humankind.

But before Dostoevsky was able to be done with this character on any level, he went on one more gambling binge. It was as though he had to personally hit bottom one last time. The situation was desperate. Dostoevsky had been suffering from a series of epileptic attacks that were emotionally devastating. His wife, in her third pregnancy, was nervous, thin, and unable to sleep. Because her husband's condition worried her, she resorted to an extreme proposal—that Dostoevsky go to play roulette in Wiesbaden. So, in April 1871, Dostoevsky went to Wiesbaden to gamble and lost everything. In despair he hoped to seek out the help of a Russian priest, for a priest had rescued him before. Like a madman, he rushed to an Orthodox Russian church. Paradoxically, he found himself in a synagogue instead and ran back home confused. At midnight he sat down and wrote to his wife about the experience. That day, for two reasons, he had no intention of gambling. First, he feared the continued effect of his gambling on her. Three nights ago he had had a dream in which he had seen Anna's hair turn white. Moreover, just the previous night he had dreamed about his father who had ". . . appeared to me in a terrifying guise, such as he has only appeared to me twice before in my life, both times prophesying a dreadful disaster, and on both occasions the dream came true. And now, when I think of the dream I had three nights ago, when I saw your hair turn white, my heart stops beating—ah, my God, what will become of you when you get this letter!"[39] Now, Dostoevsky assured Anna that his obsession with gambling was finished. In her last message to him, although she had sent him money, Anna had firmly expressed her concern. In response, Dostoevsky wrote:

> I felt so ashamed about the 30 thalers I had *robbed* you of! Believe me, my angel, all year I have been dreaming of buying you a pair of earrings, which I have not yet given back to you. You had pawned all your possessions for me during these past 4 years and followed me in my wanderings with homesickness in your heart! Anya, Anya, bear in mind, too, that I am not a scoundrel but only a man with a passion for gambling. (But here is *something else* that I want you to remember, Anya: I am through with that fancy forever. I know I have written you before that it was over and done with, but I never felt the way I feel now as I write this. Now I am rid of this delusion and I would bless God that things have turned out as disastrously as they have if I weren't so terribly worried about you at this moment. Anya, if you are angry with me, just think of how much I've had to suffer and *still* have to suffer in the coming three or four days! If, sometime later on in life you find me being ungrateful and unfair toward you—just show me this letter!)[40]

Continuing, Dostoevsky explained that he had only some small change left, and he was confused and afraid. He hoped she would save him once more by sending him thirty thalers so he could get home. He knew she had every right to think he would only gamble it away again, but he was not insane: now he knew that gambling again would be not only the death of her but also the end of himself. From now on he would work for her and Lyubov and he would reach his goal—to provide well for them. Through this experience he had undergone a moral regeneration and grown stronger. He had had a rebirth. He was a "new man."

> . . . it seems as if I have been completely morally regenerated (I say this to you and before God), and if it had not been for my worrying about you the past three days, if it had not been for my wondering every minute about what this would do to you—I would even have been happy! You mustn't think I am crazy, Anya, my guardian angel! A great thing has happened to me: I have rid myself of the abominable delusion that has *tormented* me for almost 10 years. For ten years (or, to be more precise, ever since my brother's death, when I suddenly found myself weighted down by debts) I dreamed about winning money. I dreamt of it seriously, passionately. But now it is all over! This was the *very* last time! Do you believe now, Anya, that my hands are untied?—I was tied up by gambling but now I will put my mind to worthwhile things instead of spending whole nights dreaming about gambling, as I used to do. And so my *work* will be better and more profitable, with God's blessing! Let me keep your heart, Anya, do not come to hate me, do not stop loving me. Now that I

> have become a new man, let us pursue our path together, and I shall see to it that you are happy![41]

Although the letter continues with a few "if onlys" ("if only we could get back to Russia quickly!" and "possibly Stellovsky will save us,") Dostoevsky concludes: "Let there be no mistake, now I am yours, all yours, undividedly yours. Whereas, up till now, *one-half* of me *belonged* to that accursed delusion."[42] His vow came true; Dostoevsky never gambled again.

It makes sense that Dostoevsky had his last gambling binge while writing *The Possessed,* in which he confronted head-on the psychology of possession by the Demon Lover. Here he looked squarely into the psychological and spiritual consequences of nihilism—of "self-will run riot," a phenomenon he had begun to analyze on the personal level in *Crime and Punishment* and which he felt was happening on a larger level in the apocalyptic guise of socialism. What happens, he asked, when humans believe they are utterly free, unbound by the higher power of their Creator? Writing was difficult: new characters presented themselves and Dostoevsky revised, even discarded and destroyed, much that he had written. At one point his long struggle became too much for him and the novel collapsed; every week while writing it he had suffered a series of epileptic fits. But later on he wrote to his niece:

> . . . when I resumed work on my novel, I all of a sudden realized where the hitch was, where I had gone wrong. And, at the same time, in a moment of inspiration, I perceived a new, fully structured plan for the novel. Everything had to be radically changed. Without the slightest hesitation, I crossed out everything I had written (roughly speaking 15 sheets) and restarted the whole thing from the 1st page. A whole year's work was thus destroyed. Ah, Sonechka, if you only knew how difficult it is to be a writer, I mean, to endure this way of life.[43]

A new character was developing, a sinister, yet tragic figure who "comes straight from my heart."[44] The character was Nikolai Stavrogin, a man of "ungovernable wildness" and "superhuman strength" whose tragedy is that he had a vision of the eternal, holy longing and a dream of the golden age, the earthly paradise of universal love among humans. In the despair of defiance, Stavrogin refuses that vision and intoxicated with his own demonic power, cynically gives himself over to experimenting with others. Revulsed by his own base actions (he confesses to seducing and raping a young girl who later commits suicide), he feels no repentance and spirals downward in his demonic demise. Bored, he joins the revolutionaries whom he despises, just as he despises himself. Stavrogin knows that without faith, without Christ, without the healing of the soul of Mother Earth, he will destroy himself. But although he acknowledges the existence of God intellectually, he refuses this gift. For his heart is possessed by the devil. There are only two choices: "to believe" or "to burn everything"—"to be or not to be." Stavrogin chooses the "burning," which is enacted in the "intoxicating," bewitching fire set by his most faithful follower, Peter Verkhovensky, a killer, slanderer, and arsonist who embodies Stavrogin's worst qualities.[45]

Stavrogin becomes possessed by the devil and is visited by him in hallucinations. Renouncing the Creator, he finally commits suicide. Born with the gifts of beauty, elegance, brilliance, power, and charisma, he chooses to use them destructively. He has raped the feminine, subjugated women, abused Mother Earth. Thus, all his attempts at love are aborted. In this novel, Dostoevsky worked out the facets of the Demon Lover, whose fascination and power he knew from his own struggle with addiction as well as his early experience of revolutionary activity. While writing it he hit bottom in his gambling, thanked God for his release from this addiction, and confronted the moneylender Stellovsky—thus attesting to the transformative power of the creative process.

In the summer of 1871, Dostoevsky received a large payment from the journal which was printing *The Possessed* in installments. This money and his new decisiveness enabled him to risk the return to Russia. He feared the lifeblood of his writing would dry up if he did not return. Worried about the customs inspection, Dostoevsky burned several of his notebooks. The family made it across the border. Although his creditors still plagued him, Anna, as his business manager, was able to persuade the creditors that they would be repaid if they left Dostoevsky free to write. If he was put in debtors' prison, she argued, he would be unable to write—thus they would never receive their payment. Anna also helped him realize his dream to publish and distribute his own works—beginning with the novel form of *The Possessed* in 1873. Anna was also transforming her co-addiction to her own way of creativity as financial manager and publisher.

By the time Dostoevsky returned to Russia he had many more admirers than when he left. The four years abroad had also facilitated a significant transformation within the author. Upon his return one of his friends wrote that Dostoevsky had matured during this period; even in the deprivation of exile he had written several novels, cared for his children and wife, and endured the death of a child, emerging from these difficult experiences with a new spirituality that was evident not only in his writing but also in his facial expressions.[46]

Although life in Russia was not easy, the following years were probably the happiest and most peaceful of his life. Despite the harsh judgment of some of the critics, Dostoevsky's work was becoming important to his public. As his status grew, he was even asked to pose for a portrait by Perov, the famous Russian painter. When, shortly after their return, Anna gave birth to a son, Fyodor, Dostoevsky was overjoyed. To cover the costs of living he became editor of a journal, in which he created a special section entitled *The Diary of a Writer*, a new form of philosophical-literary journalism. After two years he resigned to work on another novel, *A Raw Youth*. Here Dostoevsky portrays the family life of the "haphazard household," showing the formlessness of the contemporary Russian family.

Writing this novel was difficult because Dostoevsky was having respiratory difficulties, the first signs of the lung disease from which he eventually died. Several times he was sent to Germany for cures in the spas, where he was put on a strict diet and regular hours. Although the doctor advised that intellectual effort was stressful and harmful to the cure, Dostoevsky still tried to write. But the environment was contrary to his creative process.

For one thing, he usually wrote at night. At home a typical day for him would start late in the morning, after eleven. For an hour or so he would brood over the dreams and thoughts of the previous night, pray, drink his tea, do gymnastics, then wash and dress. After lunch, he would dictate the previous night's work to Anna, who would take it down in shorthand and recopy it so he could make the necessary corrections. Then she would transcribe it again and send it to the printer. He would then play with the children, and at four o'clock would go out for a meditative walk, returning for dinner at six. There followed an hour or so of storytelling to the children, an evening stroll with Anna, and supper at nine. After the house was quiet, Dostoevsky would sit down to work, writing straight until near morning, when he would go to bed.

Despite the interruptions of several cures, *A Raw Youth* was finished in 1875, the same year that his second son, Alexei, was born. The novel centers on a young man seeking structure for his life. Youths need a moral idea of what is right and what is wrong, which this society fails to provide. Feeling the lack of spiritual fatherhood, the raw youth is angry at his father; yet he is drawn toward him with the fascination of a love-hate attraction. In compensation for his father's life of humiliation, the son has set his sights on making money. But he also wants to pierce the enigma of his father; he wants to know the man and to judge him. The father, Versilov, is a moral idealist, but his life does not correspond to his ideas, for he is caught between two women—one representing the pure heavenly world of light and the other representing the dark world of passion. Although the actual father cannot be a model for his son, another character can be: the pilgrim, Makar Ivanovich Dolguruby, first envisioned by Dostoevsky in *The Life of a Great Sinner*. Makar, who becomes the raw youth's spiritual father and mentor, speaks the religious faith of the Russian people:

> What is the mystery? . . . Everything is a mystery, dear; in all is God's mystery. In every tree, in every blade of grass, that same mystery lies hid. Whether the tiny bird of the air is singing, or the stars in all their multitudes shine at night in heaven, the mystery is one, ever the same.[47]

Recalling his pilgrimage to the monastery, Makar tells how, for the first time, he understood that the meaning of life is a mystery and to be on earth is a wondrous thing and awesome to the heart. Dying, too, is an act of splendor if one has fulfilled one's days on earth, honoring the gift of life and the event of death, thus rejoicing in the mystery. Makar embodies Dostoevsky's vision of love and creativity, a vision that is finally expressed in *The Brothers Karamazov*.

Completing *A Raw Youth* in 1876, Dostoevsky resumed the publication of *The Diary of a Writer*, in which he conversed with his readers on matters of contemporary concern, always from his own unique combination of personal, philosophical, literary, psychological, and religious perspectives. The highly successful *Diary* also contained artistic works, including several stories and the literary seeds of *The Brothers Karamazov*. It became an important part of Dostoevsky's spiritual growth, for through this personal yet public dialogue his faith in Russia and its people was rekindled. *The Diary* included Dostoevsky's reflections on the ecstasy to be found by honoring Mother Earth; he felt that one of the spiritual tasks of humans was to care for the earth as a mother does for her child. "There is something sacramental in the earth, in the soil," he wrote.[48] The *Diary*'s large subscribership wrote Dostoevsky hundreds of letters each year, which delighted him. But as the pile of unanswered letters grew, so did his burden of guilt. Writing letters was not his forte, and it took precious time from his novels; even so he tried to answer some of them. Finally he had to stop work on the *Diary* to begin what was to be his last and greatest novel, *The Brothers Karamazov*. During these years (1876–1877) Dostoevsky studied the lives of children, and his observations and love for children became a central theme in *The Brothers Karamazov*. He also wrote three artistic works, including *The Meek One*, which presents the conflict in the psyche between the obsession for power by the Demon Lover and its disastrous effect on the feminine.

While writing *The Brothers Karamazov* (1877–1880) Dostoevsky was influenced by the philosopher Vladimir Solovyov, who became his closest friend. Their relation was much like that of Alyosha and Father Zossima. The young Solovyov explained the meaning of history as a divine-human process with its mystical transfiguration grounded in the feminine wisdom of Sophia. Dostoevsky himself experienced this in his moments of ecstatic vision of world harmony, which he felt deeply in the mystical love for Mother Earth. For Dostoevsky, to "water the earth with tears of gratitude and love" became one of the highest expressions of human love for God. Another influence on Dostoevsky was the philosopher N. F. Fyodorov, who proposed the idea of a unified humankind: to do away with the enmity and struggles that divided humans the living sons must join together for the resurrection of their dead fathers. With the universal loving union of all humankind as the aim, Fyodorov believed that the Kingdom of God could appear on earth as the culmination of the cosmic force of the "God-manhood" process. To Dostoevsky this meant that redemption of the father was essential and that parricide, the murder resulting from the hatred of sons toward their fathers, was the central tragedy. The plot of *The Brothers Karamazov* revolves around these ideas.

While Dostoevsky was writing out all these thoughts, his three-year-old son, Alyosha, for whom the hero of *The Brothers Karamazov* was named, died of epilepsy inherited from his father. Dostoevsky poured his grief into the novel with his anguished writings about the suffering of children. At this time Dostoevsky visited the monastery at Optima Pustyn for several days, where the elder spoke to him about the purifying transformation from lament to serenity that was possible for Anna and Fyodor, if they could accept, endure, and forgive. According to Anna, Dostoevsky returned comforted and wrote the novel with great inspiration.

The Brothers Karamazov is discussed in the next chapter. In the context of Dostoevsky's life it is important to note here his statement that he wrote the entire novel to show that "a pure and ideal Christian is not an abstraction but a tangible, real possibility that can be contemplated with our own eyes and that it is in Christianity alone that the salvation of the Russian land from all her afflictions lies."[49] He considered this theme to be completely original. Its embodiment lay in the artistic portrait of the monk Father Zossima.

Dostoevsky considered the blasphemous rejection of the absurdity of God's creation—based on what he thought to be an irrefutable argument, "the senselessness of children's suffering"[50]—to be one of the most important underlying themes of his novel. Through the portrayal of Zossima's character, he hoped to refute this blasphemy. His refutation was not a matter of thought, but rather of the heart, based on the life of a truly pure, humble, and sublimely hopeful human being. Dostoevsky knew his portrait of Zossima might be considered ridiculous from a mundane point of view. But from the deeper dimension of the inner life of the soul, it was his answer. As he wrote:

> . . . there were certain artistic imperatives: I needed to draw a character who was both humble and sublime, whereas real life is full of the ridiculous and is only sublime in its inner meaning; and so, to satisfy the demands of art, I was also forced to touch upon some of the coarser aspects of existence when telling the life story of my monk. Then, there are also some of the monk's teachings, which people will inveigh against as being absurd because they are too exalted. I know very well that they are absurd in the everyday sense, but, in another, deeper sense, they seem quite appropriate.[51]

Zossima was modeled on two real Russian monks: Father Amvrosy, the elder who had consoled the author upon his son's death, and St. Tikhon Zadonsky, whom Dostoevsky had taken into his heart with enthusiasm earlier and whose religious and moral writings he had studied ardently. Tikhon took great joy in the presence of the Creator in the created world and loved to immerse himself in nature. For Zossima, too, the beauty of nature attests to the joy of creation, and love transforms the earth into paradise.

The Brothers Karamazov portrays many of the inner archetypal figures of addiction. Zossima's character embodies recovery. Zossima's philosophy that the acceptance of suffering and guilt gives one the strength to forgive oneself and others, and that "in saving others you will save yourself," is a vision of the twelve steps. His belief in redemption through love is reminiscent of the way the twelve-step fellowship works.

In November 1880 Dostoevsky completed *The Brothers Karamazov*, the culmination of his entire spiritual life and creative work. Since the characters were all figures in his own psyche, he could describe them and their interactions with one another superbly. He knew their story was not only his own personal story, but a universal story of humanity as well. The novel, a tremendous success, brought forth the adoration of the Russian people, many of whom hailed Dostoevsky as their prophet. When he gave his speech at the unveiling of the monument to Pushkin in Moscow in 1880, the people flocked to him in throngs. The next day, when Dostoevsky read his speech at the Meeting of the Friends of Russian Literature, he was hailed again. He wrote to Anna:

> This morning I read my speech at the meeting of The Friends [of Russian Literature]. The auditorium was packed. No, Anya, you'll never be able to imagine, to conceive the effect that speech produced! My successes in Petersburg were nothing compared to this—just plain *nothing!* When I appeared on the stage, the auditorium thundered with applause and for a very, very long time I wasn't given a chance to begin. I bowed and made signs, begging them to let me read—but to no avail: elation, enthusiasm (all because of *The Karamazovs*!) At last I began reading. At every page, sometimes at every sentence, I was interrupted by bursts of applause. I read in a loud voice, with fire. . . . And when, at the end, I proclaimed the *universal oneness* of mankind, the hall seemed to go into hysterics, and when I finished, there was—I won't call it a roar—it was a howl of elation. People in the audience who had never met before, wept, sobbed, embraced each other, *and swore to become better, not to hate each other any more but to love one another.* The order of the meeting was shattered. Everyone rushed up to me on the stage: grandes dames, girl students, state secretaries, male students—they all hugged and kissed me. All the members of our Society who were on the stage hugged me, kissed me, and all of them, to a man, literally cried in their elation. They kept calling me back for a half an hour, waving their handkerchiefs. Suddenly—to give you an idea of what went on—two old men I'd never seen before came up to me. "For 20 years we have been enemies, have never spoken to each other, but now we've embraced and made up. It is you who have reconciled us. You're our saint, you're our prophet!" "Prophet, prophet!" people were shouting in the crowd.[52]

Even Turgenev, with whom Dostoevsky had long been at odds, embraced him with tears in his eyes. Later he was crowned with a laurel wreath in the name of Russian women; he was elected as honorary member of the Friends of Russian Literature. And he was told his talk "*wasn't simply a speech but a historic event!*"[53]

But despite the intoxication of this day honoring Dostoevsky's genius, the critics later attacked him maliciously. He later remarked, "The entire literary world, without exception, is hostile to me—*only* the readers of Russia love me."[54] In the same letter, written only three months before his death, while he was trying to complete *The Brothers Karamazov* as well as an issue of the *Diary*, he complained of the burden of his writing, the pressures from the public and the effect upon his health. It was a period that he compared to his penal servitude in Siberia.

> I can't write off the top of my head, I must write artistically. I owe that to God, to poetry, to my reputation as a writer, and, literally, to the entire Russian reading public, which is waiting for the ending of my work. And that is why I sat and wrote literally day and night. From August right up until today, I haven't answered a single letter. Writing letters is torture for me, but people keep bombarding me with letters and requests. Would you believe that I do not have time to read a single book or even a newspaper? I do not even have time to talk to my children. And I don't talk to them. And my health is worse than anything you can imagine. A catarrh of the respiratory passages has developed into emphysema, an incurable disease (suffocation, insufficient air), and my days are numbered. Owing to the pressure of work, my epilepsy has also become more acute. . . . I literally don't have a minute to attend to my own most pressing and sacred duties: I have neglected everything, abandoned everything, and I'm not speaking of myself. It is night now, after 6 a.m., the town is beginning to wake up, but I haven't gone to bed yet. And the doctors tell me I must avoid overexertion; that I must sleep at night and not sit for 10 or 12 hours bent over my desk. Why do I write at night? Because no sooner do I wake up at 1 p.m. than my bell starts ringing without letup: one comes asking me for one favor, another for another favor, a third makes demands on me, and a fourth demands insistently that I solve some sort of "accursed" unsolvable problem for him, warning me that, if I don't do it, he will shoot himself (although I may never have set eyes on him before). Finally, there are all sorts of delegations—university students, male and female, high-school students, individuals from various charitable organizations—asking me to read at their evenings. And when am I supposed to think, to work, to read, to live.[55]

Nevertheless, Dostoevsky completed the novel, went to the literary salons, and planned to resume publication of the *Diary*. He was now accepted in high society and even presented the completed novel of *The Brothers Karamazov* in person to the future emperor of Russia. In the last issue of the *Diary*, he proclaimed the Church lay in the Russian people, and that the duty of the rulers of Russia was to listen to the people's truth. He also predicted that Russia was not only European but would civilize Asia. Dostoevsky spent his last living days anxiously fearing that the article would be censored. But he died before it was published, and the authorities did not dare touch his last words.

Before his death, in January 1881, Dostoevsky was planning the sequel to *The Brothers Karamazov*. All the characters would be twenty years older, with Alyosha the major hero. But while writing in his study, he began to cough blood. After several hemorrhages, he lost consciousness. When he awoke, he asked for a priest for confession. He pledged his undying love to his wife and children and reminded them of the model of the prodigal son who humbled himself, asking God for forgiveness, and was received with rejoicing. Three days later, on January 28, Dostoevsky died. He was buried in the graveyard of the Alexander Nevsky monastery, where rest many of the most famous composers, artists and writers of Russia. Thirty thousand people attended his funeral, at which there were fifteen choirs and seventy-two wreath-bearing delegations. Dostoevsky's death was mourned on every level. He was to become one of the greatest figures in world literature. He was truly a person who passed from the bondage of the Demon Lover to the service of the Creative Daimon, and he left a great gift. His soul was on fire with the flame of divine creation. And, like the legendary firebird of ancient Russia, he consciously sacrificed himself, leaving the brilliant plumage of his writing to water the earth and to shine with the transcendent gift of beauty and love and hope for those who look to see it.

16: THE WORK OF THE HEART

> You are working for the whole, you are acting for the future. Seek no reward, for great is your reward on this earth: the spiritual joy which is only vouchsafed to the righteous man. Fear not the great nor the mighty, but be wise and ever serene. Know the measure, know the times, study that. When you are left alone, pray. Love to throw yourself on the earth and kiss it. Kiss the earth and love it with an unceasing, consuming love. Love all men, love everything. Seek that rapture and ecstasy. Water the earth with the tears of your joy and love those tears. Don't be ashamed of that ecstasy, prize it, for it is a gift of God and a great one.
>
> —Fyodor Dostoevsky, *The Brothers Karamazov*

WHEN I WAS in my early twenties, I read Dostoevsky's *The Brothers Karamazov* for the first time. Immediately, I identified with it for, like the brothers, I, too, was the child of an alcoholic father and had suffered the ravages of addiction. Each of the characters, I felt, reflected a part of myself. Their sufferings and intense questioning of the meaning of life, and their urgency about whether a good God could be reconciled with the horrors of evil, were the very questions burning deep in my heart too. For over a quarter of a century I lived with this novel, reading it many times, discussing it in my courses, always finding in it new perspectives and insights that opened up my heart and soul. I knew that sometime I would need to write about this book, although then I did not know the context. For, by living with *The Brothers Karamazov*, I learned more and more about my own struggles with good and evil, and the different sides of myself that participated in this battle. And always, when I finished that course of inner confrontation that Dostoevsky set before me, I felt a new sense of regeneration and deepened faith. Finally, in the last few years, as a result of my own struggles with the devastation of addiction, not only as the child of an alcoholic father but as an alcoholic myself, I realized *The Brothers Karamazov* as a story of the transformation of addiction. In it I could see the roots of the twelve steps as the work of the heart embodied in this transformative process.

The Brothers Karamazov shows how each member of a family either succumbs to the demons of addiction or transforms. The novel is not only about a specific family possessed by the madness of addiction, but also is a story of the addictive predicament of the human condition. The book portrays the soul's struggle between its own contradictions: the battle between good and evil raging deep within the human heart. And it affirms that those who dare to descend into The Abyss of the human soul, who boldly face both the spiritual longings and the demonic forces in those depths, can die and be reborn. Dostoevsky's epigraph for the novel was the following passage from the Bible:

> Verily, verily, I say unto you, except a corn of wheat fall into the ground and die, it abideth alone, but if it die, it bringeth forth much fruit.[1]

The Brothers Karamazov centers around the murder of the father, Fyodor Karamazov, a lecherous drunk who was violent and cruel to his wives and who abandons and taunts his sons. Each of the four Karamazov sons has, in his own way, been wounded by the unbridled and dissolute father, who has lived his life addictively, with no regard for others. This suffering has generated within each son the burning question of the meaning of life. The enigma of their uncaring, self-indulgent father and their painful childhoods have forced the brothers to face the relationship between the suffering of the innocents and the existence of God—the conflict of good and evil. Ivan, the most analytical and intellectual son, questions how one can ever reconcile the suffering of innocent children with the existence of God or with a divine plan for higher harmony. This is a question asked by anyone who has suffered from addiction—whether as an addict or as someone close to an addict: "Why me? Why must I suffer?" This question must be faced directly in the process of recovery to transform addiction into creativity, for it leads one to question the meaning of life. In the novel, each of the Karamazov brothers deals with this question in a different way. In the Karamazov family, as in the addictive patriarchy, the mother is missing and has been abused by the father. It is the missing mothers and the abused feminine that must be redeemed for transformation.

1. The Children of Addiction

Each major character in *The Brothers Karamazov* symbolizes a different archetypal figure within the psyche of the addict. The father, Fyodor Karamazov, portrays the addict who is caught in denial. Karamazov is crude, corrupt, cynical, and greedy. He has abused his wives and mistresses. His only concerns are making money and satisfying his sensual appetities. He, himself, is a "moneylender," who binds others to him through debt. He lives unconsciously, hostage to his own addictions. In his drunkenness, he acts the buffoon, offending those around him, often provoking them to shame, embarrassment, rage, or even to violence. With the exception of the gentle Alyosha, all of his sons hate him. And even Alyosha is ashamed when Fyodor foolishly jokes about faith in front of Father Zossima, who is Alyosha's spiritual father. But Zossima, who sees through Fyodor, speaks to all addicts in denial when he says to him:

> Do not be so ashamed of yourself, for that is the root of it all. . . . Above all, don't lie to yourself. The man who lies to himself and listens to his own lie comes to such a pass that he cannot distinguish the truth within him, or around him, and so loses all respect for himself and for others. And having no respect he ceases to love, and in order to occupy and distract himself without love he gives way to passions and coarse pleasures, and sinks to bestiality in his vices, all from continual lying to other men and to himself. The man who lies to himself can be more easily offended than any one. You know it is sometimes very pleasant to take offence, isn't it? A man may know that nobody has insulted him, but that he has invented the insult for himself, has lied and exaggerated to make it picturesque, has caught at a word and made a mountain out of a molehill—he knows that himself, yet he will be the first to take offence, and will revel in his resentment till he feels great pleasure in it, and so pass to genuine vindictiveness.[2]

A typical addict in denial, Fyodor only partially hears what Zossima says to him and proceeds to act the drunken fool. Soon he is back in the depths of self-deception. His behavior provokes those around him to contempt and anger, even murder or hatred.

This is especially true for Dimitri, the oldest of the brothers and the one most like his father. Of the brothers, the impulsive Dimitri has most openly expressed contempt and hatred for his father, who abandoned him at an early age. After an unhappy and disorderly childhood, Dimitri became an army officer who led a wild, sensual life of romantic affairs, drinking, gambling, orgies, and duels. Undisciplined and subject to moodiness and bad temper, Dimitri suffers from guilt, shame, and self-hatred as a result of his behavior. But underneath, Dimitri is a natural man with an open heart, a poetic soul, and a capacity for suffering, humility, and endurance that enables him to face his inner conflicts and undertake the journey toward spiritual rebirth. This strength differentiates Dimitri from his father, who does not dare look within. Dimitri's inner conflicts reach a painful point after he threatens to kill his father and is then accused of his actual murder.

Dimitri has fought with his father over the settlement of an inheritance from his mother's estate. He also feels his father has been trying to seduce Grushenka, a woman with whom he himself is passionately in love. All of the brothers, who have returned to their father's village, are worried about the potential for violence between Dimitri and his father, particularly since each bears the inner torment of their father's abuse. Two particular incidents arise in which Dimitri attacks his father—once verbally and once physically.

Once, even in the healing presence of Father Zossima, with whom the brothers had gathered hoping to reconcile these conflicts, Dimitri was provoked by his father's insults and challenge to a duel, and flew into a rage, shouting, "Why is such a man alive? . . . Tell me, can he be allowed to go on defiling the earth?"[3] Foreseeing the suffering through which Dimitri would have to pass in order to be transformed, Father Zossima silently bowed down before Dimitri's feet. Another time, when he heard that his father had offered Grushenka money if she would spend the night with him, Dimitri fell into a jealous rage, physically attacked Fyodor, and threatened to kill him later. People gossiped about both events, so that later, when the father is actually murdered, Dimitri, as the natural suspect, is accused of the crime.

The passionate Dimitri is both a Gambler and a Romantic who continually seeks ecstasy, whether it is the ecstasy of falling into love or the ecstasy of falling into The Abyss. His suffering has shown him the difficult contradictions of the soul: through his longing for love and his hatred of his father, Dimitri knows the inner conflict of good and evil. As he says to Alyosha:

> I can't endure the thought that a man of lofty mind and heart begins with the ideal of the Madonna and ends with the ideal of Sodom. What's still more awful is that a man with the ideal of Sodom in his soul does not renounce the ideal of the Madonna, and his heart may be on fire with the ideal, genuinely on fire, just as in his days of youth and innocence. Yes, man is broad, too, broad, indeed. I'd have him narrower. . . . The awful thing is that beauty is mysterious as well as terrible. God and the devil are fighting there and the battlefield is the heart of man.[4]

Just as the battle between God and the Devil is raging in the heart of Dimitri, so it is within Ivan, the middle Karamazov brother. Like all of the Karamazov sons, Ivan has suffered from his father's rejection. But he uses reason and logic to defend himself against the pain of his childhood and to try to understand the paradox of God's existence with the existence of evil and suffering. Ivan accepts God's existence, for otherwise the existence of the world could not be explained. Moreover, he believes also in God's omnipotence and in the underlying order and harmony of the universe.

But God's creation—the world with its evil, injustice, and imperfection—Ivan rejects. And Ivan can love humans only at a distance, in the abstract. For him, the world, with all of its brutality and suffering, is horrifying. Perhaps the roots of evil, Ivan says, can be traced back to the Fall of humans from the Garden of Eden. Perhaps humankind could not exist without the knowledge of good and evil. Even so, Ivan argues, life in this world is not worth the price of the unjust suffering of one innocent child.

> Listen! I took the case of children only to make my case clearer. Of the other tears of humanity with which the earth is soaked from its crust to its centre, I will say nothing. I have narrowed my subject on purpose. I am a bug, and I recognize in all humility that I cannot understand why the world is arranged as it is. Men are themselves to blame, I suppose; they were given paradise, they wanted freedom, and stole fire from heaven, though they knew they would become unhappy, so there is no need to pity them. With my pitiful, earthly, Euclidian understanding, all I know is that there is suffering and that there are none guilty; that cause follows effect, simply and directly; that eveything flows and finds its level—but that's only Euclidian nonsense, I know that, and I can't consent to live by it! What comfort is it to me that there are none guilty and that cause follows effect simply and directly, and that I know it—I must have justice, or I will destroy myself. And not justice in some remote infinite time and space, but here on earth, and that I could see myself.[5]

If the sufferings of children are an evil necessary for human knowledge and freedom and for the higher harmony, Ivan is unwilling to accept the existing world. It offends his thirst for justice. Even forgiveness by the wounded ones themselves offends Ivan's righteous indignation. Thus, Ivan blurts out in the despair of defiance:

> Is there in the whole world a being who would have the right to forgive and could forgive? I don't want harmony. From love for humanity I don't want it. I would rather be left with the unavenged suffering. I would rather remain with my unavenged suffering and unsatisfied indignation, *even if I were wrong.* Besides, too high a price is asked for harmony; it's beyond our means to pay so much to enter on it. And so I hasten to give back my entrance ticket, and if I am an honest man I am bound to give it back as soon as possible. And that I am doing. It's not God that I don't accept, Alyosha, only I most respectfully return Him the ticket.[6]

Ivan's attitude, as Alyosha gently points out, is rebellion. Such rebellion resembles The Underground Man's resentment of unavenged suffering, which often hardens into the figure of The Judge, who puts himself above all others, even God. Indeed, Ivan's thinking seems to lead to only one conclusion: If God and his world cannot be honored, "everything is lawful," even murder, a proposition that Ivan had been discussing also with his half-brother, Smerdyakov. This shows how The Underground Man's cynicism eventually leads to The Killer.

Ivan is in hell because he cannot accept the discrepancy between his thirst for perfection and his murderous feelings toward his father. Worse yet is his anger and resentment toward a God who allows the tears and agony of the innocent. Ivan is caught between his own logic and emotions, between doubt and faith. Although secretly he yearns for love and forgiveness, he also rejects it because of his need for control, power, and certitude. Finally he goes mad because he cannot resolve his inner conflict or accept a world that can neither assuage his thirst for perfection nor fulfill his need to control it with reason.

Alyosha tells Ivan that forgiveness is the only solution. Forgiveness is the necessary edifice on which the redemption of suffering is based and is embodied in Christ, the innocent one who accepted his suffering in sacrifice to redeem the sins of others. But Ivan rejects both Christ and forgiveness. He writes a poem about the Grand Inquisitor who, like Ivan himself and The Underground Man as well, acts as pope and Judge, finding humans too weak, too fearful, too rebellious, to bear the burden of freedom. Humankind prefers security and happiness to the freedom of conscious choice between good and evil, argues Ivan in his poem. Humans prefer someone to worship and give them their bread, someone to keep their conscience by giving them rules, and someone to submit to and hold their power for them. The Grand Inquisitor, who in the poem has taken over this control and power through the Church, threatens to take Christ prisoner and burn him at the stake. For Christ threatens all control by offering freedom to humankind. It is the loving, forgiving Christ in himself that Ivan is trying to kill in order to maintain the power and control of his own self-righteousness. He also secretly longs to find this loving and forgiving person in another—his brother Alyosha.

For, along with his rational rejection of God's world, Ivan longs for life regardless of logic, for "loving with one's inside, with one's stomach."[7] When Ivan confesses this philosophy, Alyosha cries out in sorrow.

> But the little sticky leaves, and the precious tombs, and the blue sky, and the woman you love! How will you live, how will you love them? With

> such a a hell in your heart and your head, how can you? No, that's just what you are going away for, to join them . . . if not, you will kill yourself, you can't endure it![8]

After this conversation, Ivan rushed off to his father's house to prepare for his departure abroad the next day. As he neared the house he was overcome by an intolerable depression. Something was irritating him beyond all bounds, and as soon as he saw his half-brother, Smerdyakov—Fyodor's epileptic son by a mute and retarded village woman—he knew that this was the source of his vexation. He loathed this man, even though he had before taken interest in talking to him and had once thought him to be rather original. Ivan had even expressed his philosophy of "everything is lawful" to Smerdyakov who now, as though in some secret complicity, expressed his kinship with Ivan as "two clever people" who understood each other.

Abused and rejected, Smerdyakov, who had been spawned in one of Fyodor's drunken debauches, also hated his father. He compensated by being vain and cynical. Now, Ivan was frightened of him. For Smerdyakov had a tricky way of parodying his ideas, insinuating that Ivan would be responsible if their father was murdered. In the addict's psyche, Smerdyakov is The Trickster who can trick the addict into continuing his destructive way but at the same time also sets things into motion for a change.

At this meeing, Smerdyakov intimated to Ivan that he had had a premonition of an epileptic fit. If that were to happen and Ivan were to leave, there would be no one to protect Fyodor against Dimitri, who knew that Fyodor was trying to seduce Grushenka with 3,000 rubles. Smerdyakov now implied to Ivan that if he were to leave he would be responsible for the murder of their father. Ivan laughed and declared that he would be leaving in the morning. But that night he suffered in a nervous state of irritability and resentment. He hoped to get away from all these family complications and escape the past for a new life. But underneath he felt a sense of hopelessness, betrayal, and gloom, and the feeling that he was indeed a scoundrel. The very day Ivan left, Smerdyakov had the predicted fit, falling down the cellar steps, unconscious. Fyodor was left unprotected. But Fyodor didn't care—Smerdyakov had told him earlier that this was the night Grushenka might come.

2. Alyosha's Abyss

Meanwhile, although Alyosha was worried about his father and his brothers, he was even more worried about Father Zossima, who was deathly ill. He rushed to his cell and was able to hear the last words of the elder—the story of his conversion. Like the Karamazov brothers, Zossima too had been ruled by his passions, but something had changed his life. As a young man he had been a proud and vain military officer who had led a licentious life of drunkenness and debauchery. Once he had been so jealous of a rival that he had insulted him and challenged him to duel. On the eve of the duel, he struck his servant so brutally that his face was covered with blood. When he woke up the next morning, he wept, so ashamed at his cruelty toward another human being. He remembered the words of his brother who had died young, dedicating himself to the spirit of Christ's love. At this memory, Zossima, on his knees, begged his servant's forgiveness. At the duel, his opponent had the first shot and missed. Then Zossima, instead of shooting, threw his pistol into the woods and asked his opponent to forgive him. After this turning point, he dedicated himself to his spiritual transformation. Through his humiliation he saw that greed for power and pleasure led only to isolation and to shame, dishonesty and guilt. He gradually came to believe that all humans are guilty in so far as they are finite beings and thus imperfect. Only by acknowledging this guilt and by taking on the suffering of others, could they be transformed. For Zossima this meant a life of sacrifice and service; a life of fellowship with all human beings. Moral judgment and blame, he said, only add to the evil in the world. Zossima emphasized that the worst sin of all and the hardest spiritual agony is to be unable to love, saying Hell is "the suffering of being unable to love."[9] Just before his death he exhorted the monks:

> You are working for the whole, you are acting for the future. Seek no reward, for great is your reward on this earth: the spiritual joy which is only vouchsafed to the righteous man. Fear not the great nor the mighty, but be wise and ever serene. Know the measure, know the times, study that. When you are left alone, pray. Love to throw yourself on the earth and kiss it. Kiss the earth and love it with an unceasing, consuming love. Love all men, love everything. Seek that rapture and ecstasy. Water the earth with the tears of your joy and love those tears. Don't be ashamed of that ecstasy, prize it, for it is a gift of God and a great one; it is not given to many but only to the elect.[10]

Now Zossima grew pale, smiled at the monks, sank to his knees, and kissed the earth in ecstasy. In joyful prayer he surrendered his soul to God and died. Zossima is an example of a man who lived an addictive life, hit bottom, and transformed spiritually. His philosophy contains many facets of the twelve steps.

Alyosha was in great grief at the elder's death, for Zossima had been his spiritual father and life model. Zossima had been especially fond of Alyosha, who reminded him of his own saintly brother who had died in youth. Of all the Karamazov brothers, Alyosha was the gentlest, most modest, and even tempered. An inward, even dreamy person, he had the gift of loving and drawing forth that love from others. Although his mother died when he was only four, he remembered her love vividly. He particularly cherished the memory of her lifting him up before an icon of the Holy Mother and consecrating him to her special care. Indeed, he seemed to be especially blessed, for he was a trusting person; yet he was not naive nor simple-minded, and he was clear-eyed and radiant with health. Alyosha accepted life without judgment or condemnation; he accepted life on life's terms, though at times one could see he was in grief. Even his father felt a deep affection for him, although he could only express it with drunken tears.

In the Karamazov family, Alyosha served as mediator. To him both Dimitri and Ivan confessed their secret desires and fears. Alyosha was worried about both his brothers, for he knew the hell they held in their hearts. He worried that Dimitri's impulsive anger might overwhelm him and that he might kill his father in a drunken rage. He worried that Ivan's skeptical and cynical state of mind might drive him mad. But when Father Zossima died, his only concern was for the one he loved most in the world. Zossima's death turned out to be Alyosha's trial by fire. After the elder's body was prepared for burial, it decomposed and began to stink more rapidly than was natural, until all had to acknowledge this strange occurrence. Instead of the miracle many had expected there was a scandal over this "breath of corruption." One of the more ascetic monks even implied that this was a sign of Zossima's evil.

Father Zossima's stinking body caused a crisis in Alyosha's life. His heart bled at the injustice and dishonor to the beloved elder, and the words of Ivan about "higher justice" started crowding into his mind. When the shallow seminarian Rakitin taunted him by offering him vodka and sausages, Alyosha took them and replied: "I am not rebelling against my God; I simply don't accept His world."[11] Alyosha resented that this "holiest of holy men," upon whom all his love had been so concentrated, should be exposed to such mortification and the spiteful jeering of the superficial masses: ". . . the sting of it all was that the man he loved above everything on earth should be put to shame and humiliated!"[12] When Rakitin saw Alyosha in such a crisis, he spotted a chance to bring about the fall of a rival. So, in the manner of Mephistopheles, he suggested they visit Grushenka, and Alyosha agreed to go. Thinking Grushenka was a fallen woman, Alyosha in rebellion sought in her his own ruin. Grushenka had the air of a seductress and seemed to be a woman who would manipulate men for money. At first she offered Alyosha champagne and sat on his lap. But when Rakitin told her that Alyosha was rebelling against God over Zossima's death and humiliation, Grushenka understood Alyosha. Immediately she blessed herself, making the sign of the cross, and got off his lap, ashamed at her attempted seduction of him. Alyosha, when he realized Grushenka's compassion, thanked her and told her that she had helped him rise from the depths. To Rakitin he said:

> . . . don't taunt me with having rebelled against God. I don't want to feel angry with you, so you must be kinder, too. I've lost a treasure such as you have never had, and you cannot judge me now. You had much better look at her—do you see how she has pity on me? I came here to find a wicked soul—I felt drawn to evil because I was base and evil myself, and I've found a true sister, I have found a treasure—a loving heart. She had pity on me just now . . . Agrafena Alexandrovna, I am speaking of you. You've raised my soul from the depths.[13]

Grushenka had been having her own spiritual crisis. When Alyosha heard how she had been abused by men, he understood her suffering. He also recognized the treasure in her soul. In return, his compassion restored her own humiliated heart: she realized she had been living in resentment toward the man who had wronged her, and that she needed to learn to forgive. She said: " 'Perhaps my heart is only getting ready to forgive, I shall struggle with my heart. You see, Alyosha, I've grown to love my tears in these five years. . . . Perhaps I only love my resentment, not him.' "[14]

Grushenka and Alyosha had each pitied, loved, and forgiven the other. The forgiveness was a gift that had a healing effect on each other's hearts. As Grushenka said, falling on her knees before Alyosha: "I've been waiting all my life for someone like you, I knew that someone like you would come and forgive me. I believed that, nasty as I am, someone would really love me, not only with a shameful love!"[15] The love between Alyosha and Grushenka in this moment is the love of the "divine wedding." It was a mystical meeting between two souls who understood each other's guilt and shame and who were able, in their acceptance, compassion, and forgiveness of each other, to bear the burden of each other's guilt. Thus each enabled the other to be open for the divine wedding. Their meeting represents the healing energy that occurs when recovering addicts meet with each other.

Indeed, that night Alyosha had a vision of the divine wedding when he returned to the monastery. Father Paissy was reading by Father Zossima's coffin the story of the wedding at Cana from the gospel of St. John. The two were alone in the cell with their beloved Zossima. Although the smell was not gone, nevertheless Aloysha now felt a "sweetness in his heart" and "a sense of the wholeness of things." As Father Paissy read, Alyosha dozed off, musing that Christ's first miracle was at this marriage; its meaning was to help people enjoy the blessing of life. Then in a dream he, too, was at the marriage in Cana. Father Zossima was present as well, alive and joyful, and, taking Alyosha's hand, he bid him rise and rejoice and join them. All were there, Zossima said, because each once had given an onion to another. That is, each person present had helped another as Alyosha and Grushenka had helped each other that day. (Grushenka had told him the fable of a wicked old woman who had give an onion to a starving beggar woman. This gift was her possibility for redemption.) Zossima said:

> We are rejoicing. We are drinking the new wine, the wine of new, great gladness; do you see how many guests? Here are the bride and bridegroom, here is the wise governor of the feast, he is tasting the new wine. Why do you wonder at me? I gave an onion to a beggar, so I, too, am here. And many here have given only an onion each—only one little onion. . . . What are all your deeds? And you, my gentle one, you, my kind boy, you too have known how to give a famished woman an onion today. Begin your work, dear one, begin it gentle one! . . . Do you see our Sun, do you see Him?[16]

When Alyosha replied that he was afraid to look, Zossima answered:

> Do not fear Him. He is terrible in His greatness, awful in His sublimity, but infinitely merciful. He has made Himself like unto us from love and rejoices with us. He is changing the water into wine that the gladness of the guests may not be cut short. He is expecting new guests, He is calling new ones unceasingly for ever and ever. . . . There they are bringing new wine. Do you see they are bringing the vessels. . . .[17]

Hearing this Alyosha felt the tears of rapture rising from his soul. As he reached toward this vision, he cried out and awoke. Immediately he arose, looked at Zossima for the last time, and with new ecstasy flooding his soul, went out into the world.

". . . his soul, overflowing with rapture, yearned for freedom, space, openness. The vault of heaven, full of soft, shining stars stretched vast and fathomless above him. The Milky Way ran in two pale streams from the zenith to the horizon. The fresh motionless, still night enfolded the earth. The white towers and golden domes of the cathedral gleamed out against the sapphire sky. The gorgeous autumn flowers, in the beds round the house, were slumbering till morning. The silence of the earth seemed to melt into the silence of the heavens. The mystery of earth was one with the mystery of the stars. . . . Alyosha stood, gazed, and suddenly threw himself down on the earth. He did not know why he embraced it. He could not have told why he longed so irresistibly to kiss it, to kiss it all. But he kissed it weeping, sobbing and watering it with his tears, and vowed passionately to love it, to love it for ever and ever. "Water the earth with the tears of your joy and love those tears," echoed in his soul.

What was he weeping over?

Oh, in his rapture he was weeping even over those stars, which were shining to him from the abyss of space, and "he was not ashamed of that ecstasy." There seemed to be threads from all those innumerable worlds of God, linking his soul to them, and it was trembling all over "in contact with other worlds." He longed to forgive everyone and for everything, and to beg forgiveness. Oh, not for himself, but for all men, for all and for everything.

"And others are praying for me too," echoed again in his soul. But with every instant he felt clearly and, as it were, tangibly, that something firm and unshakable as that vault of heaven had entered into his soul. It was as though some idea had seized that sovereignty of his mind—and it was for all his life and for ever and ever. He had fallen on the earth a weak boy, but he rose up a resolute champion, and he knew and felt it suddenly at the very moment of his ecstasy. And never, never, all his life long, could Alyosha forget that minute. "Some one visited my soul in that hour," he used to say afterwards, with implicit faith in his words.[18]

This was Alyosha's transformation. He had "fallen" to the bottom of the abyss when his beloved Zossima had been treated so unfairly, and he had closed his heart in resentment, addicted to his idealism about Zossima. But when he was able to reach out to another, his heart opened and he experienced the ecstatic wedding vision, which remained deep within him the rest of his life. After this, Alyosha did as Zossima had said—he left the monastery and went on his "sojourn in the world."[19] For Alyosha now understood the challenge of human life—not only the guilt and the suffering, but also the mystery of love and forgiveness. And, having had this experience, he was able to share that gift with others. Immediately he went out to find Ivan and Dimitri to see if he could help them.

3. Dimitri's Transformation

Just as Alyosha was passing through his Dark Night of the Soul, so was Dimitri. He had been "literally rushing in all directions, struggling with his destiny and trying to save himself."[20] His biggest fear was that he would lose Grushenka. As soon as he had seen her: "The storm broke—it struck me down like the plague. I'm plague-stricken still and I know that everything is over, that there will never be anything more for me."[21] As a romantic, Dimitri's worst addiction was to love. The dark side of his romantic longing, which could drive him to kill, was jealousy. After he heard of Smerdyakov's fit and Ivan's departure, he went to Grushenka's house, only to find her gone. Certain she had gone to see his father, in a jealous rage he picked up a brass pestle and ran like a madman to his father's house. Just before this, he had gone to borrow money to pay the debt he owed to his fiancée, Katerina. When he was refused the money, "he walked like one possessed"[22] and beat himself up in shame, for he felt if he did not repay Katerina he could not marry Grushenka. And now he was denied both possibilities. In a suicidal mood, he did not care or even know what he was doing. At his father's house he hid in the garden and watched Fyodor lean out of the window in expectation. Even though he realized Grushenka had not arrived, he was overwhelmed with repulsion and anger at his father. He was beginning to lose all control, but he did not kill his father. For as he later said, it was as though "God was watching over me then."[23] Just then Fyodor's servant, Grigory, woke up. Recognizing the intruder, he ran after him, calling, "Parricide." In the confusion, Dimitri smashed Grigory's head with the pestle. Horrified, he wiped the blood away with his handkerchief to see if he had broken the skull. But then he ran away, leaving the blood-stained pestle and taking the bloody handkerchief with him. All this became part of the circumstantial evidence used against him later.

Dimitri then learned that Grushenka had gone to her old and first Polish lover. In his longing he rushed after her.

> All was confusion, confusion in Mitya's soul, but although many things were goading his heart, at that moment his whole being was yearning for her, his queen, to whom he was flying. . . .[24]

When he got there, a drunken orgy was in progress, and Dimitri spent his remaining money on the wild party. By paying the Pole money to leave, he won Grushenka over, and the two declared their love for each other. Grushenka asked Dimitri to forgive her for tormenting him; she now knew her love for the Pole to be only an idealized memory. The lovers then went blissfully to sleep. They were awakened by the police, who had come to arrest Dimitri. His father had been murdered, and the evidence pointed to Dimitri as the killer.

At the preliminary investigation, Dimitri confessed that he hated his father and had wanted to kill him. But he proclaimed his innocence of that crime. However, he was afraid that accidentally he had killed Grigory. Relieved when he found out the servant was still alive, Dimitri relaxed, not understanding how serious his position was. When questioned, Dimitri told his story in such a way that his case looked even worse, especially since he refused to disclose how he happened to have the money to pay for the drunken orgy. (He felt ashamed to reveal that he had squandered the remainder of Katerina's money and thus had lost all possibility to repay that debt.) The fact that he had so much money was linked to the 3,000 rubles missing after Fyodor's death. When asked if Smerdyakov, the only remaining suspect, might be the murderer, Dimitri replied that he was too cowardly to kill.

Then Dimitri was told by the prosecutor to undress before everybody. His underclothes and socks were dirty and he felt guilty and inferior. The prosecutor began to trap him in all his statements, using the evidence against him. After Dimitri realized how serious his position was, he was forced to confess that he had spent Katerina's money, a matter of much shame. His great secret was received with hisses. Dimitri fell into complete humiliation.

This humiliation forced Dimitri to take the "soul's way through suffering," to endure an inner trial. Like many addicts, Dimitri had always thirsted for the spirit and for transformation. Typically, he had sought escape through external circumstances. For example, he had put all of his hopes on marrying Grushenka—Romantic that he was—threatening suicide when he thought he couldn't have her. Up to this time, Dimitri's mind worked like this:

> Then, oh, then a new life would begin at once! Of this different, reformed and "virtuous" life ("it must, it must be virtuous") he dreamed feverishly at every moment. He thirsted for that reformation and renewal. The filthy morass, in which he had sunk of his own free will, was too revolting to him, and, like very many men in such cases, he put faith above all in change of place. If only it were not for these people, if only it were not for these circumstances, if only he could fly away from this accursed place—

> he would be altogether regenerated, would enter on a new path. That was what he believed in, and for what he was yearning. But all this could only be a condition of the first, the *happy* solution of the question.[25]

Held a hostage in this trial, Dimitri was forced to face the contradictions in his soul, to make the inner journey and confront his guilt. He now had to do the work of the heart. As a Romantic, Dimitri had always been overwhelmed by his jealousy, so possessed that he was driven to thoughts of murder, driven to The Killer in himself. He had threatened to kill many rivals, above all his father; and he had threatened to kill himself. The contradictions to which Dimitri's jealousy drove him are described as follows:

> It is impossible to picture to oneself the shame and moral degradation to which the jealous man can descend without a qualm of conscience. And yet it's not as though the jealous were all vulgar and base souls. On the contrary, a man of lofty feelings, whose love is pure and full of self-sacrifice, may yet hide under tables, bribe the vilest people, and be familiar with the lowest ignominy of spying and eavesdropping. . . . It is hard to imagine what some jealous men can make up their mind to and overlook, and what they can forgive! The jealous are the readiest of all to forgive, and women know it. The jealous man can forgive extraordinarily quickly (though, of course, after a violent scene), and he is able to forgive infidelity almost conclusively proved, the very kisses and embraces he has seen, if only he can somehow be convinced that it has all been "for the last time," and that his rival will vanish from that day forward, will depart to the ends of the earth, or that he himself will carry her away somewhere, where that dreaded rival will not get near her. Of course, the reconciliation is only for an hour. For, even if the rival did disappear next day, he would invent another one and would be jealous of him. And one might wonder what there was in a love that had to be so watched over, what a love could be worth that needed such strenuous guarding. But that the jealous will never understand. And yet among them are men of noble hearts. It is remarkable, too, that those very men of noble hearts, standing hidden in some cupboard, listening and spying, never feel the stings of conscience at that moment, anyway, though they understand clearly enough with their "noble hearts" the shameful depths to which they have voluntarily sunk.[26]

Dimitri had to transform his jealous heart into a trustful heart. He had already experienced trust and a love higher than the sensual with Grushenka. But once out of her presence he still tended to be suspicious. Too, he had to learn to trust himself, to love himself generously in a spiritual way. His shame and guilt and self-loathing over his suspicious, jealous, and angry nature stood in his way. At the trial, Grushenka was brought in after all the other witnesses against him. She testified that Dimitri had told her in anger that he wanted to kill his father, but she also said, "I never believed it. I had faith in his noble heart."[27] When Dimitri heard this, he said to Grushenka, "Have faith in God and in me. I am not guilty of my father's murder!"[28] And Grushenka, thrilled, told the prosecutor she believed him. "As he has spoken now, believe it! I know him. He'll say anything as a joke or from obstinancy, but he'll never deceive you against his conscience. He's telling the whole truth, you may believe it."[29] This gave Dimitri fresh courage; Grushenka's faith in him had restored his heart. Grushenka went downstairs to await the verdict. Suddenly overcome with fatigue, Dimitri fell asleep and had a dream.

He was riding in a cart through the sleet and snow somewhere in the steppes. In a village he saw a row of peasant women along the road, all gaunt from hunger. One woman held a baby who was shivering from the cold and crying for milk. But the mother's breasts were all dried up, and the child cried and cried, reaching out its little hands all blue from the cold. "Why are they crying?" Dimitri asked, as his cart dashed by without a care, "Why is the babe weeping, and why don't the mothers feed it and keep it warm?" The peasant driver replied that the people were too poor because the village was burnt out. It was as though Dimitri had not understood before and now all the questions of human suffering burst out from his own weeping heart. He cried out:

> Tell me why it is those poor mothers stand there? Why are people poor? Why is the babe poor? Why is the steppe barren? Why don't they hug each other and kiss? Why don't they sing songs of joy? Why are they so dark from black misery? Why don't they feed the babe?" And he felt that, though his questions were unreasonable and senseless, yet he wanted to ask just that, and he had to ask it just in that way. And he felt that a passion of pity, such as he had never known before, was rising in his heart, and he wanted to cry, that he wanted to do something for them all, so that the babe should weep no more, so that the dark faced, dried-up mother should not weep, that no one should shed tears again from that moment, and he wanted to do it at once, at once, regardless of all obstacles, with all the recklessness of the Karamazovs.
>
> "And I'm coming with you. I won't leave you now for the rest of my life, I'm coming with you," he heard close beside him Grushenka's tender voice, thrilling with emotion. And his heart glowed, and he struggled forward towards the light, and he longed to live, to live, to go on and on, towards the new, beckoning light, and to hasten, hasten, now, at once![30]

At this moment Dimitri awoke and was asked to sign the protocol of the proceedings. Still in ecstatic gratitude from the dream, he noticed that some kind person had put a pillow under his head while he was sleeping. His "whole soul was quivering with tears."[31] His trial of suffering and the gift of joy in his dream had purified his heart. The dream was the beginning of his spiritual purification; an experience similar to that of his brother Alyosha, although neither of them knew it. Signing the paper which stated that he be held in prison, Dimitri cried out:

> Gentlemen, we're all cruel, we're all monsters, we all make men weep; and mothers, and babes at the breast, but of all, let it be settled here, now, of all I am the lowest reptile! I've sworn to amend, and every day I've done the same filthy things. I understand now that such men as I need a blow, a blow of destiny to catch them as with a noose, and bind them by a force from without. Never, never should I have risen of myself! But the thunderbolt has fallen. I accept the torture of accusation and my public shame. I want to suffer and by suffering I shall be purified. Perhaps, I shall be purified, gentlemen? But listen, for the last time, I am not guilty of my father's blood. I accept my punishment, not because I killed him, but because I meant to kill him, and perhaps I really might have killed him. Still, I mean to fight it out with you. I warn you of that. I'll fight it out with you to the end, and then God will decide.[32]

Like many addicts, Dimitri was unable to see his life clearly until he was struck by a thunderbolt. He had to be taken hostage and imprisoned before he could acknowledge the depths to which he had fallen. But once he underwent the public accusation and humiliation and his inner trial by fire, he understood not only his own suffering, but the suffering of all humans. And in accepting that suffering he was able to open up his heart to others.

Once in prison, Dimitri continued to pass through the spiritual purification of suffering. A "new man" had risen up in him, a side of himself that had previously been hidden. He longed to go to Siberia, he told Alyosha, where through penance he might find a human heart in his fellow sufferers, the convicts from the underground, and "at last bring up from the dark depths a lofty soul, a feeling, suffering creature; one may bring forth an angel, create a hero!"[33] He wanted to go to Siberia for "the babe," for *all* children whether they were big or little. In prison, he said, one could not exist without God.

> You wouldn't believe, Alexey, how I want to live now, what a thirst for existence and consciousness has sprung up in me within these peeling walls. . . . And what is suffering? I am not afraid of it, even if it were

> beyond reckoning. I am not afraid of it now. I was afraid of it before. . . . And I seem to have such strength in me now that I think I could stand anything, any suffering only to be able to say and to repeat to myself every moment "I exist." In thousands of agonies—I exist. I'm tormented on the rack—but I exist! Though I sit alone in a pillar—I exist! I see the sun, and if I don't see the sun, I know it's there. And there's a whole life in that, in knowing that the sun is there.[34]

Yet Dimitri was also struggling with doubts about God's existence, which had been planted by Rakitin and Ivan. Nor could he bear to be separated from Grushenka if he were found guilty and sent to Siberia. Ivan had proposed a plan for him to escape to America with Grushenka. After they became American citizens, they could safely return to Russia and work the land. Before the trial Dimitri was tormented about this possibility, afraid it would mean betraying the "new man," the "Hymn to Joy," and the "babe." But after he was finally convicted of the murder of his father, a crime he did not commit, he decided to escape with Grushenka. For, as Alyosha pointed out, he was really innocent of his father's blood and was not yet ready to be such a martyr. His awareness of suffering would remain a constant spur to "the new man." Alyosha's comments to Dimitri were similar to the advice given to addicts in the Big Book of AA, where the daily aim of spiritual progress is stressed rather than perfection.

Dimitri's redemption was to transform his dark earthy passion into the divine flame of Eros—a higher love and energy that can transform the world. The cosmic source of Dimitri's transformation rested not in the patriarchal principle but in ancient Mother Earth. Intuitively he knew his salvation could come only from the creative birth-giving force of Mother Earth. Even before he knew how to be faithful to the creative principle, he had sung some verses of Schiller's "Hymn to Joy" to Alyosha:

> Would he purge his soul from vileness
> And attain to light and worth,
> He must turn and cling forever
> To his ancient Mother Earth.[35]

But at the time, possessed by his romanticism and sensuality, he did not know how to be faithful to Mother Earth. Dimitri's dream had showed that the mother's milk was dried up because the women were poor, starving, and cold, as was the babe. This image inhibited his reckless gaiety when he drove by the burnt-out village without stopping. It inflamed his heart with pity and compassion, bringing forth his own tears for the innocent and his ardent desire to help them. This desire to help all the women and children in the world also meant compassion and redemption for the feminine side and the child within himself. In the dream, Grushenka said she would always be with him. Just as she had said this in the dream as his inner feminine partner, so in the external world she made this vow to Dimitri, bowing deeply before him at the end of the preliminary investigation. For the inner transformation that Grushenka herself had undergone through her "divine wedding" encounter with Alyosha had prepared her to acknowledge the resentment in her heart toward men, and to forgive instead. Having suffered and forgiven, she now had faith in her own goodness, and was able to love Dimitri with an open and trusting heart. And inwardly she was developing a firm spiritual resolution. Both Grushenka and Dimitri were still passionate earthy people. But the love in their hearts was transformed into the spiritual resolution to give back to Mother Earth by working the land.

4. Ivan's Conflict

Five days after his father's death, Ivan returned to discover that his father had been murdered and that Dimitri was charged with the crime. Secretly, Ivan was tortured with guilt because Smerdyakov had implied that if Ivan were to leave his father's house that fateful night, the murder would rest on his shoulders. Ivan feared that Smerdyakov was the murderer, which meant that *he* was responsible. But his innate dislike of Dimitri combined with Dimitri's violent and muddled accusations of Smerdyakov made Ivan wonder if Dimitri was guilty after all. If this were so, he might be relieved of his own guilt. Underneath it all, Ivan was suffering from the conflict between his atheism and his faith in God. Earlier, Father Zossima had intuited that this inner conflict was tearing Ivan apart:

> The question is still fretting your heart, and not answered. But the martyr likes sometimes to divert himself with his despair, as it were, driven to it by despair itself. Meanwhile in your despair, you, too, divert yourself with magazine articles, and discussions in society, though you don't believe your own arguments, and with an aching heart mock at them inwardly—That question you have not answered, and it is your great grief, for it clamours for an answer.[36]

Ivan had asked Zossima whether this question could be answered in the affirmative, and the elder had replied:

> If it can't be decided in the affirmative, it will never be decided in the negative. You know that that is the peculiarity of your heart, and all its suffering is due to it. But thank the Creator who had given you a lofty heart capable of such suffering; of thinking and seeking higher things, for our dwelling is in the heavens. God grant that your heart will attain the answer on earth—and may God bless your path.[37]

Ivan's heart was now torn asunder to such an extent with this conflict that already he had suffered hallucinations in which he was visited in his room by "the devil," who conversed with him at length. Ivan was not quite sure whether the devil was a real entity or an inferior part of his own personality. In these talks with "the devil" Ivan always felt desperately the need "to justify himself to himself,"[38] a need he felt even more strongly whenever he encountered Smerdyakov. Since his return Ivan had been under tremendous stress and feared he was going mad. Katerina, the woman Ivan loved, also feared for Ivan's sanity.

On the day that Alyosha had visited Dimitri in prison, he also went to see Ivan. He remembered poignantly Dimitri's parting words to "love Ivan," although Dimitri had also said "Ivan is a tomb." He found Ivan looking very ill. Ivan asked Alyosha if he knew how people went out of their minds, but when Alyosha replied, Ivan told him to change the subject. Then Alyosha showed Ivan a letter from Lise, a young girl Ivan had been visiting. Lise was ill and afraid she was possessed by demons; she told Alyosha that she had an urge to evil and that in her dreams demons came to take her away. With empathy, Alyosha responded that he too sometimes had strange dreams, and Lise was helped by his openness. Now, Ivan tore up Lise's unopened letter and called her a little demon, insinuating that Lise was a wanton woman offering herself to him. Shocked, Alyosha asked why Ivan had insulted a sick child on the verge of insanity. He had hoped Ivan could help her; but Ivan replied, "If she is a child I am not her nurse."[39] However, Ivan knew in his heart that his cruelty to Lise was his own refusal to help save The Madwoman in himself. Soon the conversation between Ivan and Alyosha turned to their father's murder. Ivan lost control and asked Alyosha who he thought was the murderer. Helplessly, Alyosha burst out, "You know who," and then said, "*it wasn't you* killed father."[40] Then, speaking from some higher center beyond his own will, Alyosha added:

> You have accused yourself and have confessed to yourself that you are the murderer and no one else. But you didn't do it: You are mistaken; you are not the murderer. Do you hear? It was not you! God has sent me to tell you so.[41]

Trembling, Ivan accused Alyosha of having been in his room when the devil visited. But Alyosha, who could make no sense of what Ivan was saying, repeated:

> Brother, I have said this to you, because you'll believe my word, I know that. I tell you once and for all, it's not you. You hear, once for all! God has put it into my heart to say this to you, even though it may make you hate me from this hour.[42]

But by now Ivan had regained his self-control and replied coldly:

> Alexey Fyodorovitch, I can't endure prophets and epileptics—messengers from God especially—and you know that only too well. I break off all relations with you from this moment and probably forever. I beg you to leave me at this turning.[43]

Then Ivan warned Alyosha particularly not to come to his room that day and turned away. But Alyosha called after him: "Brother, if anything happens to you today, turn to me before anyone."[44]

After this encounter, Ivan went to see Smerdyakov. It was their third meeting since the murder. During the first visit, Smerdyakov was patronizing, implying that Ivan had known his father would be murdered if he left. Ivan grew angry and accused Smerdyakov of being cunning. Smerdyakov said he thought that he and Ivan were alike—"clever men" who did not believe in God. Ivan was disturbed by this comparison, but when Smerdyakov insisted innocence of the murder, he was relieved. Still, he could not stop obsessing over their father's death and his own relationship with Smerdyakov. During the second visit, a fortnight later, Smerdyakov was malicious and haughty. This time Ivan was in a fury, asking Smerdyakov directly if he were threatening him. "Have I entered into some sort of compact with you? Do you suppose I am afraid of you?" Ivan questioned.[45] Smerdyakov replied insolently:

> This is what I meant then, and this is why I said that, that you, knowing beforehand of this murder of your own parent, left him to his fate, and that people mightn't after that conclude any evil about your feelings and perhaps of something else too—that's what I promised not to tell the authorities.[46]

Smerdyakov added resentfully that by "something else" he meant Ivan's desire for his father's death. At this Ivan jumped up and hit Smerdyakov so hard that he fell down. Smerdyakov added that at their conversation at the gate, he even had sounded out Ivan on whether he wanted his father murdered. Why did Ivan go away? That showed that he wanted his father's death—otherwise he should have said something then. Furious, Ivan accused Smerdyakov of the murder. But denying it again, Smerdyakov warned Ivan that if he were to accuse him of the crime publicly, he would reveal their secret conversation and put Ivan to shame.

In a rage, Ivan left for Katerina's house. He felt guilty of the crime now, convinced Smerdyakov had done it and that he had put him up to it. He knew he had desired his father's death. Now Katerina, wanting to save Ivan, produced a letter written by the drunken Dimitri in which he had threatened to murder his father to get the money to pay back his debt to her. Although this briefly convinced Ivan of Dimitri's guilt, it did not relieve his own.

Ill and tormented, Ivan went to see Smerdyakov for a third time. On his way a drunken peasant lurched against him in the snow. Ivan angrily pushed him on the frozen ground. " 'He will be frozen,' Ivan thought, and went on."[47] He found Smerdyakov looking ill. At this meeting Smerdyakov finally admitted to the murder. While Grigory was chasing Dimitri, he had shammed an epileptic fit, killed Fyodor, and taken the money. He knew Dimitri would be blamed because of his violent threats. The next day he was stricken with a real epileptic attack and taken to the hospital. As proof of what he said, he showed Ivan the 3,000 rubles. With hatred, he told Ivan that he had only followed his words: "All things are lawful." " 'You are the real murderer,' he said to Ivan. 'I was only your instrument.' "[48] "Are you a phantom?" asked the terrified Ivan. Then, angrily, Ivan told Smerdyakov he would testify against him in court the next day. But Smerdyakov remarked that Ivan was too ill, nor did he have the courage. For Ivan, said Smerdyakov with a smirk, was the son with the soul most like his father. Moreover, Smerdyakov added that he would only deny the whole thing in court and Ivan would be shamed before everyone.

Resolving to report this encounter at the trial, Ivan walked out into the cold. He felt relief and joy at his determination to get the truth out in the open. At that moment, ill and staggering, he stumbled into something at his feet—the drunken peasant he had knocked down and abandoned earlier. Now Ivan took him to a house nearby, giving the owner some money to help pay for a doctor. Ivan felt good that he had taken the time to care for the peasant—maybe he was not as bad or as mad as he had thought. But at the turning point between the path to his room and the prosecutor's house, suddenly he decided to go home and wait until tomorrow to make his report. At that moment, his gladness at his new-found resolve slipped away.

In his room, Ivan sat down exhausted, ill and dizzy. He was reminded of something agonizing and revolting that was present and that had been there before. On the sofa opposite him he saw a familiar figure, a Russian gentleman, middle-aged and shabbily dressed in the fashion of three years prior. It was the same "devil" who had come to see Ivan before. Ivan told him he was merely a hallucination. " 'You are the incarnation of myself, but only of one side of me . . . of my thoughts and feelings, but only the nastiest and stupidest of them,' Ivan said."[49] But the devil insisted he was real, reminding Ivan that he had even accused Alyosha of having talked to "him." As Ivan was struggling with himself to deny the devil's reality, the devil told him about a philosopher who refused to believe in God and immortality. When the philosopher died he was told he could go to Heaven, but as punishment he would have to walk a quadrillion miles. For a thousand years the philosopher refused to walk, but finally he started the journey. Once within the Gates of Heaven he cried out that what he found there was worth an infinite walk. Recognizing this story as one he had invented himself as a student, Ivan cried out that the devil was not real. But the devil continued to plague Ivan with his own stories, taunting him with all his cynicism, nastiness, and the worst of his secret fears. He said he was really working for Ivan's salvation. Finally enraged, Ivan hurled an inkstand at the devil, who quipped that this act was reminiscent of Martin Luther. The sound of the glass crashing mingled with a noise at the window, which the devil said was Alyosha coming with surprising news. As happens frequently in a dream, Ivan felt as though he were in chains and could not break free, but finally he saw that there was no one on the sofa, and the object he thought he'd thrown at the devil was right before him on the table. When he went to the window, there was Alyosha, who said that Smerdyakov had just committed suicide by hanging and had left a note that said he had destroyed himself of his own will and that no one else was to blame. But Ivan was too delirious to listen to Alyosha. Instead, he raved on incoherently about the conversations with the devil and Smerdyakov, saying that the devil had already told him of the suicide. Nevertheless, he intended to go to court the next day to testify. Eventually Ivan lost consciousness. Alyosha stayed by his side praying. He had begun to understand his brother's illness better—it was the agony of his conscience. But in this very suffering lay the hope for Ivan. Alyosha thought:

> "The anguish of a proud determination. An earnest conscience!" God, in Whom he disbelieved, and His truth were gaining mastery over his heart, which still refused to submit. "Yes, . . . yes if Smerdyakov is dead, no one will believe Ivan's evidence; but he will go and give it." Alyosha smiled softly. "God will conquer! . . . He will either rise up in the light of truth, or . . . he'll perish in hate, revenging on himself and on everyone his having served the cause he does not believe in."[50]

The next day, in the middle of Dimitri's trial, Ivan entered the courtroom, looking very ill. He testified that although he had heard Dimitri threaten to kill his father, Smerdyakov was the actual murderer and had told him so before hanging himself. He also said that he had incited Smerdyakov, adding provocatively: "Who doesn't desire his father's death?"[51] As proof of Smerdyakov's guilt he pulled out the 3,000 rubles that Smerdyakov had given him. But when questioned about his proof, Ivan gave the devil as his only witness, raving incoherently about yesterday's conversation with him. Soon Ivan had to be taken from the courtroom. Amidst the confusion, Katerina jumped up hysterically, hoping to rescue him. She presented the letter from Dimitri, written when he was drunk, in which he threatened to kill his father, and accused Dimitri of the crime, saying that Ivan was ill and innocent. Earlier, Katerina had tried to save Dimitri, testifying that she had never doubted his honesty or innocence, nor had he spoken in her presence any threat to kill his father. But now Katerina said she had lied to try to save Dimitri: "I wanted to save him, for he had hated and despised me so!"[52] She then accused Dimitri of wanting to marry her for her inheritance. " 'I tried to conquer him by my love,' Katerina cried, '—a love that knew no bounds. I even tried to forgive his faithlessness.' "[53] Katerina was revealing her true character—she was a martyr who sacrificed herself continually—first for her father, then Dimitri, and now Ivan. And while she was pouring out her life to this court, the following occurred to her:

> She had loved him [Dimitri] with an hysterical "lacerated" love only from pride, from wounded pride, and that love was not like love, but more like revenge. Oh! perhaps that lacerated love would have grown into real love, perhaps Katya longed for nothing more than that, but Mitya's faithlessness had wounded her to the bottom of her heart, and her heart could not forgive him. The moment of revenge had come upon her suddenly, and

> all that had been accumulating so long and so painfully in the offended woman's breast burst out all at once and unexpectedly. She betrayed Mitya, but she betrayed herself too. And no sooner had she given full expression to her feelings than the tension of course was over and she was overwhelmed with shame.[54]

Katerina was removed from the courtroom, sobbing. Just then it was announced that Ivan was suffering from a serious attack of brain fever.

At the end of the novel Ivan's fate is left undetermined. After the trial, he was taken to Katerina's house, where he lay unconscious in a high fever. The doctors could not be positive about his recovery. Alyosha held hope for it, while Katerina feared Ivan's demise.

In terms of the patterns of addiction, Ivan embodies the archetypal figures of The Underground Man (his cynicism and isolating distance from other humans), The Outlaw (his rebellion against God's world and his philosophy that "everything is permitted"), and The Judge (his thirst for absolute justice in the form of the Grand Inquisitor, who raises himself above God and Christ). And as he says: "I would rather remain with my unavenged suffering and unsatisfied indignation, *even if I were wrong.*"[55] In many ways, Ivan is the central character of this drama of addiction. It is Ivan's recovery that is left in question. His struggle between faith and disbelief in a higher power that conflicts with his ego desire for domination is one that the addict faces. Like many addicts, Ivan is obviously ill—to the point of madness—but he is not able to make the turn and surrender to life on life's terms.

Ivan's relation to the two women in his life is also significant. Lise, the teenager whose letter he tore up and whom he refused to help, symbolizes the archetype of The Madwoman, caught in self-hatred, bent on destroying herself. Her refusal of Alyosha's engagement proposal shows she cannot accept geunuine love; instead she is driven by the demons to torment herself and offers herself to a man, like Ivan, who will brutally reject her. Her relationship to Ivan shows the negative bond between The Madwoman hungry for a love she can never have and the rational, patriarchal Judge who rejects her brutally. Katerina symbolizes the co-dependent side of his nature. A typical co-addict, she sacrifices herself first to save her father, then Dimitri, and finally Ivan. Her martyrdom—as she finally admits to herself—comes not from the wholeness of forgiving love but from her own wounded pride. Addicted to her own nobility, she helps others in order to fulfill her need to be dominant and morally superior. Like Ivan, she is an unforgiving Judge. But she does suffer from her treachery at the trial. At the end of the novel, Alyosha pleads with her to see the ill Dimitri who hopes to give and receive forgiveness. Begrudgingly, Katerina finally visits him, but she cannot yet forgive. As she says: "My forgiveness is no good to you, nor yours to me; whether you forgive me or not, you will always be a sore place in my heart and I in yours—so it must be."[56] Nevertheless, the two pledged undying love for each other, a pledge more of an impulsive moment than a long-lasting amend. When Grushenka came in just as she was leaving, Katerina asked her forgiveness too. But Grushenka sensed her plea as coming from her pride and martyrdom, a fact that Katerina later confirmed to Alyosha. "I asked her forgiveness because I wanted to punish myself to the bitter end," she said with fierce resentment.[57] Nevertheless, Katerina arranged to pay for the escape of Grushenka and Dimitri and she offered to pay for the funeral of Illusha, a poor sick boy whom Alyosha had helped. But, like Ivan, her last words to Alyosha were: "Leave me, please!"[58] The feminine counterpart to Ivan, Katerina cannot completely transform since she is unwilling to surrender her addiction to control and dominance.

In addition to these two feminine addictive figures, Ivan must also confront two deadly shadow aspects of himself—each a product of his disbelief. First there is the devil, the spirit of his own self-destructiveness. Ivan's dialogue with the devil externalizes his internal dichotomy between faith in something higher and atheistic disbelief. Every addict has had this dialogue with the devil in himself and knows the desperate attempt to retain some contact with reality, just when he is at odds with the highest reality, God. For along with atheism goes the futility of redemption. In Ivan's legend of the Grand Inquisitor he had represented the devil as a magnanimous figure who had great pity for humankind. But he hallucinates the devil as merely a clever, banal fellow, the symbol of boredom and wornout materialism, a manifestation that Ivan finds insufferable, for it wounds his pride. As the Devil says:

> You are really angry with me for not having appeared to you in a red glow, with thunder and lightning, with scorched wings, but have shown myself in such a modest form. You are wounded, in the first place, in your aesthetic feelings, and secondly in your pride. How could such a vulgar devil visit such a great man as you! Yes, there is that romantic strain in you . . .[59]

Just as the devil repeats to Ivan the nastiest and stupidest of his thoughts, so Ivan's other shadow figure or "double," Smerdyakov, acts out his philosophy and reduces it to the hideous crime of parricide. Ivan's theory was that if there is no God, "everything is permitted." Acting on this philosophy, Smerdyakov kills the father. Though both Ivan and Dimitri desire their father's death, Smerdyakov is the actual killer in this drama of addiction. Smerdyakov is also a Trickster; he shams a fit and tricks Dimitri and Fyodor as well as Ivan. Smerdyakov shows The Trickster turning into The Killer. Yet, the murder of the father initiates the suffering and makes possible the redemption through which Ivan and Dimitri must pass. As The Trickster, Smerdyakov pushes the brothers over the edge into The Abyss, where they hit bottom and are forced to face themselves. Thus Smerdyakov has two aspects as Trickster-Killer. He initiates the transformation process, forcing the individual to make a choice. But he himself personifies self-destruction and lack of redemption, for his disbelief leads him not only to kill his father but also to commit suicide. As a nihilist he despises everyone. He harasses Ivan to the point of madness. In his hatred of humanity he puts himself outside the law (The Outlaw). In his final acts of parricide and suicide, he gives himself over completely to demonic self-will, i.e., the Demon Lover. Through his nihilism, Smerdyakov symbolizes the unredeemable aspect of addiction. Ivan comes so strongly under Smerdyakov's influence and harassment because he cannot turn his will over to something higher than his own limited rational ego. Thus his inner conflict brings him to the bottom of The Abyss in the unconsciousness of "brain fever." But having seen all these sides of himself, he now has the possibility to make the existential act of surrender, if, by the grace of God, he is given a second chance.

Thus, in *The Brothers Karamozov* one can see the various archetypal figures of addiction in operation, meshing and interweaving throughout the novel. Dimitri is The Romantic and The Gambler, the seeker of ecstasy and excitement through sensual passion. His transformation from addiction to a creative response occurs when he moves beyond his passions and turns his will over to the higher love of the babe, the feminine, and the new man within himself. His addictive love relation to Grushenka is transformed from the dark Romantic's jealous desire to possess to a higher soul-mate relationship in which they will work together to regenerate the earth. Grushenka is transformed from a Madwoman hungry for the love of men, yet angry and revengeful because she has been abused by them. Thus, like The Madwoman, she takes pleasure in rejecting and hurting men in turn. Through the "divine wedding" she experiences with Alyosha, she discovers a pure spiritual love in herself that enables her to forgive herself and extend that forgiveness to men.

Ivan is an Underground Man and Judge addicted to perfection. Because of his resentment of God's "unjust" creation, he rejects life and judges everyone against the unmerciful standards of his logic and reason. Through his judgment he puts himself above others, even God. At the same time, he tries to dodge judgment through his philosophy that "everything is permitted." It is unclear whether he will live to transform. But there is hope because, having recognized his existential guilt and confessed in court, he has humbled himself before other humans, surrendering the dominance of his rational judgment to a higher power. His madness can be seen as a descent into the irrational chaotic realm of The Abyss, the dark night of his soul's journey, which could open him to the divine fire of love and creativity. The young girl he rejects, Lise, represents The Madwoman whom he persecutes in himself, the one who is already conscious of the way the Demon Lover can possess the soul. Lise's fate is left in question. Her rejection of Alyosha's love shows her downward direction, but her conversation with him leaves open a possibiilty for redemption. Katerina, with whom Ivan is in love, is addicted to her own self-image and nobility. She, like Ivan, is a martyr and a Judge. Typical of the co-addict, she gives her money away to Dimitri even though she knows he will spend it on her rival, Grushenka. Katerina feels superior to Dimitri and Grushenka, whom she judges to be bad, just as the co-addict feels superior in comparison to the wanton addict. When Ivan becomes sick, her energy turns from Dimitri toward Ivan. Again, like the co-addict, she wants to save Ivan and, in the courtroom, judges Dimitri to be the killer.

Smerdyakov, the rejected and abused one, is an Underground Man turned Outlaw. Cunningly he follows Ivan's premise, "everything is lawful." As a Trickster, he outwits everyone and is the actual killer. He kills his father, himself, and he tries to kill the souls of Ivan and Dimitri. He tries to kill all love. But he is also the figure in the psyche who causes Ivan and Dimitri to confront themselves, thus opening up the black abyss of their dark journey to transformation.

Fyodor Karamazov is the addict caught in total denial. His is also a Moneylender and a Trickster who provokes his sons toward their own individual addictive forms of possession by the Demon Lover and toward thoughts of murder. Fyodor is the "dark father" possessed by addiction who, as hostage, dies unredeemed, passing on the wounds of addiction to his children.

In contrast is the transformed father, Zossima. As a former addict, he has experienced the darkness of the fall. But he has transformed. The bottom of his abyss was his cruelty to his servant; his regeneration is his philosophy of love and forgiveness. Just as he described to Fyodor how shame and self-deception lead to addiction, so Zossima describes the predicament of societal addiction as the slavery to which the modern world has descended:

> Interpreting freedom as the multiplication and rapid satisfaction of desires, men distort their own nature, for many senseless and foolish desires and habits and ridiculous fancies are fostered in them. They live only for mutual envy, for luxury and ostentation. To have dinners, visits, carriages, rank and slaves to wait on one is looked as a necessity, for which life, honour and human feeling are sacrificed, and men even commit suicide if they are unable to satisfy it. We see the same thing among those who are not rich, while the poor drown their unsatisfied need and their envy in drunkenness. But soon they will drink blood instead of wine, they are being led on to it. I ask you is such a man free? I knew one "champion of freedom" who told me himself that, when he was deprived of tobacco in prison, he was so wretched at the privation that he almost went and betrayed his cause for the sake of getting tobacco again. And such a man says, "I am fighting for the cause of humanity."
>
> How can such a one fight, what is he fit for? He is capable perhaps of some action quickly over, but he cannot hold out long. And it's no wonder that instead of gaining freedom they have sunk into slavery, and instead of serving the cause of brotherly love and the union of humanity have fallen, on the contrary, into dissension and isolation, as my mysterious visitor and teacher said to me in my youth. And therefore the ideas of the service of humanity, of brotherly love and the solidarity of mankind is more and more dying out in the world, and indeed this idea is sometimes treated with derision. For how can a man shake off his habits, what can become of him if he is in such bondage to the habit of satisfying the inumerable desires he has created for himself? He is isolated, and what concern has he with the rest of humanity? They have succeeded in accumulating a greater mass of objects, but the joy in the world has grown less.[60]

Zossima also foresees that isolation is dividing humanity, that "moneylenders" are devouring the commune, that addiction is on the rise. The life of addiction, Zossima says, results in the abuse of children. He asks: ". . . 'is that what a little child's heart needs? He needs sunshine, childish play, good examples all about him, and at least a little love.' "[61]

In accepting his own existential guilt as part of the human condition,

Zossima affirms the possibility of forgiveness. Only if one has accepted one's own guilt, is forgiveness possible. Zossima knows the secret of the twelfth step: "In saving others, you will save yourself." For, we all share the sorrows and joys of human existence. Once this is seen and accepted, the affirmation of life as a gift is possible. In fact, "Life is a great joy," says Zossima. "You can save the entire earth. All are happy, all are beautiful, all could establish paradise right now." Paradise, too, is deep within the soul, together with the forces of darkness. Having experienced the tension of the light and dark, the forces of good and evil within himself, Zossima affirms that one can choose the light, but not without first having experienced and accepted the dark. Love and forgiveness are the forces that can transform the world into paradise. The earth's beauty proclaims the glory of Creation. If we love the earth, if we "water it with our tears of joy," we will participate in its healing and feel the divinity of others and the mystical unity of the cosmos. Zossima teaches about the "steps" of the soul's ascent on the spiritual ladder to God. These steps, like the twelve steps, require acceptance of suffering, humility, surrender, faith in a higher power, taking responsibility for our own sins and for all humans, confession, forgiveness, prayer and meditation, and the gift of love for others. These steps are the way to redemption and to rapture. In their enactment one experiences ecstasy and the gifts of creation. Zossima's transformation from addiction into creativity is one that regenerates the earth, redeeming the missing mother and the abused feminine and uniting all beings from the mysterious center of the human heart, which is guided by the divine creative fire of love.

Alyosha is the transformed son who carries on Zossima's message in the world. Originally, Alyosha's addiction was to idealism and to projecting divinity onto a finite being such as Zossima. But, through his transformation, Alyosha sees the real task is to unite with others as God's children and to carry love and forgiveness into the earthly world. This mystical bond draws all humans together and passes from one to another in a redemptive thread of ecstasy that "waters the earth with tears of joy" and is "in contact with other worlds." This is the meaning of his dream of the "divine wedding." After his own recovery, Alyosha tries to help his brothers Dimitri and Ivan, and his "sisters" Grushenka, Lise, and Katerina. He also reconciles the children of the village with the dying boy, Ilusha. Son of an impoverished drunken father and crazed mother, Ilusha symbolizes the suffering child of a dysfunctional family, whose shame alienates him from the other children. Alyosha becomes a model for the school children and tells them how important their reconciliation with Ilusha is and how this good memory of childhood will aid them all their life. They have gathered together around the final event of Ilusha's death, and this memory of their unity will make them better human beings. Through their love and generosity for one another, they will overcome evil and the fear of life and learn to love life instead. At the end of *The Brothers Karamozov* Alyosha exhorts the children, symbolic of the child within us all, and the youthful hope of the recovering addict, to remember and love life everlasting. Alyosha reminds us of our creative human future and redemption, which is made possible through the work of the heart.

> Certainly we shall all rise again, certainly we shall see each other and shall tell each other with joy and gladness all that has happened![62]

17: THE HEALING FIELDS

The clearing rests in song and shade.
It is a creature made
By old light held in soil and leaf,
By human joy and grief,
By human work,
Fidelity of sight and stroke,
By rain, by water on
The parent stone.

We join our work to Heaven's gift,
Our hope to what is left,
That field and woods at last agree
In an economy
Of widest worth,
High Heaven's Kingdom come on earth.
Imagine Paradise.
O dust, arise!

—Wendell Berry, *Sabbaths*

FORGIVENESS—ESSENTIAL TO any healing process—is required of all addicts in their recovery. It is also a central part of the creative process, for in order to create we must continually forgive ourselves for our inability to embody the perfect vision; we must forgive ourselves for our finitude. The dictionary lists one meaning for forgiveness as: to grant pardon for an offense or a debt, e.g., to "forgive" the interest owed on a loan. Another meaning is to stop feeling resentment against an offender. In the Lord's Prayer, too, we ask the higher power to forgive us our debts as we forgive our debtors. These meanings harken back to the notion of guilt as a debt, which was discussed in the chapter on The Moneylender. The task of forgiveness is to make amends by forgiving oneself and others for specific offenses and by correcting one's faults. In accord with a dictionary meaning, to *amend* means to grow or become better by reforming onself, by improving one's life, thus acknowledging authentic guilt, the debt of existence that we owe our Creator. Ultimately, making an amend means changing one's life in accord with the flow of creation, which is the existential truth of the amends process. The result of making an honest amend is that one feels good about oneself. It is a healing process. As recovering addicts make amends they find that their low self-esteem begins to vanish. An amend differs from an apology.

> Apologies are certainly sometimes called for, but apologies are not amends. Amends are made by acting differently. I can apologize a hundred times

> for being late for work and this will not "mend" the tardiness. Appearing on the job at or before the starting time gives reality to my penitence. What I say about my behavior does not demonstrate change. It is my actions that do this. Step Nine is very definitely an action Step.[1]

To make an amend one must wait patiently for the right time. Prior to that one has to be ready and willing. Often, when one feels unwilling to make an amend, it means that the resentment behind the offense has not really been cleared away. Then one needs to ask for help, to pray for the resentment to be removed and for guidance regarding when and in what way to carry out this action. Ultimately, the making of amends is a lifelong process of reconciling the gift of our creative being with the higher power. It is the process of atonement, i.e., "at-one-ment" with ourselves, others and the cosmos.[2] The amends process is a mending of relationships and rebuilding. It restores the wholeness in our lives and the earth on which we dwell.

Paul Tillich said this about forgiveness:

> There is no condition for forgiveness. But forgiveness could not come to us if we were not asking for it and receiving it. Forgiveness is an answer, the divine answer, to the question implied in our existence. An answer is answer only for him who has asked, who is aware of the question.[3]

According to Tillich, love presupposes forgiveness, just as it presupposes the feeling of unity, of belonging to the divine. Ultimately it is the feeling of rejection by God that makes us unable to love. When we are hostage to that feeling of rejection, we feel alienated from the higher harmony. This feeling of estrangement, which the addict knows so well, leads to the feeling of being judged by an oppressive power, which in turn engenders hostility toward life. We saw this dynamic operating in the characters in *The Brothers Karamazov*. There, forgiveness was the key to redemption—asking for forgiveness, being able to receive it, and giving forgiveness in return. Forgiveness engendered love and the feeling of mystical unity, the experience of the higher harmony. This happened in the encounter between Alyosha and Grushenka. In forgiving each other, each received forgiveness. Through the love they felt for each other, each felt transformed and regenerated. Dimitri, too, had the experience of accepting guilt, asking for forgiveness, and being reborn. But the alienated ones, Ivan and his "double," Smerdyakov, could neither ask for nor give forgiveness. Thus, Ivan went mad and Smerdyakov killed himself after killing his father.

Tillich points out that nothing greater can happen to a human being than the experience of forgiveness, for forgiveness overcomes estrangement, hostility, and rejection. It reconciles, reunites, and puts the human being at one (atonement) with the cosmos and its Creator. As Tillich wrote of the prostitute who is forgiven by Christ:

> Her state of mind, her ecstasy of love, show that something has happened to her. And nothing greater can happen to a human being than that he is forgiven. For forgiveness means reconciliation in spite of estrangement; it means reunion in spite of hostility; it means acceptance of those who are unacceptable; and it means reception of those who are rejected. Forgiveness is unconditional, or it is not forgiveness at all.[4]

Tillich maintains that God's forgiveness is unconditional, "in spite of" what we do, not "because of" what we do. Sinners are not forgiven *because* they humiliated themselves: this would imply that we have to make ourselves feel guilty, rejected, and unworthy in order to deserve forgiveness. Rather, the existential reality of forgiveness is grounded in our human condition. Forgiveness is often confused with pardon, granted by the righteous ones to the wrongdoer, releasing him or her from punishment. But this notion stems from the notion of a wrathful, oppressive, judgmental god and only engenders hostility and estrangement. In contrast, genuine forgiveness always reunites and overcomes estrangement. Love is grounded in forgiveness and reconciliation, not in rejection and wrathful judgment. With compassionate forgiveness, everything changes. Then we can feel the divine healing occur within us: "Like a fiery stream, his healing power enters into us, we affirm him, and with him, our own being and the others from whom we are estranged, and life as a whole."[5]

Implied in what Tillich has to say here is the addict's experience of the Dark Night of the Soul, the fall into The Abyss. When an addict makes amends, this experience has been accepted as the refining of the soul for love. The addict has faced and acknowledged his dark side through step four, and in step five acknowledged it before another human in the presence of God. Steps six and seven ask for the removal of defects and for forgiveness from the higher power. And steps eight and nine, the steps of amends, actualize the miracle of forgiveness that is part of human destiny. This is what finally reunites us with the creative ground of our being. The amends process transforms our estrangement, and we are reunited with our creativity. As Tillich says:

> Our hostility toward life is manifested in cynicism and disgust, in bitterness and continuous accusation against life. We feel rejected by life, not so much because of its objective darkness and threats and horrors, but because of our estrangement from its power and meaning. He who is reunited with God, the creative Ground of life, the power of life in everything that lives, is reunited with life. He feels accepted by it and he can love it. He understands that love is greater, the greater the estrangement which is conquered by it. In metaphorical language I would like to say to those who feel deeply their hostility toward life: Life accepts you; life loves you as a separated part of itself; life wants to reunite you with itself, even when it seems to destroy you.[6]

For Tillich, it is the greater ground of healing—forgiveness and love—that enables people to bear their own self-doubts and their doubts about the love of others. For, like Alyosha and Grushenka, we are all longing for the acceptance of others. But it is in the cosmic source of ultimate acceptance that we are all united. This was the divine vision that Alyosha had after his encounter with Grushenka. When he saw that the connective threads of all the realms were linking with his own soul and the Creator, he longed for forgiveness.

This ecstatic moment of ultimate acceptance and forgiveness transcends linear clock time. It is a cosmic moment that breaks through our ego's version of events. Heidegger, in his revisioning of the question of being, emphasizes the mystery of time and being at our core. Our important "moments," he says, are not those we calculate or control, not those that follow from cause to effect. Rather they are moments that break through and come toward us from a vast and mysterious future, thrusting us back on our past as they gather us into a moment of presence: an ecstatic moment (ec-stasis) in which we stand out from our ego-selves and are present to all that is. For example, we experience this in times of love, creation, visions, awe before art or Nature. This is one of the great gifts of our existence—it includes all the dark and all the light as one great revolving cycle of unity. Rilke calls it the "point where it turns," the center of stillness that is the center of all creativity. This is the transforming moment of creative conversion. As Tillich writes:

> Decisive spiritual experiences have the character of a breakthrough. In the midst of our futile efforts to make ourselves worthy, in our despair about the inescapable failure of these attempts, we are suddenly grasped by the certainty that we are forgiven, and the fire of love begins to burn. That is the greatest experience anyone can have. It may not happen often, but when it does happen, it decides and transforms everything.[7]

That forgiveness is essential in the healing process can be seen in the story of the following woman, now three years into her recovery from the disease of alcoholism. Forgiving all those whom she had harmed due to neglect or resentment was part of her amends process. But, perhaps more essential was forgiving herself for the ravages of a disease that so dissolved her boundaries to the external that she allowed others to project their own creative and erotic desires upon her, blocking the fulfillment of her own creativity and love life. Forgiveness of herself and others enabled her to let go of the past and live creatively in the present. During her recovery, the mystery of forgiveness seemed to come from a force and future greater than herself, which brought her before her past and consequently the whole of her life. Her recovery was a healing and nurturing process that engendered creativity in her marriage and in her photography.

There was a history of alcoholism in her family. Ellen's father was an alcoholic and so was her mother, from whom she was separated at the age of three. Raised by her father and stepmother, she grew up with the fear that she might be sexually promiscuous and alcoholic like her mother. Desperately, she wanted to be better than her mother and not allow the same things to happen to her. So, she drank to excess only rarely. But, like her mother, she did have a daughter out of wedlock at a very early age. Two years later, she had another daughter. A single mother in her twenties, she felt that motherhood stabilized her for some time. She also studied photography during this period.

At twenty-nine, however, she became involved in a seven-year relationship with a man whose profession required social entertaining and participation in community events. At this time she began to drink socially, which helped her relax. Gradually, Ellen began to *need* alcohol to be the gracious partner her lover wanted to present to the world. Proud of his creativity, she served as his beautiful muse. But meanwhile she was giving up her own creativity for his, and she realized she must return to art school full-time. There was a lot of drinking in that environment—even during classes in the daytime. Drinking seemed to loosen up the creative process and also helped her talk more fluently about her work. Ellen was still a periodic drinker, but with some humiliating results. She would have to leave a community event because of drunkenness. Expensive long-distance charges began to appear on her phone bill for calls she couldn't remember having made. Worse, she began to become less attentive to her children. She did not even realize that her youngest daughter was developing a severe problem with drugs and alcohol.

In addition, there had been a traumatic event with her father. One evening on a visit home, Ellen and her father had been drinking and talking when, without warning, he started making love to her. At first she resisted, but then something inside her gave way. Overwhelmed, she dissolved in the confusion of the boundaries between nurturing love and sexuality. She made love with her father only once, but it was enough to throw her into a terrible confusion about who she really was. After this she also got into kinky sexuality with her partner. The fears of being just like her mother seemed to be coming true.

When she was thirty-five, her father died of cancer. She spent his last days with him at his bedside, where he was given "Brahmin cocktails," a variety of painkillers, including speed and cocaine. She drank some of this concoction, too, and doing so, she felt, put her "over the edge" of her addiction. Later, on reflection, she realized that she had had a death wish herself. At the same time, realizing the fragility of life, she became frantic and didn't want to be wasting it. The day after her father died, she changed her name. At the same time she questioned the long relationship in which she had been giving up her creativity.

Her drinking accelerated swiftly, although Ellen did not yet consider herself to be an alcoholic. She had graduated from art school where she had been a "star." Frantic to leave the relationship, which had been devouring her creativity, she finally took her paints and chalks, her camera equipment and her Laurie Anderson tapes, and rented a room of her own. From morning to night she worked on her art. Although she was not drinking so heavily at this point, typically she would have her first beer at ten thirty in the morning. In the seven-year relationship she had felt "trapped," unable to create within the confines of a controlling lover who expected her to be *his* muse and *his* bridge to the world. The choice seemed to be either to create or to be in relationship. To do both seemed impossible.

With a room of her own, able to create whenever she wanted, she felt free. In this new "high," she fell in love with her landlord. After a whirlwind romance, they were married within five months. As is usually the case in the first months of romance, each was on his or her best behavior. In this case, both were secretly trying to control their drinking. Her husband offered to support her financially in order to give her the time and space to devote her energy to art.

This was her opportunity. But now she started drinking very early in the morning, beginning with Kaluha. She felt that the drinking gave her tremendous energy, helping her to focus and be brutal with her priorities in her art. But soon the drinking took over—her work became messy; she was too sleepy to work. Moreover, her work lost its thread of meaning. And her business began to suffer. She was photographing parents with their children, and often by the time they came for their appointments she was on her way to being drunk. Hiding the Kaluha bottles became an important part of her daily routine. The drinking was also beginning to interfere with her domestic life. For she was already drunk by dinner time and was too sleepy to be present when her husband came home. He, too, had his secret drinking problem, but his drinking pattern was different. Thus, in terms of their drinking, the couple was not in "synch."

By now she was worried, for neither her relationship nor her creativity were working, due to her drinking. She could only manage abstinence for two or three days. Failing in both her relationship and her creativity brought Ellen to confront herself. Although for a brief time she tried to blame the marriage, she finally realized her drinking was not due to outer factors in her life. Instead, the drinking seemed to have a life all of its own. She finally had her "last drunk," which to this day remains a reminder of the terrible depths to which she had fallen. After a spree that had started early in the morning, she realized she'd like to live in a tree so tall that no one could reach her. She climbed a mountain, and in her drunken exhilaration, she started down in the rain, laughing and shrieking like a madwoman, running so fast she could not stop. As she approached her home, the exhilaration began to wear off. In the rain, her face smudged with mascara, she stood outside her home looking in at her husband and children. One of the children looked out and screamed at the frightening figure outside. That scary madwoman standing in the rain did not look like their mother.

The next day she decided to do something about it. She tried AA. In the beginning she had a hard time—she felt she was too smart and artistic to be a part of this group—but she kept going to meetings because she was desperate. Although initially the "religious" aspect was difficult for her to accept, this later became one of the most comforting and meaningful parts of her recovery program. Reflecting on her recovery process, she said:

> The most meaningful part of recovery for me has been the forgiveness—forgiveness of other people and of myself. For this to happen I had to realize I wasn't so special; that I was a part of the human race rather than alienated from humankind. Humbleness was a key. Life is a battle and a struggle, and yet it has also a lot of grace and beauty in it. When, with the clarity of being sober, the petal really begins to open, you can see so much deeper into the depths of the flower of being.

The amends process has been essential in her recovery, an ongoing process of healing. Even before AA, she had begun an inner dialogue of forgiveness with her father. With both daughters the amends process is ongoing, as it is with her husband and his children and her friends. Trying to be present on a daily basis for her stepchildren is part of the amends to her daughters as well. For it is putting loving presence into the well of the human condition. Ellen sees her portraits of parents and children as part of that same amends process, for her work is an expressive gift about the creative possibilities for human relationship.

> The amends process is a process of being honest, facing up to the fact that we've offended and hurt others, accepting that dark side of ourselves and being willing to stand up to it and say humbly we are sorry for the grief and pain we caused. When we make amends we also forgive ourselves, so we try not to judge ourselves or others for the past. We try to release the past and make room for the new and the present. It is as though forgiveness comes to us from the future, gathers us up in the whole of its greater mystery, releases us from the past, and enables us to re-create our lives in the present. Whenever we carry around a guilt, or anger, or resentment it is poisonous. So making amends is a constant process of clearing one's inner house. We have to learn how to know the feeling is there, how to understand that feeling, and how to let it go.

Another gift of her recovery has been the creative marriage that has resulted. Soon after she first went to AA, her husband came also. Participating in the twelve-step program together, they have been able to become honest and open with each other and build up trust. She said:

> Our marriage would never have made it without the program. The twelve steps form the hub of a wheel for a relationship. We take risks with each other. We both want to be ourselves, who we are, rather than acting out the other's projection. In the program we deal with this daily. Every day we do an inventory to try to clear things out before negative energies build up. In relationships my major problem was with asserting myself, saying *no* to the other person. I was always trying to please people and take care of other's moods. Now that my mind is clear and I have a better sense of my own boundaries, I know what I can and cannot do; what I want and

> what I don't want. Now I realize I, too, have a right to be angry. So, in this relationship I can be angry with my husband when that feeling comes up. I know now that I don't have to take care of him, or be his soul figure, muse, or his link to life. We can then discuss our feelings, and if we can be honest and listen to each other, the anger and resentment can be surrendered. Before, it seemed I had only one option when I got angry—either I had to stuff my feelings or go off on my own and leave. Now, with our constant open and honest dialogue, I do not feel the compulsion to flee. Creativity and relationship no longer appear to me as "either/or." Since working the twelve steps I feel free, clear, and strong enough to endure the tension of a creative relationship. But it takes a lot of work on a daily basis.

With respect to her creative process and recovery, she found that for nearly the first year of her sobriety, she couldn't work. This is not unusual, for the body and psyche of the addict have been so badly injured that healing takes time. Finally, her creativity broke through to even more exciting levels than before. She said:

> At first I couldn't work. I was terrified of the blank piece of paper. But once I started I became more of a risk taker. I've changed from color to black and white. And I'm always looking for new solutions. I don't waste energy doing only what is safe. Now I try to bring in an unknown into the photographic situation. Or, if suddenly it is there, I allow it to be. I don't try to control so much. I experiment with different lighting. When I was drinking I did color work that was more controlled because of the lighting. Then I couldn't take risks because I wasn't all there. Now I throw in the risk and accept the struggle. I'm willing to plant new seeds, unknown seeds, and let them sprout as they will.

Making an amend is like sowing new seed; it is a way of healing fields that have become infested with a plague. Addiction is a plague upon the soul's fields, a toxic attack on heart and spirit. It is a devastation of the earth on which we live. Making amends is an act of responsibility for the destruction caused by that disease—whether by individuals or by nations.

Central to this process is forgiveness. For one individual to make an amend to another, he or she must acknowledge and accept his or her own part in the destructive activity, regardless of the other person's side of the transaction. The shadow must be brought forth out of hiding. It must be faced without the condemnation or self-justification of The Judge, who would deny and thus repeat the process. Making amends requires, above all, humility. The destructive result of addictive activity is always humiliating, and that must be transformed into humility. The front we present, the mask or persona of perfection, must be stripped away. This requires forgiveness of oneself and of the other. Without forgiveness, we are left in power plays. Forgiveness allows us to let go of our resentments and the spiritual cynicism that holds grudges. Forgiveness is the spiritual nurturing that sows the ground with new seeds of love and creativity. It fosters gratitude for the gift of life and the opportunity to nurture others and the earth.

In *Sabbaths* the poet-farmer Wendell Berry expresses a healing process that provides personal and metaphysical images for the making of amends. Ever alert to the destructive forces that threaten peace on earth, Berry nevertheless affirms the possibility of the healing "Upon an old field worn out by disease/Of human understanding; greed and sloth."[8] If we look at human history, Berry points out:

> Our making shakes the
> skies
> And taints the atmosphere.
> We have ourselves to fear.
> We burn the world to live;
> Our living blights the leaf.[9]

Yet, despite the nuclear waste of our greedy and addictive age, despite "the putrid air," the "corrosive rain," "the ash-fall of Heaven-invading fire," despite the toxic atmosphere of neglect and greed, Berry, from his knowledge of the working of the word as well as the working of the soil, holds out a vision of hope that relies on cooperation with nature's cyclic design. The "old field" is a metaphor for the soul's "disordered history" as well as the diseased land, and needs "re-clearing," Berry writes. It needs "change made/without violence to the ground."[10] As in the case of addiction, the wrongdoing was easy, says Berry. Just one day of neglect defies creation. Berry describes such a day, familiar to the addictive state of mind:

> Suppose the day begins
> In wrath at circumstance,
> Or anger at one's friends
> In vain self-innocence
> False to the very light,
> Breaking the sun in half,
> Or anger at oneself
> Whose controverting will
> Would have the sun stand still.
> The world is lost in loss

Of patience; the old curse
Returns, and is made worse
As newly justified.
In hopeless fret and fuss,
In rage at worldy plight
Creation is defied,
All order is unpropped,
All light and singing stopped.[11]

To right this day of ruin is not easy: it takes work and patience, humility through the knowledge of the dark, and the cooperation of earthly workers with the unseen heavenly design.

The field, if it will thrive, must do so by
Exactitude of thought, by skill of hand,
And by the clouded mercy of the sky;
It is a mortal clarity between
Two darks, of Heaven and of earth. The why
Of it is *our* measure. Seen and unseen.[12]

The human mind alone comes to its limit, Berry writes, and becomes lost in the dark thicket of an unknown order that "stirs great fear and sorrow in the mind."[13] From this comes neglect, greed and ignorance, sloth and haste, and the resulting disorder. But our history summons us to correct the wrongs done to the earth and the soul. The human measure, "the mortal clarity," is to take on this work of healing with the patience and endurance born of faith. As Berry writes to his son:

Wrong was easy; gravity helped it.
Right is difficult and long.
In choosing what is difficult
we are free, the mind too
making its little flight
out from the shadow into the clear
in time between work and sleep.

There are two healings; nature's
and ours and nature's. Nature's
will come in spite of us, after us,
over the graves of its wasters, as it comes
to the forsaken fields. The healing
that is ours and nature's will come
if we are willing, if we are patient,
if we know the way, if we will do the work.
My father's father, whose namesake

you are, told my father this, he told me,
and I am telling you: we make
this healing, the land's and ours:
it is our possibility. We may keep
this place, and be kept by it.
There is a mind of such an artistry
that grass will follow it,
and heal and hold, feed beasts
who will feed us and feed the soil.

Though we invite, this healing comes
in answer to another voice than ours;
a strength not ours returns
out of death beginning in our work.[14]

Thus the healing comes when we are open to listen to the summons and have the faith and diligence to do the work. Even in the winter's dark cold silence, if we look, we can see this faith in nature.

Though the spring is late and
cold,
though the uproar of greed
and malice shudders in the sky,
pond, stream, and treetop raise
their ancient songs;
the robin molds her mud nest
with her breast; the air
is bright with breath
of bloom, wise loveliness that asks
nothing of the season but to be.[15]

Through fidelity to this joint process of human work responding to heaven's gift of creation, the fields are cleared and recleared in a healing harmony of being, which includes the balance of work and rest: "The field is made by hand and eye./By daily work, by hope outreaching wrong."[16] But in rest we learn to receive and to dwell, for "Where we arrive by work, we stay by grace."[17]

Thus, through the healing of our lives and of our earth, we make an amend for the damage we have caused by our neglect. And this effort to reclear the field is a work of creation. As Berry writes: "Who makes a clearing makes a work of art."[18]

18: THE DWELLING

> . . . all that really matters: that we safeguard that little piece of You, God, in ourselves. And perhaps in others as well. . . . we must defend Your dwelling place inside us to the last. . . . I shall never drive you from my presence.
>
> —Etty Hillesum, *An Interrupted Life*

THE HEALING PROCESS of recovery prepares a clearing, a sacred space in which to dwell. This dwelling is the silent source from which the creative life arises. Meditation and prayer, the foundation of the eleventh step of recovery, allows us to dwell in this silent spring of life. In the practice of step eleven, we can pray to be a channel for the creative process.

Meditation is a practice in which one attends to being in the moment. It transforms the addict's tendency to lose the genuine gift of life in fantasies of the past or future. When one meditates one dwells with the presence of what is. Thus, one can respond to the gift of that moment of life. Meditation is a practice of letting go. One sits, attending to the breath, and allows what appears to be and also allows it to go. The addictive tendency to cling to people, places, or things, to try to control and possess, is surrendered. Through this meditative attention to being, clarity arises. One can finally see in the mirror of one's being. Rumi expressed this way of being as the practice of polishing the mirror of God in order to see the great luminosity shining through.

Caring for the clarity by dwelling in this way brings with it a sense of finally being "home," a sense of serenity and bliss. One settles into the silent sacred space with an attentive openness to whatever is there. But the stillness that occurs is not static; it is a process of opening to the whole of being—to whatever presents itself, including suffering and joy, death as well as life.

Meditation is a practice that joins mind and body. Thus it is a practice of earthly care, of compassion toward all beings. The spiritual teacher Tai Situ, Rinpoche, talks of various steps along the path of Tibetan Mahayana Buddhism. The first is taking the vow to be a bodhisattva, to put the enlightenment of all other beings ahead of the enlightenment of oneself. This means developing "bodhicitta," loving-kindness and compassion. The bodhisattva practice entails "giving and taking."

> With the outbreath we breathe out all our goodness and wisdom, which we share with everyone. . . . when we are able to do tonglen for our most hated enemy then we are able to do it for all sentient beings.[1]

Thus the bodhisattva practice is a way of honoring and dedicating one's life as a gift to the cosmos. Through meditation, this way of being becomes a practice, a generous way of dwelling that can change the world creatively.

Meditation develops trust in simply being. As one sits in an attentive yet relaxed bodily posture, the body becomes well grounded. When one sits in the meditation posture, one's arms and hands are open and receptive. With each breath one acknowledges what appears and turns back to the openness of the outbreath, honestly seeing one's experience from moment to moment. In this way one can see the various cycles of emotions and thoughts, the habitual patterns that tend to dominate and take over one's life. For those caught in addictive patterns, meditation is a way to become aware of these modes of bondage and to practice letting them go. Since, in meditation, one does not "judge" what appears, but simply notes it and lets it go, it is possible to fully experience the feelings that make us want to escape through drinks or drugs. We can acknowledge the fears, anger, resentment, guilt, and self-indulgence that possess us without having to repress them or act them out, and then simply let them go. We can acknowledge our confusing emotions as part of a process that can lead to wakefulness, generosity, and creativity, instead of addiction. By awakening to the vast openness through meditation, we can surrender the duality of constricting power plays between "I" and "other." In this way meditation opens us up to the greater nature of indwelling love.

The turning point for one recovering alcoholic was not at the darkest bottom of the abyss. Rather, it came relatively early in his alcoholism, when he joined his wife in the practice of meditation. Up to that point he had not yet damaged his profession. Nor had he been in jails or hospitals. Neither did his "creativity" seem to suffer from his drinking. Thus, compared to many, he was a relatively "high bottom" alcoholic. But his relationship to his family was being damaged by his drinking, and the quality of his life and creativity was much more superficial than the depths to which this man eventually was able and continues to reach.

As a puer (eternal boy), he had an enormous urge to fly. In contrast to Icarus, who flew too close to the sun, this man, through meditation, was able to see and acknowledge his addiction early enough to keep himself from flying too high. Through the gift of early sobriety, he has been able to ground himself so that he can embody his visions more discriminately. His relations with both family and friends, as well as his creative work, have deepened and expanded. For his sobriety has been a grounding process. In sobriety he became aware that his children's needs were greater than his own and he was able to accept his own inner "senex" (Latin for "old man") side. From puer son-lover he developed into being a father.

Early in childhood he felt the call to creativity. "I was always dancing to a different tune because I had so much 'coyote' and 'Hermes' energy. I was a sensitive child born into an uncomplicated 'salt of the earth' family in the Midwest, and I felt so different, an embarrassment to the rest of the family, that I often wondered if I had not really originated from and been left there by the gypsies." A "happy drunk," his father was always stirring things up and operated a "still" in the basement, So, right in his childhood home the alchemical process was brewing beneath the ground level in the form of the "spirits in the still." But his father also abused his gift for words by verbally cutting down his wife and children at mealtimes. Thus the family environment was frought with double messages. It was only later, when he was old enough to drink with his father, that they could connect through their outrageous humor. Drinking became a pattern in his teens and in college. Like his father, he was a happy drunk and gradually became a maintenance drinker, always living on the edge of a buzz.

Creatively, he was always at a high pitch. He started out in music but switched to theater arts. Eventually he turned to film work and became a set designer. He created out of chaos, from which a design would emerge in an incredible surge. As the intoxicated high-flying puer, he always kept his senex side drowned in drink, and this prevented him from reaching the more profound depths of his creativity. The drinking that fired his puer energy also fostered his irresponsibility: he pushed off all the practical concerns and work onto his wife. Nor was he present at home as a father for his children. Instead he was always performing center stage. Thus there was no genuine dwelling in the home, and he was not emotionally present to his family.

Eventually, his wife went her own spiritual way, beginning to practice transcendental meditation. When he decided to join her, he was instructed not to drink for a week prior to the initial program of meditation. At this program, sober, he found that sitting still and quieting the mind was a revelation. Yet, after meditation he was hyperactive and wanted a drink. The contrast between sitting and his usual frenetic life-style was striking to him. Nonetheless, after the initial period of meditation was over he resumed drinking and tried to compensate with exercise. But instead of compensating for the drinking, the exercise expanded the growing circle of consciousness into which unexpectedly he had been thrust. Finally, he realized the booze was counter-productive to his new clarity and so decided to stop drinking.

Synchronistically, he had some help from the "gods." While working on *The Invasion of the Body Snatchers*, a coworker who was an alcoholic but had been off booze for some time had a relapse. He saw this man "turn suddenly from Dr. Jekyl into Mr. Hyde." Vividly he saw how alcohol could indeed invade the body and snatch the soul away, and how it had done so to his own. It was at this point that he made a deep commitment to his recovery.

When, after many months, the booze was finally out of his system, he felt a change in his meditation. It was easier to go into the meditational mode, easier to stay there and easier to come out. And his clarity lasted longer. With the booze gone, he also experienced many attitudinal shifts. Previously, alcohol had taken up much of his time and energy. Now he exercised more, which made his body feel good and gave him overall tone and even an aerobic high. He also began to encounter people with a different view of the world. He went to holistic seminars. He realized that for the most part his soul had been asleep; when he was drinking, the only place it had continued to work was in music. He began reading again, particularly in the area of spiritual transformation.

Other changes occurred. He became aware of "right livelihood," that what he did and how he did it affected the world. With his change in values he realized that the images and scenes he created in film and theater affected people. He began to discriminate between the jobs he accepted, refusing to do commercials that advertised products he considered unhealthy or harmful.

Previously, in his addictive mode, he had separated the opposites, particularly those of puer and senex. As he said:

> I got high on the puer and kept the senex drunk in the unconscious. Now in sobriety, I try to hold the tension of the puer and senex together. I am awake to both energies and I honor both. The senex energy, for example, helps make the necessary discriminations about which scripts to accept and which to refuse. It helps me to sit and it grounds me. Even Hermes is purer. Before, that energy was flying so high and was so intoxicated that it was out of touch with clear vision and communication. Also, in sobriety, other energies have awakened, energies that had been anesthetized through my drinking. Take the Zeus energy, for example, which helps me make decisions for the good of the community. When I was drinking, my decisions often came from an egoistic place of self-centeredness. Saturn,

too, has become positive now and helps me set good limits. Before, when I drank, my Saturn was always complaining. And even my Dionysus has been transformed. With my reborn Dionysus *I am making a new wine of creation.* Deliberately I stomp those grapes now and go through that alchemical process consciously. Before, my creation was unconscious and unfocused. There was too much chaos and hurtful stuff. So sobriety has really led to my individuation, i.e., to a conscious effort to become whole.

Before, when he kept the senex drunk, he lived off the puer energy. But he didn't stretch himself or push the mind to do more. He was never afraid that he would lose his creativity if he stopped drinking. Rather, he sensed that the drinking was constricting his creativity. So he was "willing to dare sobriety." Now, in sobriety, the positive senex helps him to work creatively by setting aside times for various disciplines. For example, he makes it a practice to memorize a poem a week, and that works down in the depths. Out of this have emerged more forms of creativity—writing poems, public readings, mask making, and teaching all these forms. Nine years into his sobriety, this is the way he now understands the call of creativity.

The most profound creation is to create me—to create a whole and healthy life. If "I am circling around God," as Rilke expresses it in one of his poems, I help God in creation. I aim for optimum wellness: I try to expand my mind as far as it can go, and I try to expand the area of my influence in the world through work. In my creativity, I have always used myself as a lightning rod by receiving the lightning bolts from the gods and letting them bounce off. But when I was drinking I missed so many of those wonderful bolts from God. Now, in sobriety, I work to clear my body and my psyche to be purer vessels so I can receive more, letting the profound work of creation occur down in the depths and come out again in new forms, as for example, in mask making or poems. Before, when I was drinking, I went into the depths unconsciously. Now, in my new sober life, I can go down consciously even into the pain I created from my drinking. And, if I allow the process to work down there, good things can come out, even from that havoc. I also consciously take a poem or a myth or a fairy tale down, work with it, and bring it back up in the form of a mask or a song. If I allow it, all sorts of experiences, even the most painful ones, are transformed down there into gold.

One of his favorite poets, Antonio Machado, in the following two poems expresses the transformation that can happen when one learns to dwell receptively, to watch and listen and be open to what is:

Last night, as I was sleeping,
I dreamt—marvellous error!—
that a spring was breaking
out in my heart.

I said: Along which secret aqueduct,
Oh water, are you coming to me,
water of a new life
that I have never drunk?

Last night, as I was sleeping,
I dreamt—marvellous error!—
that I had a beehive
here inside my heart.
And the golden bees
were making white combs
and sweet honey
from my old failures.

Last night, as I was sleeping,
I dreamt—marvellous error!—
that a fiery sun was giving
light inside my heart.
It was fiery becasue I felt
warmth as from a hearth,
and sun because it gave light
and brought tears to my eyes.

Last night, as I slept,
I dreamt—marvellous error!—
that it was God I had
here inside my heart.

~

Is my soul asleep?
Have those beehives that labor
at night stopped? And the water
wheel of thought,
is it dry, the cups empty,
wheeling, carrying only shadows?

No my soul is not asleep.
It is awake, wide awake.
It neither sleeps nor dreams, but watches,
its clear eyes open,
far-off things, and listens
at the shores of the great silence.[2]

In contrast to the blind addictive way of living ruled by clinging and control, Heidegger suggests another way to be that has its daily roots in dwelling and corresponds to the mysterious movement of Being—a way which he calls *Gelassenheit.* Translated literally, *Gelassenheit* means "Let-be-ness," or what we might call repose or serenity. This is a way of care that honors the sacredness of others and the earth, the mystery of human existence in time and space. Consider how we experience time, Heidegger suggests. When we live by "clock time" to deal with practical business affairs, we often count the passing time in boredom, frustration, or resentment. But when we are devoted to what we are doing, we experience time quite differently. When transported by a symphony, an hour of clock time may be like one ecstatic moment. In contrast, ten minutes of a boring duty may seem to last interminably. In ecstatic time we "stand out" beyond our ego concerns and are fully present to the mysterious happening in the moment. The temporal movement now comes toward us from the "future," i.e., the unknown regions of our being, gathering us up in all the past history of our lives and moving us into a mysterious moment of presence in which we are open to all that is. This moment of opening and presence to what is happening is ecstatic, for we are dwelling in a whole and holy realm that is greater than our ability to control. This moment of presence transports us. In such a moment we are inspired because we feel the holy presence, even in the ordinary. Anxiety often announces such a moment because it breaks through and disrupts our methods of control. But if we allow ourselves to be with the terror, it can announce the dark side of Being opening us up to the greater whole of life and death.

Creativity comes from such a way of time and being, from the unknown regions of our existence. It is not primarily a linear process. Nor is the process of recovery from addiction. Both creativity and recovery require us to reach into the depths of our being over and over again, just as we move through the cycles of birth, death, and rebirth.

In his later writings on creativity, Heidegger discusses dwelling. Often, he says, we objectify the notion of dwelling, literalizing it as a quantifiable and mathematically measurable space to use for shelter. Or, we reduce it to a symbol that has no bearing upon the way we live our lives. But these dualistic approaches falsify our human nature, which is to dwell. Heidegger traces the word back to its roots, and finds the following flow: the German word *Bauen* (*Buan*), a word for building, means to dwell; it means to remain, to stay in a place, just as the neighbor (*Nachgebauer*) is the one who dwells nearby. Add to this the Gothic word *Wunian*, which means to be at peace; reaching further into that word we find *Friede*, which means the free. From there we can continue to *das Frye*, which means preserved from harm and danger, safeguarded—to spare. From this Heidegger finds the meaning of dwelling to be the "preserve of peace."

> To free really means to spare. The sparing itself consists not only in the fact that we do not harm the one whom we spare. Real sparing is something *positive* and takes place when we leave something beforehand in its own nature, when we return it specifically to its being, when we "free" it in the real sense of the word into a preserve of peace. To dwell, to be set at peace, means to remain at peace within the free, the preserve, the free sphere that safeguards each thing in its nature. *The fundamental character of dwelling is this sparing and preserving.*[3]

Dwelling, or caring for the preserve of peace, involves the "fourfold," a relationship of four, uniting the earth, the sky, the divinities, and the mortals. We, as human beings, are in the fourfold via dwelling. Heidegger describes each one as follows:

> Earth is the serving bearer, blossoming and fruiting, spreading out in rock and water, rising up into plant and animal. . . . The sky is the vaulting path of the sun, the course of the changing moon, the wandering glitter of the stars, the year's seasons and their changes, the light and dusk of day, the gloom and glow of night, the clemency and inclemency of the weather, the drifting clouds and blue depth of the ether. . . . The divinities are the beckoning messengers of the godhead. Out of the holy sway of the godhead, the god appears in his presence or withdraws into his concealment. . . . The mortals are the human beings. They are called mortals because they can die. To die means to be capable of death *as* death. Only man dies, and indeed continually, as long as he remains on earth, under the sky, before the divinities.[4]

To preserve the fourfold in its essential being *is* dwelling: this means to save the earth, to receive the sky, to await the divinities, and to initiate our own nature—to live and to die a good death. In contrast to the obsession with power and control, which brings us before our destruction to face the "world's night," dwelling is a receptive way of care and preservation that allows the world's creation to emerge. Thus, Heidegger describes dwelling as follows:

In relation to the earth:

> Mortals dwell in that they save the earth—taking the word in the old sense still known to Lessing. Saving does not only snatch something from a danger. To save really means to set something free into its own presencing. To save the earth is more than to exploit it or even wear it out. Saving the earth does not master the earth and does not subjugate it, which is merely one step from spoliation.[5]

In relation to the sky:

> Mortals dwell in that they receive the sky as sky. They leave to the sun and the moon their journey, to the stars their courses, to the seasons their blessing and their inclemency; they do not turn night into day nor day into a harassed unrest.[6]

In relation to the divinities:

> Mortals dwell in that they await the divinities as divinities. In hope they hold up to the divinities what is unhoped for. They wait for intimations of their coming and do not mistake the signs of their absence. They do not make their gods for themselves and do not worship idols. In the very depth of misfortune they wait for the weal that has been withdrawn.[7]

And in relation to their own mortality:

> Mortals dwell in that they initiate their own nature—their being capable of death as death—into the use and practice of this capacity, so that there may be a good death. To initiate mortals into the nature of death in no way means to make death, as empty Nothing, the goal. Nor does it mean to darken dwelling by blinding staring toward the end.[8]

For mortals to dwell requires them to stay with things in such a way that gathers the fourfold and allows a site, opening a sacred space made possible by virture of the mortal's care. According to Heidegger, a sacred space is not simply there outside human experience as an external object. Nor is it merely an inner experience existing a priori purely inside the human mind. Rather, it requires the mutual gathering of the fourfold through the "building" or creation of a thing. Take, for example, the building of a bridge. Through this process the bridge that crosses a stream unites the banks of the earth, revealing a landscape of stream and meadows that is also open in readiness to the sky's changes. The bridge also allows the mortals to cross the waters and journey from one side to another, and it opens up the possibilities that lead and escort the mortals to many different ways. Thus the bridge is always reminding mortals of their way to the last bridge, to their death. And silently the bridge brings mortals before the holiness of the divinities, through the artfully created statues of the ancient figures of saints or goddesses of the bridge. In this way the bridge allows and opens up a location, a site for the fourfold in its space. The ancient meaning of the word for space, Heidegger points out, is that a place has been cleared and freed for settlement within a boundary. Thus, "Space is in essence that for which room has been made, that which is let into its bounds."[9] And this is a process that happens when humans dwell and stay with things in the preserve of peace. Our very failure to be concerned and care for dwelling presupposes and brings our attention to dwelling as the fundamental way of human being. Letting ourselves dwell as humans is thus essential to our way upon this earth. "*Only if we are capable of dwelling, only then can we build.*"[10] This can be seen, for example, in the Black Forest in the building of a farmhouse two centuries ago through the peasants' dwelling. The care for the fourfold via dwelling gave a natural ordering to the building of the house.

> Here the self-sufficiency of the power to let earth and heaven, divinities and mortals enter *in simple oneness* into things ordered the house. It placed the farm on the wind-sheltered mountain slope looking south, among the meadows close to the spring. It gave the wide overhanging shingle roof whose proper slope bears up under the burden of snow, and which, reaching deep down, shields the chambers against the storms of the long winter nights. It did not forget the altar corner behind the community table; it made room in its chamber for the hallowed place of childbed and the "tree of the dead"—for that is what they call a coffin there: the *Totenbaum*—and in this way it designed for the different generations under one roof the character of their journey through time.[11]

Just as the Black Forest farmhouse was built with thoughtful gratitude by peasants dwelling with the fourfold "*in simple oneness,*" so in both creating and recovery can we rebuild our lives with honor. But such dwelling and building, Heidegger reminds us, "comes from the workshop of long experience and incessant practice";[12] it comes from listening to the dialogue of building and thinking in our lives. This is a process that requires continual learning, the daily questioning anew of what it means to dwell. To dwell, we have to bring our Care to the fourfold: to the earth, sky, divinities, mortals. Resentment interferes with dwelling. This is why step ten—the daily process of inventory and amends for resentments, fears, angers, inflations, and other negative energies—is essential to the dwelling. These need to be cleared away each day to restore the sacred to the dwelling place. And step eleven, the daily practice of prayer and meditation, allows us to be open to the call that summons us to dwell.

Heidegger refers us to an ancient fable in which "Care" originally gave humans their being.[13] Once, when she was crossing a river, "Care" noticed some clay and began to give it shape, meditating upon what she had just created. She had taken the clay from the body of Earth and had asked Jupiter to give it spirit. Care wanted to give this new being her name. But both Jupiter and Earth disputed, each claiming they had a right to the name, for Earth had given of her body, while Jupiter had given his spirit. Saturn (Time) was called upon to settle the dispute, and his decision was accepted as just: due to the dispute the name would be "homo," since it is made from "humus" (earth). Jupiter would receive the spirit at death and Earth would receive the body. But during its lifetime the new being would always belong to Care ("Devotedness"), for it was *she* who had first shaped it. Creative life flourishes through dwelling in this devoted way of Care.

19: THE GIFT

> There is only one real deprivation, I decided this morning, and that is not to be able to give one's gift to those one loves most. . . . The gift turned inward, unable to be given, becomes a heavy burden, even sometimes a kind of poison. It is as though the flow of life were backed up.
>
> —May Sarton, *Journal of a Solitude*

> But still existence for us is a miracle; in a hundred places it is still the source. A play of absolute forces that no one can touch who has not knelt down in wonder.
>
> —Rainer Maria Rilke, *Sonnets to Orpheus*

EVERYONE WHO IS recovering from the struggle with addiction knows the miracle of the gift. Having faced death and sacrificed the ego's desire to control, life has been restored to them. Freed from the bondage of an addictive mode that drains vitality and ends in isolation, paranoia, and a state of possession, the recovering person is given the gift to create each day anew and to give to others the fruits of his or her caring and creative energy. Gratitude for the new opportunity to lead a spiritual life, praise and celebration for life's mystery, thankfulness for the challenge to create, trust in Nature's process—these are some of the gifts of recovery. The Promises, as set forth in the Big Book, show some of the old addictive patterns that will be transformed and some of the new creative possibilities that will emerge.[1]

Gratitude for the chance to give the fruits of this spiritual awakening is itself an essential part of the Gift. This is the meaning of the twelfth step of recovery. The word "grateful" has a double meaning. It reminds us both of the gratuitousness of all that is and the fullness of our response. Existence is not our own creation; we did not make ourselves. Rather, we were thrown into being gratuitously. We were given our existence, with its light and dark and its highs and lows. How we respond to what we are given is our part in the act of creation. Those of us who are addicts know that we can respond to the gratuitousness of this deadly and baffling disease with resentment and an angry heart. We can be at war with what we were given. Or, having experienced the depths to which it takes us, we can in full humility stand in awe before the deep mysteries of creation that gratuitously give life and take it away, and be grateful daily for life. The latter response is a "thanks-giving" from the grateful heart.[2] Giving thanks is a sacramental celebration of our creation on this earth and, as Heidegger points out, entails the meditative way of thought and being that honors the mystery of creation with care. Prayer and meditation are ways to affirm the gift of life within us. The creation and recovery that can happen in a twelve-step meeting are also a ritual recognition, a thanksgiving and wonderment at life and death. There, as recovering addicts share stories of their high flights, their falls into the depths, and their resurrection, having survived the circuitous journey that was given to them through addiction, they give thanks daily for their creation. And they try to respond with gratitude by re-creating their lives in a spirit of serenity that flows with life as it happens.

This was also the transformation of thanksgiving that Alyosha and Dimitri offered after their respective flights into idealism and romance and their consequent falls into the bitter abyss of resentful rebellion against God's "injustice." Finally they were able to accept and forgive themselves and their Creator. Alyosha and Dimitri also were each given a dream in which they felt the holy presence of life. In humility, each bowed down before the gift and ecstatically embraced Mother earth, honoring Nature's feminine creative source, watering the ground with tears. This ecstatic moment entered their hearts to dwell throughout their lives. It was a gift that enabled them to give to others, just as Dostoevsky, having transformed the torment of his addictions, was able to give the great works of his creation to humankind.

In the moment of the gift everything is fresh—received and given with childlike joy and spontaneity. Feelings flow; laughter and tears embrace, even though they may well up from the darkest abyss. Like Dionysus, who was dismembered and born anew, the gift intoxicates and regenerates. One feels enthusiasm—intoxication with divine energy (for enthusiasm originally meant to be inspired by the gods). The gift comes from the organic source; it is an outpouring of creation, a mystery to which we can only pay homage in awe, wonder, and thanksgiving.

The novelist and poet Boris Pasternak, even though suffering from "exile" in his native land, expressed thanksgiving for creation after a life-threatening illness:

> In that moment, which seemed like my last, I wanted more than ever to talk with God, to praise all things visible, capture them and record them. "Dear Lord," I whispered, "I thank you for applying the paint so richly and that in your creation of life and death you speak to us in splendour and music. I thank you that you have made me an artist, that creativity is your school, and that all my life you have been preparing me for this night." And I exulted and wept for joy.[3]

The gift is to live creatively—to be open to receive and to give back something new from our experience. Every day is a thanksgiving. In giving there is an outpouring, just as the mountain stream generously pours out of the rock-rimmed canyon that has received and channeled the heaven-sent rain, giving the water of life to those dwelling on earth. With nature's gift we can dwell together celebrating the wedding of sky and earth, mortals and divinities. Or, we can merely drink from these waters thoughtlessly, unthankfully quenching a thirst. The gifted way of being requires a certain intentionality—the recognition that one has been graced with the outpouring energy of life. The "gifted" ones recognize the greater nature of what has been bestowed and offer the self as a channel to pass that gift on to others, just as the canyon offers itself to channel the water passing through it. Thus, inherent in the gift is the notion of sacrifice—offering oneself generously as a channel for creation. Heidegger has noted the inherent etymological connection of gift and sacrifice.[4]

In the creative process, the artist receives the gift of inspiration. Although this inspiration usually is preceded and followed by diligent effort and work, the artist is transported by the sudden outpouring of the creative idea, just as in nature we find ourselves suddenly in awe of the flow of the majestic mountain stream or the golden fire of an autumn leaf. These moments of giftedness are ecstatic; the artist feels the sacred celebration occurring in the soul.

Creative people do not take credit for these inspirations; they honor them as gifts. As Dostoevesky said:

> . . . a poem is like a natural precious stone, a diamond in the poet's soul, complete in all its essence, and so this is the first act of the poet, as a *maker and creator*, the first part of his creation. We can even say that it is not he who is the actual creator but rather life itself, the mighty essence of life, God, living and real, manifesting his power in the diversity of creation here and there, and most often, in great hearts and in powerful poets, . . . the creation suddenly appears in the poet's soul too completely, with too much finality and readiness . . . the poet's soul is the mine in which the diamonds are formed and outside of which they cannot be found. Then comes the poet's *second* act, no longer so profound and mysterious, but only his artistic performance: once he has received the diamond, he must polish and mount it. At this point the poet is not much more than a jeweler.[5]

Both the receiving of the gift and the work to polish the jewel and pass it on to others requires sacrifice—one must offer oneself up as an open channel. The energy behind such a sacrifice comes from our spiritual longing. If we divert that longing through addictions to romance, substances, possessions or power, we lose access to the creative. The film director Andrey Tarkovsky emphasizes the centrality of spiritual longing and the sacrifice the artist must make to serve the gift of creation.

> Art is born and takes hold wherever there is a timeless and insatiable longing for the spiritual, for the ideal: that longing which draws people to art . . . in artistic creation the personality does not assert itself, it serves another, higher and communal idea. The artist is always a servant, and is perpetually trying to pay for the gift that has been given to him as if by a miracle. Modern man, however, does not want to make any sacrifice, even though true affirmation of self can only be expressed in sacrifice. We are gradually forgetting about this, and at the same time, inevitably, losing all sense of our human calling.[6]

Tarkovsky, who eventually defected from Russia to Europe, found that the enemy to creativity was the materialism invading this planet, an obsession with consumerism and technological power that he observed in both the West and the East. We are now at a crossroads, he observed, and the individual is faced with the choice of following the road of blind consumerism or the path of spiritual responsibility, "a way that ultimately might mean not only his personal salvation but also the saving of society at large; in other words, to turn to God."[7] This requires the step of self-sacrifice. Hence the theme of his last film, *The Sacrifice*, was both a gift and a sacrifice, as Tarkovsky was dying of cancer while he was creating it. *The Sacrifice* is a poetic parable about a man oppressed by depression, weary of the venomous atmosphere of his marriage and the inauthenticity of society, frustrated by the emptiness of human speech, and with horror facing the imminent catastrophe of world destruction. The one joy in his life is his young son. Receiving the gift of love from a simple peasant woman (whose medial nature is perceived by others as witchlike), he offers himself up to God as a sacrifice. Taking a vow of silence, he resolves to break with the life he has been leading and burns up his house, symbolically destroying all paths back to his former life. He is one of the mortals who "turns sooner into the abyss," even though that is perceived as madness. But as Tarkovsky says: "that is precisely why I see Alexander as a man chosen by God. He can sense the danger, the destructive force driving the machinery of modern society as it heads towards the abyss. And the mask must be snatched away if humanity is to be saved."[8] Alexander is symbolic of the contemporary person who needs to understand that "life's path is not measured by a human yardstick but lies in the hands of the Creator, on whose will he must rely."[9] In the end Alexander's son waters the parched and barren tree with faith that it will burst into life, and that his father's sacrifice was the gift of the "holy fool." *The Sacrifice* reveals humans in the abyss of extremity, where the choice to live can only be made daily in faith. This is the abyss in which contemporary society is plunged. The Gift is the sacrifice made in faith that the tree of life, if watered with fidelity and care, will burst into bloom.

The sacrifice required in all creativity and in recovery from addiction is turning one's life over to the creative spiritual energy with complete abandon. In Tarkovsky's view such sacrificial love "involves no less than total giving."[10] Ultimately the choice we all must make is between creativity and addiction. If we see the suffering and wounds of our addictive life as a lesson that can be passed along to others, we can transform the "wound" into a gift. Having lived through a life-threatening crisis we can become healers. As Tarkovsky states, "it is always through spiritual crisis that healing occurs. A spiritual crisis is an attempt to find oneself, to acquire new faith."[11] Through acceptance of the crisis, we can embody the archetypal transformation of the "wounded healer," which entails bearing the burden of our wounds and transforming them. To bear means to give birth.[12] Hence there comes the spiritual challenge to choose to transform addiction into creativity. Understood in this way, the wound is the gift to transform. The very abyss we experience in despair and suffering can be the "creative womb."

Central to the nature of the creative gift is that it is passed along to others. The artist receives the inspiration, feels the call to create, accepts the burden of the tension of opposites, works to shape the vision for others to receive. In that process the transformation that occurs in the creative act is given to the recipient. Thus, the recipients begin to experience in themselves the same call to creativity that the artist felt. In this way the creative work or act becomes a spiritual form of communion. Tarkovsky expresses this bond as follows:

> Touched by a masterpiece, a person begins to hear in himself that same call of truth which prompted the artist to his creative act. When a link is established between the work and its beholder, the latter experiences a sublime, purging trauma. Within that aura which unites masterpieces and audience, the best sides of our souls are made known, and we long for them to be freed. In those moments we recognize and discover ourselves, the unfathomable depths of our own potential, and the furthest reaches of our emotions.[13]

Thus, through the creative gift there comes into being a community of traveling companions on the spiritual path. From this communion emanates a generous eros that is healing and inspiring and which passes around the circle between receiver and giver. Thus arises the mysterious love of the "I-Thou" relationship, which Martin Buber said can heal our broken world and make it whole. This is also the bodhisattva's gift of compassion. Creative people feel this gift of spiritual healing from the artists and writers who have inspired them, experiencing a sense of indebtedness to their mentors. In turn they hope to transform what they have received into a gift for others through their own creative work. Without this creative transformation there would be no gifts given or received. This energy of creative love through spiritually transformative giving is the very same that happens through the twelfth step, the act of gratitude and giving through which a person shares experience, strength, and hope with others. This helps enable the process of recovery from addiction.

The Gift opens us, expands our being, makes us whole, and forms the healing ring of love. The healing cycle of giving frees a sacred space of openness and loving that sweeps the dancers into its spiraling round. This movement is itself creative energy that frees the dancers. The Gift is loss of ego and an experience of unity with all beings in which the universe is a cosmic weaving of radiating colors and textures shining forth in their threads of difference and unity or a great symphony in which the different instruments sound out in a harmony of tones. What a contrast this generous creative energy is to the possessive stranglehold of addiction!

The ancient Russian legend of The Firebird is a story that shows how creative energy is freed from the bondage of possession by the Demon Lover through an act of spiritual sacrifice. The sacrifice comes from the transcendent feminine energy as a gift of beauty for all to honor and celebrate with thanksgiving.

Once upon a time there was an orphan girl, Maryushka, who could embroider more beautifully than anyone else in the land. Although she was gentle, modest, and quiet, her fame spread over the land and beyond the seas to merchants who came to see her wonderful work and offer her riches if she would come away with them. But Maryushka modestly declined these offers, for she wanted to stay in the village where she was born. And so the merchants left, singing her praises wherever they went. One day a sorcerer, Koschei the Immortal, heard of Maryushka's work, and it angered him to learn there was a beauty in the world which did not belong to him. Changing his form to a handsome young man, he flew far away to Maryushka's home. As was the custom, when he met Maryushka, he bowed low to her and asked to see her embroidery. Whereupon she took out her fine needlework and offered it to him to see. The sight of so much beauty that a simple country girl could create, and that he himself did not possess, drove Koschei into a frenzy. So, with a cunning tone, he proposed to Maryushka and asked her to be his Queen. She could live in a palace of jewels, eat off plates of gold, sleep on eiderdown, and enjoy the golden apples and birds of paradise singing in his orchards. But Maryushka refused his offer—she would not embroider for him alone. She loved the green pastures and woods and the village where she was born, where the townsfolk found joy in her work.

When Koschei heard her answer, he was furious. Instantly he changed her into a beautiful firebird. He himself became a great black falcon and swooped upon the lovely firebird, grasping her tightly in his talons and flying off with her into the skies. But Maryushka resolved to sacrifice her life in order to leave her beauty for others on the earth. So she shed her brilliant rainbow-colored feathers, which, one by one, floated to the ground. And now these feathers of the firebird shine with magic as gifts for all those on earth who love beauty and seek to create it for others.

Appendix: The Twelve Steps

1. We admitted we were powerless over alcohol—that our lives had become unmanageable.
2. Came to believe that a Power greater than ourselves could restore us to sanity.
3. Made a decision to turn our will and our lives over to the care of God as we understood Him.
4. Made a searching and fearless moral inventory of ourselves.
5. Admitted to God, to ourselves, and to another human being the exact nature of our wrongs.
6. Were entirely ready to have God remove all these defects of character.
7. Humbly asked Him to remove our shortcomings.
8. Made a list of all persons we had harmed, and became willing to make amends to them all.
9. Made direct amends to such people wherever possible, except when to do so would injure them or others.
10. Continued to take personal inventory, and when we were wrong promptly admitted it.
11. Sought through prayer and meditation to improve our conscious contact with God as we understood Him, praying only for knowledge of His will for us and the power to carry that out.
12. Having had a spiritual awakening as the result of these steps, we tried to carry this message to alcoholics, and to practice these principles in all our affairs.

NOTES

Preface

1. A codependent is a person addicted to other people, places, and things. Codependents usually fill themselves up with the problems of others, rather than focusing upon and living their own lives. They look for their center outside of themselves. In this way they betray themselves and lose the relation to their own creativity. I am using the term "co-addict" specifically to refer to a partner who is addicted to an addict. For the sake of grammatical convenience only, I use the masculine gender with reference to the addict—addiction is *not* gender related.

2. The Ghostly Lover is the archetypal energy in the psyche that promises us magical union with the divine and can lead to creativity and spirituality but often gets projected on an external person, place, or thing instead. The Demon Lover is the inner demonic energy that can fascinate and possess our soul, becoming our master and draining us of our very life's blood. In literature, Dracula is an example of the latter. For detailed descriptions see *On the Way to the Wedding: Transforming the Love Relationship* (Boston: Shambhala Publications, 1986).

3. Throughout the book the word *creativity* is used in two senses: in the larger sense of leading a creative life and in the specific sense of creating works of art, literature, music, etc. (The context makes clear which is meant.) People can be creative in the transformation of their life, or they can be creative by producing a work of art, or both. It is a mistake to reduce or discount a work of art just because the artist's life was addictive. This would be to fall into the error of psychological reductionism or focusing on pathology in biography ("pathobiography"). Often artists who were addicted can paint for us with chilling accuracy a portrait of those addictive aspects in ourselves, thus giving us the possibility of recognition and catharsis. Many transcend via their art to express universal truths. For many of these artists, their art is their life. Some addicted artists, like Dostoevsky, are able to heal themselves through their art, while others in the process of creating the work of art seem to remain unhealed in their personal lives. In contrast many people who lead seemingly "mundane" lives are extraordinarily creative in daily existence. Søren Kierkegaard calls this creative person the "knight of faith."

4. I have used the example of the twelve-step program because it has been a successful channel of healing through which recovery has occurred. This example does not negate other ways of recovery, as shown in the personal stories of those recovering addicts who chose other paths. The Twelve Steps are listed in the Appendix.

Chapter 1, "The Hostage"

1. See David L. Miller's etymological analysis in *Christs: Meditations on Archetypal Images in Christian Theology* (New York: The Seabury Press, 1981), p. 194. Miller points out that "addiction to substances" is a metaphor of the original religious meaning and not the reverse. Note, too, the inherent etymological connection between addiction and being in debt to a moneylender in the Roman usage.

2. For an analysis of Dracula and the Demon Lover archetype see *On the Way to the Wedding: Tranforming the Love Relationship*.

3. Carl Gustav Jung, *Symbols of Transformation*, Vol. 1, trans. R. F. C. Hull (New York: Harper Torchbooks, 1962), p. 112.

4. Andrey Tarkovsky, *Sculpting in Time,* trans. Kitty Hunter-Blair (New York: Alfred A. Knopf, 1987), pp. 42–3.

5. Rollo May, *Love and Will* (New York: W. W. Norton, 1969). See pp. 122–180 for a discussion of the daimonic.

6. The artist Pieter Brueghel, recreating this scene in his painting "The Fall of Icarus," shows an additional feature of addiction—the denial of the masses. In the painting Icarus is depicted plunging into the sea while the people on land are so absorbed in what they are doing that they do not see the tragedy. This can be symbolic of a culture so absorbed in controlling practical interests that people are unaware of the Fall of addiction happening in themselves and their society, thus promulgating the cultural denial of addiction.

7. Thomas Wolfe, *The Autobiography of an American Novelist,* ed. Leslie Field (Cambridge: Harvard University Press, 1983), pp. 35–6.

8. Erich Neumann, *Art and the Creative Unconscious,* trans. Ralph Manheim (New York: Harper and Row, 1966), p. 186.

9. Tarkovsky, pp. 221–2.

CHAPTER 2, "THE MONEYLENDER"

1. Faust sold his soul to the devil when he accepted Mephistopheles's offer to take the moment so beautiful he would want it to last forever. In "The Soldier's Tale," the soldier traded his violin (symbolizing the music of his soul) to the devil in exchange for a book that could forecast all future events.

2. Eugene O'Neill, *The Iceman Cometh* (New York: Random House, 1957), p. 10.

3. Ibid., 235.

4. Ibid., 116

5. Ibid., 225.

6. Ibid., 233.

7. Ibid., 238.

8. Ibid., 241.

9. White Lady is a name commonly used by drug addicts to refer to cocaine.

10. Martin Heidegger, *Being and Time,* trans. John Macquarrie & Edward Robinson (New York: Harper & Brothers, 1962), pp. 325 ff. For an application of Heidegger's philosophy to psychotherapy, see Medard Boss, *Psychoanalysis and Daseinanalysis* (New York: Basic Books, 1963).

CHAPTER 3, "THE GAMBLER"

1. For a detailed description of Dostoevsky's relationship to Stellovsky and the way he creatively transformed his addiction to gambling, see the chapter on Dostoevsky's transformation, "The Soul on Fire."

2. Fyodor Dostoevsky, *The Gambler,* trans. Andrew R. MacAndrew (New York: W. W. Norton and Company, Inc., 1981), p. 5.

3. Ibid., 7.

4. Ibid., 28.

5. Ibid., 32.

6. Ibid., 100.

7. Ibid., 102.

8. Ibid., 144.

9. Ibid., 156.

10. Ibid., 174–5.

11. Fyodor Dostoevsky, *Selected Letters of Fyodor Dostoevsky*, trans. Andrew R. MacAndrew, ed. Joseph Frank and David I. Goldstein (New Brunswick, NJ: Rutgers University Press, 1987), pp. 252–3.

12. Robert L. Custer, a specialist in addictive diseases, describes this in a preface to Robin Moore's *Compulsion: The True Story of an Addictive Gambler* (New York: Doubleday, 1981), p. vii.

13. Ibid., 445.

Chapter 4, "The Romantic"

1. Herman Glaser, ed., *The German Mind of the 19th Century* (New York: Continuum Publishing Corp., 1981), p. 34.

2. Ibid., 33–4.

3. Friedrich Nietzsche, *The Gay Science*, trans. Walter Kaufmann (New York: Random House, 1974), p. 328.

4. Friedrich Nietzsche, "Nietzsche Contra Wagner" in *The Portable Nietzsche*, trans. Walter Kaufmann (New York: Viking Press, 1960), p. 670.

5. Ernest Newman, *The Wagner Operas*, Vol. 1 (New York: Harper and Row, 1983), p. 206.

6. Ibid.

7. Richard Wagner, *Tristan and Isolde*, trans. Andrew Porter (New York: Riverrun Press, 1981), p. 72.

8. Ibid., 73.

9. Ibid., 77.

10. Ibid., 77.

11. Ibid., 81.

Chapter 5, "The Underground Man"

1. *Alcoholics Anonymous* (New York: Alcoholics Anonymous World Services, 1976), p. 66.

2. Friedrich Nietzsche, *The Birth of Tragedy and The Genealogy of Morals*, trans. Francis Golffing (Garden City, NY: Doubleday and Co., 1956), p. 172.

3. Ibid., 177.

4. Friedrich Nietzsche, *Thus Spake Zarathustra*, in *The Portable Nietzsche*, trans. Walter Kaufmann (New York: Viking Press, 1960), pp. 180–1.

5. The shadow is an unintegrated part of the personality, which the ego often perceives as repugnant and tries to deny or conceal, usually by projecting it on others. At the universal level, the shadow fuels the propensity for evil.

6. Fyodor Dostoevsky, *Notes from Underground*, trans. Constance Garnett (New York: Dell Publishing, 1960), p. 25.

7. Ibid., 26–7.

8. Ibid., 33.
9. Ibid., 53.
10. Ibid., 34.
11. Ibid., 34.
12. Ibid., 50.
13. Ibid., 56.
14. Ibid., 106.
15. Ibid., 115.
16. Ibid., 131.
17. Ibid., 139.
18. Ibid., 140.

Chapter 6, "The Outlaw"

1. Albert Camus, *The Rebel,* trans. Anthony Bower (New York: Random House, 1956), p. 22.
2. Ibid., 17.
3. Ibid., 22.
4. Ibid., 301.
5. Ibid., 302–3.
6. Ibid., 303.
7. Ibid., 304.
8. Ibid., 304.
9. Ibid., 306.
10. Ibid., 306.

Chapter 7, "The Trickster"

1. Carl Gustav Jung, *Four Archetypes,* trans. R. F. C. Hall (Princeton, NJ: Princeton University Press, 1973), p. 150.
2. Jack London, *John Barleycorn* (Santa Cruz, CA: Western Tanager Press, 1981), pp. 315ff.
3. Ibid., 320.
4. Ibid., 5–6.
5. Ibid., 9.
6. Ibid., 43.
7. Ibid., 49.
8. Ibid., 53–4.
9. Ibid., 60.
10. Ibid., 74.
11. Ibid., 115.
12. Ibid., 116.
13. Ibid., 114, 119–20.
14. Ibid., 125–6.

15. Ibid., 130.

16. Ibid., 131.

17. Ibid., 159.

18. Ibid., 228.

19. Ibid., 247.

20. Ibid., 298–302.

21. Ibid., 305.

22. Ibid., 308.

23. Ibid., 316.

24. Ibid., 338.

25. Ibid., 342.

26. Ibid., 342.

27. Ibid., 343.

28. Andrew Sinclair, *Jack: A Biography of Jack London* (New York: Pocket Books, 1979), p. 4.

29. Ibid., 193.

30. Ibid., 200.

31. *The Letters of Jack London*, eds. Earle Labor, Robert C. Leitz III, and I. Milo Shepard (Stanford, CA: Stanford University Press, 1988), pp. xxiii–xxxv.

32. Sinclair, 228.

33. *The Letters of Jack London*, Vol. 3, p. 1503.

34. Ibid., 1169.

35. C. G. Jung, *Letters*, ed. Gerhard Adler and Aniela Jaffé, trans. R. F. C. Hull (Bollingen Series, 95), Vol. 2 (1951–1961) (Princeton, N.J.: Princeton University Press, 1975), pp. 623–625.

36. C. G. Jung, *Four Archetypes*, 136.

37. For an insightful analysis of Krishna as Trickster see John Stratton Hawley, "The Thief in Krishna," *Parabola Magazine* (Summer 1984), pp. 6–13.

Chapter 8, "The Madwoman"

1. Walter F. Otto, *Dionysus: Myth and Cult*, trans. Robert B. Palmer (Bloomington, IN: Indiana University Press, 1965), p. 109.

2. Ibid., 143.

3. Ibid., 140–1.

4. Carole Angier, *Jean Rhys* (New York: Viking Penguin, 1985), p. 65. (Jean Rhys did not want a biography to be written about her. Angier's book acknowledges Rhys's wish so it is a study of her work in the context of her life.) The biographical material in this chapter comes from Rhys's diary, stories, and letters, and Angier's study.

5. Jean Rhys, *Good Morning, Midnight* (New York: W. W. Norton, 1986), p. 11.

6. Ibid., 54.

7. Ibid., 90.

8. Ibid., 41.

9. Ibid., 43–4.

10. Ibid., 10.

11. Ibid., 45.

12. Ibid., 52.

13. Ibid., 68.

14. Ibid., 68.

15. Ibid., 72.

16. Ibid., 107.

17. Ibid., 94.

18. Ibid., 90.

19. Ibid., 124.

20. Ibid., 140.

21. Ibid., 143.

22. Ibid., 144.

23. Ibid., 145.

24. Ibid., 172–3.

25. Ibid., 190.

26. As was her custom, Rhys drank a bottle of wine before the ending of *Good Morning, Midnight* came to her through the image of the madman in the dressing gown. Even then she was not sure if that ending was right, but her husband took the book away from her and sent it off to the publisher. Angier, pp. 66–7.

27. Ibid., 62.

28. Ibid., 71.

29. Jean Rhys, *The Letters of Jean Rhys*, ed. Francis Wyndham and Diana Melly (New York: Viking Penguin, Inc., 1984), p. 38.

30. Jean Rhys, *Smile Please: An Unfinished Autobiography* (Berkeley: Creative Arts Book, 1979), p. 132.

31. Rhys received awards from the Royal Society of Literature, the W. H. Smith Literary Award, and when she was 88, the CBE (Commander of the Order of the British Empire) Award for her service to literature.

32. Jean Rhys, *Letters*, p. 158.

33. Ibid., 159.

34. Ibid., 301.

35. Rhys, *Smile Please*, p. 133.

36. Ibid., 140.

37. Ibid., 133.

38. Jean Rhys, *Wide Sargasso Sea* (New York: W. W. Norton and Co., 1982), p. 61.

39. Toward the end of her life, Rhys related to David Plante, a writer who was helping her record her autobiographical memories, an experience in which she felt hope and joy for herself and everyone. She said to Plante: "There must be something after. You see, we have such longings, such great longings, they can't be for nothing." David Plante, *Difficult Women* (New York: E. P. Dutton, 1984), p. 57.

40. *Alcoholics Anonymous* (New York: Alcoholics Anonymous World Services, 1976), p. 312.

41. Diane Wolkenstein and Samuel Noah Kramer, *Inanna: Queen of Heaven and Earth* (New York: Harper & Row, 1983), p. 62.

42. Ibid., 64.

43. Ibid., 68.

CHAPTER 9, "THE JUDGE"

1. For a detailed analysis of this syndrome, see the discussion in Marion Woodman's *Addiction to Perfection* (Toronto: Inner City Books, 1982). See also Jan Bauer's discussion of women and alcoholism in *Alcoholism and Women* (Toronto: Inner City Books, 1982).

2. Albert Camus, *The Fall,* trans. Justin O'Brien (New York: Random House, 1956), p. 12.

3. Ibid., 19.

4. Ibid., 25–7.

5. Ibid., 30.

6. Ibid., 33.

7. Ibid., 70.

8. Ibid., 78.

9. Ibid., 80–1.

10. Ibid., 47.

11. Ibid., 64.

12. Ibid., 98–9.

13. Ibid., 101.

14. Ibid., 103.

15. Ibid., 108.

16. Ibid., 109.

17. Ibid., 109–10.

18. Ibid., 110.

19. Ibid., 111.

20. Ibid., 115.

21. Ibid., 116.

22. Ibid., 115.

23. Ibid., 117–18.

24. Ibid., 128.

25. Ibid., 130.

26. Ibid., 131.

27. Ibid., 133.

28. Ibid., 136.

29. Ibid., 140.

30. Ibid., 142–3.

31. Ibid., 144–5.

32. Ibid., 147.

33. Leo Tolstoy, *The Death of Ivan Illych,* trans. Aylmer Maude (New York: New American Library of World Literature, 1960), pp. 125–27.

34. Ibid., 131.

35. Ibid., 133.

36. Ibid., 134.

37. Ibid., 138.

38. Ibid., 137–8.

39. Ibid., 138.

40. Ibid., 146.

41. Ibid., 146.

42. Ibid., 147.

43. Ibid., 148.

44. Ibid., 151.

45. Ibid., 152.

46. Ibid., 154.

47. Ibid., 155.

48. Ibid., 155.

49. Ibid., 156.

50. Elisabeth Young-Bruehl, *Hannah Arendt: For Love of the World* (New Haven: Yale University Press, 1982), p. 452.

51. Arts Anonymous is a twelve-step program that focuses on nurturing and affirming the creative process and surrendering the "drugs" that inhibit people from creating.

Chapter 10, "The Killer"

1. Fyodor Dostoevsky, *Crime and Punishment,* trans. Constance Garnett (New York: Bantam Books, 1982), p. 25.

2. Ibid., 7–8.

3. Ibid., 13.

4. Ibid., 14.

5. Ibid., 23.

6. Ibid., 20.

7. Ibid., 361.

8. Ibid., 64.

9. Ibid., 80.

10. Ibid., 97.

11. Ibid., 97–8.

12. Ibid., 104.

13. Ibid., 165.

14. Ibid., 27.

15. Ibid., 200.

16. Ibid., 278.

17. Ibid., 280.

18. Ibid., 287.
19. Ibid., 351.
20. Ibid., 359–60.
21. Ibid., 360.
22. Ibid., 361.
23. Ibid., 361.
24. Ibid., 363.
25. Ibid., 377.
26. Ibid., 377.
27. Ibid., 392.
28. Ibid., 438.
29. Ibid., 448.
30. Ibid., 449.
31. Ibid., 451.
32. Ibid., 466.
33. Ibid., 467.
34. Ibid., 471.
35. Ibid., 472.

CHAPTER 11, "THE WORLD'S NIGHT"

1. Martin Heidegger, *Poetry, Language, Thought,* trans. Albert Hofstadter (New York: Harper and Row, 1971), pp. 116–17.
2. Ibid.
3. Ibid., 91.
4. Ibid., 92.
5. Ibid., 92.
6. Ibid., 92.
7. Etty Hillesum, *An Interrupted Life: The Diaries of Etty Hillesum (1941–1943),* ed. J. G. Gaarlandt (New York: Washington Square Press, 1985), p. 214.
8. Ibid., 186.
9. Ibid., 162.
10. Ibid., 162.
11. Ibid., 161.
12. Ibid., 172.
13. Ibid., 171.
14. Ibid., 162–63.
15. Ibid., 165.
16. Ibid., 13.
17. Ibid., 14–15.
18. Ibid., 17–18.
19. Ibid., 31.
20. Ibid., 94.

21. Ibid., 27.
22. Ibid., 30.
23. Ibid., 235.
24. Ibid., 99.
25. Ibid., 87.
26. Ibid., 100.
27. Ibid., 139.
28. Ibid., 151.
29. Ibid., 140–41.
30. Ibid., 107.
31. Ibid., 149.
32. Ibid., 234.
33. Ibid., 204.
34. Ibid., 243.
35. Ibid., 247.
36. Ibid., 255.
37. Ibid., 44.
38. Ibid., 186–87.
39. Elie Wiesel, "Of Hope and the Abyss," *New York Times*, Sunday, June 7, 1987.

Chapter 12, "The Abyss"

1. Martin Heidegger, *Poetry, Language, Thought*, trans. Albert Hofstadter (New York: Harper and Row, 1971), p. 118.
2. Thomas Wolfe, *The Autobiography of an American Novelist*, ed. Leslie Field (Cambridge, MA: Harvard University Press, 1983), p. 35.
3. Jakob Boehme, in *Encyclopedia of Mysticism and Mystery Religions*, ed. John Ferguson (New York: Crossroad Publishing Co., 1982), p. 30.
4. See Marie-Louise von Franz's discussion in *Creation Myths* (Zurich: Spring Publications, 1972), pp. 114–43.
5. Rollo May, *The Courage to Create* (New York: W. W. Norton and Co., 1975), p. 93.
6. Rainer Maria Rilke, *Sonnets to Orpheus*, trans. M. D. Herter Norton (New York: W. W. Norton and Co., 1962), p. 95.
7. Rainer Maria Rilke, *Letters of Rainer Maria Rillke: 1910–1926*, trans. Jane Bannard Greene and M. D. Herter Norton (New York: W. W. Norton and Co., 1969), p. 325.
8. See Phyllis Kenevan's discussion in "Nietzsche and the Creative Consciousness," in *Man and World* (The Hague: Martinus Nijhoff: 1982), p. 383.
9. Ibid., 388.
10. Friedrich Nietzsche, *Beyond Good and Evil*, trans. (New York: Vintage Books, 1966), p. 197.
11. Friedrich Nietzsche, *Twilight of the Idols*, in *The Portable Nietzsche*, trans. and ed. Walter Kaufmann (New York: Viking Press, 1960), p. 554.

12. C. G. Jung, *The Spirit in Man, Art and Literature,* trans. R. F. C. Hull (Princeton, NJ: Princeton University Press, 1971), p. 90.

13. Ibid., 91.

14. Thomas Wolfe, p. 36.

15. Erich Neumann, *Art and the Creative Unconscious,* trans. Ralph Mannheim (New York: Harper and Row, 1966), p. 133.

16. Ibid., 196–97.

17. C. G. Jung, *Symbols of Transformation,* Vol. 2, trans. R. F. C. Hull (New York: Harper and Brothers, 1962), pp. 292–93.

18. C. G. Jung, *The Spirit in Man, Art and Literature,* p. 82.

19. Rainer Maria Rilke, *Letters to a Young Poet,* trans. M. D. Herter Norton (New York: W. W. Norton and Co., 1963), pp. 67–68.

20. Rainer Maria Rilke, *Letters: 1910–1926,* p. 255.

21. Joseph Campbell, *Myths to Live By* (New York: Bantam Books, 1988), p. 237.

22. Rainer Maria Rilke, *Letters to a Young Poet,* p. 69. For an analysis of Rilke's creative process (his descent into the abyss and his creative response), see *On the Way to the Wedding* (Part III).

Chapter 13, "Dark Night of the Soul"

1. The Bill W.–C. G. Jung Letters were first printed in the 1963 issue of *The AA Grapevine,* published by Alcoholics Anonymous. They have been reprinted in *Parabola,* Summer 1987, pp. 68–71.

2. Ibid.

3. Ibid.

4. Evelyn Underhill, *Mysticism* (New York: New American Library, 1974), p. 386.

5. Ibid., 381.

6. Ibid., 383.

7. Ibid., 386.

8. Ibid., 400.

9. Ibid.

10. See the analysis of *Paris, Texas* in *On the Way to the Wedding* (chapter 8).

11. St. John of the Cross, *Dark Night of the Soul,* trans. E. Allison Peers (Garden City, NY: Doubleday and Co., 1959), pp. 109–10. Jeremiah vividly bewails his suffering in the Dark Night of the Abyss, complaining:

"I am the man that see my poverty in the rod of His indignation; He hath threatened me and brought me into darkness and not into light. So far hath He turned against me and hath converted His hand upon me all the day! My skin and my flesh hath He made old; He hath broken my bones; He hath made a fence around me and compassed me with gall and trial; He hath set me in dark places, as those that are dead for ever. He hath made a fence around me and against me, that I may not go out; He hath made my captivity heavy. Yea, and when I have cried and have entreated, He hath shut out my prayer. He hath enclosed my paths and ways out with square stones; He hath thwarted my steps. He hath set ambushes for me; He hath become to me a lion in a secret place. He hath turned aside my steps and broken me in pieces, He hath made me desolate; He hath bent His bow and set me as a mark for His arrow. He hath shot into my veins the daughters of His quiver. I have become a derision to all the people, and laughter and scorn for them all the day. He hath filled me with bitterness and hath made me drunken with worm-wood. He hath broken my teeth by number; He hath fed me with ashes. My soul is cast out from peace; I have forgotten good things. And I said: mine end is frustrated and cut short, together with my desire and my hope from the Lord. Remember my poverty and my excess, the wormwood and the gall. I shall be mindful with remembrance and my soul shall be undone with me in pains."

12. Ibid., 107.

13. Ibid., 100.

14. Ibid., 111.

15. Ibid., 128.

16. Ibid., 33–34.

17. John Ferguson, *Encyclopedia of Mysticism and Mystery Religions* (New York: Crossroads Publishing Co., 1982), p. 19.

18. Evelyn Underhill, *Mysticism*, p. 340.

19. Ibid., 338–39.

20. Evelyn Underhill, *Mysticism*, p. 348.

21. Theodore Roethke, *The Collected Poems of Theodore Roethke* (New York: Doubleday & Co., 1975), p. 129.

22. William Heyen, "The Divine Abyss: Theodore Roethke's Mysticism," in *Profile of Theodore Roethke*, compiled by William Heyen (Columbus, OH: Charles E. Merrill, 1971), p. 116.

23. Roethke's poem "The Abyss" appears in *Collected Poems*, pp. 211–14. The entire poem is given here, interspersed with my commentary as it relates to the parallel journeys of the mystic, the poet, and the recovering addict.

24. Underhill, 319.

25. Underhill, 426.

26. See Victor Danner's article "Intoxication and Sobriety in Sufism," *Parabola*, Summer 1987, p. 48.

27. Ibid., 52.

28. *Parabola*, Summer 1987, p. 71.

Chapter 14, "The Battleground"

1. See Heidegger's analysis in "The Origin of the Work of Art" in *Poetry, Language, Thought*, trans. Albert Hofstadter (New York: Harper & Row, 1971), pp. 17–78.

2. See the twelve steps in the Appendix.

3. Thomas Wolfe, *The Autobiography of an American Novelist*, ed. Leslie Field (Cambridge: Harvard University Press, 1983), pp. 61–62.

4. C. G. Jung, *Symbols of Transformation*, Vol. 2, trans. R. F. C. Hull (New York: Harper & Brothers, 1962), p. 337.

5. For a detailed analysis see *On the Way to the Wedding*, pp. 77–107.

6. Rollo May, *The Courage to Create* (New York: W. W. Norton & Co., 1975), p. 21.

7. Ibid., 59.

8. Jules Henri Poincaré, "Mathematical Creation," in *The Creative Process,* ed. Brewster Ghiselin (New York: New American Library, 1952), p. 38.

9. *Alcoholics Anonymous* (New York: Alcoholics Anonymous World Services, 1976), p. 60.

10. Rainer Maria Rilke, *Requiem,* trans. J. B. Leishman (London: Hogarth Press, 1957), p. 141.

11. *Alcoholics Anonymous,* pp. 58–59.

12. Matthew Fox, "Creation Spirituality" in *Creation,* November–December 1987, p. 9.

13. Ibid.

14. *Illuminations of Hildegaard of Bingen,* with commentary by Matthew Fox (Santa Fe, NM: Bear and Co., 1985), p. 27.

Chapter 15, "Soul on Fire"

1. Konstantin Mochulsky, *Dostoevsky: His Life and Work,* trans. Michael A. Minihan (Princeton: Princeton University Press, 1967), p. 8.

2. *Selected Letters of Fyodor Dostoevsky,* eds. Joseph Frank and David I. Goldstein, trans. Andrew MacAndrew (New Brunswick, NJ: Rutgers University Press, 1987), p. 14.

3. Mochulsky, p. 87.

4. Geir Kjetsaa, *Fyodor Dostoevsky: A Writer's Life,* trans. Siri Hustvedt and David McDuff (New York: Viking Penguin, 1987), p. 57.

5. Mochulsky, p. 103.

6. Ibid., 57.

7. Ibid., 114ff. Dostoevsky, moving from romantic idealism to socialism, became involved with a group of young revolutionaries who believed in utopia and sought to prepare the people for an uprising to abolish serfdom and establish earthly universal harmony among humankind.

8. Ibid., 132.

9. *Selected Letters,* pp. 51–53.

10. Mochulsky, p. 151.

11. *Selected Letters,* p. 68.

12. Mochulsky, p. 158.

13. Ibid., 162.

14. *Selected Letters,* p. 90.

15. Fyodor Dostoevsky, *The House of the Dead,* trans. Constance Garnett (New York: Dell Publishing Co., 1959), pp. 112–13.

16. Mochulsky, pp. 190–91.

17. Ibid., 194.

18. *Selected Letters,* pp. 212–13.

19. Mochulsky, p. 241. In later life Polina continued her torturous relations with men. Just before Dostoevsky's death, in 1880, she married a man sixteen years her junior, whom she later left for a still younger man. Yet she refused to grant him a

divorce. Her husband compared her to Catherine de Medici, and her father said, after she came to live with him, "A human devil has come to live in my house and now I can not bear to be in it." (Kjetsaa, p. 163)

20. Mochulsky, p. 243.

21. Kjetsaa, pp. 169–70.

22. Fyodor Dostoevsky, *Notes from Underground,* trans. Constance Garnett (New York: Dell Publishing Co., 1960), p. 56. (Italics added.)

23. Kjetsaa, p. 119.

24. Mochulsky, p. 323.

25. Anna Dostoevsky, *Dostoevsky Reminiscences,* trans. and ed. Beatrice Stillman (New York: Liveright Publishing Corporation, 1975), p. 30.

26. Kjetsaa, p. 212.

27. Ibid., 211.

28. *Dostoevsky Reminiscences,* pp. 131–32.

29. Kjetsaa, p. 209.

30. *Selected Letters,* p. 252.

31. Heavy cigarette smoking, however, was one addiction that Dostoevsky did not overcome; it eventually led to his death by emphysema.

32. Kjetsaa, pp. 217–18.

33. *Selected Letters,* pp. 261–62.

34. Fyodor Dostoevsky, *The Idiot,* trans. Constance Garnett (New York: Bantam Books, 1958), pp. 218–19.

35. In Russia the "holy fool" (*Yurodivyj*) feigns idiocy to conquer spiritual pride, thus exposing himself to the world's humiliations. But the holy fool's humility is his strength, and through it he bears the divine gift of prophecy.

36. *Selected Letters,* p. 331.

37. Ibid., 338.

38. Ibid., 346.

39. Ibid., 353–54.

40. Ibid., 354.

41. Ibid., 355.

42. Ibid., 357.

43. Ibid., 336.

44. Ibid., 341.

45. Other characters in *The Possessed* symbolize different aspects of Stavrogin's possession. His teacher, Stepan Trofimovich Verkhovensky, embodies the liberal utopian idealism of the 1840s. Dostoevsky felt that idealistic fathers engender nihilistic sons—hence Stepan's son, Peter Verkhovensky, proclaims destruction by preaching the spread of drunkenness and debauchery, the stifling of genius, and the spreading of fires, lies, and riots. (In nineteenth-century Russia, the utopian idealism prevalent in the 1840s was followed by nihilism in the 1860s. In twentieth-century America one can note a parallel: the hippie idealism of the sixties has been followed by the yuppie materialism of the eighties). Another character, Shigalov, is a theoretician whose proclamation of limitless freedom ends in limitless despotism. Another character, Kirilov, is an ecstatic caught between his blissful vision of paradise and his

knowledge of evil. Finding it impossible to live in this paradox, he proclaims the idea of "man-godhood"—only self-will can change humankind. Thus he kills himself to prove his point and to "kill" God, for he wants to free humans from the idea of God. To kill oneself, Kirilov finally declares, is the highest expression of self-will. Still another character, Shatov, is a prophet of the Russian people as bearers of God. Refusing to worship Stavrogin and challenging him instead, he is killed for his convictions by Peter Verkhovensky.

46. Kjetsaa, p. 249.

47. Fyodor Dostoevsky, *A Raw Youth*, trans. Constance Garnett (London: William Heineman Ltd., 1950), p. 351.

48. Mochulsky, p. 559.

49. *Selected Letters*, pp. 469–40. Dostoevsky is referring specifically to the Russian Orthodox Church.

50. Ibid., 465.

51. Ibid., 487.

52. Ibid., 506.

53. Ibid., 506. In his speech in honor of Pushkin, Dostoevsky had proclaimed the poet as a spiritual prophet, the first to show the oppression of the Russian wanderer who was estranged from the soil, and the first to show the solution in humble love and work on the land.

54. Ibid., 513.

55. Ibid., 512.

Chapter 16, "The Work of the Heart"

1. The epigraph is from John 12:24.

2. Fyodor Dostoevsky, *The Brothers Karamazov*, trans. Constance Garnett (New York: Random House, Inc., 1950), pp. 47–48.

3. Ibid., 84.

4. Ibid., 127.

5. Ibid., 289.

6. Ibid., 291.

7. Ibid., 274.

8. Ibid., 312.

9. Ibid., 387.

10. Ibid., 386–87.

11. Ibid., 410.

12. Ibid., 408.

13. Ibid., 422.

14. Ibid., 428.

15. Ibid., 429.

16. Ibid., 435.

17. Ibid., 435.

18. Ibid., 436–37.

19. Ibid., 437.

20. Ibid., 441.
21. Ibid.
22. Ibid., 471.
23. Ibid., 476.
24. Ibid., 497.
25. Ibid., 443.
26. Ibid., 461–62.
27. Ibid., 613.
28. Ibid., 614.
29. Ibid., 614.
30. Ibid., 615–16.
31. Ibid., 616.
32. Ibid., 617–18.
33. Ibid., 720.
34. Ibid., 720–21.
35. Ibid., 126.
36. Ibid., 79.
37. Ibid., 79–80.
38. Ibid., 772.
39. Ibid., 730.
40. Ibid., 731–32.
41. Ibid., 732.
42. Ibid., 733.
43. Ibid., 733.
44. Ibid., 733.
45. Ibid., 746.
46. Ibid., 747.
47. Ibid., 755.
48. Ibid., 758.
49. Ibid., 775.
50. Ibid., 796.
51. Ibid., 834.
52. Ibid., 839.
53. Ibid., 839.
54. Ibid., 841.
55. Ibid., 291.
56. Ibid., 928.
57. Ibid., 930.
58. Ibid., 930.
59. Ibid., 786.
60. Ibid., 376–77.

61. Ibid., 378.

62. Ibid., 940.

Chapter 17, "The Healing Fields"

1. *The Twelve Steps of Alcoholics Anonymous,* interpreted by The Hazelden Foundation (New York: Harper and Row Publishers, 1987), p. 89.

2. Ibid., 95.

3. Paul Tillich, *Best Sermons,* ed. G. Paul Biscle (New York: McGraw-Hill, 1955). In *Parabola,* Fall 1987, p. 42.

4. Ibid., 40.

5. Ibid., 42–3.

6. Ibid., 43–4.

7. Tillich, p. 45.

8. Wendell Berry, *Sabbaths* (San Francisco: North Point Press, 1987), p. 35.

9. Ibid., 65.

10. Ibid., 51.

11. Ibid., 33–4.

12. Ibid., 36.

13. Ibid., 36.

14. Ibid., 52–3.

15. Ibid., 53.

16. Ibid., 67.

17. Ibid., 67.

18. Ibid., 67.

Chapter 18, "The Dwelling"

1. Susan Walker, ed., *Speaking of Silence: Christians and Buddhists on the Contemplative Way* (Mahwah, NJ: Paulist Press, 1987), p. 84.

2. *Times Alone: Selected Poems of Antonio Machado,* trans. Robert Bly (Middleton, CT: Wesleyan University Press, 1983), pp. 43–5.

3. Martin Heidegger, *Poetry, Language, Thought,* trans. Albert Hofstadter (New York: Harper & Row, 1971), p. 149.

4. Ibid., 149–50.

5. Ibid., 150.

6. Ibid.

7. Ibid.

8. Ibid., 151.

9. Ibid., 154.

10. Ibid., 160.

11. Ibid.

12. Ibid., 161.

13. Martin Heidegger, *Being and Time,* trans. John Macquarrie and Edward Robinson (New York: Harper & Brothers, 1962), pp. 242–43.

Chapter 19, "The Gift"

1. *Alcoholics Anonymous* (New York: Alcoholics Anonymous World Services, Inc., 1976), pp. 83–4. The Promises read as follows:

"If we are painstaking about this phase of our development, we will be amazed before we are halfway through. We are going to know a new freedom and a new happiness. We will not regret the past nor wish to shut the door on it. We will comprehend the word serenity and we will know peace. No matter how far down the scale we have gone, we will see how our experience can benefit others. That feeling of uselessness and self-pity will disappear. We will lose interest in selfish things and gain interest in our fellows. Self-seeking will slip away. Our whole attitude and outlook upon life will change. Fear of people and of economic insecurity will leave us. We will intuitively know how to handle situations which used to baffle us. We will suddenly realize that God is doing for us what we could not do for ourselves.

"Are these extravagant promises? We think not. They are being fulfilled among us—sometimes quickly, sometimes slowly. They will always materialize if we work for them."

2. See David Steindl-Rast's article "Standing on Holy Ground" in *Speaking of Silence*, ed. Susan Walker (Mahwah, NJ: Paulist Press, 1987), p. 28. Rast points out that the Catholic ritual of the Eucharist (The Lord's Supper) is such a Thanksgiving. For an analysis of the work of art as a gift and its relation to market societies see: Lewis Hyde, *The Gift: Imagination and the Erotic Life of Property* (New York: Random House, 1983).

3. Boris Pasternak, *Pasternak: Selected Poems*, trans. Jan Stallworthy and Peter France (Middlesex, England: Penguin Books, 1984), pp. 38–9.

4. Martin Heidegger, *Poetry, Language, Thought*, trans. Albert Hofstadter (New York: Harper & Row, 1971), p. 173.

5. Fyodor Dostoevsky, *Selected Letters of Fyodor Dostoevsky*, ed. Joseph Frank and David Goldstein, trans. Andrew R. MacAndrew (New Brunswick, NJ: Rutgers University Press, 1987), pp. 307–308.

6. Andrey Tarkovsky, *Sculpting in Time*, trans. Kitty Blair-Hunter (New York: Alfred A. Knopf, 1987), p. 38.

7. Ibid., 218.

8. Ibid., 227.

9. Ibid., 228.

10. Ibid., 217.

11. Ibid., 193.

12. Martin Heidegger, *Poetry, Language, Thought*, p. 200. From the old High German word *beran* comes the word *gebaren*, meaning to carry, to gestate and give birth.

13. Tarkovsky, p. 43.

CREDITS

The author thanks the following publishers for permission to reprint material copyrighted or controlled by them.

Alfred A. Knopf and Hamish Hamilton Ltd. for permission to quote from *The Fall* by Albert Camus, translated by Justin O'Brien, © 1956 by Alfred A. Knopf, Inc. *The Rebel* by Albert Camus, translated by Anthony Bower, © 1956, renewed 1984 by Alfred A. Knopf, Inc. Reprinted by permission of Alfred A. Knopf, Inc. and Hamish Hamilton Ltd.

Andre Deutsch Ltd. for permission to quote from *Letters of Jean Rhys* by Francis Wyndham and Diana Melly.

Atlantic Monthly Press and Collins Harvill Publishers for permission to quote from *A New Path to the Waterfall*, © by the estate of Raymond Carver. Used by permission of the Atlantic Monthly Press and Collins Harvill Publishers.

Doubleday and Faber and Faber Ltd. for permission to quote from "Pure Fury," © 1958 by Theodore Roethke, "The Abyss," © 1963 by Beatrice Roethke, administratrix of the estate of Theodore Roethke, and "In a Dark Time," © 1960 by Beatrice Roethke, administratrix of the estate of Theodore Roethke, from *The Collected Poems of Theodore Roethke* by Theodore Roethke. Reprinted by permission of Doubleday, a division of Bantam, Doubleday, Dell Publishing Group, Inc., and Faber and Faber Ltd.

E. P. Dutton for permission to quote from *Mysticism* by Evelyn Underhill. Published in 1961 by E. P. Dutton. All rights reserved. Reprinted by permission of the publisher, E. P. Dutton, a division of Penguin Books USA, Inc.

Harper and Row for permission to quote from *Good Morning Midnight* by Jean Rhys and from *Poetry, Language, Thought* by Martin Heidegger, translated by Albert Hofstadter, © 1971 by Martin Heidegger. Reprinted by permission of Harper and Row, Publishers, Inc.

Andrew R. MacAndrew for permission to quote from *The Gambler* by Fyodor Dostoevsky, translated by Andrew R. MacAndrew (W. W. Norton & Co., 1981). Reprinted by permission of the translator.

Macmillan Publishing Company for permission to quote from *Notes from the Underground* by Fyodor Dostoevsky, translated by Constance Garnett (New York: Macmillan, 1923).

New Directions Publishing Corporation for permission to quote from *A Season in Hell and the Drunken Boat* by Arthur Rimbaud, translated by Louise Varese, © 1961 by New Directions Publishing Corporation. Reprinted by permission of New Directions Publishing Corporation.

North Point Press for permission to quote from *Sabbaths* by Wendell Berry, © 1987 by Wendell Berry. Published by North Point Press and reprinted by permission.

Pantheon Books for permission to quote from *An Interrupted Life: The Diaries of Etty Hillesum, 1941–1943* by Etty Hillesum, translated by Arno Pomerans, translation © 1983 by Jonathan Cape, Ltd. Reprinted by permission of Pantheon Books, a division of Random House, Inc.

Penguin Books for permission to quote from "The Death of Ivan Ilyich" from *The Cossacks and Other Stories* by Leo Tolstoy, translated by Rosemary Edmonds (Penguin Classics, 1960), © 1960 by Rosemary Edmonds. *Jean Rhys* by Carole Angier, © 1985 by Carole Angier.

Princeton University Press for permission to quote from *Dostoevsky: His Life and Work* by Konstantin Mochulsky, translated by Michael Minihan, © 1967 by Princeton University Press. Excerpts reprinted by permission of Princeton University Press.

Random House for permission to quote from "The Iceman Cometh," from *Selected Plays of Eugene O'Neill*, © 1946 by Eugene O'Neill.

Riverrun Press for permission to quote from *Tristan and Isolde*, ENO/ROH Opera Guide #6. Libretto translation by Andrew Porter, © 1981, 1983 by Andrew Porter. Reprinted by permission of Riverrun Press, Inc.

Rutgers University Press for permission to quote from *Selected Letters of Fyodor Dostoyevsky* by Joseph Frank and David I. Goldstein, editors, translated by Andrew R. MacAndrew, © 1987 by Rutgers, the State University of New Jersey.

W. W. Norton for permission to quote the lines from "Sonnet 13," Part Two, from *Sonnets to Orpheus* by Rainer Maria Rilke, translated by M. D. Herter Norton, © 1942 by W. W. Norton & Company, Inc. Copyright renewed 1970 by M. D. Herter Norton. Reprinted by permission of W. W. Norton & Company, Inc., The Hogarth Press, and the estate of Rainer Maria Rilke.

Wesleyan University Press for permission to quote from *Times Alone: Selected Poems of Antonio Machado* translated by Robert Bly, translation © 1983 by Robert Bly. Reprinted by permission of Wesleyan University Press.

Diligent efforts were made in every case to obtain rights from copyright holders. In a few instances, the efforts were unsuccessful. The author and publisher are grateful for the use of this excerpted material.

INDEXES

SUBJECT INDEX

Title Index

Name Index